# Studies of the New Testament and Its World

*Edited by*
JOHN BARCLAY
JOEL MARCUS
*and*
JOHN RICHES

# Conflicting Mythologies

# Conflicting Mythologies

*Identity Formation in the*
*Gospels of Mark and Matthew*

JOHN K. RICHES

T&T CLARK
EDINBURGH

T&T CLARK LTD
59 GEORGE STREET
EDINBURGH EH2 2LQ
SCOTLAND

www.tandtclark.co.uk

First published 2000


ISBN 0 567 08744 1




British Library Cataloguing-in-Publication Data
A catalogue record for this book is available from the British Library

Typeset by Waverley Typesetters, Galashiels
Printed and bound in Great Britain by Bookcraft Ltd, Avon

# Contents

# Preface

The origins of this book go back to graduate seminars held in the then Department of New Testament Language and Literature in the University of Glasgow in the early 1980s. Ernest Best was preparing his Sprunt Lectures, subsequently published as *Mark: the Gospel as Story*, and during one winter we worked our way through the drafts of each chapter. Their great strength lay in Best's ability to suggest a living context for Mark's narrative, imaginatively to recreate the rhetorical situation between Mark and his readers. For Best, Mark was essentially a pastor addressing a beleaguered and persecuted community and offering them moral guidance and spiritual consolation. The story of Jesus' miracles, death and resurrection spoke of a power which could overcome all obstacles and sustain the community through the fires of persecution. The story of the disciples' faltering progress in understanding Jesus' message and moral instruction would provide comfort to those who themselves were in danger of breaking under the pressures to betray one another and their faith.

There was here a sustained attempt to link the Gospel to the emergence of a particular kind of Christian sensibility, one which was in many ways opposed to the Barthian readings of scholars like E. Schweizer, which contrasted the miracles with the cross and portrayed the disciples as incurably blind until the final and decisive revelation of God in the cross. Best's own pastoral experiences in a Northern Ireland which has suffered much at the hands of those with black and white theological convictions had made him deeply suspicious of such theological assertiveness and overconfidence.[1] The kind of faith which Best found reflected in Mark's narrative of the disciples was symbolised by the restoration of the blind man of Bethsaida's sight in stages.

---

[1]  I suggested as much in my *A Century of New Testament Study*, 1993, and in conversation Best has expressed his agreement with the views there.

All this remains an enduring contribution to Markan studies. But there are other elements in the Gospel which are less well grasped in such a reading. The element of drama which derives from the cosmic struggle between Jesus and the powers of darkness, which stands right at the beginning of the Gospel with the brief narrative of the Temptation, is largely (dis)missed by Best; for him the real struggle is for the hearts and minds of men and women, as is symbolised by the story of the Agony in the Garden. There is, too, little attempt to plot the relationship between Mark's telling of his story and the theological traditions with which he is in dialogue. Best's interests were focused more on the manner in which Mark preserved and shaped the traditions which he received.

It has, then, been a matter of great fortune over the last seven years to have had as a colleague Joel Marcus, whose contributions to Markan studies have strikingly complemented those of Ernest Best. Marcus stands in the line of those who, like James Robinson, have read the Gospel as dominated by the cosmic struggle between Jesus and Satan. He is also someone who has paid great attention to the various ways in which Mark interacts with different traditions of Jewish theology, not least with the Isaianic theme of the Way of the Lord. For Marcus it is above all Jewish apocalyptic which provides the dialogue partner for Mark and which in turn leads him to stress both the cosmic conflict between Jesus and Satan and to portray the disciples in darker colours: in the battle for their hearts, Satan too is at work, responsible for Peter's all too human thoughts about Jesus' predictions of his suffering.

The discussion with these two scholars provides a good deal of the dynamic of the following pages, not only in the discussions of Mark; many of the issues raised by these contrasting approaches are present also in the discussions of Matthew. I mention them here partly by way of thanks to two colleagues who have been wonderfully generous with advice and support over the years, partly by way of introduction to the two interwoven themes which form the subject of this book. What, in the first place, is one to make of the fact that two colleagues, for whose scholarship one has only respect, offer quite radically opposed views of the same text? The answer to that dilemma that I advance in this volume is that they are both trying to impose too consistent, too monolithic a reading on to Mark's mythical narrative. Mythologies are not simple, one-stranded narratives, though they have often been presented in this way. Rather, in their attempts to try to make sense of the dilemmas of particular societies and cultures, they tend to draw on conflicting accounts of the nature of the world and society. They take traditional stories which express very different views of the way things are and weave them together in ways which, while they hardly suggest a definitive cosmology, may nevertheless enable their readers/ hearers to make sense of, and to impose some kind of meaning on, their experience.

Mark, like many of his contemporaries, wrestles with two very different accounts of the origins and resolution of evil. This has been most clearly pointed out by Martin de Boer, who too has played his part in the genesis of this book. On one view, evil results from demonic invasion of the world: those who sin, sin because they are led astray by the powers of darkness, who control and hold them in bondage. Only rescue from the powers of darkness and their ultimate defeat and destruction can resolve the world's ills. On another view, sin is the direct result of human disobedience, archetypally represented in Adam, which can be overcome only through the revelation and teaching of God's will, the institution of punishments and rewards and, ultimately by the judgement of all. It is quite possible to read Mark (and to a lesser extent, Matthew) through either of these lenses, but that fact only reinforces the conviction that in either case the singular perspective fails to capture the particular nature of the Gospel narratives, their dialogue with opposed views of reality. The title of this book, *Conflicting Mythologies*, seeks above all to make the point that we need to be sharply aware of the fundamentally dialogical character of the Gospel narratives. There is a struggle in the Gospels to make sense of the world and of human experience in terms of some over-arching cosmology: but all the time that search is paradoxically conducted in terms which are opposed to each other, so that there is always a subversive element in the narrative, working against any final resolution of the world's dilemmas.

The other element in the book is represented by the subtitle: *Identity Formation in the Gospels of Mark and Matthew*. In writing their narratives the Evangelists were assisting in the development of new religious sensibilities, of a new religious ethos, which will spawn a remarkable variety of religious communities in the following centuries. Again Best's and Marcus' readings underline the very different moods and sensibilities which can be derived from the Gospels. Is Christian discipleship to be thought of as a struggle between the divine and the human will, as a slow leading towards greater obedience, trust and understanding? or is it fundamentally determined by a moment of apocalyptic illumination, by the giving of a mystery, such that the world will never seem the same again?

While questions about the nature of early Christian mythology have largely dropped out of sight over the last forty years, questions about the formation of Christian identity have been vigorously pursued. New social scientific perspectives have been brought to bear, more or less sensitively. Discussion has focused around the sectarian nature of the groups. There has been a growing tendency to see the Gospels of Mark and Matthew as marginal groupings within Judaism, struggling for control of the tradition in the crisis of the second half of the first century. In what follows I attempt to build on these discussions. At the same time I have chosen to focus on two particular topics which played a major role in the formation of ancient senses of identity: kinship and descent, on the one hand, senses of sacred space, on the other hand. How did the Gospel narratives serve to reshape inherited senses of identity, which were so closely tied to descent from Abraham and from Jewish parents and to a sense of attachment to the Land?

It is perhaps misleading to speak about the second half of the title as a *sub*-title. The two halves are more closely interrelated, constituting two poles of the work. Here I owe a debt to the work of Clifford Geertz. Geertz argues that religious cultural systems are compounded of two interrelated and mutually reinforcing elements: world-view and ethos. The central symbols of a culture can be read both as 'models of' and as 'models for' reality. The sense of reality which is conveyed by such symbols reinforces the moods, attitudes and values which are prevalent within the group. Equally, those moods and attitudes confer a unique sense of factuality upon the accepted cosmology. What I try to show is how the senses of identity which are generated by the Gospels are strongly influenced by the underlying mythologies, and indeed show the same kind of tensiveness which is a characteristic of those mythologies, with their inherent, fundamental oppositions. Much social scientific and social historical work on the New Testament has been unduly functionalist, concerned only with the way that the beliefs of the group/s functioned to produce a more or less coherently structured society. This flight from a consideration of the ideological contents of the New Testament texts may have many reasons and motivations in the guild of scholars; it can hardly serve even the goal of examining the social function of the texts. Without first reconstructing the beliefs advanced in those texts, it is hard to see how one can profitably talk about their social function.

I have incurred many debts in the writing of this book. In the first place, it has taken up much time which might and should have been spent with my family and they, particularly my wife Nena, have been greatly patient about this. Nena it was, too, who made it possible for me to spend two and half months in wonderful isolation at St James' Hospital, Mantsonyane, in central Lesotho. While she went off every morning to face the challenges of working in a rural African hospital, often without any kind of back-up, I was able to retire to the peace of my study, looking out onto the Maluti mountains. My thanks too go to the staff at the hospital, especially Dr Theo Thakens, for the way they made us welcome during our stay. It was here that much of the first draft was written.

There are many other important debts. Dr Geoffrey Green and his staff at T&T Clark have been, as ever, immensely accommodating. Dr Ralph Waller of Manchester College, Oxford, invited me to spend a fortnight with them at the start of a period of leave, which provided a splendid opportunity for uninterrupted study. The Humanities Research Board of the British Academy awarded me a grant under their Research Leave scheme in 1997, without which this book would still be unfinished. The Department of Theology and Religious Studies in Glasgow generously matched this award. Numerous colleagues have contributed much in discussion and detailed comment. The Post-graduate Biblical Studies Seminar in the Department has provided a vigorous and constructive forum and I am grateful to all those who have contributed. I would particularly like to mention John Barclay, who has been a wonderfully supportive colleague over the years, always ready to spend time reviewing some idea or to share his great knowledge of first-century Diaspora Judaism.

Two scholars have gone beyond the call of duty in working over my drafts, Joel Marcus and Dale Allison. They have not only done so with great attention and understanding, even where my views are not their views, but they have done so to the very tight timetable which had to be kept. To have afflicted the inflexibility of the RAE schedule on scholars outside these overmanaged Isles is something for which I can only apologise. The help and encouragement, the advice and cautions, the references and ideas they offered were of immense value. I can hope only that they will not feel that I have squandered their largesse. They are certainly not to be held responsible for the final result. To them and to 'Paddy' Best I dedicate this book.

JOHN K. RICHES
*July 2000*

# Abbreviations

| | |
|---|---|
| AB | Anchor Bible |
| *ABD* | D. N. Freedman, ed., *Anchor Bible Dictionary*, 6 vols. |
| AGAJU | Arbeiten zur Geschichte des Antiken Judentums und des Urchristentums |
| AnBib | Analecta Biblica |
| AThANT | Abhandlungen zur Theologie des Alten und Neuen Testamentes |
| *BJRL* | *Bulletin of the John Rylands Library* |
| *CBQ* | *Catholic Biblical Quarterly* |
| EKKNT | Evangelisch-katholischer Kommentar zum Neuen Testament |
| *EvTh* | *Evangelische Theologie* |
| FRLANT | Forschungen zur Literatur des Alten und Neuen Testaments |
| HNT | Handbuch zum Neuen Testament |
| HTKNT | Herders theologischer Kommentar zum Neuen Testament |
| *HTR* | *Harvard Theological Review* |
| ICC | International Critical Commentary |
| *JBL* | *Journal of Biblical Literature* |
| *JJS* | *Journal of Jewish Studies* |
| *JR* | *Journal of Religion* |
| *JSNT* | *Journal for the Study of the New Testament* |

| | |
|---|---|
| JSNTSup | Journal for the Study of the New Testament Supplement Series |
| JSOT Press | Journal for the Study of the Old Testament Press |
| *NovT* | *Novum Testamentum* |
| *NTS* | *New Testament Studies* |
| *OTP* | ed. J. H. Charlesworth, *Old Testament Pseudepigrapha* |
| *RevExp* | *Review and Expositor* |
| SBLDS | Society of Biblical Literature Dissertation Series |
| *SE* | *Sacris erudiri* |
| *SEA* | *Svensk exegetisk arsbok* |
| SNTSMS | Society for New Testament Studies Monograph Series |
| SNTW | Studies of the New Testament and its World |
| StANT | Studien zum Alten und Neuen Testament |
| *ThLZ* | *Theologische Literaturzeitung* |
| WUNT | Wissenschaftliche Untersuchungen zum Neuen Testament |
| *ZNW* | *Zeitschrift für die neutestamentliche Wissenschaft* |

# 1

## Identity and change

*Early Christian identity in the Roman world at the turn of the era*

Times of major political and social change often occasion changes in
the ways that people see, not only their external circumstances, but
themselves as well. Christianity is formed in the century after the
Roman Principate emerged to give (relative) peace and security to the
Mediterranean world. A world consisting of diverse nations worshipping
a great variety of gods is welded together into an empire, held together
by a politically, economically and militarily strong centre. A vastly
impressive international engineering enterprise links together parts as
remote from each other as southern Scotland and the Nile valley, the
lower Rhine and Armenia. Colonies spring up which bring the new
technologies to Iron-Age peoples. The Graeco-Roman cities of the
Mediterranean, already a melting pot of different peoples, thrive as
commercial and mercantile centres in this new age of (relative: 2 Cor
11:25–27!) security and ease of travel. Themselves the purveyors of a
Hellenistic culture that was spread three hundred years earlier through
the campaigns of Alexander of Macedon, they now become the centres
for the forging of new senses of identity and belonging in this brave
new imperial world. Cities in Asia Minor will vie for the privilege of
hosting the imperial cult; they will also provide a home for the new
cults which will sweep through the newly united territories: cults of Isis
and Mithras, Demeter and Jesus Christ. A battle will ensue for the soul
of this new Empire. Will it be won over to the traditional deities of
Rome in an enlarged pantheon generously incorporating the deities of
other nations? Or will the newly-arrived cults replace the old? What
new virtues will inspire and curb the passions of the new rulers under
their monarchical princeps?[1]

---

[1]  See Syme, 1960, 440–58. See esp. 442: '*moribus antiquis res stat Romana virisque*', quoting
Ennius, quoted by Cicero in *De re publica* (Augustine, *De civ Dei* 2:21).

It is in this new world that Christianity emerges as a series of small religious groupings, all claiming to be followers of a Jewish teacher-prophet from the Galilee, part of the Roman province of Syria. Though the origins of the groups are rural, they will rapidly spread through the cities of the eastern Mediterranean, from Antioch through Asia Minor and Greece to Rome. They will leave few archaeological traces of these early years; nor do they feature often in imperial records. What they leave behind are writings: a series of letters, accounts of the spread of the movement and the 'acts' of its leading figures, a strange book of revealed mysteries, and a number of accounts of the life, teaching and death of Jesus Christ. For this purpose they made their own a new form of writing material, the codex, less venerable than the scroll, but more convenient both for small notes and excerpts and even for longer narratives such as the Gospels. These books achieved remarkable distribution throughout the Empire and would, alongside the more venerable scriptures of the Jews, be accepted within less than three hundred years as the official sacred texts of the Empire.

The enquiry undertaken here will not be concerned with tracing out the history of the emergence of Christianity into prominence and eventual imperial dominance. What I want to ask is rather this. Within this world of massive political change, how were the self-understandings of those who became members of these small Christian groups affected, changed, by their affiliation to this new cult? Specifically, what evidence of such transitions, such reshaping of senses of identity do we find in the Gospels of Mark and Matthew?

We move, that is to say, from the larger consideration of the politics of Empire to the literary activities of groups more or less on the margins of mainstream political and social life. Their group consciousness, as we shall see, is heavily determined by their Jewish roots, symbolised most obviously by their thoroughly Jewish saviour. At the same time, their relations with other (non-Christian) Jewish groups have become particularly painful and they are on their way to becoming a quite separate religious group. This imparts a somewhat ambivalent status to the young churches. They are on the one hand bodies who can claim antiquity for themselves, who can claim the authority of inherited traditions, something which carried enormous weight in the world of the first century. On the other, they are deviants within their own wider grouping. They will be drawn to the attention of the authorities precisely by the disorder which they cause among groups of Jewish resident aliens in the cities of the Mediterranean. Their appeal to ancient traditions may give reassurance to the conservatives; their message of the dawn of the kingdom of God will have carried too much of the frisson of the new.

All of this suggests, at the very least, that their sense of their own identity in these early stages of the movement will have been quite fluid. For people's sense of who they are is a function not only of their own aspirations and views of themselves, but of the way that other members of their group and also outsiders see them. There will have been enough conflict of view among such different parties for Christians to have found it difficult to settle into an easily accepted sense of their place and identity in the world of the first century.

## Christians among Jews and Gentiles

Not all members of the early Christian congregations were Jews. The presence of Gentiles from an early stage raised other pressing questions about the nature of the identity of the groups and their members. Admission of Gentiles to the Christian *ecclesiai* without circumcision was the surest sign that these new groups were not Jewish. Everyone knew that circumcision was the mark of a Jew. There were, it is true, some Jews who tried to conceal their circumcision, but such practice was regarded as deviant and anomalous. The fact that the church in Antioch, at an early stage, contained uncircumcised members, and that the circumcised and uncircumcised ate together, so far as it became known (and it was certainly known to some as far away as Jerusalem), will have sent extremely mixed signals about the identity of this new group. It is hardly surprising, then, that it was in Antioch that the new group first earned the name of Christians (Acts 11:26).

But if the presence of uncircumcised members in the Christian congregations raised questions about their Jewishness, the fact that Gentiles were being incorporated into a group which claimed Jewish roots and ancestry would equally raise sharp questions about the place of such congregations within the multicultural world of the Graeco-Roman city. Jews after all made the clearest of distinctions between themselves and the adherents of all other religious cults. To become a Jew was to turn away from the worship of idols and to worship the one, true God. Jewish monotheism was set sharply against the burgeoning polytheism of the many cults of the cities. Jews had inhabited the cities of the Mediterranean for centuries and had intermingled quite freely, though by no means always without friction and conflict. They had, in Alexandria, attended Greek schools, performed naked in their games and drunk deep at the well of Greek culture. Alexandria was also the scene of fierce conflicts between Jews and the Greek-speaking citizens.[2] Jewish refusal of pagan worship remained one clear mark of their identity. Did now the presence of uncircumcised Gentiles within the Christian congregations represent a turning away from this refusal? Did it represent one further step on the way to assimilation with the wider culture? What were the practical, cultic limits to 'being all things to all people' (1 Cor 9:22)?

### The Gospels as evidence of Christian senses of identity

Such questions have been widely treated in discussions of the Pauline churches and their controversies over the admission of the Gentiles. They have equally gained some attention in discussions of the canonical Gospels. It is, however, less easy to make direct connections between narratives about the life and death of Jesus and the way such narratives may have shaped the identity of his later followers, than it is to make such connections where the Epistles are concerned. The Epistles, after all, deal directly with controversies within the early church specifically about table-fellowship, about the admission of the Gentiles and whether they should be circumcised, whether Christians might eat food which had been offered to idols, whether they were allowed to participate in meals in temples. By contrast, the Gospel of Matthew, which by general agreement is written in the context of a growing split between Matthew's congregation and the synagogue, makes no direct reference to the question of circumcision *at all*. This is not to say that there are no such direct references to inter-communal disputes: the Fourth Gospel refers on a number of occasions (9:22; 12:42; 16:2) to people being 'put out of the synagogue' (ἀποσυνάγωγος γενέσθαι). The Gospel of Matthew does indeed contain Jesus' commission to the disciples to go and make disciples of all nations. Even so, these all occur in the context of a narrative about Jesus' life and death and we therefore need a careful strategy, if we are successfully to negotiate our way back behind the text

---

[2] After a pogrom in 38 CE Philo led a delegation to Rome, unsuccessfully asking for the full rights of citizenship for Jews. In 66 CE Philo's apostate nephew savagely suppressed a Jewish riot (Josephus, *Bell* 2:487–98). The Jewish community was largely destroyed in the revolt under Trajan, 115–17 (Eusebius, *Hist Eccl* 4:2). For a full study, see Barclay, 1996, 19–395.

to the actual situation in the life of the church which the Evangelists may be referring to and possibly seeking to influence.

The pioneer in such attempts at reading the history of the Gospels was J. Louis Martyn, who attempted to read the narrative of the Fourth Gospel as a 'two-level drama'.[3] What at one level was the story of the healing by Jesus of a man born blind and the subsequent divisions within a small Jewish community in Galilee, can also be read as the story of the conversion of a Jew to belief in Jesus as the Son of Man (Messiah?) and the conflicts consequent upon it in the synagogue from which the Johannine community emerged. Martyn quite properly worked from a basic instinct about the art of storytelling, namely, that good storytellers seek to make links between the past events which they narrate and the present experience of their hearers. The tell-tale clue to all this in the story of the man born blind is the reference to his parents' fear of being put out of the synagogue (John 9:22). It is hard to know what aspect of Jewish practice this might have referred to in the Galilee of Jesus' life-time and it is therefore most plausible to suggest that it refers to practices in the synagogue at the time of the writing of the Gospel.[4] It is not difficult to find such tell-tale traces of concerns and issues close to the heart of the other Evangelists. Jesus' command to the disciples to go and make disciples of all nations at the end of Matthew's Gospel is one such; so too is his statement in 21:43, 'Therefore I tell you, the kingdom of God will be taken away from you and given to a nation producing the fruits of it.' Clearly here are sayings attributed to Jesus, whether presented as statements of the earthly or the risen Lord, which relate to questions of the early church's relations with Jews and Gentiles, questions which in turn have left their deposit in the

[3] Martyn, 1968. It should be noted, however, that Martyn's book is not an attempt simply to divert the course of New Testament studies from what at the time, under Bultmann's influence, was largely an enquiry into the theological senses of the Gospel. Rather, it was an attempt to link the way in which, for the Evangelist, the history of community mirrors that of Jesus to the Evangelist's understanding of the action of the Spirit. It was precisely about history *and* theology. This intention has been closely followed by some, like Rensberger, 1988. Nevertheless, the dominant trend in Gospel studies over the thirty years since Martyn's book has been away from their theological interpretation and towards a greater concentration on the social setting and conflicts of the communities which are thought to lie behind these works.

[4] There has, of course, been considerable scholarly debate over Martyn's proposal and the very similar proposal made by Davies, 1963, 275–9, that the reference was to the liturgical use of the revision of the *Eighteen Benedictions*, the so-called *Birkath ha-Minim*; see the long note in the second edition of Martyn's book, 1979, p. 56, n. 75.

Epistles and Acts. It is therefore hardly surprising that scholars have devoted much time over the last two decades to following up such clues and attempting to construct a social setting and indeed history of the Evangelists' communities.

Nothing in the book will be intended to undermine such efforts. They will prove invaluable in the present undertaking. But at two points I want to enter a caution. The first has been made recently and power-fully in a collection of essays edited by Richard Bauckham.[5] Bauckham argues that it is unlikely that any of the Evangelists would have pro-duced something as complicated and demanding of time and expense as a Gospel purely for his own congregation. From the start they would have been intended for the other Christian communities of the Mediterranean area. This is a good simple point, powerfully made. It does not completely undercut the present trend of Gospel studies. The concerns which recent scholarship has identified as being peculiar to one particular community (say Matthew's) would in any case hardly have been restricted to his community alone. If Matthew wanted to address an audience outside the immediate circles of his own church, he would still have wanted to deal with questions concerning their relations to Jews and Gentiles. Importantly, however, it makes the point that the Evangelists had wider horizons than is sometimes suggested by scholars who tie the Gospels into very tightly defined situations in the history of the first-century church. Maybe, too, they were less interested in addressing immediate and pressing problems in the lives of their own community than in the preservation and presentation of the com-munity's traditions about Jesus. Such an enterprise would certainly not have been without implications for the lives of people in the Evangelists' own community. But, as we shall attempt to show, they are engaged in a wider dialogue both with Jewish expectations and belief and with the Christian tradition, something clearest in Matthew's handling of Mark. They are engaged in a process of forging the community's beliefs and ethos, in tracing out the contours of the sacred universe in which they now find themselves. After all, if it was particular problems they were interested in, would it not have been better to address them less indirectly, and therefore less ambiguously?[6] Matthew might well not

---

[5] Bauckham, 1998.
[6] The fact that scholars disagree over Matthew's position on the circumcision of Gentile converts should alert us to the fact that a Gospel would have been a very blunt weapon for attacking these sorts of controversies. See the discussion in Sim, 1996 and 1998.

have been able to avoid alluding to such debates in the course of his narratives, but this does not mean that dealing with them was his primary concern. Maybe the kinds of controversies which recent studies have foregrounded were more in the nature of tools for reflection, debates around which reflection about wider issues of cosmology and the ethos of the community would crystallise.

The second point is this. The tendency within recent social historical studies of the early church communities has been either to seek to place them in relation to known controversies within the early church or to evaluate the communities from which the Gospels sprang, using sociological criteria. To what extent and in what sense did they function as sects?[7] Such analyses have undoubtedly yielded useful results, even if there are clearly grounds for caution in applying categories derived from empirical work on twentieth-century social groups to similar groupings in the first century.[8] The pioneer in this field of early Christian history was Wayne Meeks, who in a number of creative and original articles[9] looked at the way that certain motifs were used in the Gospel of John to foster a particular kind of sectarian mentality. More recent studies have attempted to apply such analyses to the Gospels in much greater detail,[10] considering the extent to which Matthew in his Gospel has sought to consolidate his – sectarian – community over against the dominant Jewish community. The harsh language of the Gospel against the Jewish leadership betrays its sense of marginalisation. It was, relatively speaking, 'more concerned with world-maintenance than being open to the world . . . interested in community formation, and not primarily

---

[7] See the cautious and suitably differentiated discussion in Markus, 1980. Markus' discussion of the differences in the modes of self-definition between the second- and third-century churches is couched largely in terms of their different treatment of doctrinal diversity: whereas, in the second century, a measure of doctrinal diversity was acceptable, so long as the boundaries were drawn clearly enough over against Gnostics and others; in the third century there was a growing tendency to seek doctrinal uniformity and to define all deviant beliefs as heresy. In this respect the later church assumed certain aspects of sectarian mentality: 'a need for uniformity and homogeneity, a need to outlaw deviance from its communion as "heresy" and an inability to preserve the ecumenicity of diverse traditions' (15). There is a nice balance here between attention to matters of cosmology and world-view in the study of early Christianity and a concern with the social function of such beliefs.

[8] For a measured assessment of work in the field of Matthaean studies, see Stanton, 1992, esp. 85–107.

[9] See esp. Meeks, 1972.

[10] See esp. Overman, 1990; Saldarini, 1994; Sim, 1998.

world transformation'.[11] Ulrich Luz, in his magisterial commentary on Matthew, has also spoken, in terms taken from E. Troeltsch rather than Bryan Wilson, about the sectarian nature of the community, characterising it more in terms of its doctrine and ethics than of its boundary formation and social interaction with the dominant social group in its environment. For Luz, Matthew's theology is the theology of a minority group which takes Jesus as its leader in its quest to establish its own way of life, based on obedience and love. It is perfectionist, practising a religion based on law, where grace is essentially 'practical assistance to the believer'.[12]

## Kinship and sacred space as key identity factors

Such works will form invaluable discussion partners in what follows, but I also wish somewhat to change the direction of the enquiry. Rather than focusing on particular debates within the church, or examining the particular manner in which the Gospels may have contributed to the consolidation of the early Christian communities, I want to look at certain topics, which were of widespread importance in the ancient world in the determination of a person's identity: kinship and geography. Josephus, in his *Life*, is at pains to stress the nobility of his descent: '[m]y family is no ignoble one, tracing its descent far back to priestly ancestors' (*Vita* 1). Concern with purity of ancestry was a mark of Judaism; maintaining purity of priestly descent, according to Josephus, was an important part of guaranteeing that they properly fulfilled their function as guardians of the national records (*c Ap* 1:28–38). In this they were like, indeed somewhat superior to, the Egyptians and Babylonians. Kinship, belonging to a particular blood-line, was of the greatest importance in defining who a person was.

So too was territory. One has only to think of the grandest of all grand narratives in the ancient world, the story of Odysseus' wanderings and return home, to realise how deep-seated was the sense of attachment to a particular place, to the hearth and the family. Language, particular religious and national festivals and customs are, too, all of major importance, but perhaps nothing is celebrated in narrative with quite

---

[11] Overmann, 154.
[12] Luz, 1989, 192–3, quotation, 193: 'Gnade versteht sie zentral als Hilfe in der Praxis.'

the same fervour as Odysseus' sense of belonging to Ithaca – unless it be the story of the Jews' attachment to the Land of Israel. The Hebrew Scriptures give pride of place to the story of the original entry and possession of the Land, with its long pre-history of slavery, exodus and desert wanderings; but the motif of home-coming continues to run through the subsequent history of exile and restoration. Isaiah's cry, 'In the desert prepare the way of the Lord', evokes deep resonances in later generations and stands as a motto over the Gospel narratives (though in both Matthew and Luke it yields its place of pre-eminence to the genealogies with which they both begin).

Such narratives of exile, wanderings and home-coming which underline the central importance of territory in the ancient world are not simply accounts of the travels of men and women. They are stories in which the gods are actively involved. Some places are dear not only to human beings but also to the gods. Odysseus' return, long after the other Greeks have returned from Troy, is decreed by the gods. Despite the worst that Poseidon can do, he is guided back to Ithaca by Hermes and there greeted by Athene. In similar ways Moses is divinely called to lead the Israelites out of bondage into the promised Land. They are led by the pillar of fire and accompanied by the presence of the Lord in the ark. Finally, under Solomon, the Temple is built in Jerusalem as a 'house for my name' (1 Kings 5:5).

In these narratives, territory is portrayed as more than physical geography: it is 'home' and, moreover, a home which lies under the 'sacred canopy' of the gods.[13] It is sacred space, a hallowed and protected haven; but, equally, it can be used in the most terrible punishments which God can inflict on his people: the overrunning by enemies, occupation, exile, desecration of the Temple itself, the 'abomination of desolation' (Dan 9:27; 11:31; 12:11; Mark 13:14). Similar motifs occur in the *Odyssey*: Odysseus' long exile and wanderings from which he is released only by divine decree, the invasion of his home by the suitors, and their threatened desecration of Penelope. That is to say, these stories not only impress on their readers a deep love of and longing for home, for a 'haven where they would be' (Ps 107:30, BCP); they also locate the known world within the boundaries of a sacred universe, peopled with divine beings.

[13]   Berger, 1969. See too Smith, 1978 and 1987.

The use of cultural anthropology in this study

Such stories, to draw on the cultural anthropologist Clifford Geertz, present both a 'model for' and a 'model of' reality. The sacred geography which they present powerfully suggests to their hearers and readers patterns of behaviour, 'powerful, pervasive, and long-lasting moods and motivations',[14] which constrain, often in unsuspected ways, the manner in which they act. As Geertz suggests, such symbolic artefacts impart cultural codes which have analogous roles in human societies to the genetically transmitted codes which control the behaviour of beavers in animal societies.[15]

Geertz's work is widely known and used, not least among biblical scholars. What I should like to emphasise here is twofold. In the first place, Geertz lays stress on the mutual reinforcement which is provided by the two ways in which such cultural symbols are read: as cosmology and as ethos. The more people act in accordance with the ways of conceiving the world which are suggested by their shared narratives, rituals and other symbolic products, the more such patterns of action seem to confer on their conceptions of the world an 'aura of factuality'. The more realistic a society's conceptions of the world become, the more its members will be constrained to act in accordance with them. There is then every reason in attempting to understand the way such important reservoirs of cultural meaning as the Gospels would have shaped their readers' identities in the first century, to give proper attention to the kind of cosmology that they would have imparted. We should avoid a simple functionalism, simply looking, for example, at the way in which the text of Matthew may have served to legitimate the sectarian community for which he was writing. How could it legitimate anything *religiously*, if it was not setting forth some form of trans-cendental framework within which to place his community? Reductive functionalist readings of cultural artefacts like the Gospels, which attend only to their social function, their ethos, to the exclusion of consideration of their cosmologies, fail thereby to consider the interaction between cosmology and ethos, which as Geertz suggests, is a crucial element in the functioning of religions as cultural systems. As Geertz so elegantly puts it, 'We have been trying to stage *Hamlet* without the Prince quite long enough.'[16]

---

[14] Geertz, 1993, 90.
[15] Geertz, 1993, 93.
[16] Geertz, 1993, 109.

Second, I want to caution against a too deterministic use of Geertz. Cultural codes may be analogous to genetic codes; they are not identical with them. The patterns of behaviour of beavers are predictable in a way which human patterns of behaviour, even in the most routinised forms of existence, are not. This is not to deny that there are indeed societies where the constraining force of cultural codes is extremely powerful. But two considerations must be set alongside this: first, that even in such societies instances of deviant behaviour may occur; second, that the same set of cultural symbols may be read to produce interestingly different cosmologies and types of ethos.

Geertz himself is clearly aware of these matters. He is intrigued precisely by the question how adherents of particular cults behave, when faced with everyday realities away from the rituals and observances which inculcate a particular world-view, values and attitudes. He is aware, that is to say, that there may be less than straightforward compliance, less than full internalisation of the codes and their given interpretation, on the part of individual members of the group at any time.[17] He is perhaps less aware of the diversity of cosmologies which can be formulated on the basis of one set of symbols and their articulation in particular narrations, rituals and so on. He certainly recognises the looseness of the connection between the symbols of a particular group and the general ideas of order which they generate.[18] It will, however, be part of our enquiry to look closely at the variations in the senses of order which are promoted by Matthew's redaction of Mark, and at the same time have an eye to the basic beliefs and attitudes which these two texts have in common. Part of the fascination of Synoptic studies, particularly in its more recent emphasis on the editorial contributions of the Evangelists, has been to present us with a picture of the way that, within an agreed framework of beliefs and a largely agreed narrative, significant variations in world-view and disposition could nevertheless be suggested. It is true, doubtless, that repetition serves to inculcate a basic message and that the promulgation of different Gospels may have

[17] Geertz comments: 'Religious belief has usually been presented as a homogeneous characteristic of an individual, like his place of residence, his occupational role, his kinship position, and so on. But religious belief in the midst of ritual, where it engulfs the total person, transporting him, so far as he is concerned, into another mode of existence, and religious belief as the pale, remembered reflection of that experience in the midst of everyday life are not precisely the same thing', 1993, 119–20.

[18] Thus, Geertz speaks of symbols as formulating 'however obliquely, inarticulately, or unsystematically, general ideas of order', 1993, 98.

11

served this goal. But it is also hardly thinkable that Matthew and Luke would have laboured so long, if they had not thought that their efforts would in some ways address, clarify, and set out more securely, the boundaries, the lineaments of their world.

## Cosmology and myth

This brings me to a further general, theoretical point about religious cosmologies or myths. Discussion of the mythology of the New Testament has ebbed, since the heyday of the demythologisation debate of the 1950s and 1960s. What was characteristic about the portrayals at that time of, say, the Gnostic redeemer myth, was its imagined coherence and roundedness.[19] Myths were sustained stories about the gods which could be told or summarised in a more or less straightforward manner. In practice, such a point about myths was rarely emphasised: it was simply taken for granted that the story or stories which made up or gave expression to a particular myth fitted together into an overall, logically consistent pattern. Such a view runs counter to the account of myth which is offered by Claude Lévi-Strauss, perhaps twentieth century's most omnivorous of myth-collectors. For Lévi-Strauss, myths are fundamentally oppositional. They give voice to oppositions which, so Lévi-Strauss holds, are projections of the deep structures of the mind. Such stories with their different codes – geographical, social and cosmological – express and seek to mediate between different patterns of social organisation and different ways of viewing the world. Ultimately the purpose of the myth is to expose and admit the paradoxes which lie at the heart of human societies.

I do not propose to follow Lévi-Strauss very far: the complex structural analyses of the myths which he offers seek a neatness and organisation which is strikingly at odds with the more piecemeal view of the relation of religious cosmologies to their basic symbols which we just noticed in Geertz. Nevertheless, Lévi-Strauss' emphasis on the oppositionality of myth, the ways in which it seeks to mediate between different views of reality, different explanations of human origins,[20] and of the origins of evil, is one that fits well with the evidence of first-century Jewish mythologies, as well as with the Greek myths that Lévi-Strauss discusses.

---

[19] See, for instance, Schmithals, 1971.
[20] See here Lévi-Strauss' account of the Oedipus legend, in Lévi-Strauss, 1955, 433.

Martin de Boer[21] has argued that first-century Jewish eschatology was of two kinds: one cosmic dualist, which saw the root of evil as lying in the invasion of the world by demonic forces which held men and women in bondage and which could be overcome only by a final battle between God and the demonic forces (*1 Enoch 1–36*); another forensic, which saw the source of evil as lying in the human will, of which the resolution resides in some final assize (*2 Baruch*). These two views may be found in isolation but more often they are found in some kind of dialogue within the same work. One of the tasks of this essay is to look at the relative weighting which is given to these different views of evil and its remedy in Mark and Matthew.

Brief statement of aims and methods

How then are we to proceed? To recapitulate briefly. The task is to examine the Gospels of Mark and Matthew for evidence of the emergence of new senses of self-identity among the communities and circles which formed their intended readership. Such senses of identity, following Geertz, are forged by the reading of sets of religious symbols to provide both a 'model for' and a 'model of' reality. We should not imagine, however, that such views of ethos and world order were set out in any systematic manner.[22] It is probably much closer to the mark to say, with Geertz, that they were formulated in ways which were oblique, unsystematic and even inarticulate. Moreover, it is likely that people's attention was drawn to such matters by particular issues, either of cosmology or ethos, which had a certain topical value within their society. Within the circles around Jesus it is likely that the topic of the 'kingdom of God', the manner in which and the time at which God would establish his rule over Israel and the world, was of burning interest. This clearly raised issues about 'the order of existence', about Israel's earlier history, about the place within God's plans for the Gentiles, for his 'enemies', for his faithful subjects; but it also raised issues about

---

[21] de Boer, 1989.

[22] It is this which deters me most from what had been my original intention, which was to write a 'New Testament theology'. The title has too much of the sound of a systematic theology, and sets up constraints on the author to produce a rounded and coherent whole out of what is a set, albeit a very rich set, of symbolic presentations of Christian models for and of reality. The task of constructing more systematic, philosophically filtered accounts of the Christian world-view (with and despite all its diversity) would be undertaken (and constantly revised) in subsequent centuries. It is not the intention of this present volume to anticipate that later work of cosmological and ethical construction.

ethos, about the ways in which God's subjects should prepare for, anticipate and co-operate in the establishment of that rule. Similarly, questions which were of particular importance for people's understanding of themselves, questions about their attachment to the Land, their ties of kinship and family, would also raise questions about the order of things, about the history of their people in the land, its invasion by other nations, their exile and return, the destruction of the Temple and its rebuilding. And such matters, equally, would be linked to stories of the Patriarchs, of their place within the Land, stories, for example, of Abraham's burial at Hebron, so that notions of kinship and attachment to place would be interlinked.

What then I propose to do is to take two of these common topics, descent and attachment to the Land, and to use them to lead us into a discussion of the world-view and ethos of the first two Gospels. We are interested, that is to say, not just in the extent to which the motif 'sons of Abraham' is replaced by notions of 'brothers and sisters of Jesus', but in the consequent changes in world-view, of God's purposes in history, his manner of resolution of the world's ills, and the inter-related changes in human 'moods and motivations', attitudes and values, which this may have occasioned. Precisely because of the *interactive* nature of cosmology and ethos, we cannot simply treat questions of identity-formation in isolation from wider questions of cosmological belief, or vice versa. Thus, as we treat each Gospel, we shall first look carefully at the use of particular narrative features, characters, motifs and metaphors, which in turn address or give expression to questions of kinship and of attachment to place. As we conduct such detailed studies, we shall notice how such motifs are interwoven with various cosmological features, address questions of the world's ills, their origins and divine resolution. Finally, at the end of our discussion of each Gospel, we shall attempt to draw together some of these wider themes into a more comprehensive account of the cosmological beliefs which they express.

There are many difficulties in making the transition from the Gospel texts to the kinds of theological beliefs, attitudes, moods and motivations which they may have inspired in the communities and members who read them. These difficulties will be particularly acute in our reading of Mark, where we take our starting point. We can neither be very sure what traditions he inherited, nor can we be very clear what the original setting of the Gospel was. We shall then be dependent, more than elsewhere, on an imaginative reconstruction of the views of kinship and sacred place which Mark's text may have suggested. Certainly we shall want to set Mark's work in the wider context of contemporary notions of kinship and sacred space and our next chapter will attempt to give at least a sketch of such ideas. But in the end, we shall have to rely much on a close reading of the text to discern its use and weighting of the narrative codes which it employs.[23]

The situation improves significantly, however, when we come to consider Matthew. For here we have a gift which is perhaps under-appreciated by writers on the New Testament. We have wonderfully full evidence of the growth of a literary history. This history, of course, does not stop with Matthew, nor indeed with Luke and John, but extends into the rich fields of the non-canonical Gospels. In employing the term 'literary history', I have particularly in mind the work of Hans-Robert Jauß.[24] Texts, says Jauß, are not so much world-depicting (weltabbildend) as world-building (weltbildend). They provide us with the cultural language and symbols to construct a new vision of the world. They create a literary history, in which a community's understanding of reality is forged by its engagement with the text (and its own life-experiences). This is a process which may go through many stages. The view of reality adopted by the community at any time in response to a given text, changes the horizon of expectations with which subsequent generations will approach and interpret the same text, leading to the formation of rather different imaginative reconstructions.

This view of the history of the appropriation of texts (and the production of other literary texts as part of that history) rests on an understanding of the reading process whereby the community of readers itself has an active and creative role in the reading of texts; it 'fills in the gaps' which are left in the narratives and dialogues; and this filling out of elements which have been left undetermined in the text, precisely initiates the process of imaginative reconstruction of the text by the reader, without which the text remains mute.[25] Such gaps, Iser argues, are not so much omissions on the part of the intentional

---

[23] In this we shall not be working in any way *de novo*. There are excellent examples of this kind of work on literary texts and on Mark in particular. I have been especially helped by Nancy Shumate's perceptive and close reading of Apuleius, in Shumate, 1996.

[24] Jauß, 1970.

[25] See esp. Iser, 1990, 284–301.

object ('Bestimmungslücken des intentionalen Gegenstandes') but rather represent opportunities for the reader to occupy the text with his imagination. Hence there is a reciprocal process between the text and the reader: the reader brings his or her 'horizons of expectation' to the texts which inform the manner in which the text is imaginatively realised when read. But this reading in turn informs and indeed modifies the 'horizons of expectation' of the community, so that subsequent readings will vary as new ways of realising the meaning of the texts emerge. Such 'readings' may be of many different forms: they may be the imaginative acts of the individual reader reading in private; they may be public 'performances' of one kind or another: sermons, lectures, dramatic presentations and readings. They may also take the form of retellings and reformulations of the original text, as in the many retellings of the Genesis stories, or indeed as in the Synoptic Gospels.

The bearing of Jauß's notion of literary history on the Gospels is not hard to seek. What we have in Matthew is a reconfiguration of Mark's symbolic world, which he has constructed out of the Gospel traditions, notably as presented in Mark's Gospel, though with significant other manifestations (as in 'Q'). Like any other texts, Matthew has to be read as a whole. But as we investigate his reworkings of the themes and motifs relevant to our chosen topics in Mark, we shall more easily discern the emphases he wished to place, the ways in which he has sought to realise the Markan text in his own rewriting. Matthew is a reading of Mark, albeit one which we also have to read. Identifying the ways in which Matthew modifies Mark's cosmology and ethos, as reflected in his presentation of the motifs associated in Mark with kinship and sacred space, will certainly be a somewhat easier task than simply reading Mark from cold. It may, in a measure, also help to confirm or modify our views of Mark. Being aware of what, for example, Matthew omits from Mark, may well help us to realise not only what is unimportant or offensive to Matthew, but also to check our views of what was characteristic of Mark.

Most importantly, it will give us an insight into the ways in which the rereading and subtle recasting of symbolic worlds can help to shape the communities which accept their authority. This process of appropriation of the symbols of the Gospel tradition leads to the production of texts which were to have enormous generative power over the next two thousand years.

*Relation of this study to contemporary discussions of self-identity*

This study, it will be apparent, is first and foremost, an essay in a kind of historical cultural anthropology. As such it might appear to be of merely antiquarian interest. But such studies are rarely taken without an eye to questions and concerns contemporary to the writer. The question which intrigues me and which motivates this study is this: in what way may the close study of the genesis of these texts, of the early stages of this complex literary history, shed light on our contemporary concerns with the identity of the self? Is there something which we may learn from the study of these complex interactions within a particular religious and cultural context, which goes beyond an understanding of the processes involved in this particular history of identity-making to address even the questions of substance which tax those who observe our own rapidly changing cultures?

The contemporary search for identity is conducted in a world where society is undergoing massive change: traditional modes of regulating community life and the life of the individual are being challenged as more and more the economic and cultural processes in which men and women are involved are globalised, stripped of any local significance, and equally of any reference to local mores or traditions (disembedding). Such processes are self-referential: they are judged by their own internal criteria, how successfully they meet their own aims and objectives. In this sense they are creative of their own meaning. Society itself becomes immensely dynamic and so potentially dangerous. People live through periods of unprecedented change and have to struggle to find some basis of trust and confidence in an increasingly unfamiliar world. Their own identity itself becomes a self-regulating project.[26] This high modern view of the nature of the 'project of the self' contrasts sharply with the ways in which in traditional societies a person's sense of identity was received. Here people's identity was principally defined in terms of their place within a particular community, the role which they filled within the community, their kinship relationships, their economic and social status. Their behaviour was judged in terms of the existing norms within that society: honour and shame was apportioned on an agreed basis. Giddens' point is that there is a close interrelationship between the self-regulating projects of modern institutions and the ways in which people

---

[26] Giddens, 1991.

today have to seek to construct their own self-identity. People tell a constantly revised and revisable story about themselves. They are engaged in a search for themselves which is self-reflexive, where they constantly review and revise their views of their lives and their life-projects.

This concern with the self and with the construction (or discovery) of self is, it has been powerfully argued by Charles Taylor,[27] a truly modern phenomenon. It emerges at the time of the breakdown of the *ancien régime* with its system of *préférences*. Philosophers like Rousseau argued that what was essential or foundational for the value of a person was not his or her conformity to a set of widely-held values, or indeed his or her position within a particular society but the sense of self, *le sens de l'existence*. In simple terms: it is important, above all important, that we should be who we are, that we should be true to ourselves and *not* to some imposed view of who we should be. However, while such demands for the authenticity of the individual represent one side of the changing nature of the search for self-identity, there is another, which is more concerned with the role of inherited cultural group traditions in the formation of the individual's identity and the need for society to recognise such groups, rather than to disparage or to discriminate against them. This again goes back to intellectual traditions from the late eighteenth century, notably expressed in the work of the German preacher and philosopher J. G. Herder. For Herder, it was the inherited language, art and culture of a people which gave it its particular character and genius and this was of vital importance for the development of the individuals within it. Such views strike a rich chord in present debates about the state's duty to support and further the rights of minority groups, whether based on ethnicity, gender, sexual orientation, language or whatever, even at the expense of other, universal, human rights. The 'politics of recognition' has become a major issue for multicultural societies like those of North America and Europe.

These analyses of the modern project of the self raise some major questions for the Christian tradition and for modern Christian attempts at self-definition. Such questions cannot be answered simply in terms of our historical enquiry into the nature of early Christian identity-formation: they can only be answered by further dialogue with those who debate these issues in our modern society. Nevertheless, it is first

[27] Taylor, 1989 and 1991.

necessary to state the questions and then to see how far the historical analysis may help to inform our subsequent judgements.

If Christianity emerges in a 'traditional' as opposed to a 'modern' setting, that is, in one where a person's identity is largely conferred on them by the accident of birth into a particular station within a particular community with its own particular sacred cosmos, then does it have anything at all to contribute to the modern 'project of the self' with its emphasis on reflexivity, on the self-regulating and self-referential nature of that project, in short, with its outright rejection of a transcendental framework for the self?

Further, how are those who seek to develop a sense of their own identity in dialogue with the New Testament texts to address the complex issues raised by Charles Taylor in relation to multiculturalism? Are they to see their identity as specifically tied to that of a particular religious group and culture, and therefore to stress the need for a due politics of recognition which would if necessary support the rights of such communal groupings over against the rights of individuals to free expression?

Finally, how far can the search for a Christian identity be conceived of as a search for 'authentic existence', if, as Taylor argues, such ideas are developed polemically against the notion of an existence which has its place within a received hierarchy of being? Can the notion of authenticity escape the charge of a radical ethical relativism and is such relativism in any way compatible with the ethics of the New Testament writings?

I hardly expect this study to provide direct answers to such questions. Theology, as David Tracy has suggested, is essentially a conversational activity.[28] We should not then expect an enquiry like the present one itself to produce the kind of contemporary reading of the Gospels which would directly address our present questions about multiculturalism and self-identity. What I hope for it is threefold. First, that it will demonstrate that creativity and diversity of reading are a feature of the Gospels' literary history and that all attempts to impose singular readings on them is doomed, in the long run, to be subverted by their inherent plurality. Second, it may show that the 'traditional' world and society from which these texts sprang was less rigidly determined than some of our contemporary debates suggest; that, moreover, within such

---

[28] Tracy, 1988.

traditional societies, with their strong transcendental frame of reference, there is ample evidence of changing senses of identity, of different forms of self-definition, even within closely related communities. The gap between traditional and modern, or 'high modern' societies, massive though it is, should not be exaggerated. And third, it may show something of the resources of our Gospels which have enabled at least some of their readers to discover new and fulfilling modes of existence which are not oppressive of those outside their group.

# 2

# Jewish identity in the world of the Mediterranean cities: themes and variations

## Introduction

Jews in the Diaspora: their cultural codes

Two things, at least, can be said about Mark and Matthew with some considerable confidence: they were both written in the first century CE in one or other of the Graeco-Roman cities which ringed the Mediterranean; and they both treat the Jewish Scriptures as authoritative. These two indications, taken together, make it compelling to locate these books in the world of the Jewish communities living outside the Land itself. One might add, if looking for further obvious pointers to their origins in the Jewish Diaspora, that they were written in *koine* Greek, the lingua franca[1] of the Mediterranean world of commerce, the military and government.

What this means is that these Gospels have to be read as emanating from a family of religious communities which enjoyed a highly complex and varied set of relationships to their surrounding culture. Jews in the Diaspora regarded the world of the Hellenistic cities with everything from total acceptance, through critical enthusiasm, to profound suspicion and enmity. They spoke its language and translated their sacred writings into it. Many Diaspora Jews attended its schools and took part in the commercial and cultural life of the cities. Nevertheless, they stood out as a distinctive religious and ethnic group with their own ties of blood and distinctive customs. They were also in an obvious sense aliens, in that they acknowledged, again with differing degrees of enthusiasm, their belonging to the Land of Israel with its sacred priesthood and,

---

[1] The original application of the term was to the language spoken in the Mediterranean ports from the time of the Crusaders to the eighteenth century, 'based on Italian, Spanish, French, Arabic, Greek and Turkish' (*The New Collins Concise English Dictionary*). *Koine* is first encountered in the fifth century. Like the later lingua franca, properly so-called, it was widely established as a result of military campaigns, in this case those of Alexander the Great.

until its destruction, one Temple.[2] After its destruction, Jews across the Mediterranean will have shared the same sense of humiliation and revulsion at the public display of the Temple vessels and furnishings and at the coins which were minted depicting Judaea in chains. Jews everywhere were now compelled to pay their former contributions to the Temple in Jerusalem into the *fiscus iudaicus*,[3] which was initially applied to the rebuilding of the temple of Jupiter Capitolinus.

The variety of Jewish communities in the Diaspora at this period means that we should be hard put to depict the precise nature of the relationship between our Gospels and the communities from which they sprang and their local synagogue. It is, in the first place, difficult to give precise and accurate locations for our Gospels.[4] Second, as we have already indicated, one should be cautious about reading the Gospels too narrowly, as addressed solely to particular small Christian communities, confronting quite specific issues. Apart from the difficulties involved in identifying the precise historical setting of each of the Gospels, the present enquiry has necessarily a broader focus. One can reasonably ask what the bearing of the Gospels may have been on particular issues which concerned the churches at the time of their composition. One may also ask what sort of view of the world, what sort of community ethos such texts helped to shape.

To answer this latter question, it is less important to know the precise setting of a particular Gospel, than to have as keen an awareness as possible of the various codes, linguistic, social, geographical, ritual, physical, through which Jews and, following them, the Evangelists, expressed – in a variety of ways – both their sense of their identity and their vision of the world. We shall then be in a position to judge how far the Evangelists have used the same codes, and to what extent they may have modified them or substituted others; above all, to what particular sense

---

[2] Philo, *Spec Leg* 1:67–8. The highest and most holy temple of God is the whole universe with heaven as its sanctuary, but because it is right not to inhibit those who want to give thanks or ask for forgiveness by offering sacrifice, one Temple has been established, 'for he judged that since God is one, there should also only be one temple'. This means that those who live outside the land have to bring themselves to 'leave country and friends and kinsfolk and sojourn in a strange land'.

[3] Josephus, *Bell* 7:218.

[4] Such attempts have, of course, been made and it is proper that they should be. Hengel, 1985, esp. 1–30, argues strongly for a Roman location during the year of the four emperors (69 CE); there are also, however, strong arguments to be made for a Syrian location during the Jewish War; see Marcus, 1992a. For a full discussion of Matthew's location, arguing for Antioch, see Sim, 1998, 40–62.

of identity and visions of reality they gave expression through the use of such codes. Clearly, it will be helpful to give examples of the ways in which such codes were employed in different Jewish groups.

Our purpose in this chapter then is to examine as far as possible the cultural codes in use in Jewish communities at the turn of the era as they related specifically to kinship and sacred space. These codes would have formed an important part of the cultural arsenal of the emerging Christian communities, as they sought to give shape to their own sense of identity. They were a part of a wide range of such codes which covered all aspects of life.[5] There were genealogical codes, relating to descent and kinship; codes relating to matters of 'practical' social intercourse: fellowship at meals, participation in Gentile assemblies, codes relating to the body and dress: not least circumcision and the wearing of 'phylacteries and tassels' (Matt 23:5); codes which defined the cult and the relation of places, people and materials to the cult, such as purity regulations, classifications of different families and individuals as priests, levites, and so on, definitions of places and things as more or less sacred and profane; there are codes relating to the great figures and events of the past, the 'forefathers', Abraham, Moses, the prophets and the Exodus, the desert wanderings, exile, return.

Simply to list in a cursory way the symbolic resources available to Jews is to be aware of the richness of their cultural heritage, and of the impossibility of giving any kind of comprehensive account of the way such codes functioned in the Jewish Diaspora. We shall accordingly concentrate attention in this chapter on those codes which bear most directly on the topics which form the major focus of this book. That is to say, we shall look first at matters of sacred geography: of the place of the Land and the Temple in Jewish life, the way it defines the position of those who live outside the Land, the relation of such distinctions to notions of sacred and profane, and the way such distinctions govern the details of daily life both within and outwith the Jewish community. This will be followed by a treatment of descent, kinship, family relationships, relationships to the great figures and events of the past. Again, it will be apparent that even such an attempt to limit the treatment will in one

---

[5] In his enormously helpful book, John Barclay, 1996, distinguishes between social and symbolic resources for identity formation and 'practical distinctions' and 'the ethnic bond'. As a broad classification this is helpful enough, but it should not be allowed to obscure the fact that 'separatism at meals' is as much a 'symbolic resource' as is the appeal to Moses or to descent from Abraham.

way do no more than provide a convenient framework within which to treat virtually all symbolic codes available to Jews at the time. Inevitably, some aspects will receive at most a cursory treatment here. Further discussions will be given in the notes in later chapters as required.

Finally, I shall attempt to say something about the ways in which such codes were employed in the formation of Jewish cosmology in the first century. In particular, I want to see what role notions of kinship and descent, on the one hand, and sacred space, the Land and the Temple on the other hand, played in Jewish hopes in an age of catastrophe. Faced with such evidence of forces inimical to themselves and, apparently at least, to the purposes of God, how did Jews account for the presence of such dark powers and what hopes did they entertain for their overcoming and their own release and restoration?

Such questions received very different answers. As a result, the various articulations of sacred geography we shall notice are predicated on very different views of the origin and ultimate destiny of evil in the world. For such geographies and the maps which they evoke are not by any means simply aids to navigation, even though they may draw on contemporary cartography. Rather they map out a particular view of the divine cosmos and of its alien and contrary forces; they may disclose the final resting places of the wicked and the just, and the places where the future sources of blessing are already stored up. And different geographies may give rather different clues to such final mysteries. Not all such 'maps' will be revelations of hidden mysteries; some will be staking claims to divinely-sanctioned territorial boundaries, whether achieved or still longed for. The same *pari passu* is true of the ways in which views of social and national identity are spelled out: they too may express very different ideas of the nature of Jewish identity, of the forces which threatened it both from within and without, and of the manner in which such conflicts would be resolved. And we shall find evidence of contrasting, indeed of fundamentally opposed views, within the self-same texts and sources.

## Jewish identity in the Diaspora and the Land: notions of sacred geography

Jackson and Henrie define sacred space as

> that portion of the earth's surface which is recognised by individuals or groups as worthy of devotion, loyalty or esteem. Sacred space is sharply discriminated

from the non-sacred or profane world around it. Sacred space does not exist naturally, but is assigned sanctity as man defines, limits and characterises it through his culture, experience and goals.[6]

## Jubilees

Such a notion of sacred space is easy enough to apply to biblical and post-biblical ideas of sacred territory.[7] A second-century text, *Jubilees*, gives a clear example, though one which contains some surprises:

> And he knew that the garden of Eden was the holy of holies, and the dwelling of the Lord. And Mount Sinai (was) in the midst of the desert and Mount Zion (was) in the midst of the navel of the earth. The three of these were created as holy places, one facing the other (8:19).

Strikingly, the sanctuary on Mount Zion is not described as the most holy, the holy of holies, nor as the dwelling of the Lord: these descriptions are reserved for the garden of Eden, lying in the extreme east.[8] Equally interesting is the fact that the holiness of the Land is not defined in terms of concentric circles radiating out from the Temple as the centre of holiness, even though the notion of ὀμφαλός, the navel of the earth, is borrowed from Ezekiel 38:12. Rather, we are offered a vision of a triangle of three holy places, facing each other and creating, as it were, a field of forces which renders the territory in between sacred.

Definitions and demarcations of space are here intimately related to notions of kinship and descent. Spaces are distinguished by virtue of their divinely sanctioned donation to specific peoples. The *Jubilees*

---

[6] Jackson and Henrie, 1983, 94. As we shall see, sacred space in Judaism may be graded according to degrees of holiness; nevertheless, this does not undermine the fundamental nature of the distinction between sacred and profane.

[7] Even though within the overall distinction between sacred and profane there may be degrees of holiness, the distinction itself is still sharply drawn.

[8] This may reflect traditions which denied that the *Shekhina* was present in the Second Temple. Certainly Ezekiel contains the notion of the departure of the glory of the Lord from the Temple, as judgement on the profanity and immorality of the Jerusalemites (Ezek 8–11), as he portrays its return in the vision of the final, eschatological Temple. If, as is widely held, the book of Ezekiel is the product of the exilic period, then clearly the immediate reference of such prophecies is to that period, not to the period after the return and the rebuilding of the Temple under Zerubbabel. But this in no way precludes such prophecies being transferred by later generations to the period of the Second Temple itself. Nevertheless, the text in *Jubilees* does not speak of the profanation of the Temple; it simply subordinates it to the paradisal sanctuary.

text is part of a retelling of Genesis 10, in which the Table of Nations is taken up and given a much more detailed geographical setting than in the original text.[9] As Philip Alexander[10] has argued, the *Jubilees* text provides a *mappa mundi* based on Noah's division of the world between his sons Ham, Shem and Japheth and also locates within that threefold division the nations descended from their offspring. The world is conceived as circular, with Zion lying at the centre of the circle, which is in turn surrounded by water. The lands of Shem are bounded on the west by the Great Sea (the Mediterranean), to the north by the River Tina (the Don); to the south by the River Gihon (the Nile) which comes from a more easterly direction, and in the east, where Paradise is located, by the waters of the abysses. The territories of the descendants of Japheth lie to the north, of Ham to the south. Sacred geography also justifies Israel's claim to the Land, not least by locating Canaan's lands in the extreme north-west of Africa rather than in Palestine. *Jubilees* goes on to relate Canaan's violent seizure of 'the land of Lebanon as far as the river of Egypt' and the curses which his father and brothers imposed on him in consequence (10:27–34).

This map, as Alexander points out, takes over many of the features of Ionian geography, notably its division of the world into three continents: Europe, Asia and Libya. Unlike the Ionians, however, it locates the *omphalos* not at Delphi (so Pindar, Aeschylus), but at Zion and orientates the map on a east–west axis running from Paradise through Zion to the Straits of Gibraltar and a north–south axis through Sinai and Zion. In this way the key sites of Jewish history are given a pivotal position in the cosmos. Geography affirms that Israel's story is the central story of the world. The holy sites are located within or in direct relation to the land of Israel, thus distinguishing it from all other territory. Nevertheless the map, with its close links with the Table of Nations, affirms also that nations and peoples are part of God's world and purposes, with their own legitimate claims to land and territory. There is, that is to say, both a remarkably universal character to the *Jubilees* 'map': all nations have their allotted place; and a clearly

---

[9] Gen 10 is based on a P-table of Noah's descendants, who live 'each in their own lands, each with his own language, by their families, in their nations' (10:5). It is filled out by material from a J-table. Only the J-material contains specific geographical references to enable the reader to locate the different ethnic groups; see vv. 19 and 30.

[10] Alexander, 1992.

particularistic one: the major sacred sites are located within Israel's territory.

In view of the apparently ecumenical assumptions of the *Jubilees* map, it is interesting to note the sharply dualist nature of the presentation of Israel's relation to the other nations in the book as a whole. The nations may have all been given their allotted place within the created world; they may all be descended from Noah; but this does not mean that they will therefore all continue to enjoy their portion of the earth forever. Their disobedience is such that they will all be destroyed. The sharpest formulation of this distinction between Israel and the nations comes in the section on circumcision, following the circumcision of Abraham and his household ( *Jub* 15:25–32). There the circumcised, as the sons of the covenant, are distinguished from the children of destruction who 'are destined to be destroyed and annihilated from the earth'. Israel is sanctified in the 'presence of the angels of the presence and the angels of sanctification . . . so that they might be with him and with his holy angels'. Only in one respect is this fierce particularism tempered: the people of Israel is not simply coterminous with the descendants of Abraham. Not all Abraham's descendants are to be included: 'For the LORD did not draw Ishmael and his sons and brothers and Esau near to himself, and he did not elect them because they are sons of Abraham, for he knew them'. Equally his choice of Israel was not limited to Abraham's descendants: 'And he sanctified them and gathered them from all the sons of man because (there are) many nations and many people, and they all belong to him.' There are, however, important limits to this kind of universalism. As in Qumran (1QS3–4), God has set spirits to rule over the nations to 'lead them astray from following him'. By contrast with the Two Spirits passage in Qumran, where God appoints a Prince of Light to rule over Israel, *Jubilees* has: 'over Israel he did not cause any angel or spirit to rule, because he alone is their ruler and he will protect them and he will seek for them at the hand of his angels and at the hand of his spirits and at the hand of all his authorities, so that he might guard them and bless them and they might be his and he might be theirs henceforth and forever' (16:32).

*Jubilees* is certainly one of the most interesting of the attempts in early Jewish literature to trace out a map of the world. It is the earliest example of a type of map of the world which, according to Alexander, 'predominated in European culture down almost to the time of Columbus'. It is, for example, the basis of the Hereford *Mappa Mundi* of *c.*1290.[11] It is not unique among Jewish literature: there are further attempts to map out the world in *1 Enoch* 76–77 and 17–36, which are arguably influenced by Eastern rather than Ionian cartography.[12] There are further treatments of the Table of Nations in Josephus, *Ant.* 1:122–47, and Pseudo-Philo, *Liber Antiquitatum Biblicarum* 4:1–10. The importance of *Jubilees* for our purposes is not to argue that this represents the standard view of the world for Jews in our period, but to show how such maps were constructed and the ways in which they might influence a writer's (and his community's) understanding of his people's place in the world.

*Jubilees*' comprehensive picture of the existing world is drawn from motifs from the biblical narratives and Jewish cultic ideology and blended with contemporary geographical knowledge. The Table of Nations claims to give a comprehensive account of the world's peoples. *Jubilees* follows this by allocating the different ethnic groups territories within the known map of the world. But it is not just a straight distribution of peoples: within the map, specifically within the territory of Shem, there are special places marked out from all the rest, Paradise, Zion and Sinai, on which the map is centred. What distinguishes these is their holiness: they are places where God has shown himself or where indeed he dwells.

Such a map provides one articulation of the cosmology of the writer, which may then interact with the political, social and moral attitudes and values of his community in different ways. *Jubilees*, by wide consensus, is held to date from the period of the Maccabean revolt. Its writer is to be placed among the party of the Hasidim, probably before the period at which the Qumran sectaries split away from the Pharisees. Its context, that is to say, is marked by the profound experience of persecution, proscription of the Law and desecration of the sanctuary under the Seleucids, and, more arguably, by growing conflict and dissension among the party of the Hasidim. This context is reflected in

[11] The extent to which the text of *Jubilees* was directly responsible for this is debated. Alexander, 1992, 982, comments: 'It is unclear whether the Christian T-O maps go back to the lost drawings of the *Jubilees* map, or whether they are derived from the written text of *Jubilees* alone. *Jubilees* was certainly known to some Christian authors in its Greek translation, and it seems to have influenced the patristic *Diamerismos* literature, which is concerned with dividing up the world among the sons of Noah.'

[12] Alexander, 1992, 984–85, refers here to the Babylonian *mappa mundi* in the British Museum and suggests that the maps in *Jubilees* and *1 Enoch* represent two schools, one looking to the west, the other to the east.

its retelling of the Abraham story, in which the universalistic aspects of the map's cosmology are in large measure subordinated to the particularistic motifs implicit in the singling out of Israel's sacred sites. When the author came to retell the story of Abraham and the birth of the Jewish nation, Jews' recent experience of torture and oppression under the Seleucids would have precluded a simple treatment of Israel as one among the many peoples of the earth.[13] The radical opposition between Israel and the nations who have oppressed it, cannot tolerate such a flattening of the distinction between the two. A far sharper contrast is required, which is drawn both in terms of sanctification/defilement, corruption ( *Jub* 21:21) and in terms of a dualist distinction between the peoples whom the spirits lead astray and Israel over whom God alone rules ( *Jub* 15:31–32). But equally, the writer's own experience of the divisions within Israel during that period and the Hasidim's own insistence on obedience to and zeal for the Law (1 Macc 2:42) must have left their mark on the retelling of the story. It would explain why for him not all descendants of Abraham were 'sons of the covenant'. What ultimately distinguishes the true sons of Abraham is their adherence to a particular programme of renewal of the Law. Thus there is no inconsistency in his affirmation that the 'sons of the covenant' can be drawn from all the 'sons of man because (there are) many nations and many people'. The universalising map may still serve as a caution against overconfidence in kinship and descent.

There are aspects of the *Jubilees* map to which we need to return. We noticed above the remarkable linking of three holy sites in Shem's territory Zion, Sinai and Paradise, with Paradise being described in terms usually applied to the inner sanctum of the Temple as the holy of holies, the dwelling place of God. This maps out a sacred area extending from the centre of earth in Zion, to the east in the Garden of Eden and to the south at Sinai. The Book of *Jubilees* itself is set on Sinai. It is portrayed as the second book of law which is delivered to Moses by the angel of the presence on Sinai ( *Jub* 1:26–28). The book opens with God summoning Moses to the mountain. There he reveals to Moses what is to happen to Israel ( *Jub* 1:4–29; see also 23:14–31) after the establishment of the covenant. Israel will apostasise and forsake 'my

---

[13] The immediate pre-history of the Seleucid persecution, the Hellenistic 'reform' which introduced institutions like gymnasia and stadia into Jerusalem, will hardly have well disposed the author to any form of assimilation or accommodation to the nations.

ordinances and my commandments and the feasts of my covenant and my sabbaths and my sacred place, which I sanctified for myself among them, and my tabernacle and my sanctuary, which I sanctified for myself in the midst of the land so that I might set my name upon it and might dwell (there)' ( *Jub* 1:10). Those who repent will be gathered from the nations: 'I shall build my sanctuary in their midst, and I shall be with them' (1:17). They will be called 'sons of the living God' (1:25).

Thus the chronicles which the angel of the presence gives to Moses encompass the history of the world from the day of creation to the 'day of the new creation when the heaven and the earth and all of their creatures shall be renewed according to the powers of heaven and according to the whole nature of earth, until the sanctuary of the Lord is created in Jerusalem upon Mount Zion' ( *Jub* 1:29). It looks then as if the location of the holy of holies in the Garden of Eden in the world map is a reflection of a belief that at the time of the writer the Lord had withdrawn from Zion.[14] The restoration of God's presence to Zion will mark the inauguration of a new paradisal existence.[15]

We may perhaps see here further evidence of the way that the writer's situation has affected his re-presentation of the patriarchal narratives. Priestly ideology asserted that God's presence in the Temple was a guarantee of the integrity of the Land.[16] If, however, the people sinned

[14] The motif of the abandonment of the Temple is quite common; see 1 Kings 9:6–9; Isa 64:10–11; Jer 12:7; 22:5; Ezek 8:6; 11:22–25; 12:7; Hag 1:9; Tob 14:4; *1 Enoch* 89:56; 4QFlor 1:5–6; 4Q179; *T Levi* 15:1; Josephus, *Bell* 6:300; *2 Bar* 8:2; *4 Ezra* 1:33; Tacitus, *Hist* 5:13; *Gos Phil* 84:27–28. For further discussion, see Davies and Allison, 1997, 321–2. If this does indeed refer to God's abandonment of the Temple, then the writer is more sectarian than Wintermute in his Introduction allows. He appears to belong to a group which rejects the Temple cult as contaminated and faithless. This is supported by the strong polemic against the Temple lunar calendar (which *Jubilees* links with all kinds of unfaithfulnesses and abominations 1:12–14) and also by his rejection of the mitigation of sabbath law, which the Maccabees had introduced to prevent their wholesale slaughter (1 Macc 2:40–41; cf. *Jub* 50:13).
[15] This is reflected in *Jubilees'* treatment of the Enoch passage in Gen 5:18–24, where Genesis' 'Enoch walked with God (*'elohim*); and he was not, for God took him' is expanded into the story of Enoch's location in Paradise. There he 'offered the incense which is acceptable before the Lord in the evening (at) the holy place on Mount Qater'. Enoch is thus portrayed as 'the instigator of the ritual of evening incense, which was part of normal daily service in the Temple in Jerusalem', *OTP*, 2, 63, n. m. The passage here speaks of four sacred places, adding Mount Qater to the list in the map, and specifically notes that Mount Zion will be sanctified in the new creation for the sanctification of the earth.
[16] The view is expressed powerfully in the Psalms (cf. e.g. Ps 18, 48), and in popular narrative, e.g. Judith (cf. Achior's speech, 5:5–21), and the story of Apollonius, 4 Macc 4.

and contaminated the Land and polluted the Temple through their immorality and idolatry, then God would leave the Temple and abandon the Land.[17] *Jubilees'* sense of the absence of God from the Temple (*Jub* 1:13), even though Zion is still designated a holy place, is given expression in the future predictions, which, in the narrative, are the clearest reference to the time of the writer. The experience of invasion, desecration and subsequent division over the implementation of the Law, both in military and cultic matters, has led the writer to see his own time as fundamentally one of rebellion from God, as one where the divine presence has departed from the Temple.[18] The root cause is Israel's forsaking God's ordinances and 'the feasts of my covenant and my sabbaths and my sacred place' (1:10). But this rebellion has led them to sacrifice their children to demons' (1:11), so that the 'spirit of Beliar rules over them' (1:20). Nevertheless, they will repent and God will circumcise them spiritually. 'And their souls will cleave to me and to all my commandments. And they will do all my commandments. And I shall be a father to them, and they will be sons to me. And they will all be called "sons of the living God"' (1:23–25).

We have seen that there are distinguishable motifs in the sacred geography of *Jubilees*. Superimposed on the map of the world, with its apportioning of territories to the different nations, distinguished by lineage and custom and language (Abr[ah]am learns the original language of paradise, Hebrew, *Jub* 12:25–27) is a different system of boundary drawing, that between sacred and profane. These different ways of marking out territory are not simply coterminous. The sacred places of Zion, Sinai and Eden mark out the central axes of the world; they all fall in Shem's territory, but they do not coincide with the borders of the Land. Sinai is forever associated with Moses and the desert wanderings of the people; Eden is the lost paradise from which Adam and his descendants have been cast out, which yet foreshadows the expected restoration of the presence of God in the Temple.

## Other views of Land and Temple

Such views had deep roots in Scripture. Leviticus portrays the Land as the sacred realm from which God has vomited out the Gentiles because

---

[17] Ezek 9–11.

[18] In this sense one might compare CD 1's characterisation of the early period of the renewal movement: 'They perceived their iniquity and recognised that they were guilty men, yet for twenty years they were like blind men groping for their way.'

of their abominations (Lev 20:22–26). Jews, therefore, must make a clear distinction between clean and unclean animals to remind themselves of the distinction between themselves and the lawless Gentiles, lest they too corrupt the Land and meet the same fate. On this view, which is developed more fully in the discussions of the Temple in Ezekiel 40–48 and in Haggai and Zechariah,[19] the Temple is the centre of holiness in the Land, with its high point in the inner sanctuary and with concentric circles of holiness radiating out from the central place.[20] For Ezekiel, the power and life which flows from the rebuilt Temple, once the glory of the Lord has returned, is symbolised by the waters which flow out of the Temple (47:1–12). Similar motifs are to be found in Haggai (2:10–19) and Zechariah (2:8–9; 8:9–13).

As William Horbury has argued, this close connection between the Temple and the Land is also a feature of later narrative and psalm. In such presentations of Israelite history, '[c]olonization of the *land*' is 'presented as leading directly to assembly in the *sanctuary*'.[21] This is true of the song of Moses and the children of Israel in Exodus (15:17), as it is of Psalm 78:53–54, especially in its Septuagint version (77:53–54):

> he guided them in hope, and they were not afraid,
>> and the sea covered their enemies,
> and he led them into the mountain of his sanctuary,
>> this mountain which his right hand possessed.

Such reworkings of the Exodus traditions are prevalent in both Hebrew and Greek Jewish sources of the turn of the era.[22] They provide, as we shall see towards the end of this chapter, the basis for apocalyptic predictions of the gathering in of the nations to a new sanctuary (*1 Enoch* 89–90) and for the belief in a coming divinely prepared temple, based on Exodus 15:17 LXX:

[19] See discussions in Meyers and Meyers, 1987, liv-lix, and chart 8.
[20] See, for example, P. Alexander's characterisation in *ABD* 2, 978, 'a simple model of the world is generated by the notion that the Land of Israel is holy in contrast to the rest of the world; Jerusalem is holier than the rest of the Land; the Temple precinct in Jerusalem is holier than the rest of Jerusalem; and the holy of holies in the Temple is holier than the rest of the Temple'. For fuller discussions, see Smith, 1987, Levenson, 1976, Davies, 1994, esp. 138–54; 1991.
[21] Horbury, 1996, 207–24; here 208.
[22] Horbury, 1996, 209, lists: 11QT cols. 2–3; cf. Exod 34–35; Philo, *Hyp* 6:7, cf. *Vita Mos* 272; Josephus, *Ant.* 4:199–200.

> Leading them in, plant them in the mountain of thine inheritance,
> In thy ready dwelling, which thou, Lord, didst make,
> The sanctuary, Lord, which thy hands made ready.

Here the 'sanctuary which thy hands made ready' of Exodus 15:17 is 'already taken to promise a pre-existent God-given Temple in the third century BCE'.[23] Its influence is also felt in the LXX translations of Isaiah 54:11 with ἑτοιμάζω and in the use of the phrase 'ready dwelling' from Exodus 15 for God's habitation: 1 Kings 8:39, 43, 49 LXX; 2 Chronicles 6:30, 33, 39 LXX; Psalms 33(32):14 LXX. What is interesting here is the way that entry into the Land and the establishment of the worship on the Temple mount are fused together almost as one event.[24] Again the LXX translation of Psalms 78(77):53–54 provides clear evidence of this process:

> he guided them in hope and they were not afraid, and the sea covered their enemies; and he led them into the mountain of his sanctuary, this mountain which his right hand possessed.[25]

Intense hope for the future restoration of the people to the Land and the Temple is reflected too in Jewish prayer.

> Gather all the tribes of Jacob,
> and give them their inheritance, as at the beginning.

This prayer, from Sirach 36:11–17, continues:

> Have mercy, O Lord, upon the people called by thy name,
> upon Israel, whom thou hast likened to a first-born son.

> Have pity on the city of thy sanctuary,
>> Jerusalem, the place of thy rest.

> Fill Zion with the celebration of thy wondrous deeds,
> and thy temple with thy glory.

---

[23] Horbury, 1996, 210.

[24] Cross, 1973, 108 (cited Marcus, 1992, 33) believes that this fusion occurs already in the Hebrew: 'The old Exodus-Conquest route, the way through the wilderness, becomes at the same time the pilgrimage way to Zion. The march of the Conquest abruptly shifts into the festal, ritual procession to Zion', referring to Isa 35:8–10; 40:3–5; 44:24–28; 51:9–10; 62:24–28 (Marcus suggests this last citation refers to 62:10–12 and adds 52:1–12).

[25] Compare MT: 'He brought out his people like sheep, guiding them like a flock in the desert, leading them safe and unafraid, while the sea engulfed their enemies. He brought them to his holy land, the hill-country won by his right hand.'

And similar petitions are made and developed in 2 Maccabees 1:27–29 and in the *Eighteen Benedictions* at the turn of the era.

## 1 Enoch

All the views we have looked at so far work broadly within the overall narrative of the promise of the Land to Abraham, Israel's liberation from bondage in Egypt and the possession of the Land. For those in exile, this story inspires and shapes their hopes. God will restore the former glory and the exiles will return to Zion. In some forms of apocalyptic writing, however, the human predicament is cast in such dark tones that only a total renewal of the earth can provide a solution. Thus in the 'Book of the Watchers' in *1 Enoch* (chs 1–36), the human predicament is attributed to the descent of fallen angels to the earth, who father giants by the women to whom they have been fatally attracted and lead men and women astray (19:1–2), teaching them all kinds of sin and the arts of war and so filling the whole earth 'with blood and oppression' (9:9). God intervenes through his faithful angels; the Watchers are bound and the Flood forms the climax to the first judgement of the world (10:1–3). Yet the spirits descended from the Watchers continue to plague the earth and will continue to do so till the 'great age is consummated' (16:1). Then the Creator, the God of Israel, will put an end to the angels' dominion and will purify the earth. The final resolution will be in the form of a 'cosmic confrontation' (de Boer) between God and the Watchers. 'The God of the universe . . . will come forth from his dwelling. And from there he will march upon Mount Sinai and appear in his camp emerging from heaven with a mighty power. And everyone shall be afraid, and Watchers shall quiver' (1:4–5). Knowledge of this divine purpose has been revealed to God's elect, who bear witness to the Creator and who will be vindicated in the age to come.

The terms in which de Boer describes this invasion of the world are significant for our discussion: 'By leaving their proper heavenly abode, these angels have caused cosmic disorder (15:3, 9–10), bringing about the pollution, corruption, and perversion of both nature and history'.[26] Such a story is remarkably cosmic in scope, by contrast with other Jewish hopes for a return from exile and a restoration of national sovereignty, for a restoration of the sanctuary and its worship. In the

---

[26] de Boer, 1989, 174.

first place, the disaster which has befallen the world is a universal one. Its origins lie not in Israel's (or even Adam's) disobedience, but in a heavenly rebellion which has infected the earth and corrupted it. The wars which beset the world are seen as the product of the sinful knowledge brought by the Watchers. There is no suggestion that the nations are waging war on Israel as instruments of God's punishment. War and the weapons of war are part of the general human condition brought about by the dissemination of knowledge by the Watchers. What needs to be rectified is not just the exile and the devastation which has befallen Israel, but the state of the world.

Israel nevertheless plays a role as God's chosen: not so much as the nation in which the Lord's glory will be manifest in Zion, but as God's elect, to whom the mysteries of God's purposes have been revealed. God appears, not on the Temple mount but on Mount Sinai, and it is there (at least according to the first five chapters) that the final judgement occurs. It is the God of the Torah who comes with his hosts to destroy the sinful Watchers and their spirits who pollute the world. According to the later chapters, the accursed will be judged, after the general resurrection (*1 Enoch* 22) on the holy mountain in Jerusalem, and consigned to Gehenna, while the righteous will be blessed (27:1–4).

It is striking how little the key events of Israel's history feature in this schema. God's descent for judgement from heaven to Mount Sinai (*1 Enoch* 1:4) contrasts with Deuteronomy 33 where God comes from Sinai. Strikingly in this section, the behaviour of the unrighteous is not explicitly condemned in terms of the law. True, the unrighteous have not 'done the commands of the Lord and have turned away and spoken harsh words with [their] impure mouths against his greatness' (5:4), but the main weight of the discourse lies on the contrast between the steadfastness and reliability of things in the natural order and their fickleness.[27] The only biblical narratives referred to in any detail are those of the Watchers and the Flood. God's rule will be established when he comes to sit on the 'high mountain' (Zion) and when the Tree

---

[27] In this respect, Collins, 1998, 49, somewhat overstates his case: 'The sinfulness of the wicked is demonstrated in contrast to the orderliness of nature, not by the special revelation of Sinai.' It is, indeed, the failure of the wicked to live faithfully in accordance with the Law which is the main thrust of the charge against them. Of them it cannot be said, as it is of the 'all his work', that 'everything functions in the way in which God has ordered it' (5:2). Nevertheless, the commandments which the wicked have failed to do are still the commandments given on Sinai.

of Life will be transplanted to the Temple and its fruits given to the elect (25). God is King; there are no references to Davidic or priestly messiahs. The emphasis, that is to say, is far less on the history of the particular misfortunes and failings of Israel and their remedies,[28] far more on the general pollution and corruption of the world and its removal. In the light of this, it is not surprising to read that 'all the children of the people will become righteous, and all nations shall worship and bless me' (10:21). The final resolution of the world's woes is universal, not just the vindication of Israel, but the return of the whole world, Jews and Gentiles alike, to acknowledge and worship its creator.

So far we have noticed some only of the geographical references in *1 Enoch* 1–36, the references to Sinai and Zion. One of the striking features of the 'book' are the narratives of Enoch's journeys which take him to the ends of the earth and into the very heavens. As with *Jubilees*, it is possible to construct at least an outline map of the cosmos from these journeyings. The divine court in heaven is depicted as a temple. Enoch is shown the prison of the fallen angels in *1 Enoch* 18 and the place where 'the spirits of the souls of the dead' are kept till judgement in chapter 22. His journeys take him to the hidden places of the earth: to the ends of the earth, to the Garden of Eden and to the portals of heaven. He concludes his account of his journeys by blessing God for his great works, which have been done to 'manifest his great deeds to his angels, the winds, and to the people, so that they might praise the effect of all his creation' (36:4). Again, by contrast with *Jubilees*, there is little or no concern with the apportionment of territory to different peoples. Ethnic distinctions and different peoples' attachments to their lands do not play a part in this map-drawing. The emphasis is rather twofold. First, it is eschatological rather than geopolitical, focusing on the places where the wicked and the righteous will be placed after judgement. Second, as John Collins has suggested, it is designed to demonstrate that God is in control of his world, even when things seem out of joint. 'Whatever crisis pollutes the earth, the foundations

---

[28] As Collins notes, 1998, 74, there are other sections of *1 Enoch*, the Apocalypse of Weeks and the Animal Apocalypse, which 'show a heightened group identity', which he connects to the emergence of a Jewish renewal movement at the time of the Maccabean revolt. He comments: 'It is of interest that in these apocalypses, written in a time of conflict, the cosmological interests of the apocalyptic genre recede, and the historical interests come to the fore.'

of the cosmos, its outer regions and the places of judgement remain intact, as of course does the heavenly court.'[29]

Emphasis on the foundations of the world, rather than on territorial boundaries, does not mean that there is no sense of holy as opposed to profane spaces. The problem is that the whole world, apart from its hidden places (Eden, the mountains where God dwells, the portals of the heavens), has been polluted by the presence of the spirits of the Watchers. In this respect all territorial distinctions are irrelevant. Sinai and Zion are referred to only as the places to which God will come from heaven to restore his rule and to sanctify his world. As such they will become places of judgement and restoration, sources of life (25:5). This recasting of geography and history seems to take us from the realm of history into that of myth. The story of the Watchers is scarcely, *pace* Collins, typological.[30] Typology occurs where similar patterns of divine action are discerned between historical events in the present and those of the sacred-past, between for example, return from exile and the exodus. The connection between the mythological story of the Watchers and the situation at the time of Seleucid rule can only be made by allegorising the story of the Seleucid rulers and presenting them in mythological terms, as indeed is done in the Animal Apocalypse (*1 Enoch* 83–91). But to do this is to leave behind the realm of a typological identification of patterns of God's actions in history and instead to cast the whole of history as a mythological struggle between good and evil. In the same way geography is mythicised: the world presently inhabited by the people of Israel is presented as a world where geographical boundaries no longer have meaning, for the world is overrun by evil spirits who cannot be contained by political frontiers. The significant divisions are between the places prepared for the wicked and those prepared for the chosen righteous, between the hidden places and the polluted world.

It would be possible to multiply examples of Jewish use of the symbols of Land and Temple, but I hope to have shown sufficiently both the importance of such symbols and their flexibility in use. There was no single way of deploying such symbols to give a coherent understanding

---

[29] Collins, 1998, 58.
[30] Collins, 1998, 51: 'the use of the pseudonym Enoch . . . imposes the setting of the fictive author on the historical situation. A typological view of history is thereby implied. The crises of the Hellenistic age are presumed to bear some analogy to the story of Enoch and the Watchers'.

of sacred space. All might agree that the Temple Mount was or had
been a sacred place, but this would not preclude radical disagreement
at any particular time on the question whether or not the divine presence
dwelt there. It was acknowledged on all sides that Israel had to take
possession of the Land from the Canaanites: accounts of the legitimacy
of this conquest varied considerably. Nevertheless, it was an inescapable
part of Jewish heritage that the Lord God had given them a Land in
which to dwell, that he had promised to protect them in the Land, if
they would obey his commandments, and that such beliefs took concrete
form in the conviction that when God was present in the Temple his
people would flourish. Like it or not,[31] Jews were a people with a strong
attachment to the Land and the Temple, wherever they lived. But, like
it or not, apart from a brief period under the Hasmonaeans, Jews had
no independent control over the Land from the time of the destruction
of the Temple by the Babylonians in 586 BCE to the establishment of
the modern State of Israel.[32] It was a reality to be hoped for rather than
one possessed. And as oppression grew more terrible, it is hardly
surprising if there grew up darker visions of the human predicament,
views of the world as subject to demonic agencies who radically defile
it. On such a view, the problem goes deeper than the displacement of
the people of Israel or the occupation of their land by foreign forces.
Only when the cosmic powers which pollute the whole world are
destroyed will the new age dawn.

## Kinship and descent

### Genesis

If attachment to the Land represents one major facet of Jewish identity
over the ages, a sense of belonging to a particular people represents
another. As we have seen in our discussion of *Jubilees*, it is the Table of

[31] A rabbinic legend (*Tos Sukkah* 4:28), cited by Horbury (215), tells of one, Miriam, who
when the Temple was defiled at the time of Antiochus stamped on the altar crying
'Wolf, wolf (cf. Gen 49:27 LXX) 'you destroyed the wealth of Israel, but did not help
them in their hour of affliction': a bitter complaint against the extortion of the Temple
cult, full of a sense of betrayal. Miriam is portrayed as an apostate, who married a Greek.
Horbury comments: 'Here resentment at the expense of the sacrifices – the half-shekel
levy for this purpose (Exod 30.13) was not always readily paid in Judaea (*Mekhilta*,
*Yithro, Bahodesh*, on Exod 19.1) – is coupled with sceptism.'
[32] See Wilken, 1992, 7: 'What had been a charter of entitlement to a land that belonged to
others became a hope of repossessing the land that had been taken from them.'

Nations in Genesis 10 which forms the basis of the map of the world traced out in the story of Noah's division of the world between his three sons and their offspring. Homelands are not mere territory, though without territory they would not exist; they are places inhabited by the memories and experiences and aspirations of a particular people. This is nowhere clearer than in the promise of the Land to Abraham: 'I will give to you and to your descendants after you, the land of your sojournings, all the land of Canaan, for an everlasting possession; and I will be their God' (Gen 17:8). Those who possess the Land do so by virtue of their descent from Abraham to whom it was promised. In *Jubilees'* account, this goes hand in hand with the promise of the lands between the Nile and the Don to Shem and his descendants (which in turn disinherits the Canaanites).

Yet this motif of physical descent from Noah–Shem–Abraham is not allowed to go unqualified, either in Genesis, or in subsequent commentary. Genesis while setting out Abraham's descent from Shem clearly enough, opens its narratives of Abraham with the divine call to go out 'from your country and your kindred and your father's house' (Gen 12:1). It is explicitly Abraham's faith and obedience which is counted to Abraham for righteousness (Gen 15:6). Even the notion of descent from Abraham, of 'Abraham's seed', is not defined in purely biological terms. The story of the covenant in Genesis 17 repeatedly refers to those with whom the covenant is made as 'descendants' ('seed', Gen 17:7, 8, 9, 10); it further defines them (at least as far as males are concerned) as those who are circumcised: whether 'born in your house, or bought with your money from a foreigner who is not your offspring' (17:12). The category of 'seed', descendant, is being stretched and extended to include membership of the wider socio-economic unit of the household, offspring and slaves.[33] Moreover, what now defines Abraham's seed (whether offspring or purchased) is the covenant relationship to God, signified by circumcision. This is the mark of their election by God and of their obedience to him. It is then adherence to Jewish law and custom: circumcision and other Jewish observances, which mark them out from other peoples and are constitutive of the

---

[33] We have already noticed in *Jubilees* how this tendency to stretch the notion of physical descent from Abraham coupled with physical circumcision can lead to the adoption of more overtly fictive kinship terms to describe the faithful in Israel. God will circumcise their hearts and the hearts of their descendants; they obey his commandments and 'they will all be called "sons of the living God"' (1:23–25).

Jewish ethnos. So, to a lesser degree, is language. In a word, the people whose presence and history in the Land turns it into a homeland is to be identified partly by their descent from Abraham, and partly also by incorporation into the group through purchase (?marriage) and adherence to custom and language. And in turn, the Land itself, their living in it and their longing for it from without, welds them into a particular people with particular attachments.

And yet, while there are indeed a number of motifs which tend towards particularism in the Abraham narrative, there are others which have a more universalist tendency. Abraham is to be the father of many nations, as his new name makes clear (Gen 17:4). He is the father of Ishmael as well as of Isaac. He is the one in whom all nations will be blessed/will bless themselves (12:3).

It is interesting to see how these various motifs of Abraham's call, physical descent, purchase, incorporation into the covenant, circumcision, faith and righteousness, and the motifs associated with the name Ab-raham are developed in the literature of the turn of the era.

## Jubilees

*Jubilees*, we have already seen, works with a broad cosmic view of things, at the same time as it draws very sharp lines between 'the sons of the covenant which the Lord made for Abraham' and the children of destruction (15:26). The conflictual element is built into the story of Abraham's departure from Ur where he burns the house of idols. God's call to him to leave all and go to Canaan comes in response to Abram's prayer for deliverance from evil spirits lest they lead him astray 'from following you, O my God' (12:20). What is crucial in the narrative is the choice between being ruled over by spirits and following God.

This then has the effect of relativising (to a degree) matters of physical kinship and their physical sign, circumcision, and indeed of economic ownership. The sons of the covenant are gathered from all the sons of man, because there are many nations and many people, and they all belong to him. Physical descent is not all. Even though *Jubilees* has a touching story of Abraham seeking a blessing for him from God (15:18–20), it also notes that God did not draw near to Ishmael because he knew him (15:30), implying, presumably, that God knew that Ishmael would be disobedient. On the other hand, Israel's particular place in the divine purposes and love is strongly affirmed: the Land is for the children of Israel, not of Ishmael. God will set (evil) spirits over the nations to lead them astray, whereas he, together with his angelic forces, will protect Israel, that 'they might be his and he might be theirs henceforth and forever' (15:32). Even though the promises to Abraham are tied to the commandment, which 'was ordained for the covenant' (15:29) and Israel will disobey and incur God's wrath, God will not finally reject them. Repentance and a spiritual circumcision will restore them and make them 'sons of the living God' (1:23–25). The passage echoes Hosea 1:10, which is also in the context of the restoration to God of the people of Israel *after* their rejection as 'not my people'. Throughout this retelling there is a strong sense of a symbolic universe which is capable of many realisations being pressed here in a strongly particularist rather than a more universalist direction.

## Josephus

There are similar particularising and universalising traits in Josephus' retelling of the story of Abraham. Unlike *Jubilees* he does not include the story of God's distributing the Land between the posterity of Japheth, Shem and Ham. Rather he engages in some rather forced etymology to link the various descendants with known place-names and so to locate them in Europe, Asia and Egypt. In this he agrees largely with *Jubilees* in placing Japheth's descendants in Europe, Shem's in Asia and Ham's in Africa. Significantly, he seems to regard those who first settled an area as its rightful inhabitants, with the exception of the Canaanites. Their settlement of Canaan is described simply: 'Chananaeus, the fourth son of Ham, settled in the country now called Judaea and named it after himself Chananaea' ( Josephus, *Ant* 1:134). The reason why they are not the rightful inhabitants has nothing to do with land-rights as such, whether divinely conferred or acquired by right of first settlement; it is because of the curse which fell on them as a result of their father Ham's dishonouring of his father Noah (*Ant* 1:142). Thus on Josephus' view, the world is widely populated by the sons of Noah: there is certainly no suggestion that the peoples outside Judaea are of wholly different descent. But their rights to their lands are conferred by settlement. Israel alone provides an exception to this rule: the Land was given to it by God, in part as punishment for Ham's dishonouring of his father, in part as a reward for Abraham's faith. There are other traits which equally distinguish Israel from the nations, notably circumcision, which is expressly said to be given 'to the intent that his posterity should be kept from mixing with others' (*Ant* 1:192). On the other hand, Abraham's relations with the surrounding nations are portrayed in a somewhat less antagonistic manner. He is a philosopher who develops arguments which persuade him of the truth that there is one God; one who began to have 'more lofty conceptions of virtue than the rest of mankind, and determined to reform and change the ideas universally current concerning God' (*Ant* 1:155). This certainly gets him into trouble with the Chaldaeans and other Mesopotamians (*Ant* 1:157), but also allows him to instruct the Egyptians concerning their customs and to teach them arithmetic and astronomy (*Ant* 1:168). In this way he is portrayed as a wise man, with an international reputation for his intelligence, rhetorical skills and sagacity. This contrasts with *Jubilees'* portrait of the one who burns down the traditional gods of the Chaldaeans. It is not difficult to see how Josephus in Rome, writing to persuade Romans of the trustworthiness and venerability of the Jewish religion, should want to make this change of emphasis. Abraham is portrayed not as the destroyer of other nations' ancestral cults, but as the purveyor of an international wisdom, one who anticipated the rational and enlightened philosophy of the Greeks and who approached other people's religion with an open mind, visiting the Egyptians 'alike to profit by their abundance and to hear what their priests said about the gods; intending, if he found their doctrine more excellent than his own, to conform to it, or else to convert them to a better mind should his own beliefs prove superior' (*Ant* 1:161).

## Artapanus

The great variety of ways in which Jewish writers could treat the theme of Jewish ancestry can hardly be better illustrated than in the work of the Egyptian-Jewish writer of historical romance, Artapanus. He engages in what John Collins has called 'competitive historiography'.[34] In the fragments of his work preserved in Eusebius (in turn drawing on the work of Alexander Polyhistor), Artapanus is almost certainly engaged in polemic against Egyptian historians who purveyed highly slanderous tales about Jewish ancestors.[35] Manetho, as we know from Josephus, portrayed Moses as a priest of Heliopolis who forbade the worship of

---

[34] Collins, 1986, 33.
[35] Josephus, in *c Ap* 1:237–50 cites the work of Manetho at length and then, as we shall see, proceeds to refute him.

the Egyptian gods and encouraged his followers to eat the sacred animals of the Egyptians. Moses, Osarsiph, allies himself with 'other priests and polluted persons like himself' (*c Ap* 1:240) and invites the inhabitants of Jerusalem (shepherds who had been expelled from Egypt) to invade Egypt. The Egyptian king flees to Ethiopia and the Jews occupy the country and commit all sorts of abominations, including using the sanctuaries of the temples as kitchens for roasting the sacred animals (Josephus, *c Ap* 1:249). Eventually, however, the Jews are driven out.

Artapanus presents a totally different account of Moses. Far from being the scourge of Egyptian religion and culture, Moses is its very founder. Just as Abraham had taught the Egyptians astrology (ctr. Philo, *De Abr* 69–71, 77 and *Jub* 12:16–20), so Moses is the teacher of Orpheus, is responsible for teaching the Egyptians hieroglyphics, for developing naval architecture and building techniques, for dividing the state into districts, even for the system of irrigation and the annual flooding of the Nile, essential for the local agriculture. Even more surprisingly, it is Moses who determines which gods shall be worshipped in each district of the land, and who promotes the cult of 'cats and dogs and ibises' (Artapanus 3.27.4). It is Moses, too, who introduces circumcision to the Egyptians (3.27.10). This is all quite remarkable. There is strong national pride: an insistence on the moral and religious superiority of the Jewish ancestors but this pride is expressed in ways which seem to turn their back on much which is central to Jewish tradition and culture.[36] For Artapanus offers a refutation of Manetho's slanders against Moses, which were, foremost, that he forbade the worship of the Egyptians' gods and desecrated their sanctuaries. His refutation displays such enthusiasm for Egyptian culture that he makes Moses its author, even involves him in the administration of its polytheistic animal cult. Thus Artapanus' assertion of Jewish national pride appeals only occasionally to the superiority of Jewish law and custom (as when he claims that Moses introduced circumcision, which was common to Jews and Egyptians – or Egyptian priests); it is all about the superiority of Jewish ancestors.

In this respect Josephus' refutation of Manetho's charges makes for interesting contrast. Much of Josephus' attack is based on the implausibility of Manetho's account: its contradictions and improbabilities. What

---

[36] Most of what is preserved concerns Moses, but there is also reference to Abraham in Fragment 1.

he does acknowledge is that there is some basis in fact in the tissue of fabrications, namely, that '[w]e have therefore Manetho's authority for saying both that our race was not of Egyptian origin, and that there was no mixture of the races'. Moses was not, moreover, leprous or impure, but ordered that lepers should reside outside towns and villages and prescribed rites for their purification (*c Ap* 1: 278–84). In his own way, Josephus, too, asserts the superiority of the Jewish race (see, too, the opening of the *Vita* and his defence of Jewish historiography based on the purity of the priestly line), its distinctiveness and apartness.

Artapanus represents one extreme of diaspora Judaism: Jews who were vigorous in their defence of their ancestry and nation, but who freely adopted the customs and religious traditions of the surrounding cultures as – literally – their own. Much of what was important to other Jews in the assertion of their identity, for example, their attachment to the land of Israel,[37] their pride in their distinctive ethos and laws, is abandoned. What sustains this Jew and presumably those who read his work with favour, was a rather quirky but strong ancestral pride. Artapanus is extreme because he fails to identify those points at which there is a clash between Jewish laws and custom and those of Egypt.

## Philo

There is, as we have seen, nothing unusual in Jewish writers wanting to stress the elements which Jewish culture has in common with those which surround it.[38] Jews, writing in Greek in the cities of the Mediterranean, were in many ways the beneficiaries of Greek education and culture. To portray Abraham or Moses as the source of various cultural goods is a popular strategy among such figures. Josephus presents Abraham as the first to discover rational arguments for the existence and providence of God. Philo in *De Abrahamo* presents Abraham as the archetypically wise man who through his contemplation of nature does all that the law will subsequently prescribe. The lives of good and blameless men recorded in Scripture are 'laws endowed with life and reason' which are the originals (ἀρχετύποι) of the particular laws, which

---

[37] In the brief account of Abraham that has survived, we learn only that Abraham came to Egypt with his family, taught them astrology, and then 'departed again for the regions of Syria, but that many of those who came with him remained in Egypt on account of the prosperity of the land' (Fragment 1). The omission of any mention of the promise of the Land of Israel to Abraham, is at the least, surprising.

[38] For a much fuller treatment of these issues, see Barclay, 1996.

are thus merely copies (εἰκόνες). Their lives are recorded to show the consistency between the written laws and nature and to demonstrate that it is no difficult matter to observe the written laws (*De Abr* 3–5). This Platonic elevation of the more general (καθολικώτεροι) laws over the particular (οἱ ἐπὶ μέρους), as originals over copies, goes hand in hand with a subordination of the manner of reception of the written law (by hearing and by instruction) to that by which the forefathers came to know the natural law: they listened to and taught themselves (αὐτήκοοι δὲ καὶ αὐτομαθεῖς, *De Abr* 6). The fathers exemplify virtues which are there for all to emulate, since they are those which are natural and universal, catholic.

Philo, however, does not actually abandon particular Jewish laws. Even for dietary laws he can find an allegorical explanation which enables him to relate them to rational principles (*Spec Leg* 4:100–31).[39] His claim is rather that in the lives of the fathers Jews have a precious tradition, which is reinforced by the 'special laws', to which they should remain faithful, for it is the source of all virtue, which is in turn a precious gift to all.

The place of physical descent in all this is then ambiguous. Jews on the one hand have every reason to be proud of their ancestors, for they are shining lights to subsequent generations. On the other hand, Abraham's faithfulness to God is demonstrated precisely by his willingness to abandon everything that binds him to his own people: 'fellow-clansmen, or wardsmen, or schoolmates, or comrades, or blood relations on father's or mother's side, or country, or ancestral customs, or community of nurture or home-life, all of them ties possessing a power to allure and attract which it is hard to throw off' (*De Abr* 67). His emigration is 'one of soul rather than body, for the heavenly love overpowered his desire for mortal things'. Philo demonstrates the immense flexibility of the tradition, with its central figures and narratives, its stress on the land and descent from the Patriarchs, on the covenant and the Law. Philo's genius is to have given a universalising reading of the tradition, while at the same time insisting on faithfulness to the particular laws, even if it is an insistence achieved only with great allegorical subtlety.

---

[39] In *Migr Abr* 93, he compares the outward observance of the laws with the body, and their inner meanings with the soul. 'It follows that, exactly as we have to take thought for the body, because it is the abode of the soul, so we must pay heed to the letter of the laws.'

Nor do the universalising tendencies in Philo stand in the way of his emphasising the importance of belonging to a stable and well-knit community. Not only does he value such ties (*De Abr* 67), he clearly considers there to be an integral link between embracing faith in the one God and becoming a member of the Jewish ἔθνος. Those who have abandoned mythical fables and their own kin should be received warmly and generously into the Jewish commonwealth (πολιτεία).[40] The proselyte's leaving his community and cult and joining the Jewish community is compared standardly to a journey from one homeland to another.[41] Behind this recurrent use lies the figure of Abraham's own migration: 'He is the standard of nobility (εὐγενείας κανών) for all proselytes, who, abandoning the ignobility of strange laws and monstrous customs which assigned divine honours to stocks and stones and soulless things in general, have come to settle in a better land, in a commonwealth full of true life and vitality, with truth as its director and president.'[42]

There is a change of mood here. Philo may see Abraham and, by extension, Judaism, as establishing a religion of nature which teaches the truths which can be achieved, in principle at least by any 'virtue loving soul in its search for the true God'.[43] He may indeed see all human beings as 'judged worthy of kinship with him [sc. God] because he shared the gift of reason'.[44] But nevertheless, the transition from other cults to Judaism is seen as one from illusion and falsehood to truth. Those who previously had ascribed the honours due to God to those who were no gods, but now 'embrace the creed of one instead of a multiplicity of sovereigns, must be held to be our dearest friends and closest kinsmen'. It is their 'godliness of heart' (θεοφιλής) which leads up to 'friendship and affinity',[45] and therefore Jews must rejoice with them, 'as if, though blind at first they had recovered their sight and had come from the deepest darkness to behold the most radiant light'.[46]

---

[40] *Spec Leg* 1:51; 4:178; *De Virt* 102–8; 212–19.
[41] πρὸς εὐσέβειαν μεθορμίσασθαι, *Spec Leg* 1:51; καλὴν δ᾽ ἀποικίαν στειλαμένους, *De Virt* 102; 219.
[42] πρὸς ἔμψυχον τῷ ὄντι καὶ ζῶσαν πολιτείαν, ἧς ἔφορος καὶ ἐπίσκοπος ἀλήθεια *De Virt* 219.
[43] *De Abr* 68: ὑπὸ φιλαρέτου ψυχῆς τὸν ἀληθῆ ζητούσης θεόν.
[44] *De Abr* 41.
[45] Elsewhere Philo can speak of this bond between the proselyte and the members of the Jewish nation as 'the most effectual love-charm, the chain which binds indissolubly the goodwill which makes us one (εὐνοία ἑνοτική)', *Spec Leg* 1:52.
[46] *De Virt* 179.

There is here the most delicate mingling of, on the one hand, a universal rationalism, recognising the divine gift of reason in all men and women and, on the other hand, a deep attachment to his own kin, in virtue of their communal piety, their 'godliness of heart'. In principle, all men and women are God's kin in virtue of their endowment with reason; in practice, such endowment finds its full and undistorted expression in the monotheistic beliefs and religious observances of the Jewish community.

Conversion to such 'godliness of heart' is a form of repentance, indeed it is the 'first and most necessary form of repentance' (*De Virt* 180). It is, as one of the virtues, not something restricted to one particular race or nation. Nevertheless, for Philo it is exemplified in the faith of Abraham and in the conversion of proselytes and in their incorporation into the company of those who are properly 'kinsfolk of God'. This new sense of kinship is neither exclusively a matter of consanguinity nor is it entirely a fictive kinship. True, the notion of kinship with God, which is attributed to every person in principle and to Abraham in particular, is one which abstracts from all ideas of consanguinity.[47] But at the same time, Abraham is the father of the Jewish nation, and those who follow him in abandoning polytheism and worshipping the one God become members of that family.

As I have said, I am not attempting here to give a comprehensive survey of Jewish views of sacred space and kinship at the turn of the era. What I hope this discussion of some passages from Philo may show is how central recurrent motifs in the literature, descent from Abraham, his abandonment of his kinsfolk and his ancestral religion, his migrations, his fathering of a great nation, can be played out in surprising ways. These are not symbols which simply determine a single and coherent world-view and ethos. On the contrary, they are capable of very varied expression, within which there may be tensions and fissures. Some will emphasise the universal; others underline the particularities of Jewish communal life. Philo portrays Abraham very much in the guise of the Hellenistic philosopher/wise man. Judaism is the exemplification of such wisdom, whose particular laws are concrete representations (εἰκόνες) of the originals which are exemplified in the lives of the Patriarchs. Conversion to Judaism is an outstanding example of

---

[47] Noah's genealogy is not given in Genesis because, says Philo, Moses wishes instead to extol his virtues and 'this is little less than an assertion that a sage has no house or kinsfolk or country save virtues and virtuous actions' (*De Abr* 31).

the virtue of repentance. As such it is a manifestation of a universal human attribute. On the other hand, it brings the proselyte out of his inherited community and into a new commonwealth of a quite concrete and particular kind. This is connected with a particular people rather than with a particular territory (for all the use of travel metaphor to describe conversion there is no specific reference to a particular land as such).[48] There is finally a sense that, however much the proselyte may be treated as a member of the Jewish group, there remain differences. Proselytes are to refrain from slandering the very cults which they have just abandoned but which others acknowledge, 'lest they on their part be moved to utter profane words against Him Who truly is'. By contrast, members of the Jewish nation are urged in the strongest tones not to 'betray the honour due to the One'. Those who have chosen darkness rather than light are worthy of summary punishment. Philo does not shrink from advocating lynch-justice for such traitors of the nation. The warmth of hospitality which is to be shown to those who wish to convert will turn to very different feelings, 'hatred of evil and love of God which urges them to inflict punishment without mercy on the impious' (*Spec Leg* 1:53–55).

This complex relationship between a universal love and honour of God, affinity with God, on the one hand, and the concrete ties of kinship and membership of a particular nation on the other hand, is symbolised effectively by the rite of circumcision. It is the inscribing into the human body of the covenant between God and his people and, as such, a mark which unites both those physically descended from Abraham and those who are not; it is also the readily identifiable mark of membership of the Jewish people.[49] There is little doubt that its particularising significance dominated. It could function as a mark of marriage-worthiness for young males who aspired to marry Jewish girls.[50] It was equally regarded by Greeks and Romans with distaste and would have been at least a cause of embarrassment to Jewish boys engaging naked in sports at the gymnasia. It was, almost certainly, required of

---

[48] See esp. *Spec Leg* 1:68.

[49] Suetonius (*Dom* 12:2) recounts how an elderly (non-practising) Jew was stripped in court in order to determine whether he was liable to the tax which was paid into the *fiscus Iudaicus*.

[50] See Barclay, 1996 411–12, citing Josephus, *Ant* 1:192: it was instituted to prevent Abraham's offspring from mixing with others; and Philo, *Quaest Gen* 3:61: it was taboo for a Jewish woman to receive 'alien seed' from an uncircumcised man.

proselytes who wished to Judaise.[51] For the writers of 1 and 2 Maccabees, the practice of circumcision was something which the Jewish martyrs had died for (1 Macc 1:48; 2 Macc 6:10). For *Jubilees*, it was the essential mark of the covenant: failure to comply with the requirement brings destruction ( *Jub* 15:26). This uncompromising statement is supported by reference to the fact that angels are by nature circumcised from the moment of their creation (15:27). The reality of the heavenly orders provides a model for the life of Israel. Philo provided a more allegorising defence of the custom (*Spec Leg* 1:8–11), alongside various medical reasons, although he indicates elsewhere (*Migr Abr* 89–93) that such allegorising should not imply the abandonment of literal compliance. Even Artapanus, as we have seen, argued that Moses had introduced the custom to the Egyptians.

## Cosmic implications

### The persistence of evil

I have suggested so far that Jews in the first century, in a considerable variety of ways, constructed for themselves an ethos in terms of certain notions of sacred space and of descent from their forefathers. They were who they were in virtue of their belonging to a particular people, with particular attachments to a particular territory. Such attachments and belonging are, in the way of things, linked to a particular view of history and of the world and, in the case of the Jews, it is a highly theological one. It is the creator-God who has called them out to be his people, who promised them the Land and who made a covenant with them, secured by the giving of the Law which they would bind themselves to keep. These strong cosmological beliefs undergird a strong sense of national identity and vice versa. The paradox is that the very claim which thus grounds Jewish identity is itself the source of the deepest self-questioning. For the claim that God has chosen Israel as

---

[51] There are some documented exceptions or reservations about the requirement: *Sib Or* 4:163–70 speaks only of baptism; Josephus, *Ant* 20:38–48: Ananius tries, unsuccessfully, to dissuade his convert King Izates, from being circumcised; Philo, *Quaest Exod* 2:2, speaks of the 'proselyte' as one who 'circumcises, not his uncircumcision, but his desires and sensual pleasures and other passions of his soul'. Cohen, 1989, takes this to refer to a class of Gentiles who venerated the God of the Jews, but did not fully convert; 'if those gentiles wanted to join the Jewish community in the here and now, they had to accept circumcision' (27). See too Barclay, 1988, 45–60, and for a slightly different view, Hall, *ABD* 1, 1029.

his people, has given them the Land and will be with them stands in marked contrast to the subsequent history of Jewish occupation of the Holy Land. From the time of the Babylonian exile to the establishment of the State of Israel only the brief period of the Hasmonean monarchy (152–63 BCE) saw any real measure of Jewish sovereignty. What had gone wrong? What explanation could be given for the extraordinary 'persistence of evil'?[52]

## Opposed cosmologies: cosmic dualist and forensic

Answers to such questions rarely come in fully systematised form. As Levenson suggests, many of the responses to this dilemma in the Bible are in form more liturgical than philosophical: pleas, taunts even, designed 'to goad the just God into action after a long quiescence' (xvii). Jeremiah 12:1–3, which Levenson quotes at this point, lays the responsibility for Israel's suffering directly at God's door. It is God who has planted the wicked and allowed them to prosper, who knows that the prophet's heart is with him and yet who delays. In face of such inaction the prophet can only plead: 'Drive them out like sheep to the slaughter, prepare them for the day of slaying!' There are, however, other modes of addressing the question of evil's persistence. Israel's suffering may be portrayed as God's punishment for disobedience. Isaiah describes Israel's terrible history of defeat and exile and ultimately return as one of God's guidance and leading. Ultimately God will make good his promises to Israel in the return to Zion; meanwhile Israel must bear the consequences of disobedience and learn to turn again to God.

But if for Isaiah the root of the problem lies in Israel's disobedience, there are other voices which attribute evil, oppression and suffering in the world, neither to God's tardiness, nor to Israel's disobedience, but to the agency of malevolent spirits. As we saw in the book of *Jubilees*, God has set evil spirits to rule over the nations, whereas he himself rules over Israel. A similar distribution of responsibilities is to be found in 1QS 3–5. God's sovereignty is not as such impugned, but the divine decree has unleashed forces on the world which will cause suffering to his people. But *Jubilees*, like other writings of the turn of the era, *1 Enoch* for example, also portrays such demonic infection of the world as the result of spiritual disobedience in heaven. The angels are seduced by the beauty of the 'daughters of the children of men' and

[52] Levenson, 1994.

mate with them, producing giants who spread corruption in the world
( *Jub* 5:1–2; *1 Enoch* 6–8; 1QapGen 2:1). Even here there are important
differences. In *Jub* 5:3–11 the wicked angels are punished and buried
and their offspring eliminated and judged. Corruption returns after
the Flood as a direct consequence of the corruption of the calendar and
the consequent confusion of sacred and profane times. In *1 Enoch* the
Watchers are buried, but their offspring continue to 'rise up against the
children of the people and against the women' (15:12) and will continue
to do so until the end of the age (16:1). On such a view evil has cosmic
origins; it stems from a deep opposition at the source of all reality. In
the words of Revelation 12:7, there is 'war in heaven'.

Here I should like to acknowledge a debt to Martin de Boer, who in
an article on 'Paul and Jewish Eschatology' has argued that there were
essentially two tracks in the Jewish eschatology of the period: one *cosmic
dualist*, which saw the origin of evil as residing in the invasion of this
world by hostile angelic forces, which enslaved or ensnared men and
women.[53] This he illustrates from the Book of the Watchers (*1 Enoch*
1–36) which attributes all sorts of evil practices to the union between
the Watchers and earthly women, who were taught the arts of war-
making and cosmetics by the heavenly partners. Such bondage is
universal and can be overcome only by divine intervention, culminating
in a cosmic battle and the defeat of the Enemy, as illustrated in *Test
Mos* 10. Another, *forensic* track is clearly to be seen in *2 Baruch* and
*4 Ezra*, and attributes evil to human disobedience, archetypally in
Adam (*2 Bar* 54:14–19). Such disobedience is the true source of sin
(*1 Enoch* 98:4–5; *Ps Sol* 9:4–5) and characterises this present age. It can
be countered only by the giving of the Law and the apportioning of
rewards and punishments at the final judgement.

There is a debate to be had here about the extent to which these two
views occur independently of each other, and how far they always occur
together in some conjunction or another. de Boer suggests that on
occasions they occur in pure form (as in *1 Enoch*, *2 Baruch* and *4 Ezra*),
while on others the two tracks criss-cross and overlap. As de Boer says,
their conjunction is evident in well-known passages such as the section
on the Two Spirits in Qumran. Here God sets two spirits over two
groups of people: the angel of light over the children of light and the
angel of darkness over the children of darkness. The framework of the

[53] See de Boer, 1989; see too de Boer, 1999.

passage is thoroughly determinist: God knows all and has determined all things. The spirits will lead the children of light into righteousness and the children of darkness into evil. At the same time, the angel of darkness attempts to lead all the sons of light astray and is the cause of evil deeds committed by members of the community. But such determinism does not in any way stand in the way of moral exhortation or the establishment of disciplinary procedures with fierce punishments in the Community Rule. The Rule from the start emphasises the importance of the oath which all members must take on entering the community 'to return to the law of Moses with all his heart and soul, following all that he has commanded, and in accordance with all that has been revealed from it to the sons of Zadok' (1QS 5:8–9). Members stand under strict discipline and are assessed every year on their understanding of and performance of the Law. It is hardly an exaggeration to say that the Community at Qumran was a voluntary community based on observation of the Law as they understood it. All its efforts and its structures were designed to stiffen the will of its members to obey the Law. Thus, views of evil both as originating in Satanic possession and as originating in the human will sit alongside each other and are apparently seen as complementary, at least, not as mutually exclusive.

Indeed, different views of the sources of evil and of the ultimate manner of its overcoming (cosmic war, a final divine assize) are combined throughout the literature of the turn of the era with remarkable freedom and without systematic rigour. This can be seen in accounts of the final resolution of the conflict between good and evil. The Book of Dreams of *1 Enoch* 83–90 contains an Animal Apocalypse which, in highly allegorical form, sets the Maccabean conflict in a wide historical setting and leads it to a triumphal, if imagined, conclusion. The characters in the visions are portrayed as animals: the main historical periodisation is constructed in terms of a succession of shepherds, who represent, respectively, the Babylonian, Persian, Ptolemaic and Seleucid rulers. Israel is presented as their flock. The Maccabean war is portrayed as a struggle between the rams, lead by one with a great horn (90:9, Judas Maccabeus) and an assortment of birds: eagles, vultures, ravens and kites. Finally, a sword is given to the sheep (90:19) and they complete the slaughter of their opponents. God descends to earth, sets up his throne and judges both the unfaithful shepherds and the blind (apostate) sheep. A new 'house' (90:28–29, Temple?) is created and the sheep are transformed into cattle. Here, too, the notion of a cosmic battle between spiritual forces is effortlessly moulded on to visions of a final assize, in which both faithless Jews and their oppressors will receive their due deserts.

The question of the relation of these different cosmological motifs (evil as springing from spiritual forces or as the result of human disobedience) will be of considerable importance as we attempt to show how such motifs are combined within the Gospel narratives. It could be argued, though it would require a much more thorough survey than is possible here, that the combination of the two cosmologies is typical of the apocalyptic writing of the period and that, therefore, the two 'tracks' rarely occur in separation. What I shall argue in much more detail is that this combination of two different views of the nature and resolution of evil is characteristic of both our Gospels.

This is an important insight into the nature of first-century Jewish and Christian mythological writing. A great deal, if not all, of such writing is engaged in a dialogue between two different views of the world. Neither on its own seems adequate to make sense of the desperate plight of humanity. Some account of human responsibility for sin and its overcoming is necessary, if human beings are not to be reduced merely to puppets in the hands of the gods, good or evil. On the other hand, were all responsibility for the present condition of the world to be loaded onto human beings, it would seem to destroy any basis for hope in a future purged of evil. If humanity were in and of itself so corrupt, what possible basis could it provide for a new world freed of sin? Only if some angelic agency is invoked, which can also shoulder the responsibility for the world's ills and which can be overcome by divine intervention, can a view of the future be constructed which provides hope for a restored humanity.

Thus these two cosmologies can be found constantly in dialogue in the writing of the period. This should in a sense not surprise us, but it is rarely acknowledged by students of the literature. This is largely a heritage from the History of Religions school which certainly constructed myths in a dominantly monological form and whose views in this respect persisted into the discussions of mythology which were sparked by Bultmann's famous essay, 'The New Testament and Mythology'.[54] By

---

[54] Bultmann, 1941, in Bultmann, 1985.

contrast, it seems that myths/mythic narratives, certainly of Judaism in the first centuries BCE and CE, more often deal in what Lévi-Strauss has called 'fundamental oppositions': they say what they have to say about the world and human patterns of behaviour by drawing on different views of reality, for example of the origins of good and evil and the overcoming of evil by good.

This view of myths as dealing in fundamental oppositions is put forward in some of his shorter, more focused, if more speculative, studies by Claude Lévi-Strauss. Lévi-Strauss argues that myths give voice to fundamental oppositions in societies. Ultimately he thinks that these oppositions are determined by the structure of our minds and that they shape the way the societies he studies organise their lives in kinship relationships, with their problems and instabilities. But these oppositions are also expressed in the way geographical space is understood and also in the development of cosmology. Thus in the Oedipus myth there are different views about the origins of humanity: are human beings 'of the earth', autochthonous, or derived from human parents? Of one or of two? Oedipus' relations to his mother and his father, in a classic understatement, are described as respectively 'overrating' and 'underrating blood-relations'.[55] In the myth such oppositions are both expressed and obfuscated: Oedipus, though born of a human mother and father, is staked out to the earth at birth. Ultimately the purpose of the myth is to expose and admit the paradoxes which lie at the heart of human societies.[56] Now this in a significant way is illuminating: it asserts strongly that myths are not monolithic constructions, imposing a particular view of the world, a particular form of society upon their readers/receptors, but rather that they function more as therapies for societies radically at odds with themselves: a Freudian-dialectical view rather than a Marxian view of myth as ideology. Such insights may be worth all the wizardry of Lévi-Strauss' virtuoso readings of world mythologies. It will be a major part of our undertaking to see how these

---

[55] Lévi-Strauss, 1955, 433.
[56] This is Leach's clearly expressed view, 1970, 58, 70–1: 'It is Lévi-Strauss' thesis that the function of mythology is to exhibit publicly, though in disguise, ordinarily unconscious paradoxes of this kind.' Cf. p. 58 where he quotes from 'The Story of Asdiwal' (GA.27–8): 'All the paradoxes conceived by the native mind, on the most diverse planes: geographic, economic, sociological, and even cosmological, are, when all is said and done, assimilated to that less obvious yet so real paradox which marriage with the matrilateral cousin attempts but fails to resolve. But the failure is *admitted* in our myths, and there lies precisely their function.'

opposed mythologies, which lie behind much first-century literature, are engaged with, what kinds of mediation between them is achieved, what views of the world are forged or suggested by the Evangelists' imaginative interplay with these two quite radically opposed cosmologies.

## Bearing of cosmology on definitions of kinship and sacred space

Finally, this chapter will illustrate briefly how the various motifs, which we have seen as formative of Jewish identity in this period, interact with these different cosmological themes.

### Circumcision

The mark of circumcision is a central Jewish symbol which clearly distinguishes members of the Jewish community from those outside. But such a symbol can easily be interpreted to give very different accounts of the nature of that distinction. In *Jubilees*, as we saw, the circumcised are identified as the 'sons of the covenant', as distinct from the 'children of destruction' (15:26). They are further associated with the angels of the presence and of the sanctification, whereas the children of destruction are under the power of evil spirits. The causes of evil and sin in the two groups are thus distinguished. The 'children of destruction' are depicted as being 'led astray' by evil spirits, whereas if Israel fails, it will be by way of conscious decision: they will leave his covenant and turn aside from his words (15:33–34). Indeed, *Jubilees* lays such stress on faithfulness and obedience and repentance, that physical circumcision alone can scarcely be a guarantee of being within the covenant. Ultimately Israel's rebelliousness will be overcome only by a radical change of heart inspired by God, a spiritual circumcision (1:23).

Similar emphasis on the demonic causes of evil and the need for complete obedience and faithfulness is found in Qumran, where we read that Abraham circumcised himself 'on the day of his knowledge' to free himself from the dominion of Mastema. So too with those who enter the community: 'on the day on which the man has pledged himself to return to the law of Moses, the angel Mastema will turn aside from following him, should he keep his word'.[57] Clearly, this is metaphorical

---

[57] CD 16:3–6 explicitly refers to the book of the divisions of the periods according to their jubilees and their weeks. Note that even here there is no suggestion that such removal from satanic influence removes the need for faithfulness and moral effort. See, too, the warning against apostasy which follows in *Jub* 15:33–34.

circumcision: the swearing of the oath of the covenant on entry into the *yaḥad* now fulfils the role of Abraham's physical circumcision. It is not that physical circumcision is abandoned but rather that the act of repentance and taking the oath of the covenant now becomes the defining mark of membership. The metaphor is used widely in Qumran: circumcised ears can hear God speak the truth (1QH 18:20); uncircumcised lips cannot speak God's message truly (1QH 2:7,18). Thus for Qumran, as with *Jubilees* (1:23), the literal sense of circumcision takes second place to the metaphorical, precisely because of the community's marginal place within Judaism: what confers a sense of identity on the members of the *yaḥad* is their oath and the distancing of themselves from the rest of the Jewish people. At the same time, their claim is that they are the true remnant of Israel (CD 1:4; 2:11).

Even for Philo, the great allegoriser, the literal sense of circumcision is still of major importance in establishing his community's sense of who they are. However much he may spiritualise or explain the meaning of circumcision, Philo does not abandon the claim that God has chosen the Jewish people over all other nations, and that circumcision remains a distinctive mark. In two places where he addresses this theme, in *Spec Leg* 1:300–18 and *Leg All* 3:88–89, he lays stress on the divine election of the Jewish people to serve God with a pure and rational worship. The argument is delicately balanced between a rational apologetic which insists that Jewish election is a sign of God's choice of the rational mind to worship him, rather than the bodily passions; and a clear affirmation that the Jews have been chosen by God as 'of special merit and judged worthy of pre-eminence over all, those who are in a true sense men'.[58] The passage in *Spec Leg* 1:300–18 is in the form of a commentary on Deuteronomy 10:12–22, which combines the command to Israel to worship God with the reminder of Israel's election. God, the universal God, to whom belong the heavens and the heaven of heavens has, nevertheless, chosen a particular people, the Jews, to worship him. But while God's choice thus underlines the importance of this particular people, true, rational worship of the universal God is the highest good, higher, that is, than the bonds of blood and kinship which bind Jews together as his chosen people. Therefore they are to circumcise the

---

[58] *Spec Leg* 1:303, cf. *Leg All* 3:88–89, where the story of Jacob and Esau in the womb is, on the one hand, allegorised to demonstrate the superiority of the rational mind over the irrational senses, but still allowed to stand as a story about two separate nations, one of which shall serve the other.

hardness of their hearts and not to harden their necks, 'pruning the superfluous overgrowths sown and raised by the immoderate appetites of the passions and planted by folly, the evil husbandman of the soul' (*Spec Leg* 1:305). Such 'circumcision of the heart' is necessary because some of these 'true men' (τοὺς πρὸς ἀλήθειαν ἀνθρώπους, *Spec Leg* 1:303) fall short of their calling. The spiritual and moral discipline of such metaphorical circumcision reinforces and is made all the more urgent by the claim that they have been chosen because of their rational nature. And for the same reason they are to receive any proselyte (Deut 10:18 LXX) who has forsaken his own kin 'in the measure that fits their case' (*Spec Leg* 1:309) and to pursue to the death any Jew who frequents pagan temples, 'for we should have one tie of affinity . . . namely, the willingness to serve God and that our every word and deed promotes the cause of piety' (*Spec Leg* 1:317). Any rational worshipper of God (at least 'in the measure that fits their case') is a worthy member of the people of God;[59] any Jew who abandons his true vocation ceases to be a member and must be expunged.

There may be traces of different cosmologies in Philo's insistence on physical circumcision, but the dominant mode of thought here is forensic and moral. What marks out the Jews from all other peoples is God's loving choice of them as his people and this is signified by the practice of circumcision. Little justification of this practice is offered which goes beyond the allegorical, certainly nothing approaching the dualist explanations in, for example, *Jub* 15. Nevertheless Philo rejects a purely allegorical interpretation which would set aside the practice altogether. On the other he argues that what sets them apart, and forms the ground of God's choice, is their rational worship of God. In this, figures like Abraham and Moses are the great exemplars. Evil in the world is the product, not of some angelic invasion, but of the disordering of the relation between the mind and the passions. The division between Jews and Gentiles, important as it is so long as worship of the one true God

---

[59] This view is apparently contradicted in *Leg* 4–5, where Israel is interpreted as 'he that sees God', such that the perception of the uncreated forms the basis of Jewish virtue, and where this vision is contrasted with what can be attained by reason: 'which cannot attain to ascend to God', *Leg* 6. It is not, however, entirely clear whether in this passage the vision refers to a particular manifestation of God to the Patriarchs (which would be privileged to Israel) or to a mystical ascent to God, which goes beyond what can be achieved by the discursive use of the reason, but which would presumably be open to souls which had 'soared above all created things and schooled themselves (πεπαίδευνται) to behold the uncreated and divine'.

is the exception in the world, is ultimately something which could be superseded if all were to turn to rational worship of God. Meanwhile God has set Jews apart to exemplify such true humanity. It is a view of the world where, whatever the appearances, God is firmly in charge, distributing his gifts and his punishments. All rational creatures can comprehend 'God's attendant powers' . . . 'the creative, the kingly, the providential and of the others all that are both beneficial and punitive' (*Leg.* 6). When one considers that this apparently calm view of God's just ordering of the affairs of the world comes at the beginning of a treatise which will describe the pogroms against the Jews in Alexandria in 38 CE, one can appreciate how resolutely Philo refuses to embrace any form of dualist cosmology to explain the misfortunes which have befallen God's chosen people.

## The Land

Are there similar connections between different Jewish geographies and differing cosmologies? In a sense we should hardly expect to find much variation at this point. The biblical traditions about the Land make it clear that it has been given to the Jews by God in recognition of Abraham's righteousness. The Jews are to live in it, in so far as they remain faithful to God's laws, otherwise he will vomit them out as he vomited out the Gentiles, because of their abominations (Lev 20:22–24). Such views are clearly represented in *Jubilees*, immediately after the passage where God has set the spirits over the Gentiles. 'And they have provoked and blasphemed inasmuch as they have not done the ordinance of this law because they have made themselves like the gentiles to be removed and be uprooted from the land' (15:34). As long as they are faithful, they will remain; otherwise God's wrath will be upon them and cast them out. There are, however, other voices within *Jubilees*. At the end of the book, in the section on the observance of the Sabbath, a different view is found: the present condition of the land is one which is Satan-infested: only when Israel is purged from all the sin of fornication, and defilement, and uncleanness, and sin and error will it be able to 'dwell in confidence in the land. And then it will not have any Satan or any evil (one). And the land will be purified from that time and forever' (*Jub* 50:5).

*Jubilees* betrays, within a fairly standard view of Israel's relationship to the Land (disobedience and rebellion leads to exile and punishment), a darker view, where the whole earth is polluted by evil spirits and bereft of God's presence. This latter view, as we saw, is found in striking form in *1 Enoch*. There, such is the universality of demons' control over the world that the old territorial boundaries make little difference. Inside or outside the Land, Satan reigns and men and women are subject to him. Only God's elect, to whom the mysteries have been revealed, are free of his control, though they must suffer nonetheless. When God descends to restore his rule, it will be on Sinai but it will be to re-establish his rule over the whole earth. The sacred sites of old will be restored but for the time being their importance is minimised. The cosmic perspective of such dualist eschatologies has the effect of diminishing the significance of the land and its borders.[60]

By contrast with this strand of apocalyptic thought which looks for the purification of a demonically infested earth in a final battle, the other strand, the forensic one, sees the culmination of God's saving action as lying in the restoration of the Land and the Temple and its worship and in the ingathering of the scattered peoples, prior to some final judgement. This strand of thought is much more concerned with history and territory, with the concrete details of the past movements of the people from Egypt to Israel, of Israel's disobedience and punishment in exile in Babylon and of its restoration and return to Zion. If the people of Israel is once again languishing in the diaspora, and if the Land itself is under alien occupying powers which pervert its laws, then this past history provides a precedent for God's expected action in the future, and indeed is interpreted in the typological mode. As we saw, Exodus 15:17 LXX, the culmination of the song of Moses and the Israelites after the crossing of the sea, has become a prophecy of the future restoration when 'the ready (ἕτοιμος) dwelling which thou, Lord, didst make, the sanctuary, Lord, which thy hands made ready' will be given to Israel.

On such a slimmed down and expurgated view of the conquest of the Land, the expected acts of redemption will closely parallel the great

---

[60] Davies, 1994, 370, notes a similar effect within early Christianity. 'The cosmic awareness of primitive Christianity – its doctrines of the new creation, the new age, the cosmic Christ, the cosmic Church, and the cosmic salvation through these, all expressed variously and with differing intensity, but all, to some degree at some point, informing the minds of Christians, could not but place all Christian speculation on geographic entities that were central to Judaism in a minor key. Judaism had this cosmic dimension also. To that extent it, too, depressed the doctrine of Jerusalem and the land. But that dimension is far more immediate and ubiquitous in primitive Christianity, and the consequent depression greater.'

events of the past. Isaiah 40 proclaims the way of the Lord in the desert. It will lead straight from the desert to Mount Zion, the glory of the Lord will return to the Temple, the exiles will be gathered in and the nations will come to worship. The trials and dilemmas of the prolonged and bloody conquest are omitted. If Marcus is right, in the first century such views were powerfully linked to the belief that Israel's fortunes would be restored by a holy war which would start in the Judaean desert and culminate in the renewal and restoration of Jerusalem and the Temple.[61] It is certainly true that expectations of a new Temple occur widely in Jewish literature of the centuries around the turn of the era.[62] The focus is on Jerusalem, but here too there is a cosmic dimension to the hopes: the whole world will come to acknowledge the glory of Yahweh which is revealed in Zion.

Isaiah 40 is taken from a corpus of texts which contains material of very diverse character. Nevertheless, it would be anachronistic to suppose that first-century readers would have distinguished sharply between the various parts of the work. The setting of the prophecies of return from exile in chapter 40 is provided by the earlier history of Israel's disobedience, and of God's punishment as he allows Israel's enemies to invade his beloved vineyard. It is, as indeed the introduction to the prophecy in 40:2 makes clear, the story of Israel's iniquity and God's fierce punishment. '[S]he has received from the Lord's hand double for all her sins.' But the punishment is not ultimately destructive: it is the means by which he leads her back into the ways of righteousness:

> He will feed his flock like a shepherd,
> he will gather the lambs in his arms,

---

[61] See the important discussion in Marcus 1992b, 12–31. Following Snodgrass, 1980, he argues that there was already, prior to the writing of Mark, a Jewish tradition of interpreting Isa 40:1–5 on which Mark was drawing. Isaiah's prophecy of a return from Babylonian exile is interpreted in the Dead Sea Scrolls, Apocrypha, Pseudepigrapha and in rabbinic traditions, to refer 'to a return of the exiles at the end of days, a return accompanied by spiritual renewal of the people and indeed of the cosmos itself' (22). Marcus further argues (citing Schwartz, 1987) that there are clues in Josephus which make it probable that Isa 40:3, and the theme of the return from the wilderness, 'played an important role in the events leading up to and including the Jewish Revolt' (22). Such use of the passage 'apparently fired Jewish hopes for an apocalyptic holy war that would begin in the Judean wilderness and climax in the liberation of Zion' (23).

[62] Tobit 14:5; *1 Enoch* 90:28f.; *Jub* 1:15–17, 26–28; *T Benj* 9:2; 4QpPs37 3:11; 11QTemple 29:8–9 and *Sib Or* 3:294; 702–20; 772–4; 5:414–33.

> he will carry them in his bosom,
>   and gently lead those that are with young
>     (40:11; cf. 42:16; 48:17; 49:10; 57:18; 63:14).

The *source* of evil and suffering in the world, for Israel and for all the nations, is primarily their disobedience: it is this, rather than the agency of fallen spirits, which brings God's punishment upon them, which is the means whereby he will re-establish his rule and restore his beloved. There are darker, more cosmic notes. In Isaiah 24 the transgression of the laws 'pollutes the earth' (v. 5). The effects of such disobedience assume universal dimensions, which at the very least anticipate later, more dualist language. A 'curse devours the earth' (24:6); the rulers make a covenant with death (28:15; cf. Wis 1:16). Such is the depth of evil which overwhelms the world, that its expurgation is also cast in cosmic terms: 'Then the moon will be confounded, and the sun ashamed; for the Lord of hosts will reign on Mount Zion and in Jerusalem and before his elders he will manifest his glory' (24:23). The figures of Leviathan and the dragon in the sea also make their appearance (27:1). However, it would be difficult to say that these ideas are in any way dominant in Isaiah. They convey vividly the ravages of human iniquity and its power, which can only be overcome by the action of God. In the end, however, this action consists firstly in disciplining the disobedient people of Israel, ultimately through sending them into exile, and then in God's punishment of the nations by subjecting them to Israel. The ultimate vision is of a time when 'the Lord God will cause righteousness and praise to spring forth before all the nations' (61:11). Peace and justice will be restored to the world. Iniquity will be banished, as all nations acknowledge the glory of the Lord in Zion. Certainly there is a correspondence between the cosmic language in which the human predicament is described and the universal dimensions of the salvation announced at the end of the book; there is not as yet the more fully developed dualism of later writings like *1 Enoch* and *Jubilees*.

These two accounts of sin and salvation clearly have very different territorial emphases. Not only is significance accorded to very different places, but the literalness with which places and events are treated varies considerably. For the more emphatically cosmological dualist view, the events of the past are not types of the events to come. They are not to be repeated: the past is to be overcome; the old age has to be replaced by the new. For the more strictly forensic view, the events of the past have a more positive significance: they represent God's great acts of redemption and the realisation of his promises to his people. Moreover, these acts are played out on the geographical stage of a world where Israel has its allotted territory and where loss of territory represents the most terrible of the punishments which God brings on his people. Salvation is conceived – literally – as return to and restoration of sovereignty over the Land. The great acts of salvation which Isaiah had prophesied in the past will again be performed. God's purposes will be finally realised as the Land is restored, the exiles return, the worship of the Temple is renewed and the nations acknowledge his glory.

It is true, as we have seen, that there is a mythological element in the Isaianic texts.[63] The triumphal way of the Lord is announced to the heavenly council: God will ride with the returning exiles and accomplish the victory. But the battle is cosmic only in the sense that God is with the Israelites. It is fought not in heaven but on the plane of history. It is nevertheless a relatively truncated history; the key events, deliverance, desert wanderings, entry into the Land, arrival at the holy mountain and the establishment of the Temple worship are emphasised; all else is fairly peripheral. The other important element is the messianic Son of David motif (e.g. Isa 9:1–7). What is absent from this story is the struggles for the possession of the Land. The way of the Lord to Zion will be a triumphal procession: his paths will be made straight; there will be no obstacles or opposition. The exiles will return along a holy way which the unclean will not be allowed to use (Isa 35:8).

The views we have been considering are more or less intensely eschatological: looking for a restoration or renewal of the world, however that is to be conceived. There are other cosmologies: Philo's neo-Platonist world-view provides a very different framework within which to think of the Temple and the Land. Here we move out of the world of eschatological expectation and into a world of eternal verities, though ones only imperfectly grasped by the many. The source of evil is not, that is, demonic possession but – universal – human ignorance and disobedience. The problem then, for Philo, is how to account for the special position of the Land and, within it, the Temple, in a view of the world which is as universalist as his. The Jewish πολιτεία is, after all, a

---

[63] Cf. Cross, 1973, 106–8, 188, who argues that the notion of Yahweh's 'processional way' through the wilderness draws on both Israelite holy war traditions and Canaanite myths of a cosmic battle. The words of Isa 40:1–5 are directed to the heavenly council who are to act as his heralds. See the discussion in Marcus, 1992, 27.

community of virtue (e.g. *Spec Leg* 2:73), and Jews are in any case
κοσμοπολῖται, citizens of the world created by God, in virtue of their
compliance with the law of nature (*Op Mund* 3). Such universalism,
indeed, is underlined by fact that the Law opens with the account of
God's creation. Moses neither delivers his account of the Law 'naked
and unembellished', nor does he invent myths or simply take over the
myths of others. Rather he offers

> an account of the creation of the world, implying that the world is in harmony
> with the Law, and the Law with the world, and that the man who observes
> the law is constituted thereby a loyal citizen of the world, regulating his
> doings by the purpose and will of Nature, in accordance with which the
> entire world itself also is administered.[64]

It is not at all clear, therefore, what place a particular land with its own
Temple-cult could have within such a scheme of things. Philo, indeed,
pays little attention to the Land as such. What he does offer in *Spec Leg*
1:66–70 is an account of the significance of the Temple. In true Platonist
fashion, he first contrasts the 'highest, and in the truest sense, the holy
temple of God' with the temple made with hands (τὸ χειρόκμητον).[65]
The whole universe constitutes the holy Temple of God in the truest
sense, with the heaven as its sanctuary and the purely rational angels as
its priests. Such priests, 'all mind through and through, pure intelligences,
with the irrational eliminated', are in the likeness of the monad, and
clearly are intended to represent the ideal of true worship. The earthly
Temple is there to provide a spur to such rational worship of God and a
deterrent to the cults of polytheism. There is to be only one Temple, for
God is one. The prohibition of sacrificial rites in the home is intended
as a discipline, the 'severest test' of their resolve. The pull between
allegiance to the local community and the Temple-cult is nicely caught
in what follows: 'for one who is not going to sacrifice in a religious
spirit would never bring himself to leave his country and friends and
kinsfolk and sojourn in a strange land, but clearly it must be the stronger
attraction of piety which leads him to endure separation from his most
familiar and dearest friends who form as it were a single whole with
himself' (*Spec Leg* 1:68). But all is not pain and grief, for those who
flock in their multitudes to the Jerusalem Temple find there a haven

---

[64] *Op Mund* 3.
[65] τὸ μὲν ἀνωτάτω καὶ πρὸς ἀλήθειαν ἱερὸν, *Spec Leg* 1:66.

and a new sense of community, where the sacrifices 'are the occasion of reciprocity of feeling and constitute the surest pledge that all are of one mind' (ὁμονοίος, *Spec Leg* 1:70). Even in the worship of the Jerusalem cult, the bonds which are forged transcend those of attachment to home and of close blood-ties: true kinship resides in the common love and true worship of God. Those who worship at the one Temple are offering the universal, rational worship of the sanctuary of the heavens.

This universalising of the particular raises the question whether Philo is Platonising Judaism or Judaising Plato. Perhaps one might answer rather obliquely. The first thing is to say that Philo has a more philosophically developed cosmology than most Jews (though we cannot know what other Jewish writers in Alexandria may have offered). What is indirect, and often contradictory in Jewish writings like *Jubilees*, is here synthesised and worked out in remarkable (some have said predictable and tedious) detail. In this sense, Philo owes a deep debt to Greek philosophy, which distances him from most other known Jewish writers of his time. On the other hand, this is not to say that there is complete harmony between Philo and Plato: there are differences both of cosmology and ethos. Plato has neither a doctrine of creation in time; nor does he accord a particular place to a particular people in the divine scheme of things. Nor it is to say that there is complete harmony between Philo's cosmology and the ethos of the community which he endorses. True, he insists that the allegorical interpretation of the law is not to supersede the literal sense. However, his allegorical interpretations far from simply reinforce the literal practices. When all is said and done, and there is a lot more saying than doing, what Philo does is what all good Jews in his community do. But that does not mean that his writing provides the major impetus for that faithfulness. What he says can be taken over effortlessly by later generations of Christians who have left the practices of Judaism far behind. Philo provides us with evidence of a form of Jewish thought whose cosmology was so universal that it subsumed the particular categories of Jewish thought and practice, the Law, the people and its worship, under general, 'catholic' cosmological and moral ideas. For Philo, this was not to degrade them or to diminish their importance. They could now be seen as the supreme examples of moral and rational behaviour and thought. It would be open to others to choose other examples and to elevate them over Philo's chosen ones.

## Conclusions

This chapter has sought to give an insight into the ways that certain central motifs and symbols in Jewish culture were used to develop a variety of senses of Jewish identity. Those who read *Jubilees* with enthusiasm, whether in the immediate aftermath of the Seleucid proscription of the Law in second-century Israel or later in Greek translation in some Hellenistic city, will have had a very different sense of their own identity and their relation to their Gentile neighbours to that shared by those steeped in the never-ending stream of treatises which came from Philo (and doubtless from others like him).

The point of the chapter has been twofold: to show the prominence of certain motifs in the Jewish culture of the time, specifically those relating to geography and kinship, and to show something of the variations in use of which they were patient. The first point is rather obvious, though surprisingly the importance of geography in the Judaism at the turn of the era has, with some notable exceptions, been largely neglected. The promise of the Land to Abraham is a central feature of the covenantal promises to Abraham; the subsequent history of the possession of the Land, of exile and return continues to inspire hopes and expectations of restoration of national sovereignty to those who live under occupation or foreign control. Such hopes will be thrown into turmoil by the crisis of the Jewish War and the destruction of the Temple.

The second point, that the themes of the Land and of descent from Jewish ancestors were patient of very different treatment, needs underlining for two reasons. The first is that the influence of certain types of cultural anthropology has tended to suggest too strongly that a given set of cultural symbols will in large measure determine the singular ethos and world-view which is held by the community which accepts them. Comparison of *Jubilees* with Philo or Josephus shows how cautiously one must treat such views. The second is a more general caveat against assuming that the occurrence of particular motifs and themes in one context can provide an immediate key to their meaning in another. We always have to be careful to see how they are articulated in any given context (even in the work of the same author), before asking how far they may illuminate apparently similar usages elsewhere. We need to tease the meaning out of each passage as far as we can, before drawing any conclusions about its meaning there or its applicability elsewhere.

While our discussions in this chapter do not therefore allow for a set of general conclusions about the nature of the various forms of Judaism which could be found at the time of the writing of the Gospels, they do permit us to draw a few very general conclusions which will be foundational in what follows. The first is simply this: that kinship and attachment to the Land were of wide significance in the establishing of Jewish senses of identity at that period *and* that there were many and varied ways in which these motifs could be used. Such motifs taken literally tend to support a particular, as opposed to a universal, sense of identity. Those who give an account of their identity in terms of their physical descent from a particular group and their attachment to a particular territory, will do so by contradistinction from those with other links of the same kind. In general terms, such senses of identity are the basis of ethnic distinctions and identities. On the other hand, as we have seen, it is possible to use such terms in more universal ways: notions of descent may be allegorised or metaphoricised. There is a natural tendency to this kind of universalising in a writer like Philo, who sees all true rational worshippers of God as worthy of being regarded as his kin (*De Abr* 41). He can combine a sense of Jewishness with this more universal sense of fictive kinship with God by virtue of the link with Abraham who, above all, embodies the rational virtues of worship of God. In a similar way, those who convert to Judaism and embrace the true worship which is inculcated by the law are also to be held (within limits?) to be the true kinsfolk of the Jews themselves. There is, as we saw, a nice blending of literal and figurative uses of kinship in Philo.

There is a rather different kind of universalising of kinship terms which occurs in some of the more sectarian Jewish writings, sectarian at least in the sense that they wish to draw sharp distinctions between themselves and other Jews. In *Jubilees* the 'sons of the covenant' are not simply to be equated with those who are born and physically circumcised as Jews; they are to be distinguished from the 'sons of destruction' who comprise those who are unfaithful to God's commandments, 'who have broken the covenant of the Lord our God' (*Jub* 15:26). In Qumran, the 'sons of light' are the men of the community, the men of the covenant, the men of God's lot (as opposed to those of Belial's lot, 1QS 2:2, 5). They are to be distinguished from the 'sons of darkness', who certainly include the Sectarians' Jewish opponents. Here it is the pressure of a certain kind of cosmic dualism which leads to this kind of relegation of particular, ethnic distinctions to a place of secondary importance. In the light of the cosmic battle between good and evil, allegiance to the good and avoidance of evil is all; physical descent and local attachments pale into *relative* insignificance, which is not to say that they lose all importance.

This brings me to a further point. By the time of the turn of the era, Jewish apocalyptic eschatology was expressed, we have been suggesting, in terms of sharply differing accounts of the nature of evil and its overcoming. In consequence, the motifs of descent from the forefathers and of attachment to the land could receive very different articulation depending on the ways in which these different cosmologies were developed in a given community or writing. In practice, writings which seem to lay most stress on a forensic cosmology tend to treat the theme of the Land most directly, often expressing specific hopes for restoration of sovereignty, and for a gathering of the dispersed, whereas those whose primary focus is on cosmic dualist accounts of evil, are most likely to play these motifs down. Demons and fallen angels know no territorial boundaries and, if they are to be rooted out, must be rooted out from the whole world. Philo, by contrast, with his Platonist view of the world, allegorises the Temple on the one hand (the true Temple is the whole universe) and yet still insists, on none too persuasive grounds, on the necessity of having one earthly temple for all people to worship in. Again, there are two different tendencies at work which serve to de-particularise traditions about the land, the cosmic dualist and the Platonic. And again, we should not necessarily expect a simple and direct relationship between the cosmology and the ethos of any given writing. Correlations there will be, a sense in which the one supports and reinforces the other, but there will often be loose ends not least because the cosmology itself is being worked on in a dialogue with two rather different views of the world.

In what follows I want to investigate how far similar tendencies are at work in the Gospels of Mark and Matthew. In so doing we shall find, not unsurprisingly, that there are many more similarities between Mark and Matthew and the apocalyptic literature which we have been reviewing than between the two Gospels and Philo. In particular, we shall see how they too tell their story in dialogue with the two strains of apocalyptic eschatology which we have identified in other contemporary Jewish texts and how in so doing notions of kinship and descent and also of geography and sacred space are extended and modified.

# 3

## Sight to the blind

*Introduction: Mark 8:22–26*

Recovery of sight and the commands to silence in Mark

In the eighth chapter of Mark's Gospel, Jesus and his disciples come to Bethsaida and encounter a blind man, brought to him (presumably) by the people of the village, who ask Jesus to touch him. Jesus leads the man out of the village, spits on his eyes, lays hands on him and asks him if he can see anything. He replies that he can see people 'like trees, walking'. Jesus lays hands on him again and now he can see plainly. The story ends with Jesus sending him home and telling him not to go back into the village.

The story is remarkable in a number of ways. It bears close resemblance to the healing of the deaf man in 7:32–37. There are echoes, in the portrayal of Jesus' healing activity, of the work of a physician, albeit one with miraculous powers.[1] But for our purposes what is most striking are two motifs: the recovery of sight occurs in stages; the healing occurs outside the village and the man is told not to return there.

It is often said that the two healings of blind men in Mark's Gospel (8:22–26 and 10:46–52) form an *inclusio*, bracketing the section in the Gospel which deals with discipleship and the cross.[2] This deliberate shaping of the section strongly suggests that Mark intends the stories of the giving of sight to the blind men to be taken symbolically, providing a clue to the reader as to how the new life of the believer is to be

---

[1] See the discussion in Theissen, 1983, 93–4, and the literature cited there.

[2] See, e.g. Best, 1983, 62: 'Jesus can both open the ears and the eyes of those who at present in the pagan world do not see or hear, and he can also do the same for those within the community who are deficient in sight or hearing in relation to what their faith means for them; as they truly see and hear they will learn to follow Jesus in the way of the cross.' Thus Best takes these as stories both of transition from paganism to Christian faith and of progress and transformation in the Christian life.

understood.[3] The new life of the follower of Jesus is a life of sight, as compared with the former life of blindness, a life of light after darkness; but illumination may not come all at once: only gradually will those who choose to follow Jesus be led to the truth about the new world which they have entered. The imagery of the blind receiving their sight from Jesus is dominant (and supported by the similar story of the restoration of the deaf man's hearing in chapter 7); but the unusual story of the man at Bethsaida receiving his sight in stages also makes the point that the disciples will come only gradually to a full comprehension and acceptance of the new life on which they have embarked.[4] This, too, is supported by the immediately preceding section, 8:14–21, in which Jesus chides the disciples, 'to whom has been given the mystery of the kingdom of God' (4:11), for their continuing lack of understanding, quoting Jeremiah 5:21: 'though you have eyes, do you not see, and though you have ears, do you not hear?'

The other striking feature of the story is its choreography. Jesus encounters the blind man as he enters Bethsaida (actually a town rather

---

[3] I assume, with the majority of scholars, that what Mark writes about the disciples is intended to be instructive for believers, which is not of course to say that they are to be imitated in every respect. Not only is much of the disciples' behaviour as recorded in the Gospel far from exemplary; the itinerant life-style which they embraced is not necessarily that of all believers. Later believers are, therefore, followers of Jesus only in an analogical sense. Belief/faith is a more embracing category than discipleship, something that is laid on all those who seek to follow the way that Jesus opens up to them, 1:15. See the useful discussion of these issues in Marshall, 1989, 134–76.

[4] This point is denied by Gnilka, 1978, 315: 'Eine detaillierte Entsprechung der stufenweisen Heilung auf der einen und der stufenweisen Einführung in das Verständnis der Person Jesu auf der anderen Seite aber führt zu weit und ist abzulehnen.' But he gives no reasons for this judgement, while he does argue strongly (with reference esp. to the connection between 8:17f. and 22–26) for a symbolic significance for the stories of the healings of the blind men. Contrast Hooker, 1991, 198: 'The constant inability of the disciples in the chapters that follow this scene to understand Jesus' teaching about suffering – a failure which is remarkably similar to their inability beforehand to understand the significance of his words and deeds – suggests that Mark regards the disciples as semi-blind until after the resurrection; until then, they are in the position of the half-cured man who could barely distinguish between men and trees.' One must surely be allowed to point forward to connections in the text, as well as backwards. Matera, 1989, argues that the disciples' incomprehension is linked to the notion of divine hardening (6:52; 8:17) which prevents them from recognising Jesus as the Messianic shepherd (6:37). However, he argues, this hardening has to be lifted in order for Peter to be able to give a 'formally correct' confession in 8:29, and this corresponds to Jesus' laying his hands on the blind man's eyes. This is puzzling in the light of Peter's almost immediate misunderstanding of the nature of Jesus' Messiahship and of the fact that there is, as Matera acknowledges, no explicit identification of this action of lifting the hardening in the text (170).

than a village, but Mark seems not to know this or not to be interested in it), takes him out and directs him back to his house, telling him not to go into the village. As commentators have noticed, this final motif is reminiscent of the commands to silence which Jesus, often quite fruitlessly, as for example in the similarly structured story of the healing of the deaf and dumb man (7:36), directs to those whom he has healed. In Bethsaida, Jesus' taking the man out of the village together with the command to go to his house, suggests an avoidance of the public realm of the village, a remaining in the private sphere of the house/home (cf. κατ᾽ ἰδίαν, 7:33) which is typically for Mark the place of revelation, of instruction (and, less commonly, healing).[5]

The purpose of the motif of the command to silence has been the subject of intense and, frankly, unresolved debate.[6] Some have highlighted the sense in which the motif underscores the revelation which Jesus brings. Wrede, appealing especially to Mark 9:9, argued that the motif was principally intended to stress the fact that the full revelation of the mystery would come only at the resurrection. H. J. Ebeling believed that the motif of the *unsuccessful* commands to silence after healings was designed to stress the theophanic nature of Jesus' ministry: even despite Jesus' commands to silence, the power of the revelation which Jesus brought was so great that people could not contain themselves. Others, however, have seen the commands to silence as indicators of the strangeness and hiddenness of the revelation, that it was a mystery which could be grasped only with great difficulty. E. Schweizer and others argued that the commands to silence, along with the motif of the disciples' misunderstanding, were intended to reinforce Mark's central theology of the cross, according to which illumination about the meaning of Jesus' person and the life of discipleship could come only in face of the cross. Gnilka commenting in this sense on 8:26 suggests that its meaning is that the process of spreading the revelation of the mystery was to be delayed until such time as the miracle-worker Jesus could be seen as the crucified one.[7] This, however, restricts the discussion to the process of spreading the Gospel, whereas, as Gnilka

---

[5] So, rightly, Gnilka, 1978, 314.
[6] See, among the mountain of literature, Wrede, 1971, Räisänen, 1990, and Tuckett, 1983.
[7] Gnilka, 1978, 314: 'Die Verbreitung der Offenbarung soll jetzt noch nicht, sondern erst zu einem späteren Zeitpunkt erfolgen, zu dem der Wundertäter Jesus als der Gekreuzigte gesehen werden kann.'

himself recognises, the motif of the healing of the blind man is concerned primarily with the question of the *disciples'* understanding. The revelation they are given is something that they appropriate only gradually; only in stages do the scales fall from their eyes. It is necessary for them, therefore, to remain apart from the wider, public world, if they are to receive full understanding. Nevertheless, Jesus sends them out and there are those who are unable to remain silent. If this is right, then what we have to ask is how the motif of secrecy-privacy/openness-publicity bears on the question of the re-orientation of the disciples' lives, self-understanding and world-view, which is expressed in the motif of gaining sight.

## The wider literary context of Mark 8:22–26

At this point we need to look at the literary context of our story within the Gospel as a whole, in order to discern the wider network of symbolism of which the motif of secrecy is a part. Specifically, we need to trace the web of associated terms and images in which the disciples are, so to speak, suspended in the Gospel. The story of the disciples starts with the call of Simon and his brother Andrew in 1:16–18, followed immediately by the call of the sons of Zebedee (1:19–20), and, in chapter 2:13–14, by the call of Levi. They follow Jesus and so witness the extraordinary series of miracles, healings and exorcisms which he performs and hear the teaching which he gives. They are drawn into the new and, to some, offensive style of living which Jesus in his itinerant existence adopts. They consort with tax-collectors and do not fast like John's disciples or the Pharisees (2:18). They forage for themselves on the Sabbath (2:23–28). Nevertheless, despite such offensive behaviour, which leads to plots against his life (3:6), Jesus' activities attract large crowds. Then in 3:13, Jesus goes up on to the mountain and 'calls those whom he wills and they go off to him'. This episode contains the making of the Twelve and the renaming of Simon and the sons of Zebedee, and leads into the Beelzebul controversy in 3:22–27, the saying about the blasphemy against the Holy Spirit, and the final scene in the chapter (3:31–35) where Jesus' mother and brothers 'call' him and he asks the crowd: 'Who are my mother and my brothers?' and declares all those who do the will of God to be his kin (3:34–35). Then, in chapter 4, Jesus gives the parable of the sower and its interpretation, which is prefaced by the announcement: 'To you has been given the mystery of the kingdom of God, but for those outside, all things are in parables, so that they may indeed see but not perceive, and may indeed hear but not understand; lest they should turn again, and be forgiven' (4:11–12). The group of disciples, which had its inception with the call of a few fishermen on the shores of the lake and the large popular following called forth by his miracles, has become an in-group centred on the revealer Jesus, sharply distinguished from the unseeing people from whom they have been called.

As the narrative progresses, this picture of a group of itinerant followers, gathered around Jesus to receive and obey the revelation which he brings, is qualified, partly by the growing evidence of their lack of understanding (4:13; 6:52; 8:4, 17–21) and faith (4:40; 6:50), and partly by their being sent out to exorcise, heal and preach (6:7–13), which they do with some success. Not only they, but also the Gadarene demoniac, when restored, is sent to proclaim 'what the Lord has done' for him (5:19). Importantly, too, the reader's understanding of the nature of this new community is developed in the section 11:20–25[8] and in the parable of the wicked tenants, 12:1–11.

To what extent does this complex of narratives cast light on Mark's use of the motifs of giving sight to the blind and the separation of the disciples from the public sphere? There are a cluster of images and motifs here: the call of the disciples; their abandonment of their trade and their households, servants and parents; their embarking on an itinerant life and enlisting in the service of a teacher–healer–exorcist; their renaming and incorporation into a new family of those who do the will of God, which includes those who have been healed and delivered from possession; their consorting with the outcast; their privileged access to Jesus' teaching and interpretation of his parables, such that they form an in-group of the elect; their relationship to the crowds and to Jewish leadership groups; and their shortcomings and difficulties within this new life.[9]

---

[8] This is most fully developed by Marshall, 1989, 159–76, but is also noticed by Lührmann, 1987, 195–6: 'Die Szene . . . spricht . . . die Leser oder Hörer an im Blick auf ihren Gottesdienst außerhalb des Tempels. Die Verschachtelung der Feigenbaumszene mit der Tempelszene ist also nicht lediglich als literarische Technik zu verstehen, sondern hat einen Sinn im Blick auf den Leser.'

[9] See, for a fuller discussion, Malbon, 1986b. Rejecting any attempt to give an allegorical reading of the disciples, the crowds and the Twelve, she writes: 'The Gospel of Mark is, however, metaphoric and imagistic, and the disciples and the crowd – especially taken together – do evoke a composite image of the followers, the fallible followers of Jesus' (123). See below for further discussion on the theme of the boundaries of the new community.

One may well ask to what extent we can expect to offer a coherent account of the interrelationships of such a variety of motifs. Given Mark's very considerable dependence on his traditional material, the precise limits of which, however, it is more or less impossible to determine, we should not in any way be surprised if there were tensions and inconsistencies in the material which Mark has assembled.[10] We should certainly not be overzealous in our attempts to find a rationale in what may be more of a collage than the product of a single conception; yet, in the end, collage[11] or no, this is what 'Mark' gave to the world and we shall discover the overlaps and breaks in his conception only once we have tried to see how it fits together.

Rather than attempting a study of each of these motifs, and the light which they shed on the motifs of blindness and secrecy/privacy/openness, we will focus attention on the motif of the family of Jesus in chapter 3. Precisely because of the way these motifs link and overlap in a loose network of ideas and beliefs, a close study of one set of motifs will cast a good deal of light on others. Later in the chapter, we shall also introduce a discussion of the parable of the vineyard.

## Discipleship and family ties

### Mark 3:20–35

One of the striking features of Mark's portrayal of the disciples lies in his use of familial motifs. The keytext in this regard is Mark 3:20–35. Here Mark has woven together two stories of confrontation between Jesus and, respectively, his family and the 'scribes from Jerusalem', who accuse him of being possessed.[12] As the text now stands, there are two main sections, 3:22–30, 3:31–35, preceded by an introduction, 3:20–21, which prepares the way for the second section. Each of the two

---

[10]  To discuss the issues here would take us way beyond the scope of this volume. Luz, 1980, focuses the difficulties here with characteristic clarity; Räisänen, 1990, is a forceful attack on any attempt to provide a cohesive account of the various motifs which together make up the Messianic secret in a broad sense. Moore, in Anderson and Moore, 1992, 84–102, advocates a deconstructive approach to the reading of the Gospels which would positively exploit the diversity of views and motifs in the texts.

[11]  Cf. my discussion of Lévi-Strauss' characterisation of 'prior' thought as *bricolage*, the forging together of concrete images and motifs from the reservoir or treasure house of shared cultural objects. Chapter 5 below, pp. 176–9.

[12]  For the analysis of Mark's role in recasting the traditional material, see Barton, 1994, 68–75; Gnilka, 1978, 144–7; Best, 1976, 309–19.

sections concludes the account of the confrontation with a saying of Jesus which is legal in form and includes the conditional formula 'whoever . . .' (ὃς ἂν . . .). This structural parallelism between the two stories confers on Jesus' family a certain guilt by association with the scribes from Jerusalem.[13] More significant than this structural linking are the similarities of content: both his family and the scribes accuse him of having lost control of himself (ἐξέστη, 3:21; Βεελζεβοὺλ ἔχει, 3:22); both are met with an apodeictic legal saying which condemns/disqualifies them (3:29, 35); both sayings could apply equally well to both groups. The scribes who plot Jesus' death are clearly acting against the will of God; the family which accuses him of being mad is blaspheming against the Holy Spirit.

The section comes immediately before Jesus' discourse, 4:1–34, and as the conclusion of the account of the beginning of Jesus' ministry and the call of the disciples which opens the Gospel. It is preceded, that is to say, by three call-narratives, 1:16–18, 19–20; 2:14–17; and the account of a further more general call and the making of the Twelve in 3:13–19. Included in this section are controversy stories, where Jesus' opponents object to the company he keeps and the behaviour of his disciples (2:14–17, 18–27; 3:1–6, 22–28). The scene in 3:31–35, with its fivefold use of 'mother . . . brother . . . [sister]' and its close association of Jesus' physical family with his scribal opponents, is clearly intended as a commentary on the nature of the community of Jesus' followers.

There are other points to notice about its setting in the immediate literary context of the Gospel. There are verbal links with the important passage 4:10–12 in the immediately following discourse, where the disciples, to whom has been 'given the secret of the kingdom of God' are contrasted with those 'outside', to whom everything has been given in parables.[14] (There is also a reflection of 4:10–12 in 3:23 where Jesus replies to the scribes in parables.) The opposition of Jesus' family surfaces again in 6:1–6, the rejection at Nazareth, and there are further passages which stress the disciples' distance from their natural families: 10:28–31, on rewards for those who have left family and possessions, and

---

[13] Cf. Bas van Iersel's interesting suggestion, 1989, 93: 'All in all, Nazareth could be described as Jesus' Galilean Jerusalem, a place fraught with opposition based upon supposed knowledge.'

[14] Cf. Barton, 1994, 72: 'Given the predominantly redactional character of 4:10–12, it is legitimate to assume that, in the mind of Mark, ἐκείνοις δὲ τοῖς ἔξω includes Jesus' natural kin, who are ἔξω (3:31b, 32b) also.' Barton refers to Kelber, 1974, 25–6.

13:12 on family betrayal. On the other hand, not all references in the Gospel to family matters are anti-familial: 10:2–9, 10–12, unequivocally uphold the marriage bond.

What are we to make of this? Mark, in 3:20–35 and in its literary echoes throughout the Gospel, is building up a range of associations for the notion of discipleship. Discipleship is linked to being called by Jesus, to leaving family and possessions, to being with Jesus, to being sent out to preach and exorcise, to being Jesus' 'mother, brother and sister', to doing the will of God, to being given the secret of the kingdom of God.

The section in 3:20–35 adds definition to some of these associations. The disciples, who sit in the house around Jesus listening to him[15] are contrasted with Jesus' relatives who accuse him of being mad, who seek to seize him (cf. the use of the same verb at Jesus' arrest, 14:44, 46)[16] to bring him back to the family, who stand outside, who are closely associated with the scribes who blaspheme against the Holy Spirit. They, by implication at least, are those who confess the Holy Spirit (cf. 13:11, who trust themselves to the Spirit), who acknowledge Jesus' authority, who are led by Jesus. The interweaving of the two stories of Jesus' family and the accusation of demon possession[17] makes the point, moreover, that Jesus' true family are those who are freed from and opposed to the powers of evil, once Jesus has bound the strong man (3:27), and freed to proclaim the good news of Jesus' 'teaching with authority' (1:27; cf. 5:19). The story of the Gerasene demoniac reinforces this later point. He begs to 'be with Jesus' (5:18; cf. 3:14), but Jesus instead sends him back to his own to tell them what 'the Lord has done for him'. This contrasts with Jesus' commands to others who have been healed to keep silence. The δαιμονισθείς, as Mark reminds us, becomes a precursor of the Christian mission, and in this way a disciple.[18]

---

[15] Strictly speaking, the contrast is with those among the crowd surrounding Jesus, who not only listen to Jesus but who then do the will of God. In the same way, those to whom the secret of the kingdom of God has been given, though contrasted with those outside who are spoken to in parables and so blinded, may still deny and betray Jesus.

[16] Jesus' arrest and betrayal is again echoed in the prophecies of his disciples' betrayal by their own kin (13:12), though, ironically, Jesus is betrayed not by his blood brother but by his fictive brother.

[17] Mark's fondness for 'sandwiching' two stories together can be seen also in 5:22–43; 11:12–25; 14:54–72.

[18] Gnilka, 1978, 27: 'Er wird somit zum echten Vorläufer christlicher Verkündigung und damit zum Jünger.'

We can see again the tensions here between two different emphases in the understanding of discipleship, one which stresses the giving of the mystery of the kingdom through private instruction to an in-group of followers, sharply distinguished from the parent group from which they come; the other, which is more concerned with openness, with operating in the public sphere, bringing the good news to the wider world and with engaging in conflict with the demonic powers.

One way of pressing the question how far these texts represent a view which stresses separation from the parent group, would be to ask how far this contrasting of Jesus' natural family with the 'family' of his followers represents a relativisation or, more, a rejection of natural ties of kinship. It can scarcely be a rejection of *all* ties of kinship, in the light of Jesus' strong defence of marriage in 10:2–12. Nor is it likely that the polemic against Jesus' family is directed against actual members of Jesus' family in the Jerusalem leadership of the church. It is too broad and general for that.[19] On the other hand, to speak only of *relativisation* of kinship ties in Mark, as does Barton, in his in many ways helpful treatment, hardly tallies with Barton's own account of the extremely negative portrayal of Jesus' actual family in 3:20–35. Of course, it is possible to read 3:35, 'Whoever does the will of God is my brother, and sister, and mother', as simply affirming the overriding importance of doing the will of God: family ties must take second place to that. But this does not quite get to the heart of the matter. Mark is attempting to identify the defining characteristics of his group. And these do not lie in ties of kinship, of family relationships, or in descent from Abraham, but in doing the will of God as taught by Jesus. Fictive ties replace natural ties *as definitive of group membership*. In this respect, one (but only one) of the key markers of Jewish identity is undermined.

It is interesting to consider the bearing of this reading on Mark's use of the apocalyptic motif of internecine conflict (13:12). This is a motif found widely in prophetic[20] and apocalyptic literature.[21] Its later usage links it to notions of some radical transformation/renewal of Israel, in no sense to the abandonment of Israel's history and links with the patriarchs and forefathers. Profound disruption of family ties is a mark of the rebellion and trauma which will precede the final resolution of

---

[19] See the more detailed criticisms of this view, as exemplified by Tyson, 1961, Trocmé, 1975, 130–7 and Crossan, 1973 in Barton, 1994, 82–5.

[20] E.g. Ezek 38:21; Amos 1:11; Hag 2:22; Zech 7:10; 14:13; Mic 7:2, 5–6.

[21] See e.g. *1 Enoch* 99:5; 100:1f.; *Jub* 23:16, 19; *2 Bar* 70:3.

Israel's ills. But Mark seems to go further: in juxtaposing Jesus' natural family and his 'true' family, in suggesting that this contrast is on a par with the contrast between the disciples and those outside, between those who are inspired by the Spirit and those who blaspheme it, he is indicating that there is now an irretrievable rupture between the community gathered around Jesus and their former kinship group. What, for Mark, is the nature of the transition from one group to the other? Is it conversion? Are the new group seen as something wholly new over against the parent body? Or are they seen as a faithful remnant? As we have seen in our previous chapter, the use of fictive kinship terms can be found in types of Judaism as diverse as Qumran and Philo.[22] How far can a comparison with such usage help us here?

## Relation to Jewish understandings of conversion

The motifs of the gift of sight and the conferral of new family relationships, which Mark weaves into his portrayal of the disciples, have strong parallels in Jewish descriptions of conversion. As we saw, Philo, writing in Alexandria in the middle of the first century CE, talks about proselytes (ἐπηλύται) as having 'abandon[ed] their kinsfolk by blood, their country, their customs and the temples and images of their gods, and the tributes and honours paid to them' and 'taking the journey to a better home (καλὴν δ' ἀποικίαν στειλάμενους),[23] from idle fables to the clear vision of truth and the worship of the one and truly existing God'.[24] Similarly, he can speak of their being offered 'the high rewards of membership in the best commonwealth (πολιτεία)' and of the remarkable moral transformation which comes over them.[25] The moral and epistemological distance which they have, so to speak, traversed in this exchange of communities and their corporate world-view and ethos is well expressed in Philo's encouragement to his Jewish readers to 'rejoice

---

[22] The same is also indicated by the Q traditions about John the Baptist, Matt 3:9, where the importance of descent from Abraham is relativised.

[23] Literally: 'having been sent away to form a good settlement', with the implication that such a settlement is far from home; see *LS*, s.v. This may reflect a certain reversal of Jewish experience: Jews living away from Jerusalem in the Jewish settlement in Alexandria think of proselytes as leaving their own communities far behind, at least figuratively, as they exchange their kinsfolk and their ancestral customs and beliefs for those of the Jews. Such exile is good, because it locates their new home in the community of those who worship God in truth.

[24] *De Virt* 102.

[25] *De Virt* 175.

with them, as if, though blind at first they had recovered their sight and had come from the deepest darkness to behold the most radiant light'.[26] Such a change of community can be described in both active and passive terms: the proselytes have abandoned (ἀπολελοιπότες) their kinsfolk and have been sent (στειλαμένοι) on their journey; they have chosen God to be their God, just as God has chosen them to be his people.[27]

There is no difficulty in discerning the points of contact between Philo's account of conversion and Mark's story of the disciples.[28] They,

---

[26] καθάπερ ἂν εἰ καὶ τυφλοὶ πρότερον ὄντες ἀνέβλεψαν ἐκ βαθυτάτου σκότους αὐγοειδέστατον φῶς ἰδόντες, *De Virt* 179. In conversation Joel Marcus has suggested that this passage may be too much influenced by Philo's Platonism to be usefully typical of Jewish understandings of conversion. I see how the passage may be read in that way, it is also important to notice the strong community emphasis that Philo gives to the phenomenon, which cuts across the essentially individualistic character of Platonism. For Plato, it is through individual enlightenment and παιδεία that one proceeds from δόξα to ἐπιστήμη. For Philo, conversion is moving from one community with one – false – set of values and understanding of God to one with another – divinely revealed and therefore true – set of values and understanding of God. Where his Platonism may influence his presentation of conversion to Judaism, is in the stress that he places on the individual initiative in the process, in his universalising understanding of kinship with God (see chapter 2 above) and in his stress on the radical change in understanding that it entails, like the conversion of those in Plato's analogy of the cave who turn from watching shadows to emerge into the light to view the objects themselves (*Rep. Bk.* 7). But does Philo's use of this analogy distort his presentation of conversion to Judaism? The stories which we have of conversion: Joseph and Aseneth, Achior in the book of Judith, and King Azates (*Ant.* 20:2–4) are certainly stories of individual conversion, though admittedly the motifs vary considerably. In a sense this discussion nicely illustrates the point that conversion in the ancient world is a puzzling phenomenon, entailing a move from one set of traditional, and therefore inherited, values to another, by individual choice. There may, of course, be other reasons why people changed allegiance from one ethnic group to another: Metilius (*Bell* 2:457), after the massacre of his soldiers by the Jews, out of fear; foreign male rulers, who wished to marry into the Herodian household (*Ant.* 20:139, cf. 16:225) but these, *pace* Sim, 1996, 175, are not conversions proper. Conversions out of free or disinterested choice show the limits of the view that ancient religion was purely a corporate phenomenon with no interiority or psychological depth.

[27] *De Virt* 184, quoting from Deut 26:17–18.

[28] Marshall, 1989, 135–9, in his treatment of faith and discipleship, assumes without further ado that the call narratives are conversion narratives, even though he follows Hengel in seeing Jesus' role as 'analogous only to that of Yahweh in the Old Testament prophetic call stories'. In his view, discipleship faith 'entails a radical conversion, a decisive break with the existing order' (137). While he sees a possible eschatological resonance in this, he believes that this motif is designed to emphasise (i) the fact that God's kingdom lays claim to the whole of existence, and so leads to a transformation of social and economic relations, even before its eschatological realisation; (ii) that the 'almost suicidal renunciation of all means of human security places the disciples in a situation of radical dependency, even of human powerlessness' (138). The question which he does not raise at this juncture is to what extent such a radical break means a radical break with existing

too, have abandoned their kin and have become part of another kinship group, albeit a figurative one. They have been sent out on a journey which will take them into strange places (and indeed the last words to the disciples in the Gospel send them on their way again (Mark 16:7)). They are portrayed as blind and having received (or being in the process of receiving) sight; and they are called by Jesus; they are chosen/elected by God (13:20); as the elect, they belong to the Son of Man (13:27).[29] On the other hand, there are clearly points where the fit is less close. There is no suggestion here that they are leaving the worship of idols and false gods, though certainly the Pharisees and the scribes (as representatives of the group which they are leaving) are accused in general terms of hypocrisy in their worship: 'This people honours me with their lips, but their heart is far from me' (Mark 7:6).[30] There is a programmatic statement of need for repentance in 1:15, but subsequently there is little stress on the moral change which the transition from their old life to the new is to bring:[31] their new life as 'fishers of

---

forms of worship and belief in Yahweh, though, as we shall see, in his treatment of 11:20–25, he does juxtapose the community of faith with the worship of the Temple. He rightly observes that 'the realities of the old order as such are not repudiated. Simon and Andrew still exhibit familial concern and evidently retain their house and maybe their boat. But these are put at the disposal of the kingdom and are no longer their means of support and identity' (138). It is a moot point how far someone can see his family as having no bearing on his identity without repudiating it.

[29]  Reading αὐτοῦ with the Egyptian and *Koine* text.

[30]  Watts, 1997, 240–3, links Mark with Isaiah's polemic against idolatry and the motif of blindness. This is interesting, but there is little evidence in Mark of idolatry as such.

[31]  Nor does the notion occur in call stories, where one might most obviously expect it, notably in the call of Lévi, where Luke has inserted 'for repentance' into Jesus' further programmatic statement: 'I came not to call the righteous but sinners', 2:17; cf. Luke 5:32. It is true that the call-stories of Simon and Andrew and James and John follow on immediately after Jesus' programmatic announcement of the kingdom and his call to repentance, but is it not slightly forcing the evidence to suggest (Marshall, 1989, 135–6) that Mark has woven these episodes into 'a small literary unit' by the dual reference to 'Galilee' in vv. 14 and 16 (cf. 'the wilderness' vv. 12f. and 'Capernaum' v. 21), by the absence of temporal markers in the section (cf. 'forty days', v. 13 and 'the Sabbath' v. 21), and by creating a 'three-step progressive sequence' by adding 'come after me' (v. 17) to the two commands in v. 15. The three-step progression works awkwardly, as one would expect some similar command in the second call-narrative. The references to 'forty days' and 'the Sabbath' are integral to their respective stories and are quite likely traditional (Mark may not be editorially active in this respect at all: Gnilka, 1978, 1, 72f.). The reference to the 'Sea of Galilee' may be Mark's (so Gnilka, ibid.), but do not the call-stories, with their reference to boats and fishing, cry out for some such location, and may this way of referring to the lake not simply be Mark's own idiosyncrasy (cf. Mark 7:31)? There is, of course, no denying the connection with the programmatic

men' is conceived of as something which will be superior to their former life, but its superiority lies less in its development of certain kinds of virtues (though there is in the later chapters a concern about servanthood and the proper exercise of power) than in its instrumentality in the coming of the God's kingdom. The true mark of this life is faithfulness to and understanding of the mystery of the kingdom into which they have been initiated.

If Philo's account of conversion to Judaism by non-Jews sheds some light on the portrayal of the disciples in Mark, then comparison with accounts of change of allegiance *within* Judaism may also assist. The Dead Sea Scrolls provide evidence of the self-understanding of those who saw themselves as having made a radical break with their former lives within Judaism, and who in consequence saw themselves as wholly distinct from their fellow Jews. Jews who had not been admitted to the *yaḥad*, the community, were no more sons of the covenant than were Gentiles. There are a number of striking features which the two groups have in common. Just as Mark portrays the disciples as having gained their sight, the Qumran writings portray the covenanters as having come from blindness to sight,[32] as being under the Prince of light, rather than under the angel of darkness.[33] Such understanding is a gift

---

statement in vv. 14–15, but the question is, how far does Mark emphasise the notion of repentance; or perhaps better, *given* the close proximity of the two, what does this tell us about Mark's understanding of repentance? As Gnilka (1978, 75) says, the call story's position after the summary gives it 'stärkere paradigmatische Bedeutung. Sie verdeutlicht, wie in der bedingungslosen Nachfolge Jesu Umkehr und Glaube verwirklicht werden können.' (Cf. Marshall's claim, 1989, 39–42, that the summary itself has a paradigmatic function, which is surely too strong: it is at most thematic.) This is important, for, as Gnilka also says: 'Die Umkehr bleibt im ältesten Evangelium eigenartig unbestimmt'; ibid. 67. It is the concrete instantiation in the narrative which gives some further definition to the term, and the first two call-narratives do not emphasise moral repentance, but as Marshall indeed notes, a 'decisive break with the existing order' (1989, 137). This seems to me a happier formulation than speaking of repentance as 'the first part of faith, which brings one into the sphere of existence opened up by the gospel', or saying that 'repentance is considered a necessary requirement for faith' (52). This sounds much too tidy, in view of the subsequent narratives. Neither is any sort of change of attitude a *condition* of being invited into the kingdom; nor is it possible, in the light of the slipping and sliding of the disciples, to think of repentance as a first necessary stage for faith. Somehow being caught up with Jesus, being associated with him, sitting at table with him, being called to follow him, being among the crowds who follow – all of these may bring people to faith in him and the reality of the kingdom.

[32] CD 1:9: 'they were like blind persons and like those who grope for the path'.

[33] 1QS 3–4.

and is only partially under human control.[34] Nevertheless, just as the disciples' understanding is only partial, and the healing of the blind

---

[34] 1QH 4:5: 'I thank Thee, O Lord, for that thou hast illumined my face by Thy covenant.' Marcus, 1984, 562, emphasises this point strongly for Mark as well as for Qumran. For both 'the autonomy that can be ascribed to human beings in matters of perception is severely limited'. Marcus sees evidence for this in the limitation of the call to hear, in the parable of the sower, to 'those who have ears', and in the stress, in the interpretation of the parable, on the different types of soil: only the one who is good soil will be 'addressable, will be able to hear'.

The issues here are delicately balanced. On the one hand, there is no denying that precisely in the passage which is one of Marcus' key witnesses, there are repeated appeals to Jesus' hearers and Mark's readers to 'hear' (not only those listed by Marcus, but also 4:3). Such an appeal to hear Jesus' message can readily be related to the programmatic statement in 1:14–15, to Jesus' call to all who hear him, to repent and believe. All this seems to stress clearly enough the need for people to respond to his preaching. On the other hand, there is no denying the strict limits which the passage puts on the ability of some to hear: 'To those outside all things are in parables that . . . they may listen and listen yet not understand.' Similarly, the interpretation of the parable, identifying different types of people with varying abilities to hear, suggests strongly that there are forces which determine a person's ability to respond to the word which lie beyond his or her control. There is, of course, a question as to how far these determinative factors are the result of the direct or indirect activity of Satan. Satan is certainly mentioned, but it is much less clear that other factors which impede people from hearing the word are in any way linked with him. It is also true that the interpretation of the parable has a strongly predestinarian ring which makes it somewhat unsuitable for paraenetic purposes. Nevertheless, while it is true that the character of the different types of soil appears fixed, their function has still to be determined. Are they simply descriptions of the various categories of people in the world, as determined by God; or do they represent types of response to the word, in a manner to make clear to the hearers what the choices are which lie before them? The emphasis on hearing throughout the passage would tend to suggest the latter.

In sum: there is no denying that the parable of the sower and its interpretation contains elements which stress the hardening of some, and that it asserts that different groups are differently constrained in their hearing of the word. On the other hand, there are clearly paraenetic elements throughout the chapter which stress the importance of the hearer's response to the word, and therefore suggest that the human will has an important role to play in the reception of the word. Satan, too, is undeniably present; but there is no explicit link between his actions towards the first soil and the trials of the seeds in the other non-productive soils. Nor is there any explicit link between the divine hardening in vv. 11–12 and the action of Satan. It is Jesus' preaching in parables which effectively blinds 'those outside', just as Isaiah's preaching in Isaiah 6 prevents the people from repenting and being healed. If Isaiah 6 (or at least my reading of Isaiah 6 as opposed to its readings in the Dead Sea Scrolls) is to be taken as an indicator of the sense of Mark 4:11–12, then it has nothing to do with angelic forces perverting the hearts of those who are not among the elect (which is also not an element within Paul's use of the term in Rom 11:25–26), and everything to do with the rejection of God's love and law on the part of his people. Certainly this latter theme is strongly stated in the parable of the Wicked Tenants in Mark 12. In short, in this crucial passage there is a good deal of 'overlap' between a cosmological eschatology, which sees evil rooted in the action of man is in stages (Mark 8:22–26), so too the covenanters are plagued by the angel of darkness, who seeks to lead them in its ways (1QS 3:20–22).[35] Like Mark's disciples in 4:10–12, the covenanters have been given a special revelation of 'marvellous mysteries' (1QH 1:21), and the role of the community is to preserve this revelation and to keep it secret from those outside (1QS 4:6; 9:17).[36] Again the covenanters, like the disciples, are the elect of God. Just as God hardens some, and causes them to be led astray, so he forgives the sins of others (CD 3:18). The covenanters are also spoken of in fictive kinship terms: sons of righteousness, of light, of truth (1QS 3:13, 22; 4:6); like the disciples, they break with ties of family, transferring their possessions into the community (after a period of probation) and adopting a celibate mode of life.[37]

---

Satan and his cohorts, and a view which sees the source of evil, and indeed of its overcoming, as lying in the human will. I do not think it is possible, however, to fuse those elements which arise from this second view with the other in such a way as to give a coherent reading in terms of cosmological dualism. Indeed, Marcus himself says as much in a footnote, when he writes, following a suggestion from J. L. Martyn, that 'there is a "mysterious interpenetration" between faith and the grace shown in revelation'. Referring to the stories of the healing of blind Bartimaeus where Jesus commends his faith (10:52), he writes, 'Thus the initiative for revelation remains with God, but proclamation and faith have roles to play within that initiative' (362, n. 20).

[35] See Marcus, 1984, 560. Marcus contends in his article that the disciples' misunderstandings are subject, in the penultimate age, 'to the blinding onslaughts of the forces of darkness' (570). While it is true that Peter is rebuked by Jesus as Satan in 8:33, and that in his denials of Jesus he emphasises his ignorance (οὐκ οἶδα; οὔτε ἐπίσταμαι: 14:68, 71), it seems to be stretching the evidence to see in the Markan narrative clear indications of demonic intervention. Ignorance is not *per se* evidence of darkening of the mind by angelic agencies; it may be the result of divine hardening or of human failure. The tragic quality of the account of Peter's denial might equally well suggest that there is an interplay here between notions of divine necessity and human choice and failure.

[36] Marcus, 1984, 563, has argued that there is a closer parallel between Mark and Qumran in respect of their understanding of the nature of the mystery which has been revealed, namely that it is about the nature of divine activity in the world, 'God's dealing with humanity'. Here he is arguing specifically against the view that the mystery in Mark 4:11 is concerned with Jesus' identity. This is well judged in context. The immediate reference is to the parables of the kingdom divided, the strong man, and the sower. But it is also clear that the notion of secrecy in the Gospel does include Jesus' identity, even if his identity is not fully revealed to *a human being* until the centurion's confession at the cross.

[37] There are interesting anti-familial traits in 1QH 9:34–36: 'Until I am old Thou wilt care for me; for my father knew me not and my mother abandoned me to Thee. For Thou art a father to all [the sons] of Thy truth, and as a woman tenderly loves her babe, so dost Thou rejoice in them.'

If Mark's association of discipleship with receiving of sight finds strong echoes in Qumran, the motif of privacy and openness fits less well with the picture of conversion into the Qumran sect. In Qumran the mystery which has been given to the community is to be preserved within the *yaḥad*. Members of the community were carefully instructed and progress was monitored annually. In Mark, despite the commands to silence, the secret is something which cannot be kept under wraps even during Jesus' life-time. More importantly, Jesus' call is not just directed to the elect, to the chosen few with whom he has surrounded himself, but to the crowds whom he also calls to follow him (8: 34).[38] More radically, it is addressed unrestrictedly to sinners (2:17).

The nature of the connection between Jesus' call to discipleship and his call (καλέω) to sinners (2:17) is a matter of dispute among scholars. Barton takes the saying in 2:17 to be indicative of the universal nature of the prophetic call to mission, which the disciples have received.[39] He does not consider, however, what the implications of Jesus' call to tax-collectors and sinners are for the nature of that call and therefore for the self-understanding of the disciples. If Jesus does not come to call the righteous, what does this say about the disciples, who like the tax-collectors and sinners have also been called? Hooker rightly opines that the association of the verb καλέσαι with the meal in v. 15[40] means that Jesus' call to sinners is of a piece with his invitation to them to dine with him. 'Open commensality',[41] admission to the intimate circle without any prior conditions (cf. Luke 5:32, 'I came . . . to call . . . sinners *to repentance*') is the characteristic of the life to which the disciples are called. As Hooker comments: 'As in the story of the leper, it seems that Jesus' own power to bring forgiveness is understood as greater than the power of uncleanness to contaminate: like a doctor dealing with the sick, he is able to venture among sinners and help them. Once again, the story demonstrates Jesus' extraordinary authority.'[42] It is, precisely, the one who dips his bread in the same dish as Jesus who betrays him and brings him to his death (14:20). Jesus' authority, ἐξουσία, to forgive sins is not just a function of his admitting people to (table-)fellowship with him; it characterises the relationship that he

---

[38]  So esp., Malbon, 1986b.
[39]  Barton, 1994, 66.
[40]  Hooker, 1991, 97, taking the house in v. 15 to be Jesus'.
[41]  The phrase is taken from Crossan, 1991, 261.
[42]  Hooker, 1991, 97.

continues to enjoy with his followers, with those whom he calls to 'be with him'. Misunderstanding, denial and betrayal are continuing marks of that relationship. This again distinguishes Mark's portrayal of conversion from that of Qumran. For there the authority of the community, its standing in the truth, is to be assured by its distancing of itself from all alien influences, as is illustrated by its elaborate purity regulations and its shunning of commerce with those outside the community.

## Call stories in 1 Kings and Josephus

Further than this, there are elements in Mark's account which are discordant with the picture of conversion portrayed both by Philo and by Qumran. This can be seen from a further comparison, this time with the story of Elijah's call of Elisha in 1 Kings 19:19–21, which provides the model for Mark 1:16–20. In this story, Elijah finds Elisha ploughing, throws his cloak over him and immediately Elisha follows him. However, there then comes an exchange between the two in which Elisha asks to be allowed to return home and kiss his father and mother goodbye. Elijah's reply is somewhat ambiguous, but in the context seems to be a curt rejection of Elisha's request. Elisha responds by slaughtering his ploughing oxen, breaking his yoke, feeding the beasts to his servants and then following Elijah.

The context of the story is worthy of attention. It is preceded immediately by the theophany to Elijah on Mount Horeb, where God speaks to him in the 'still, small voice'. This occurs in response to, and indeed, as the story stands, as a corrective to, Elijah's sense of abandonment: 'the people of Israel have forsaken thy covenant, thrown down thine altars, and slain thy prophets with the sword; and I, even I only, am left' (1 Kings 19:10, 14). God's response to this is to appoint new leaders, including a successor to Elijah, who will slay all those who have been faithless and leave the few (seven thousand) who have not bowed the knee to Baal. Thus there are considerable tensions in the story. Elijah sees himself as the only faithful one left; God tells him his duty is to gather together those who have remained faithful and to purge out the faithless from the people of the covenant. Is this a story about calling the faithless people to repentance or about the appointing of kings and prophets to draw together the faithful remnant? The final form of the text points clearly in the direction of the latter reading, for all its tensions. Later reception of the story will reinforce this view.[43] Elisha is the one called to continue Elijah's fight against the prophets of Baal and all those who would worship the dark powers.

As Martin Hengel has pointed out, the Synoptic call-stories have strong formal and material parallels to the story of the call of Elisha in 1 Kings 19:19–21.[44] They are brief, omit any psychological explanation, focusing instead on the authoritative call of Jesus and the disciples' response in abandoning their present occupations and families and following Jesus. The original form of the story in the Old Testament, it is suggested,[45] has Elijah forbidding Elisha to say goodbye to his parents (cf. Exod 4:18f.) but this is softened in the final form of the text. In Josephus, *Ant.* 8:354, a more 'charismatic' version of the story emerges and the links with the Synoptics become clear: the prophetic gift is transferred to Elisha at his call; he leaves, follows and becomes Elijah's disciple and servant – though he is allowed to go back and say farewell to his parents. What is distinctive in the Synoptics, according to Hengel, is that whereas in the Elijah/Elisha story it is God who calls, in the Synoptics it is Jesus, acting on his *Messianic authority*.[46] Hengel argues that the fundamental similarity between Jesus' call of his disciples and Elijah's call of Elisha is that Jesus called his disciples to 'participate in his mission and authority . . . by confronting the whole people, along with him, with the offer of approaching salvation and with the proclamation of the final judgement'.[47] In context, this is a judgement about Jesus himself, not a judgement about Mark's presentation of Jesus, but it is one, nevertheless, which, in view of the close literary parallels between 1 Kings and Mark, remains of interest for our purposes.

The fit between the story of Elisha's call to be God's instrument in the restoration of Israel and the call of the disciples in Mark is striking. Most of the elements in the Elisha tradition, particularly if we take Josephus' version into account, are to be found in Mark. The call is

---

[43] See Hengel, 1981, for a discussion of the reception-history of this story.

[44] Hengel, 1981, 5.

[45] So Fohrer, 1957, 21–2.

[46] Hengel, 1981, 17. Apart from the Elijah/Elisha story, there are very few other references to disciples of the prophets in the Old Testament. Hengel also argues that Elijah serves as a role model for those contemporaries of Jesus, 'zealous for the Law' who called people to follow them and who, like Judas the Galilean, could also be referred to as σοφιστής. Here Elijah is identified with Phinehas (Hengel, 1981, 24). Elijah, the איש אלהים, can also be compared with the θεῖοι ἄνδρες of Hellenistic tradition who attracted disciples (Hengel, 1981, 24–5).

[47] Hengel, 1981, 73.

made by an authoritative, charismatic figure who endows his followers with charismatic gifts (prophecy, miraculous powers, in Elisha's case; preaching, exorcism for Jesus' followers) and calls them to be his disciples, and to leave occupation and family in order to follow him in an itinerant ministry. Both Elisha and Jesus' disciples are to participate in the work of the one who has called them, a work which is directed towards Israel and its salvation and against the powers of evil.

On the other hand, there are features which distinguish Mark's narrative about Jesus and the disciples from the Elijah/Elisha cycles in 1 and 2 Kings. In the final form of the story, Elisha is called as one of those who has not bowed the knee to Baal, to gather the faithful together. There is no question of his being called out of darkness to the light, as the healings of the blind men suggest for the disciples in Mark. Again, the motifs of the disciples' misunderstanding, of Jesus' instruction of the disciples, and indeed of the revelation of the mystery of the kingdom, have no real parallels in the Elijah/Elisha story.

At other points the comparison becomes more complicated. Do the disciples inherit Jesus' mantle and continue his work in the way that Elisha does? In one sense, they do. In the mission charge in Mark 6, Jesus sends them out to do the same work that they have seen him doing in his ministry thus far; and they do indeed do it. They are enjoined to take up their cross and follow him; they will drink the cup which Jesus drinks and be baptised with the same baptism (8:34; 10:39). In another sense, they show by their repeated failure both to grasp Jesus' identity and to accept his account of his work and their final failure in the Passion, that they are in no way ready to follow in his footsteps, far less to receive double his Spirit, though they are promised that the Spirit will speak for them (13:11).

## Two views of discipleship?

What emerges from this initial survey is that there are elements in Mark's account which stress the sense in which the disciples are being forged, haltingly and with much misunderstanding and failure, into a new community of those who have abandoned their old attachments of kinship, custom, land and cultic sites, and have found a new family in the company and following of Jesus; and there are elements which show them as being called out from among the people for a particular task in the proclamation and ushering in of the kingdom of God, a task they share with Jesus and which they will indeed continue after his departure.

It is not easy to offer neat categorisations of these two different emphases in Mark's account of discipleship. One can imagine the rather different moods and attitudes which concentrating on one or other strand might generate, as one can conceive of the rather different views of the world which would accompany and reinforce them. The first view, which for convenience we can call the conversionist view, paints the world in darker colours: Jesus calls people from a world of blindness to a sight achieved only with difficulty. The disciples are associated with the social and religious outcasts whom Jesus calls and with the possessed whom he has freed. Those who are Jesus' brothers and sisters have been rescued – with difficulty and much backsliding – from a world of illusion, sin and demonic pollution, and brought into fellowship with Jesus. On the one hand, there is much dwelling on the misery of the former state, and indeed, the continuing weakness even of the converted; on the other hand are heady images of unexpected release and new-found life. The other, restorationist view lays greater stress on Israel's predicament and the announcement of the good news of the way of the Lord. The disciples are those who are commissioned to follow in the Messiah's footsteps, receiving instruction from him, being sent out to call the people to repent and follow him on the way of the Lord to Zion. The mood might seem to be more confident, rooted in the pronouncements of the fulfilment of the prophetic sayings. Israel has suffered enough and the time of restoration is at hand. And yet there is, as we shall see more fully, a deep irony in Mark's use of this imagery. The way leads to Jesus' death in Jerusalem. The disciples who follow him on the way stumble and betray and desert him. The people who flock to hear the Baptist's proclamation end up by calling for Jesus' crucifixion.

Behind these two 'accounts' of discipleship lie, I want to argue over these three chapters on Mark, the same two different views of the human predicament and its resolution which we noticed in our discussion of Jewish apocalyptic texts. On the first view, men and women are caught in a world from which only some dramatic intervention can rescue them. They are blinded, possessed; evil has dark, pervasive, even demonic roots. Its overcoming lies outside the control of men and women, unless they first 'bind the strong man'. But who is strong enough? On the other view, the focus is first and foremost on Israel, whose punishment and spiritual exile is coming to its end and whose restoration is announced. Disobedience is the problem; divine forbearance and leading is the path by which Israel will be restored. And yet, this picture of

Israel's restoration is cruelly parodied in the events of the Passion, and the promised restitution of the Temple is replaced with prophecies of its destruction. The darker mood of the first set of images seems to have cast its spell over the restorationist account. Only a more radical solution, a complete reversal of things, can bring a solution. The two views interanimate each other in ways which are suggestive rather than precisely worked out.

## Emerging senses of identity

What kind of self is beginning to emerge from these complex narratives? And, just as importantly, what kind of account are we, from our later vantage point, to give of it? We need to approach this question cautiously. Such discussions as New Testament scholars have offered have either stuck quite closely to categories taken from the social sciences, or have attempted, more flexibly, to trace the emergence of a certain kind of moral sensibility, reflected in a network of 'perceptions, beliefs and practices'.[48] In an obvious sense, what we have been attempting so far is much closer to the latter. We have been looking at the shift in sensibilities occasioned by Mark's narratives of Jesus' call and commissioning of his disciples. How would it have affected the sensibilities of those whose senses of identity were closely linked with their belief in the divine election of the Jews and of their own membership of Israel as a community separated by God from the nations? Those who previously had seen blood-ties and the ritual marks of circumcision as fundamental to their identity, were now being invited to see themselves as members of a group gathered around a Messianic figure rejected by the leaders of his people, who sent out his followers to preach the gospel not only to the Jews but to all nations. Did this involve a radical break from the parent group, or was the conversion which they underwent from one group to another within Judaism?

As we saw, there were interesting lines of contact between Mark's portrayal of the disciples and the senses of identity to be seen in Jewish groups in the diaspora and on the margins of Temple Judaism[49] in

---

[48] Meeks, 1993, ix.
[49] I use this term as a convenient, though potentially misleading, shorthand for what E. P. Sanders has described as 'common Judaism'. It refers, that is, to the centrality of the Temple cult in the observances, organisational structures and world-view of Judaism in Roman Palestine in the earlier part of the first century CE. It is not meant to imply that

Roman Palestine. Both Philo and Mark, in their use of the imagery of blindness and sight, established a clear sense of the boundaries between their own group and those outside. Similar use of the language of light and darkness can be seen in Qumran, where it is used, however, to draw sharp lines of demarcation between the covenanters and other Jews, and not only between Jews and Gentiles, as in Philo. Qumran, like *Jubilees*, also shares with Mark in its figurative use of kinship language ('sons of the covenant', 'of light', 'of righteousness'), which in a measure replaces the literal language of kinship, which is inadequate to the task of providing a self-description of the group. At the same time, the disciples in Mark are called to share in God's restoration of Israel. The opening announcement of the 'way of the Lord' sets the Gospel clearly within the confines of Jewish 'restoration eschatology' and therefore ties Mark's readers into the 'grand narrative' of the Jewish people, as does their close relationship with the Messianic figure, Jesus, which is underlined by Peter's confession in the mid-point of its own narrative. In this respect, the Gospel is much closer to the world of the Qumran writings and of *Jubilees* than to Philo or Josephus. It breathes an air of expectation of radical change which will restore the glories of the past.[50] It seeks to draw its readers into a new community with a strong sense of its distinctiveness over against other groupings. It calls people to seek a new life, in company with a divinely approved, Messianic figure who will fulfil their deepest expectations.

To ask such questions and to make the comparisons which we have made is already to begin to form a sense of the newly emerging sensibilities of this movement. We shall learn a good deal more about how such narratives affected people's sensibilities when we come to consider how they were retold, and see the different emphases which Matthew gave to them. But, as we continue to look at the Markan narrative, it may be useful to see what we can learn about these new senses of identity by comparing them to different kinds of social grouping, sectarian and ethnic, which sociologists of religion and anthropologists have described in more general, ideal typical ways. This will, *inter alia*, provide a means

---

Jews in the diaspora had no interest in the Temple (see Philo's extensive discussion in *Spec Leg* 1:66–298), nor indeed that Jewish observance in the Land was restricted to rites performed at the Temple itself.

[50] Joel Marcus has argued recently that the term 'Son of Man' in Mark should be construed as 'Son of Adam'. This intriguing thesis, if substantiated, would make precisely the point: for Mark, *Endzeit ist Urzeit*.

of exploring the relation of Mark's community to the Jewish community. Was the community for which Mark wrote a sect and, if so, to which group did it feel itself to be marginal? In what sense did that community see itself in ethnic terms?

## The community of Mark's readers as sect

Care is needed here, not least because it is all too easy to imagine that the categories of modern sociology of religion can simply be used to fill in the gaps of our knowledge[51] – as if the pieces of our sorely depleted jigsaw could now be fitted together with confidence because we have at last found the lid of the box. Not so. The ideal types of modern sociology are merely abstractions from empirical data gathered from religious movements operating in the rather different world of today. They differ interestingly from the generalisations offered by Ernst Troeltsch, based on his knowledge of the medieval period.[52] We should treat them as guides, analogies, not as rigid models.

With this caveat, what can be usefully said about the nature of sects? Wilson's summary of their ideal typical features is as follows.[53] Sects are exclusive, not permitting dual allegiances. They claim a monopoly of religious truth, which extends to all areas of life. Organisationally, they tend to be lay, anti-sacerdotal: everyone has 'some equal possibility of access to the truth'. In terms of practice, they reject division of labour, the restriction of certain kinds of activity to a particular religious class, though there may be exceptions in terms of their founders. They are voluntarist: an individual chooses to be a member and is expected to show some 'mark of merit', knowledge of doctrines, quality of life. Sects are keen to maintain standards, and may employ sanctions to ensure their maintenance, including expulsion from the group. They demand total allegiance from their members. Finally, 'the sect is a protest group'. It arises in protest against the dominant ethos of its own wider society, whether this be, as in former times, against a dominant religious grouping, such as the church; or whether, as is now more often, against the 'social, cultural, and political condition of the world'.

---

[51] See Gager, 1975, 4: 'In other words new "data" may come in the form of new models', but note the scare-quotes!

[52] See the useful discussion of ideal types in relation to sociological accounts of sects in Wilson, 1982, 95–100.

[53] Wilson, 1982, 91–3.

It is not difficult to compile a list of passages and motifs in Mark to correspond to Wilson's list. There are motifs which reinforce Mark's use of the metaphor of sight/blindness to underline the *exclusiveness* of the group. These are closely tied to the notion of *the monopoly of truth* which has been imparted to the group. It is to the disciples that 'it has been given to know the mystery of the kingdom'. By contrast, all 'those outside' are taught in parables, so that they may neither see nor understand (4:10–12). Allied to this are the commands to secrecy, which accompany Jesus' miracles and the moments of the revelation of his divine nature to demons and disciples. Mark's community is a group of *non-specialists*. The notion of discipleship is widely applicable, not restricted to a special class of functionaries: readers are invited to identify themselves with the main characters and to hear the call to lose their life in order to save it as applying directly to themselves (8:34–38). There is, it is true, a clear distinction between Jesus, the Messiah, Son of God and the disciples, as there is also between the Twelve, who actually accompanied Jesus on his earthly ministry, and the disciples who make up the company of Mark's readers and hearers. Nevertheless, the practical work of the community is not restricted to the few original leaders. True, the initial mission charge is given specifically to the Twelve, who on this occasion are also referred to as apostles (6:30); when, however, Jesus later tells of the gospel's being preached to all nations, it is related to the early church's experience of persecution (13:9–13), something which could overtake whole communities of Christians, as in the Neronian persecutions in Rome.

As in other sects, there is a clear emphasis on *choice* and on the high demands which membership of the new group will impose on those who join. The choice itself entails a 'losing of one's life' (8:34–38); they may expect to sacrifice family and property for the sake of the Gospel (10:29–30). Similarly, a fierce *self-discipline* is demanded of those who embrace the life of discipleship, which is reinforced by the consequences of eventual failure: 'If your hand causes you to sin, cut it off; it is better for you to enter life maimed than with two hands to go to hell, to the unquenchable fire' (9:43). Discipleship requires a *total reorientation*: they are to 'think the things of God, not of men' (8:33, of Peter: Ὕπαγε ὀπίσω μου, σατανᾶ, ὅτι οὐ φρονεῖς τὰ τοῦ θεοῦ ἀλλὰ τὰ τῶν ἀνθρώπων).

There can be no doubt of the strong notes of *protest* against Jews and Jewish leaders in the Gospel. These are principally directed against specific groups, scribes and Pharisees, the chief priests and elders, who are castigated for their misunderstanding of the law and presented as plotting Jesus' death. All of this could lead one to a simple assertion that the Gospel encourages a sectarian mentality on the part of its readers. But is it as simple as that?

Such a simple sketch of the Gospel's sectarian tendencies can be questioned at a number of points. The little story about the strange exorcist, 9:38–40(41), contains the surprisingly open saying: 'For he that is not against us is for us.' Best and Gnilka, independently, regard this section as traditional and see it as reflecting debates among the earliest Christians about the boundaries of the community as raised by the practice, attested in Acts (19:13–17; cf. Matt 7:22), of exorcists outside the community invoking the name of Jesus.[54] Jesus offers the somewhat pragmatic explanation (9:39) that such people will not easily be able, at least in the short term, to vilify him. The saying in 9:41 adds to the list of those who are to be regarded as being 'for us' those who sympathise with the community (those who are 'of Christ'), anyone, that is, who offers support to Christians as Christians. Whether this refers to those who offer help when Christians are under persecution[55] or to sympathisers of the Christian mission,[56] is probably impossible to decide. In either case, the community is urged not to close its boundaries with the outside world, to leave open the possibility of others joining them. Even without such formal association, however, 'they will not lose their reward'. This contrasts, of course, strikingly with the Q version of this saying, which precisely reverses the sense: 'He who is not with me is against me, and he who does not gather with me scatters' (Matt 12:30//Luke 11:23, though Luke also has the positive version, 9:50).

The history of this saying is, then, quite revealing. It confirms in one way that the sectarian tendencies which our initial sketch suggested are there; that the tendency to put tight boundaries around the group and to demand total allegiance to it, were strong and had already given rise to the traditional material contained in Mark 9:38–41. It shows, nevertheless, that there were contrary tendencies, which are reflected in this tradition and picked up and developed by Mark. At the same time,

[54] Best, 1981, 82–3; 235–6; Gnilka, 1979, 58–62.
[55] Best, 1981, 83: 'the person who assists the Christian who is in such desperate straits that even a cup of water is help'.
[56] Gnilka, 1979, 61.

the Matthaean handling of the tradition shows that the sectarian tendencies could also stiffen.

Closely related to the questions of exclusivity and tight boundaries is the question of knowledge which is specific to the group. We have already seen that Mark 4:10–12 makes a sharp division between those within and those outside, between those to whom the mystery has been revealed and those to whom everything is in parables (riddles). This conforms to the ideal-typical portrayal of the sect where all knowledge is restricted to the in-group and is to be carefully protected from those outside. There are, as is often noted, clear redactional traits in Mark which reinforce such tendencies: commands to silence, private instruction to the disciples (4:10–12, 34b; 7:17–23; 8:14–21, 31; 9:2–13, 30–32; 10:10–12, sometimes to a particular group among the disciples). There are, however, also counter-tendencies. The central teaching on discipleship after Peter's confession at Caesarea Philippi is directed to the crowds (8:34 – 9:1). The knowledge which the disciples have received is to be shared. They are called to be fishers of men (1:17), to preach and exorcise (3:14–15; 6:7), to be a lamp set on a stand (4:21–23).

## Sectarian responses to the world

The question raised by these texts is whether they suggest a reversal of the sectarian character of some of Mark's texts, notably 4:10–12, or whether they point more to a particular kind of sectarian character. Wilson has attempted, alongside his general description of sects, to provide a classification of sects, categorising them in terms of their different responses to the world. This is a discussion to which we shall return, not least when we look at the world-view, or views which emerge from the Gospel texts. Here we need first to introduce the concept of responses to the world and to list some of the types of response. This will enable us to say something about the character of Markan responses. Wilson introduces the concept of responses to the world by refining the discussion of sects in terms of their missionary activity. There is more to the notion of responses to the world than just the presence or otherwise of missionary activity within a particular group. Such responses embrace attitudes, life-styles, patterns of association and ideology.[57]

---

[57] Wilson, 1975, 20: '*Response to the world*, much more evidently than *mission*, may be manifested in many relatively unfocused, unpurposive activities, and *not only* in activities, but also in life-style, association, and ideology.'

Responses to the world may be of different kinds: Wilson is concerned with supernaturalist ones. Within those, sectarian responses are distinguished from the dominant, orthodox position which 'is that of acceptance of the world, the facilities it offers, and the goals and values that a given culture enjoins upon men'.

But what characterises people who reject the dominant position of acceptance of the world and what it offers? 'Concern with transcendence over evil and the search for salvation and consequent rejection of prevailing cultural values, goals, and norms, and whatever facilities are culturally provided for man's salvation, defines religious deviance.'[58] Members of sects, that is to say, are radically dissatisfied with what is on offer, both in terms of the kind of world that they encounter and in terms of the ways which are standardly presented for dealing with that world. They want a different world and they look for different ways of transcending the present world and its ills. Such ills, their source and the means of their overcoming, are conceived in various ways. For some, evil stems from supernatural agencies, devils, ghosts, sorcerers. For others, it may stem from human willing and be ascribed to the 'inherently evil nature of men, or to their failure in serving God, or in failing to organise their affairs in accordance with his will'. The remedy for such evil, variously conceived, which is sought, will also vary: from 'limited demand for *ad hoc* instant therapy to a programme for the reorganization of the world.'[59] It is not difficult to recognise in these two broad traits the two main varieties of Jewish apocalyptic eschatology which we reviewed in our last chapter.

Wilson offers a typology of such responses to the world.[60] Of the seven responses which he lists, four are said to be objectivist, where the principal focus is on God's action to overturn the world. God will either overturn it (revolutionists), call on people to abandon it (introversionists), to amend it (reformists) or to reconstruct it (utopians). One approach is subjectivist: God will change us (conversionists). Two are relationist: God calls us to change our perception of the world (manipulationists) or will work particular miracles (thaumaturgists).[61]

Wilson's categorisation can help us both to consider the extent to which Mark's Gospel may be said to encourage sectarian tendencies

---

[58] Wilson, 1975, 21.
[59] Wilson, 1975, 21–2.
[60] Wilson, 1975, 22–6.
[61] Wilson, 1975, 27.

and to give a more differentiated account of such tendencies as we may discern. The first question is: to what extent does Mark's Gospel encourage '[c]oncern with transcendence over evil and the search for salvation and consequent rejection of prevailing cultural values, goals, and norms, and whatever facilities are culturally provided for man's salvation'? Jesus in Mark calls his followers to engage in conflict with evil: both with evil spirits who possess men and women, and with 'the cares of the world, and the delight in riches, and the desire for other things' (4:19). But does his fight against evil lead him to reject prevailing cultural values and institutions? The answer is more difficult, not least because Judaism itself at the time was sharply divided in its response to its predicament. Groups like Qumran, Josephus' fourth philosophy, Josephus' prophets, writings like *Jubilees*, the *Testaments of the Patriarchs*, *1 Enoch*, and the *Sibyllines*, looked for a radical renewal of Jewish institutions and an end to suffering, disease and foreign domination. This contrasts with many Jews who saw, in the worship of the Temple-cult and in the extension of associated notions of purity to the local community and the home, a means of protecting themselves from the worst ravages of evil and sin. But is Jesus in Mark not portrayed as going yet further? He predicts the destruction of the Temple; Mark portrays his death as the manifestation of the *Shekhina* which has abandoned the Temple. Moreover, Jesus simply sweeps aside the food laws (7:19) which played such an important part in the development of Judaism after the destruction of the Temple. Thus we may with some confidence place Mark among the Jewish groups who looked for some radical refashioning of Jewish religious institutions and observance. At the same time, one can see clear points at which Mark parts company with Jewish restorationist groups.

## The strange exorcist

Can we go further and place Mark among the categories proposed by Wilson? The debate over the strange exorcist may serve as a starting point. Interest in and the practice of exorcism, may be a characteristic of at least two of Wilson's categories. Thaumaturgical groups may practise exorcism as a means of helping individuals to *cope* with the troubles that afflict them in this world.[62] It is not part of a wider vision of God's action to change the world itself, part, rather, of his helping individuals

---

[62] Wilson, 1975, 72.

to come to terms with it. On the other hand, revolutionist groups may see exorcism as a sign that God is at work, overthrowing the powers of darkness as part of a wider campaign radically to renew the world. As Wilson points out, millenarian cults often start out as revolutionist in character and then fall back into a thaumaturgical mode, when their initial expectations are disappointed. Occasionally, as in the case of the Kimbanguists,[63] thaumaturgical movements may be transformed (in this case, at least, through the brutality and insensitivity of the colonial rulers)[64] into millenarian movements. On a millenarian, revolutionist view, if anyone is casting out demons, then this is a sign that God is at work, that the expected radical transformation of the world is already occurring. The work of 'strange' exorcists could then be seen as confirmation of their own millenarian message. From a thaumaturgical viewpoint, the use of Jesus' name by other groups for healing purposes looks like a dangerous challenge to their own access to divine power. The text in chapter 9 may give us a fleeting glimpse of controversies in the early church before the writing of Mark, which could lead in very different directions: to a revitalising of the millenialist character of the movement, or to its refashioning as a thaumaturgical movement. It suggests, however elusively, that early Christianity may well have moved in and out of a more or less revolutionist outlook with some regularity in the early decades of the movement, before settling down into a relatively stable thaumaturgical mode. Even so, the seeds of a millenarian revolutionism remain, and from time to time, put out remarkable shoots.[65]

We must be careful not to regard Wilson's types of response as more than ideal types. In reality, actual groups will match up with different elements from the different categories. What we have seen in our brief account of discipleship in Mark is that there are both tendencies to view the world as wholly under the sway of Satan/Beelzebul and,

---

[63] Wilson, 1975, 367–73.

[64] Joel Marcus, 1999, has raised the question whether Jesus' own ministry went through a transition from thaumaturgical to revolutionist. The harsh and politically insensitive imprisonment and execution of John the Baptist may indeed have provided the occasion for such a transformation. But we should also reckon with the possibility that early Christianity may have experienced considerable ambiguity about this side of its character, and that similar changes from thaumaturgical to revolutionist may have been occasioned by the events of the Jewish War and the destruction of Jerusalem, or indeed by the Neronian persecutions in Rome.

[65] See Rowland, 1988.

therefore, to look for some radical intervention by God to subdue Satan, corresponding broadly to Wilson's revolutionist response; and also tendencies to look for an end to Israel's disobedience, and God's punishment, a return to the Land, and a restoration of the national institutions. This latter tendency is closer to what Wilson calls a reformist response: amending the institutions and behaviour of the people, though clearly the myth of the return from exile adds a thoroughly interventionist element. The first is also closely aligned to Wilson's conversionist response. This is not just a matter of national repentance, that is, of returning to the ways of the past. It is more radical, a move from darkness to light, from bondage to freedom, from the status of the outcast to admission to the family of God. What people must do here to be saved is not simply to repent and mend their ways, but 'to undergo emotional transformation – a conversion experience. This is the proof of having transcended the evil of the world. Since it is a permanent and timelessly valid transcendence, some future condition of salvation is often posited in which objective circumstances come to correspond to the subjective sense of salvation, but the believer also knows, from the subjective change, that he is saved *now*. Thus he can face the evil of the world, the processes of change that threaten men with decay and death, because he is assured of an unchanging condition *and feels this.*'[66]

## Group norms and group protest

Two further points need to be made about Mark's sectarianism. The first concerns the nature of the group's norms and the manner of their enforcement. The second concerns the nature of Mark's protest against the authorities which dominated his world. The first point can be made relatively simply. Mark's Gospel contains dominical sayings of extreme severity (9:42–48). What formal disciplinary procedures or institutions Mark's community may have had, we do not know.[67] It is hard to imagine that these sayings formed part of any functioning disciplinary code of practice. They would rather have enforced a rigorism which was largely self-imposed but reinforced strongly by the group pressure of commonly

---

[66] Wilson, 1975, 22.

[67] We shall return to these questions of group discipline, not least in the discussion of Matt 18. There, at least, we have some evidence for the development of disciplinary procedures which suggests the Matthew's community was beginning to institutionalise in ways that had not previously been attempted, or at least not successfully. The Pauline letters provide plenty of examples of similar attempts to develop such procedures.

held beliefs, beliefs which provided the essential rationale for membership of the group and therefore for the individual's personal sense of identity.

The sense in which Mark's community is one which lives not so much by a clearly formulated code of laws and social norms, but by a set of personal values which are strongly interiorised, is brought out well by the discussion of purity regulations in Mark 7. Jesus, remarkably, rejects not only the 'tradition of the elders', the oral law of the scribal tradition, which would form the basis of the later compilations of the Mishnah and the Talmudim, but also the Levitical food laws. Whatever one's view of the originality to Jesus of such sayings, the sense in which Mark himself understands Jesus' somewhat cryptic saying in 7:15: 'there is nothing outside a man which by going into him can defile him; but the things which come out of a man are what defile him' is clear: 'Thus he declared all foods clean' (7:19). The saying in 7:15 itself is profoundly ambiguous: it might be a hyperbolic statement of the priority of a 'clean heart' over against concern with purity laws. It might be an outright rejection of the notion of ritual purity which underlies a great deal of the Levitical legislation. Mark's editorial comment is of two kinds. First, in one of his few explicit authorial comments, he clarifies the nature of the earlier part of the saying: 'thus he declared all foods clean'. But second, he has Jesus define what he meant by the latter half: 'And he said, What comes out of a person is what defiles. For from within, out of the human heart, come evil thoughts, fornication, theft, murder, adultery, coveting, wickedness, deceit, licentiousness, envy, slander, pride, foolishness' (7:20–22). Such lists of vices were common enough in the Greco-Roman world[68] and occur frequently in the New Testament, where they are often used to characterise the behaviour of Gentiles.[69]

Here Mark, through Jesus' private instruction to his disciples, is identifying patterns of behaviour which are unacceptable to the group. In the section following Peter's confession (8:31 – 10:45), the instruction will deepen to include the virtues which Jesus' followers are to embrace: service, humility, self-sacrifice, renunciation of possessions and of family

---

[68] For an excellent summary of virtue/vice lists in the ancient world, see John T. Fitzgerald's article in *ABD* 6, 857–9.

[69] Vice lists occur elsewhere in the New Testament in Matt 15:19; Rom 1:29–31; 13:13; 1 Cor 5:10–11; 6:9–10; 2 Cor 12:20–21; Gal 5:19–21; Eph 4:31; 5:3–5; Col 3:5–8; 1 Tim 1:9–10; 6:4–5; 2 Tim 3:2–4; Titus 1:7; 3:3; 1 Pet 2:1; 4:3, 15; Rev 9:21; 21:8; 22:15.

ties. There is, no doubt, a perfectionist ethos at work here, a concentration on certain key qualities and characteristics which will mark out the members of this voluntarist group and which are indeed a measure of the genuineness of their decision. Yet much of what is advocated is common ground with the accepted morality of the Hellenistic world.[70] There is here, whether it is conscious or not, a sense of competitive engagement with the Hellenistic world outside the group. This strongly suggests that Mark's community saw itself as marginal, not so much to other Jewish groups vying for the control of the Jewish community, as to the social, political and cultural world of the Hellenistic cities.

This leads us, secondly, to consider the element of protest against dominant societal groupings which can be discerned in the work. Here we immediately encounter a problem. There is no doubt who are the dominant societal groupings in the narrative: the Jewish authorities, variously represented by the chief priests, the scribes, the Pharisees, the Herodians and the Sadducees, and the Romans, represented principally by Pilate. But, from the point of view of the author, of the Gospel itself, who are the authorities which dominate his society? There is such a distancing of the readers from the Jews, an assumption that (some at least of) the readers will not know some of the basic facts about the Jews so that they need explanations of Jewish customs (7:3–4), that it is hard to see the Jews as a particularly significant group within *the author's society*.[71] If what defines a sect is its protest against some other mainstream, authoritative body *with respect to which it itself is marginal*, then the community for which Mark writes can hardly be said to be a

---

[70] Burridge, 1969, suggested that millenarian groups often assume many of the characteristics of the dominant colonial powers in their area. G. Theissen's, 1989, thesis that early Christianity was a 'charismatische Wertrevolution' (a charismatic revolution of values), where characteristic virtues of the wealthy élite were taken and given a new spin, develops this kind of thesis in characteristically subtle ways. While he develops this largely within the framework of a sociology of class-conflict (see now, Theissen, 1999, 81–117) and of the appropriation of aristocratic values by the underclass, he recognises that this is also part of a wider process of what he calls a 'universalization of values and norms which had hitherto been attached to a particular *ethnos*' and now become available to others in a process corresponding to Jewish expectations and hopes. This aspect of the development of the early Christian 'sign world' 'is bound up with a "counter-current", a partial acculturation to pagan values and norms (cf. Phil 4:8)' (1999, 81–2).

[71] This is not the same as saying that for the author Judaism was not significant. His engagement with major themes of Jewish theology makes it clear that for him Judaism is the 'significant other' (Mead, 1934), in terms of which he seeks to define himself and his community. But, as Taylor argues, 1991, 32–3, such dialogue can continue even when we outgrow such others.

*Jewish* sect. It appears to see itself as quite detached from Judaism. A good deal of effort is expended by the Evangelist in showing how Jesus is hounded to death by the Jewish authorities, who are intent on destroying him, right from the start of his ministry (already in 2:6–7 he is accused of the capital crime of blasphemy,[72] and in 3:6 the Pharisees and Herodians plot his destruction). But in the wider context of the Gospel, the Jews' behaviour seems representative of the world, rather than constituting a national opposition to Jesus and his movement.

If the Jews are not the dominant group against which the Gospel of Mark is protesting, then the only other figures representative of a dominant power in the Gospel are the Romans. The problem here is that the Gospel does not appear to be written in protest against them. The Roman governor is portrayed as having being misled by the Jewish leaders who accuse Jesus of Messianic and political pretensions, not knowing that the Messiah, Son of God, Jesus has to suffer. In this respect the blame for Jesus' death is laid, in the first place, on the Jewish leaders, secondarily, on the crowds, who at the end are misled by their leaders into calling for Jesus' death. Part of this *may* be a kind of apologetic directed to the Romans to show them that Jesus was not in fact guilty of a political charge, and that Christians did not owe allegiance to an insurgent or political pretender, but rather to a very different kind of Messiah.[73] But whether or not the element of apologetic is there, Mark's Gospel is characterised by a profound sense of its apartness from and opposition to the powers of the world, whoever they may be. In one sense, this is part of his apocalyptic world-view. The world lies in the grip of Satan, so that only when Satan's forces have been overwhelmed can the kingdom of God be fully established. Until the Gospel is preached to all nations (who all lie under the grip of such

[72] Guelich, 1993, 94.

[73] In its extreme form, this view was put forward by Brandon, 1967, as part of his case for making Jesus out to have been a Zealot: Mark removed evidence of this in order to deflect the wrath of the Romans from the Christians. The wildness of Brandon's thesis should not lead one to dismiss altogether the view that there was an element of political apologetic in Mark's writing of the Gospel. There are problems, however, with such a view: how would such an apologetic have been delivered to the Romans? There is no evidence of offical awareness of Christian writings (see, e.g. Pliny the Elder; cf. Wilken, 1984). It is more likely that Mark intended his Gospel to help Christians when questioned by the authorities (13:9), even if they are told not to prepare what they will say (13:11). Lampe, 1973, has argued that Peter's denial in Mark 14 actually parallels the situation of confession vs. denial later Christians found themselves in before the authorities.

radical evil), there can be no final peace. At the end, when all nations have been reached, the Son of Man will come to gather his elect 'from the four winds'. Thus, there is a universalistic perspective in Mark: the true authority in the world is that of Jesus; *all* other authorities are destined to pass away, when his authority is finally established and recognised. In this way, the element of protest is enormous: Mark is claiming for his group that they and only they know who the true authority in the world is. The polemic is, in the end, neither anti-Jewish nor anti-Roman: it is directed against any authority which fails to recognise the ultimate, divine authority of Jesus.

## Mark and ethnicity

The question of Mark's sectarian protest, his sense of marginality to the 'world', not just of Judaism but to all powers and authorities, leads us finally to consider the extent to which identity in Mark is linked to ethnic attachments. Are the disciples, as followers of the – Jewish – Messiah Jesus, Jews? Or do they, as members of the family of God, transcend all ethnic distinctions?

To answer this, let me first consider an essay by R. Guelich[74] which portrays Mark as a Jewish Gospel which is engaged in prophetic criticism of the Jewish people, and then an article by J. Marcus which reads the parable of the Vineyarders in Mark chapter 12 as a 'sacred parody' of the vineyard motif from Isaiah 5, representing a sharp break with the Jewish nation.

### Mark as internal critic of Jews: R. Guelich

Mark, so Guelich, portrays Jesus as engaged in conflict with and criticism of the Jewish leaders. It is a story of conflict between two opposed authorities in Judaism, that of Jesus, the Messiah, Son of God, and that of the Jewish leadership groups: only at the end of the story do the (Jewish) crowds get drawn into the opposition. The conflict is about authority, not about the Law. Guelich acknowledges that there are debates about the Law, but, he comments, they are about the use of the Law as a boundary marker, 7:1–23; 12:28–34.[75] Guelich concedes that Jesus passes judgement on the Temple

---

[74] Guelich, 1993.
[75] Guelich, 1993, 99.

and so 'intends that it cease to be a cultic centre and locus for God, who is seen rather to be at work redeeming in the world through the ministry of Jesus'.[76]

Moreover, Guelich argues, Mark 'betrays very little interest in distinguishing between Jews and Gentiles': 'unless Mark makes it obvious otherwise, the characters in the Gospel are presumably Jewish. In other words, the identity and roles of the characters in Mark do not appear to reflect any conscious dissociation with the Jews or Judaism (cf. 13:9a), even though Mark's audience itself was apparently non-Jewish and [un?]familiar with certain Jewish customs'.[77] Conflicts about the Law are about Jesus' authority to 'redefine the boundary markers as they had been set by the Pharisees and even to set aside the Levitical dietary laws'.[78] Nevertheless, Jesus' affirmation of the Law (12:28–34) and the Temple cult (1:40–45) 'makes clear that Jesus is operating within the context of Judaism'.[79] We should, then, speak here at most of a form of 'Jewish-Christian anti-Judaism'.[80]

There are problems with this account. In the first place, while driving a wedge between boundary-marking laws and other laws allows Guelich to present Jesus as within the tradition of prophetic criticism of Jewish rulers, it is doubtful whether the distinction between laws as boundary-markers and laws as defining the ethos of the group (if this is Guelich's distinction) was one which Mark or his contemporary Jews would have recognised. To reject laws clearly set out in Leviticus 11 was to reject Law *simpliciter*.[81] Similarly, to replace the Temple with Jesus' ministry is to de-centre the major Jewish cultic institution of first-century Judaism and therefore represents a major break in the tradition. In this light, Mark's lack of interest in distinctions between Jews and non-Jews appears more the product of his own distancing from such ethnic markers,

[76] Guelich, 1993, 94.
[77] Guelich, 1993, 98–9.
[78] Guelich, 1993, 99.
[79] Guelich, 1993, 99.
[80] Guelich, 1993, 100.
[81] It is true that in Mark 7 Jesus is portrayed as upholding the 'commandment of God' against the 'tradition of the elders', vv. 5–8, but Mark's account makes him go beyond this to reject specific commands of the written Law. No explanation is offered here for this contradiction; in 10:5–9, Jesus does offer reasons for setting aside the Mosaic provisions for divorce. Such legislation which goes against God's intention in creation is for the 'hardness of their heart'. It is an almost Pauline (at least in Galatians) view of the Law as a temporary measure designed to deal with the worst ravages of sin, before the coming of the new age in Christ.

rather than as a reflection of the fact that he is writing from within a Christian-Jewish community.

## Mark's sacred parody of Isaiah: J. Marcus

Guelich's view contrasts very sharply with the way the tone of Mark's polemic against the Jews is read by Marcus. For him, the parable of the vineyard represents 'a sacred parody' of the vineyard image in Isaiah 5.[82] What for Isaiah was an image of 'the intimate and unbreakable personal relationship between God and Israel' has become instead merely an image of 'an impersonal contractual relationship that is readily dissolved when Israel defaults on her side of the bargain'.[83] Such a radical distortion of central Jewish beliefs can be explained only in terms of some major catastrophe, which Marcus identifies in the Jewish War. It is Christians' experience of being caught in the cross-fire of Jewish Messianic opposition to the Romans[84] (which because of their belief in Jesus as the Messiah they could not endorse) that led them to disinherit the Jews and claim for themselves the vineyard, which had previously belonged to the Jews.

There are difficulties with this account,[85] prime among which is the fact that in Mark the parable is directed against the leaders of the Jews (11:27, the chief priests and the scribes and the elders), who recognise that the parable has been told against them, but who fear to act against Jesus because of the crowd (12:12). It is difficult to see this parable as

---

[82] The phrase is taken from Roskies, 1984, 19–20.

[83] Marcus, 1998, 216.

[84] Marcus' proposal supposes a Syrian location for the Gospel (see Marcus, 1992), as opposed to a Roman location, which others, Best, 1983, and Hengel, 1985, for example, have advocated. One should be careful, however, not to exaggerate the differences between the situation of Christian Jews in Syria and Rome, as supposed in the debates we have been considering in relation to Mark. They were both outside the Land; they both lived in cities more or less under Roman control. The obvious and important difference is that in Syria the consequences of the Jewish War would be more directly felt, not least in terms of pogroms against the Jewish communities and in Jewish uprisings in the Syrian cities. In Rome, by contrast, Roman terror had been directed specifically against them. Nevertheless, there was a good network of communications in the period of the Roman Principate and as news would have travelled fast, so too would anti-Jewish feeling and inner-Jewish tension with the Jewish communities. In brief, whether we locate Mark's community in Rome or in Syria, we can be confident that its members would have been aware of fierce opposition from Jewish nationalists and felt the force of Roman political power.

[85] Much of what follows in this paragraph is indebted to work in progress by Dale Allison.

simply about the transference of Israel's relationship to God to the new community, when it is directed, not against the people as a whole, but against their leaders. Allison suggests that, in the light of the targum of Isaiah[86] and of 4QBenediction (4Q500)[87] the parable, as uttered by Jesus, will have equated the Vineyard with the Temple and so been directed against the Temple authorities. This is an intriguing thesis, as relating to the meaning of parable as uttered by Jesus, but it is less clear how it would apply to Mark. Its meaning for Mark can hardly be that control of the *Temple* will be taken away from the chief priests and scribes and given to the Jesus and the Twelve.[88] There is little in Mark to suggest that he expected his community to take over the Temple. It seems much more likely that what is envisaged is the transference of the relationship between God and his people, mediated through the Temple cult and the divine *Shekhina*, to a relationship mediated through Jesus. The leaders of the Jews (and, in the end, the crowds) reject Jesus, and it is those who accept him, follow him and do the will of God, who will receive the vineyard, enjoy this new relationship with God. There is, that is to say, a certain openness here. It is not simply that Jesus is rejected. Rather, those who reject Jesus, turn their back on their relationship to God. Those who accept him are those who will enjoy the new relationship which is to be established in Jesus, as an alternative to the Temple cult. They may be the faithful remnant of Israel, but will also include Gentiles who accept the disciples' preaching

Marcus' reading of the parable of the vineyard as a 'sacred parody' of Isaiah 5 makes clear that Mark's community had deep Jewish roots and that there had been a painful rift between them and their Jewish parent community.[89] The question is: how does Mark, now that the rift has

---

[86] Cf. *Tg Isa* 5:2: 'And I sanctified them and I glorified them and I established them as a plant of a choice vine; and I built my sanctuary in their midst, and I even gave my altar to atone for their sins; I thought they would do good deeds, but they made their deeds evil.' And 5:5: 'And now I will tell you what I am about to do to my people. I will take up my *Shekinah* from them, and they shall be for plundering; I will break down the place of their sanctuaries, and they will be for trampling.' Allison comments: 'Here the divine judgement does not mean the end of God's relationship with Israel but the destruction of the Temple.' This seems too unqualified. It may not mean the end of the relationship, but it does speak of God's withdrawal of his presence and protection of his people.

[87] Taking 'the gate of your holy height', to refer to the Temple building and the 'streams of your glory' to the channel that took the fluids from the Temple altar.

[88] Something which is altogether possible for Jesus.

[89] As indeed does his exploration of Mark's use of Scripture in *The Way of the Lord*.

occurred, attempt to orientate himself and his community? Is his attention still largely directed towards the Jews, such that his work is principally a work of polemic against Jews? Or has the story of Jewish opposition to Jesus and his followers now become symbolic of the whole world's opposition to the Christians? Here the juxtaposition of chapters 12 and 13 is crucial. In chapter 13 Jesus foretells the future. His answer to the question, 'when will these things be and what will the sign be when all these things will come to pass?' is in the form of a series of warnings, predictions and pieces of advice, which plainly refer to events and dilemmas which will overtake the Christian community. Equally clearly, the references in the discourses to the false messiahs, to being handed over to synagogues to be beaten, and to the abomination of desolation standing where it should not, can all be given a convincing Jewish reading: the experience referred to here is readily interpreted, as it indeed is by Marcus,[90] as the experience of Christian Jews within a Jewish community torn by different Messianic groups fighting for control. It seems most likely then that Christians' experience of conflict with other Jews is reflected in some of the material in this passage. But can everything which Jesus predicts be read in such terms? This seems much less likely. The need to preach to all nations, the references to standing before kings, and to being 'hated by *all* for my name's sake'[91] seem to refer to incidents in the life of the community which are not directly connected with the internal life of the Jewish community. Chapter 13 does more than record the traumatic events which have led to the sharp break with the Jewish community and produced the 'sacred parody' of chapter 12; it also reflects the subsequent experience of the group as they bring their message to all nations. It may not be a message which advocates armed resistance and uprising; but as a message about a Jewish Messianic figure, it remains one which looks for a radical transformation of the world and therefore one which would both attract

[90] Marcus, 1992a, 217–18 argues that the references in Mark 13:9–13 are to Christians being 'betrayed by family members, handed over to sanhedrins, beaten in synagogues, brought before rulers for judicial enquiry, even put to death'. Their preaching of Jesus the Messiah to the Gentiles was seen as such 'breaking of revolutionary ranks' that 'the animosity towards the Christians' became 'so general that their existence in the world' could be characterised as being "hated by all" for the sake of Jesus' name', But cf. Hengel's views on this phrase in n. 91 below.
[91] As Martin Hengel, 1985, 23, has argued, this chimes in well with Tacitus' remark, *Ann.* 15:44, 2, 4, that Christians in Rome were convicted of being the object of *odium humani generis*.

profound suspicion on the part of the political authorities and also encourage a profoundly oppositional ethos among its followers.

To what extent, then, does Mark's Gospel betray a consciousness of having left behind the close ties of kinship, culture and attachment to place, which traditionally mark out one people from another? Does the sense of radical opposition between the followers of Jesus and everyone else ('you shall be hated by all') represent a radical break with senses of identity which are predicated on *particular* ties of blood, place and custom? The parable of the vineyard certainly alludes to such issues as it takes up the biblical theme of 'inheritance': 'let us kill him, and the inheritance will be ours' (12:7). As Marcus points out, this echoes key texts in Genesis 15:4–5, 7, which link the term with both the promise of the Land and of descendants.[92] 'Both these aspects of the Abrahamic inheritance, land and descendants, seem to be in view in the Markan vineyard parable, since the passage, as we have seen, refers both to the Jewish loss of the land and to the loss of the right to be called the true Israel, the seed of Abraham.' Does this suggest that Mark sees these goods now being simply transferred to the community of Jesus' followers?

As far as the question of the Land is concerned, we have already suggested that the focus here is principally on the Temple. The crucified and resurrected Jesus now mediates the relationship between God and his people which had previously been mediated by the Temple. But what of descent from Abraham, of ties of blood and kinship?

A number of considerations suggest quite strongly that Mark, at least, represents a view of the world which has left behind such divisions between particular people with particular ties of blood and territory. As we have already noticed, following Robert Guelich, there is a strange sense of detachment from such divisions in the Gospel narrative. Mark is just not particularly interested in distinguishing between Jews and Gentiles. However, it hardly seems to follow from this, that 'the identity and roles of the characters in Mark do not appear to reflect any conscious dissociation with the Jews or Judaism'.[93] In the light of our discussion of the parable of the vineyard, this seems most unlikely. It is more probable that Mark represents a stage of Christian consciousness where such divisions belong to the world which hates them and therefore have no direct bearing on their own sense of identity.

---

[92] Marcus, 1998, 220.
[93] Guelich, 1993, 99.

The force of the parable of the vineyard, as Marcus suggests, is to offer 'a symbol of Israel's lost inheritance and forfeited relationship with God'.[94] But to what extent does this mean, therefore, that Mark is claiming the inheritance for the community of early Christians, as Marcus' remarks at the end of his essay seem to imply: 'The reuse of Isaiah 5 in Mark 12, then, illustrates how highly charged the inheritance dispute between Jews and Christians became in the first century.'[95] This is true of the treatment of the parable in Matthew,[96] but much less so for Mark, where the emphasis is on the tenants' *rejection* of the owner's servants and son, and God's rejection of them. As they kill and cast the Son out of the vineyard, so the owner will come and destroy them and give the vineyard to others. Does this do much more than underline the point that they will no longer enjoy the tenancy? This view certainly fits in with the concluding comments in the Markan version, which stress that the parable was directed against Jesus' interlocutors (presumably the high priests and scribes and elders of 11:27) and which see the future of God's dealings with his people as lying in the reversal of the Son's rejection, not that is, in the replacement of the tenants.

The quotation of Psalm 118:22 reinforces this point.[97] It switches the underlying metaphor from the vineyard to a building. In context,[98] and in the light of contemporary readings of the Vineyard metaphor, it is hard not to see a link here with the Temple and its destruction, which Jesus predicts in Mark 13:2. The cultic centre of Israel, its Temple, is to be replaced by the crucified and risen Jesus and his followers.[99] The links to Abraham, implicit in the notion of the inheritance in the parable, can again be detected in the background to these texts. Later rabbinic interpretation identified the rejected stone both with Abraham and David.[100] In 12:18–27 Mark picks up the notion of resurrection, implicit

---

[94] Marcus, 1998, 222.

[95] Marcus, 1998, 222.

[96] Matt 21:43 speaks of the vineyard being given to a people 'producing the fruits of it', which is hardly the point of the parable: where it is not the tenants' inability or unwillingness to produce fruits, but to hand them over, which is the issue. See further discussion below.

[97] One of the more frequently cited verses of the Old Testament, cited verbatim from the LXX (cf. Acts 4:11; 1 Pet 2:7, where too it has a christological reference).

[98] Cf. esp. Mark 11:15–19; 13:2; 14:58.

[99] Cf. Guelich, 1993, 94.

[100] See Billerbeck 1, 875f.

in his application of the psalm to the son killed by the tenants, and relates it to Abraham and the theophany in Exodus 3:6. The God revealed there as the God of Abraham, Isaac and Jacob, is a God of the living, not of the dead. The important sequel to the killing of the son is not just a simple transfer of the tenancy to another group but the 'marvellous' deed of God by which he raises Jesus from the dead and creates a new community out of those who lose their life to save it (8:35). In this sense Mark is wanting to stress the continuity between the God of the Exodus theophany and the God who is mediated through the death and resurrection of Jesus.

Of course, there is a sense in which this is an inheritance dispute. The quotations from the Psalm and Exodus make it abundantly clear that Mark is contesting the tradition with the Jewish leaders, not turning his back on it. The plot of his Gospel turns on the conflict between Jesus and the Jewish leaders, who fail to recognise that this is the 'way of the Lord'. But it is not a simple inheritance dispute. It is not about who is to inherit the Land, who among the physical descendants of Abraham are his true heirs. It is, rather, a dispute about discerning God's purposes in the dark history of the times, which include the destruction of the Temple. Mark's claim is, precisely, that it is to the disciples that such – eschatological – discernment has been given: 'To you has been given the mystery of the kingdom' (4:11). Such a mystery, secret, is hidden. It is revealed only to those whom God chooses. God's dealings with his people are indeed 'marvellous' and the way to the future lies via the mystery of death and resurrection, of rejection and reversal. The new life which follows the catastrophe of Jesus' death and the destruction of Jerusalem is a fulfilment which leaves its first witnesses speechless (16:8). Mark himself, that is to say, acknowledges that the continuity between God's actions and promises in the past and his future actions and fulfilment of the promises, is strange and beyond reasonable expectation. Jesus inaugurates a world which transcends the old order, its ethnic divisions included.

One further point may serve to underline the sense in which Mark has reworked old senses of ethnic identity and their associated expectations. Jewish expectations of the restoration of Zion were strongly linked to hopes of the return to the Land of the Jewish peoples dispersed throughout the world. Matthew 8:11 echoes such hopes, when Jesus predicts that 'many will come from the east and the west and sit at table with Abraham and Isaac and Jacob in the kingdom of heaven'.[101] This fulfils the promise to Jacob in Genesis 28:12–15, RSV:

> And he dreamed that there was a ladder set up on the earth, and the top of it reached to heaven; and behold, the angels of God were ascending and descending on it!
>
> 13. And behold, the LORD stood above it and said, 'I am the LORD, the God of Abraham your father and the God of Isaac; the land on which you lie I will give to you and to your descendants;
>
> 14. and your descendants shall be like the dust of the earth, and you shall spread abroad to the west and to the east and to the north and to the south; and by you and your descendants shall all the families of the earth bless themselves.
>
> 15. Behold, I am with you and will keep you wherever you go, and will bring you back to this land; for I will not leave you until I have done that of which I have spoken to you.'

In Mark 13:27 'And then he will send out the angels, and gather his elect from the four winds, from the ends of the earth to the ends of heaven', the idea is, however, redrawn. Those who will now be gathered in are the elect, those who have not been ashamed of Jesus and his words in his earthly life (8:38). Questions of ethnicity simply fall away: those who will enjoy life in the presence of the Son of Man[102] are those who confess him, the members of the congregation, of the household of faith.[103] Hooker comments on this passage: 'Now, however, the elect who will be gathered must be the members of the "new" Israel.' This is right in so far as it suggests that those gathered in are not the 'old' Israel; but it obscures the fact that there is actually no explicit reference to such ethnic distinctions here. The 'elect' who are gathered in are simply those who acknowledge Jesus as the Son of Man. The contrast here, within the context of the world-wide preaching of the disciples, is with those who reject the Son of Man. The group-consciousness of the church for whom Mark writes is shaped by the

---

[101] In fact, most interpreters think that this refers to the Gentiles coming into the kingdom, and this may well be true within the setting in Matthew's Gospel, where it is addressed to the Gentile centurion. However, Allison is surely right to argue that the allusion is to the hope of the Jews' return; cf. Isa 43:5; Zech 8:7; Bar 4:37; 5:5; *Ps Sol* 11:2; *1 Enoch* 57:1.

[102] Cf. *1 Enoch* 62:13f.; 1 Thess 4:17; Luke 23:43; Rev 20:4. Gnilka, 1979, 202 comments: 'Mit dem Menschensohn Jesus sein und leben zu können, ist der eschatologische Ausblick, den unser Evangelium mit anderen neutestamentlichen Schriften teilt.'

[103] Hooker, 1991, 319.

radical distinction between those who believe and those who do not. All other distinctions of race and ethnicity pale into insignificance by contrast.

## Conclusion

The picture which emerges from our discussion of Mark's Gospel is an intriguing one. Many of the central images and motifs suggest that our text comes from a group with a strong sense of its identity as distinctive from all other groups in the world. It is the community of the sighted, by contrast with the rest of the world which is blind; it is the family of God, by contrast with all others who do not do his will. It enjoys knowledge of the mystery of God's purposes for the world. Those who belong to it are the called, the elect, those liberated from the power of demons, whose task is to preach the Gospel to all nations. In all this there is a universality which is breath-taking in a small group of persecuted, itinerant followers of a crucified Jewish prophet.

On the other hand, they have a profound sense of their rootedness in Jewish history. The way that Jesus treads is the way proclaimed by Isaiah for the return of the exiles to Zion. It is the way of Jewish restoration through which all the nations will be blessed. They are called to a specific role in this final drama through which God will overthrow evil and establish his rule in the world. They are the disciples of the Messiah, Son of God, who suffers the same fate as the prophets at the hands of his own people, but who, along with his disciples, will ultimately be vindicated.

This sense of ambivalence towards the Jewish people and their Jewish heritage is reflected in the nature of the group's sectarianism, so far as we can determine it. On the one hand, there is no doubting the strong sense of oppositionality to the world which breathes through the Gospel. They are those who are hated by all the world 'for my sake'. They are those to whom the secret of the kingdom of God has been given, as opposed to all those outside who are deliberately blinded, whether by Satan or by God. They are the true family of Jesus, the Messiah, as opposed to all those who are ashamed of him. They are the elect, whom the Son of Man will gather in from the four winds at the end of the age. The world is divided into those who think the things of God and those who think the things of men.

And yet there is another dynamic, which to some extent modifies this unrelenting dualism. They are, in the first place, a missionary movement which is sent to preach the Gospel to all nations. They are to play a role in bringing to fulfilment of Isaiah's prophecy that the nations will bless themselves in Israel. Jesus welcomes the strange exorcist as a sign that the power of the kingdom is at work in the world overcoming the powers of darkness and evil. They are not just a thaumaturgical group, purveying spiritual power to their own; they are a revolutionist sect, filled with the expectation of a dramatic transformation of the whole world in which all may share.

But though this expectation is rooted in the prophetic vision, the final transformation will be a surprising one. The history of God's dealings with his chosen people will undergo an unexpected turn, when the one rejected by the leaders of the people will be chosen as the 'cornerstone' of the new building. The Evangelist seems to distance himself from the old ethnic divisions and markers which divided Jews and Gentiles. The same dualism is maintained between the in-group and all others; only now it is between the followers of Jesus the Messiah and the rest of the world, Jews and Gentiles included. Kinship ties are no longer constitutive of membership of the chosen group. The criteria for membership are election and doing the will of God.

All this, as we have seen, is not without its parallels in Jewish groups of the time. Philo, too, saw his community as those who lived in the light and were God's kin; the Qumranites, inspired by a darker view of the world, saw themselves as the sons of light as opposed to those ruled over by the Prince of darkness. Mark has a view of the world much closer to Qumran than to Philo, but he has nothing like the same emphasis on obedience to all the commandments of the law. Nor does he look forward to the restoration of the Temple in any but a figurative sense. His vision of the future is of the ingathering of the elect, not of the dispersion.

Thus, in the end, it is the universalising, sectarian elements in Mark's Gospel which dominate. Ethnic divisions are subordinated to the new – voluntarist – criteria for membership of the group, even if the new group takes its rationale from the history of a nation defined by just such markers. Fictive kinship replaces ties of blood. As an analogy for the bonds which unite the members of the new group it has all the power to suggest closeness and intimacy (not to mention conflict) and to suggest distinctiveness over against the other. But the point of the *analogy* is precisely that membership is no longer defined in terms of qualities which are acquired merely by the accident of birth, but in terms of a deliberate choice open to all, whether this is explained in terms of divine election or no.

# 4

# The remaking of sacred space

*Making space*

Nothing, it might seem, is so ineluctably given, as the places we inhabit.
The landscapes, the climate, the physical environment in which we
find ourselves, all these things influence our lives and yet are in large
measure not of our making. Yet a moment's reflection makes it clear
that we do not inhabit a world of nature which lies wholly beyond our
control or influence: 'man' has been constantly attempting to subdue
and modify nature, to shape his environment, through engineering,
cultivation, architecture and town-planning. And yet, no human efforts,
however prodigious, can obliterate the fact that I live on the west of an
island off the coast of continental Europe, and not in a tropical savanna
or in an Alpine valley. Geography and climate are factors which shape
us, just as we try to shape them (or at least to ward off their worst
effects). The places we inhabit are thus the product of a long history of
human interaction with 'nature'. Whether we seek to improve our urban
or our rural environment, we are caught up in a long history of human
attempts to create a bearable or indeed pleasurable environment.[1]

Such interaction between men and women and their environment
does not occur purely at the physical level. Adam's dominion over the
animals and the plants gives him power not only to hunt and cultivate,
but to name them. The way we look at the world, name it, chart it,
describe it, divide it up, call it our own, significantly shapes our relationship to it, and to other groups who may have alternative namings to
our own chosen ones. It is an integral part of our struggle for power
and control over our world.

Among such 'namings' the way we apprehend the world religiously
is of profound significance. To speak of Canaan, *Eretz Israel* or *falastin,*

---

[1] On the relation of nature and culture, see Smith, 1987, 21f. and 24–46 and discussions
in Sibley, 1995, 73f., on dead space.

is not simply to refer to a particular geographically (neutrally?) definable area (even if there were agreement about the limits of such areas), but to invoke powerful, religiously undergirded aspirations about an area which from the Late Bronze Age has been contested by different peoples and 'where a politically unified Palestinian state has never been voluntarily achieved'.[2] Any one of these designations is a contested naming which expresses the aspirations and religious beliefs of a particular group and differentiates it sharply from other contending groups. The name marks out the claim which the group puts on the land and expresses, in part at least, its sense of attachment to the land. Such acts of naming, that is to say, are strong expressions of a social identity and map not only physical realities, but also social realities and differences: they include and they also exclude.

The religious labelling of places, whether of whole areas or of particular sites within them, is by no means the only religious strategem available to people in their attempt to define, lay claim to and attach themselves to place. In ritual, narrative and poetry they may also rehearse those things which attach them to the land they inhabit or, it may be, long for from exile.[3] As we saw in chapter 2, the Tables of Nations in Genesis 10 and the Abrahamic narratives can allow the construction

---

[2] See Keel, I, 1984, 206–88 for a fascinating discussion of the different nomenclatures and boundaries of the Land. Keel concludes: 'Problematisch erscheint doch nur schon das Reden von *dem* Land, das als *ein* bzw. geeintes Land nur in der Sprache religiöser Idealisierung, nationalistischer Leidenschaft oder strategisch-faktischer Oberherrschaft bezeichnet werden kann . . . Weder die alten Israeliten noch die Philister noch irgendein anderes Volk haben jemals das gesamte Israel/Palästina besiedelt . . . Die oft bekundete ("verheißene") und angestrebte, aber praktisch nie verwirklichte Idee eines geeinten Israel/Palästina/(Syrien) geht wahrscheinlich bis auf ägypt. Großmachtansprüche aus der Spätbronzezeit zurück. Demgegenüber ist es für die Geschichte des Landes aber bezeichnend, daß ein staatlich geeintes Palästina nie freiwillig zustande gekommen ist' (287).

[3] Our concern is with literary texts and the way they create attachments, reshape a group's sense of its identity and relationship with the land they inhabit. This process of identity-shaping may indeed be closely paralleled with the way in which people's identity and status is forged in rituals and ceremonies (where rituals are occasional occurrences, including rites of passage, and ceremonies are recurrent celebrations reinforcing central beliefs and aspirations of the community), but this does not mean that we should look for more than suggestions as to how the literary texts may have been appropriated by the communities which heard/read them. See the sensitive handling of such suggestions, in Cohn, 1981, 7–23; ctr. the way in which Hanson, 1994, forces his 'social-scientific' models on his texts, which is accurately identified by Esler, 1994, though rather puzzlingly he seems to think that Hanson's article 'has laid the foundation for a significant inter-disciplinary understanding of how the Matthean text functioned in its context' (176).

of a map of the whole world with territorial boundaries and alloca-
tions of particular peoples to their particular places within it. It may go
further and allow the conferral on particular places of especial power
and authority, identifiable with their particular holiness/purity. Such
narratives, together with the rituals and psalms in which they are
rehearsed, reproduce the beliefs by which particular peoples construct
their view of the world and their place within it. At the same time, each
time such narratives are recited and such beliefs are articulated, they
may be given more or less subtle twists. Precisely as they are reproduced,
they may also be transformed. Our discussion of *Jubilees*, Philo and
Josephus was intended to disclose the basic symbolic resources of the
Jewish religion at the turn of the era, to give some indication of the
diversity of their reproduction and to indicate how such reproduction
interacted with the different cosmologies which were current. Our task
in this chapter is to consider the use which Mark made of such resources
and the manner in which he modified/transformed them.

## Aims of this chapter

However, before we launch into a detailed consideration of Mark's use
of topographical descriptions, we need to ask what we expect to get out
of such an undertaking. Two things are sometimes too quickly elided.
On the one hand, we want to discern as sharply as we may the kind of
world which Mark is mapping out. In Geertzian terms, we want to
discern what kind of view of reality is expressed in his construction of
space in his narrative. Is it close to the view of reality found in a writer
like Josephus, where Jerusalem and the Temple lie at the centre of the
Land and where other areas are more or less distanced or excluded from
this sacral sphere? Or is Mark challenging and reworking not only such
notions of sacred space, but also the notions of God's power, of order
and chaos with which such an understanding of space is linked? I shall
argue that it is the latter which is happening. On the other hand we
want to see, if we can, how such a narrative which thus redraws the
world may have affected those who heard it and read it. Again in
Geertzian terms, what kind of ethos is reflected in such a view of reality?
How do we draw out the practical, attitudinal implications of such a
view of the world? What categories would it offer people as they seek to
describe themselves, to forge a sense of their identity? What kinds of
behaviour would now be appropriate for people who made these
narratives their own? Would it for instance any longer be appropriate

to worship in the Temple (if that was still an option open to Mark's readers)? What is the 'watchfulness' referred to in 13:34–37? What kinds of self-designations would now be appropriate for readers who accepted the views of reality implicit in the Gospel? Jews? Israelites? Disciples of Christ? People of the Way?

It is important to separate out these two areas of enquiry. There is a need to counter a certain kind of reductionism which wishes to move too quickly to considering the sociological functions of religious myths and narratives before an adequate account of the world-view which they express has been given. I have argued elsewhere[4] that religious beliefs (and, by extension, the sentences, signs, rituals and so on in which they are expressed) form part of a network of linked beliefs which encompass both high-level theological claims about the nature of the world and its relation to a divine being and also beliefs about the nature of human society and the modes of behaviour proper to such a world. It follows that a full appreciation of beliefs about society and the ordering of communal and private affairs requires an understanding of their interrelationship with 'high-level' theological beliefs and vice versa.

A reductionist/functionalist reading of sacred space: Jonathan Smith

An instructive example of such reductionism is provided by debates about the interpretation of an Australian Aboriginal myth about a sacred pole.[5] As the debate involves two of the most distinguished comparative religionists of the second half of the twentieth century, Mircea Eliade and J. Z. Smith, its importance for our subject is not to be under-estimated. In the myth, the ancestor Numbakulla fashioned a pole, anointed it with blood and then climbed up the pole and disappeared into the sky. Subsequently the ancestors who remained carried the pole around with them wherever they went, and eventually broke it by accident. In Eliade's version of the myth, this accident led directly to the death of the ancestors who had been travelling around with the pole. For him, the pole 'represented a cosmic axis, for it is around the sacred pole that territory becomes habitable, hence becomes transformed into a world'. The pole connects them with the transhuman realm of the sacred, of transcendence and when the pole breaks it is 'like the "end of the world", reversion to chaos'.[6] Smith's critique of Eliade's

[4]  See Riches, 1980; Millar and Riches, 1981 and 1985.
[5]  In Smith, 1987, 1–23.
[6]  Quotations from Eliade, 1959, 32–3, in Smith, 1987, 2.

reading of the myth is sophisticated and includes a detailed discussion of Eliade's handling of the ethnographical material which records the myth. He notes tellingly that Eliade's summary of the myth omits important details connected with the breaking of the pole and the subsequent death of the ancestors (which are in fact recorded as two incidents). After each event in the myth as recorded by the original ethnographers, features of the landscape are noted which remain as a memorial to the breaking of the pole and the death of the ancestors. Eliade has omitted these details and instead construed the two events as cause and effect with the causality being construed in terms of his reading of Aboriginal cosmology. Smith's critique of Eliade is not just directed to Eliade's forcing of the ethnographic records, but to the way that this enables him in his interpretation to emphasise the cosmological significance of the story. For the point about the story for Smith is not cosmology, but etiology. In this he claims support from the numerous incidents (recorded in the original accounts of the myths, but omitted by Eliade) connected to details in the landscape: '[e]very feature of the contemporary landscape represents a "track," a deed, a work, of those ancestors'. And he quotes with approval Géza Róheim: 'in all of [these narratives] *environment is made out of man's activity* . . . Environment is regarded as if it were derived from human beings'.[7] Smith comments:

> It is anthropology, not cosmology, that is to the fore. It is the ancestral/ human alteration of and objectification in the landscape that has transformed the undifferentiated primeval space during the Dream-time into a multitude of historical places in which the ancestors, though changed, remain accessible. This is expressed in the myths, It is expressed as well in the extreme localization of the Arand *njinanga* sectional organization, with its demarcated structures of homeland and birthplace.

The undoubted strength of Smith's argument is that he can show how Eliade's wish to draw out the cosmology implicit in the narratives has led him to filter out important details in the ethnographic records. The desire to find a particular cosmology reflected in myths and narratives from widely diverse cultures is clearly fraught with danger and here Eliade has been caught out. But the fact that undue emphasis on the cosmological senses of a narrative can lead to distortion is no justification for neglecting such senses altogether; it ought to encourage a more

---

[7] Róheim, 1945, 211–13, in Smith, 1987, 11.

careful balancing of world-view and ethos in the interpretation of such myths. To summarise the main content of the stories as 'Environment is regarded as if it were derived from human beings' is at least odd in the light of the features of the ancestors which distinguish them from most human beings, their supernatural powers and their origins in the ancestral 'dream time'. Indeed when Smith claims that '[i]t is anthropology, not cosmology, that is to the fore', it is not easy to grasp the nature of the distinction he is wanting to draw. What he wants to distinguish is in fact two different accounts of cosmology, of the way the origins of the world are told. He does so by identifying different emphases and functions of these cosmologies, and then denies that Australian Aboriginal myths are *primarily* cosmologies. As a consequence he appears to feel free to concentrate his explanatory energies on elucidating the 'anthropological' consequences of these myths, rather than giving an account of how cosmological sense and anthropological function are related, which would have required a more careful account of the myth. What is it to say that Numbakulla disappears up his pole into the sky? Smith, in his turn, omits this detail from his explanations, even though it is important to Eliade, and appears to have some kind of cosmological sense. If Smith thinks it does not, he does not tell us why; if he thinks it does, but is not important, he does not tell us that either. It may indeed be that aboriginal myths are etiological myths whose function is to explain the origin of certain sacred sites, even simply to inculcate knowledge of large tracts of land to nomadic peoples; this does not mean that they are not cosmological, that the stories are not based on some account of how the world was created and got to be the way it presently is. And precisely such distinctive characteristics of their cosmology should be of interest to someone whose principal interest is in comparative religious studies.

Smith's attack on cosmological explanations *per se* can be seen more clearly in his subsequent critique of Eliade's notion of the 'Center' – 'the cosmological world-mountain where heaven, earth and underworld, are linked' – and his claim that this pattern is replicated 'in human acts of construction, in temples and palaces'.[8] Smith points out that such views, which stem from the Pan-Babylonian school of the end of the nineteenth century, have been largely discredited and that one of the key pieces of evidence cited by Eliade, the title *Dur-an-ki*, which Eliade

---

[8] Smith, 1987, 15.

translates as 'the bond of heaven and earth', 'refers to the "scar" or "navel" left when heaven and earth were separated by force in the creation myths. That is to say, *Dur-an-ki* is a term that emphasizes disjunction rather than conjunction'.[9] This is altogether fair comment: it does not, of course, remove the title from the realm of cosmology; it does strongly suggest that the cosmology is different from that proposed by Eliade, though Smith does not go on to tell us what it is.[10] Rather he has recourse to a functional account of the language. 'The language of "center" is preeminently political and only secondarily cosmological. It is a vocabulary that stems, primarily, from archaic ideologies of kingship and the royal function. In any particular tradition, it may or may not be tied to cosmological and cosmogonic myths'.[11]

Again the emphasis in Smith's interpretation is on function rather than on cosmological sense. The language of 'centre', applied to temples and palaces, has an ideological function: it serves to justify existing relations of power within the given society. But, one has to ask, could it have fulfilled those functions (and perhaps not only those), if it had not had a conventional cosmological sense which was well understood by those whom it was intended to hold in subservience? It is not easy to see how an understanding of *Dur-an-ki* which asserted the permanent dissociation of heaven and earth would have given much ideological backing to priests or kings linked to sites so-named. One of the political functions of similar assertions by later Deists, was precisely to deny doctrines of the divine right of kings and of political privilege based on theological status.

None of this should be taken as leave to ignore the important warnings that Smith makes. One-sided emphasis on the world-view implicit in religious texts at the expense of consideration of their social and ethical senses will at best produce a very abstract, generalised reading of texts; at worst, it will lead to distortion. It is certainly my intention to struggle to keep a due balance between attention to both anthropology and cosmology, however difficult in practice that may be.

---

[9]  Smith, 1987, 122, n. 3.

[10]  He does offer in the text, however, a rather different formulation of the meaning of *Dur-an-ki* to that in the earlier footnote. Here we read: 'The *Dur-an-ki* marks the place of permanent disassociation, rather than of conjunction and access between the celestial and terrestrial realms'. Smith, 1987, 16. This sounds less like a matter of emphasis, as suggested by the remark in the earlier note; more like an early form of Deism.

[11]  Smith, 1987, 17.

## A structuralist/literacy reading of Mark: Elizabeth Struthers Malbon

In this respect there is much to be learnt from a recent work in New Testament studies which shows unusual methodological sophistication: Elizabeth Struthers Malbon's *Narrative Space and Mythic Meaning in Mark*.[12] Malbon's work is an exploration of the semiotic universe which is created by Mark's narrative, specifically by its use of spatial terms. Her analysis is strongly influenced by the work of C. Lévi-Strauss and is in the first place an exhaustive study of the deployment of such terms, subdivided into geopolitical, topographical and architectural, through the narrative by Mark. Her task is first to analyse the deployment of the terms diachronically in the sequence of the narrative, and then to give an account of the schemata which underly the use of such terms at any particular point (synchronically). What she then hopes to do is to show how the manifest signs in the text give expression to non-manifest 'opposites' (order/chaos; strange/familiar; threat/promise; sacred/profane) which underly the text and which are 'mediated' by the narrative as it develops different oppositions to express such non-manifest concepts. Her aim is to show how the mythic oppositions underlying the text of Mark are progressively mediated and overcome, by being replaced with other oppositions which permit mediation. Notions of order and chaos which seem to permit no reconciliation (purity and impurity) are to be so reworked that a way out of the impasse can indeed be found.[13] In both these tasks she draws heavily on C. Lévi-Strauss, first on the account that he offers of the language of myth, where different levels of myth, geographical, economic, sociological, cosmological, each have their codes/symbolism, which function like a language, and where language is seen as reflecting a fundamentally binary 'underlying logical structure'.[14] Second, she draws on his understanding of myths as representing (and overcoming or mediating between) fundamental oppositions in the understanding of reality.

Malbon's analysis is remarkable for its careful attention to the details of Mark's text and offers a creative synthesis of the spatial imagery and terms which he deploys, which in many respects we shall be able to follow. In terms of notions of sacred *space*, Malbon proposes, what is

---

[12] Malbon, 1986.
[13] For a fuller account of her method, see Malbon, 1986, 1–14.
[14] 'Asdiwal', 146. Here as E. R. Leach has pointed out, Lévi-Strauss follows his colleague Roman Jakobsen; see Leach, 1970, 27–30.

happening is that stasis is being replaced by purposive action, movement. Out of the conflict between Jesus on the cross and the Temple emerges anew *the way*. Men and women are called to follow, to preach the Gospel to all nations (Mark 13:10), to 'go to Galilee', rather than to maintain the barriers of sacred/profane around the cult. This is illuminating. Senses of identity are being reforged, as identity is no longer linked to local attachments, the Land, Jerusalem, Zion, the Temple (a sense of identity reinforced by a sharp awareness of the profane/degrading world outside). Instead people are to be linked to a transforming power bringing order out of chaos: the rejected, suffering Son of Man will bring new life, forgiveness, reconciliation to a world which is basically opposed to these goods. This generates a highly mobile, effervescent form of religion which rejects the need for barriers and defences and is cast out defenceless into the world to transform it (Mark 6:7–13).

There are a number of points at which stresses appear in her method and its deployment. In the first place, the method is presented as a literary, non-historical one: she is concerned simply to identify the spatial relations (or 'bundles of relations') which appear in the text and to determine their diachronic and synchronic relations, by giving an account of the narrative sequences which they form and the conceptual schemata which at any point underly the sequential deployment of the terms in the narrative.[15] But such an ahistorical, purely literary approach misses an important point, that the spatial signifiers which are used in Mark's text are signifiers in virtue of their conventional senses within a particular natural language, and that the associations and expectations which they carry and which Mark is adopting or reworking are specific to the culture from which they emerge.[16] This is significant not only for

---

[15] Malbon, 1986, 3, following Lévi-Strauss, compares the literary text to a musical score which has to be read diachronically along one axis, and also synchronically along the other, '"all the notes which are written vertically making up" one harmonic unit. In other words, myths are two-dimensional. . . . Sequences tell the mythic story; schemata suggest the fundamental opposition the myth seeks to mediate'. The quotation is taken from Lévi-Strauss, 1955, 432.

[16] While an examination of their conventional significance within their culture of origin plays no part in Malbon's stated methodology in chapter one, it does in fact become more and more a part of her actual working practice, notably in the last chapter of the book, where she looks at the process of mythical mediation in Mark. A similar tendency to abandon the very sharp distinction which she makes between literary and historical readings of the text can be seen in her (very occasional) interest in Mark's intention: see e.g. sentences like 'The succeeding oppositions illustrate well Mark's challenge of normative expectations with regard to the associations of ORDER and CHAOS' (159).

the analysis of the narrative sequences, but also for the account of the mythic mediations to which she turns at the end. It is hardly possible to make the identifications which she does between spatial terms in Mark and the mythic oppositions of order and chaos, familiar and strange, promise and threat, sacred and profane, nor indeed to see how these oppositions are being reworked by their deployment in Mark's narrative, without an understanding of the associations of the spatial terms in their original cultural context. Expressed slightly differently, we might say that the symbolic resources which Mark calls on to create his spatial world are themselves culturally and historically conditioned. We need to know something of their history, and how they were connected in the minds of his readers, if we are to grasp their potential meanings.

The second point is associated. Malbon plays the structuralist game of manifest and non-manifest meanings. The surface meaning of the narrative conceals a deep meaning which is what the myth is subtly inculcating into the believer. The interpreter's task is to unearth the hidden meanings of the text and to show us what the senses of the text are by which the unsuspecting reader is bound. But in practice what Malbon has to do is to invoke the conventional senses of the terms deployed in the text (which would presumably have been at least as available to the early readers of the text as to Malbon herself) in order to identify the non-manifest meanings in the first place. This is not to say that the meanings which she identifies were never hidden or obscured or in need of clarification. But equally it would be a mistake to suggest that they were in principal 'non-manifest'. What is interesting, in the light of our discussion of J. Z. Smith's work, is that the senses which are uncovered by Malbon's analysis are not presented as anthropological as opposed to cosmological or theological. Indeed, for Malbon, the terms order and chaos which play a primary role in her analysis are said to express the other oppositions more 'cosmically'.[17] In this respect we have a surface meaning which is clearly and manifestly theological; and a deep or non-manifest meaning which is about 'fundamental

[17] Malbon, 1986, 155. Of course, Smith is aware of the cosmological significance of chaos, as Malbon points out: 'chaos is never profane in the sense of being neutral . . . Rather, chaos *only* takes a significance within a religious world-view. Chaos is a sacred power; but it is frequently perceived as being sacred "in the wrong way"'; Smith 1978, 97. Interestingly, in this earlier work, Smith does not betray the reductionist sympathies that he does in *To Take Place*. Here he writes, when concluding a discussion of two fundamental types of world-view: 'I have a sense that much will be learned from relating these cosmic views to the social worlds in which they are found' (101).

oppositions', fundamental views of the world which may be as much social as cosmic. This contrasts with, say, Mary Douglas' reading of myth, which distinguishes two levels, one literal, overtly theological and understood; the other symbolic, sociological and largely hidden, which is the 'real' meaning of the myth.[18] In the end Malbon's analysis becomes unwieldy and it would have been preferable to have teased out more of the cosmic implications of the deployment of the spatial terms *in the narrative* in order to gain as full a view as possible of the world-view in the text; and then to have proceeded to a consideration of the social and practical implications of such views: the ethos of the texts. I shall choose this way, though for reasons of space it means restricting myself to a consideration of only some of the main spatial terms and images.

Two further points, first, about Malbon's treatment of the 'fundamental oppositions' which are given expression in mythological narratives. Where Malbon gets Lévi-Strauss wrong, and where he is really interesting, is about mythic oppositions. As we have seen,[19] Lévi-Strauss argues that myths give voice to fundamental oppositions. This means that mythical narratives are constructed not just in terms of binary opposites, such as sacred and profane, but in terms of different and competing concepts of order and chaos, of which sacred and profane is one, righteousness and lawlessness another. Myths are not monolithic constructions, imposing a particular view of the world, a particular form of society upon their readers/receptors; rather they function more as therapies for societies radically at odds with themselves. Unfortunately, there seems to be little awareness of this side of Lévi-Strauss' work in Malbon's account of Mark: the distinction between chaos and order is presented as a logical distinction, not as a paradoxical opposition which needs, for the health of society, to be brought out into the open and admitted; only different views of chaos and order expressed in the same myth or mythological narrative would present such a conflict and opposition. By relating Mark's treatment of sacred space to deep tensions in the mythical cosmologies of his time, showing, that is, how such tensions are reflected in his narrative account of Jesus' progress, we may be able to shed some light on how Mark sought to address the problems inherent in such conflicting mythologies.

---

[18] See e.g. Douglas, 1966, 122–34, for an analysis of a Coorg myth, and Riches, 1980, 24–8 for a discussion of Douglas.
[19] See chapter 2 above for a fuller discussion of these points.

There is a further point, however, which needs to be made about Malbon's 'logical hierarchy', and this will take us more directly into a discussion of Markan use of spatial terms. Malbon assumes that there is a logical hierarchy of terms which underlies Mark's use. This then leads her to set out Mark's spatial terms in a 'branching tree diagram', which is basically controlled by pairs of binary oppositions, with, where appropriate, intermediate terms interspersed. Thus, for example, Jewish homeland is opposed to foreign lands, within the Jewish homeland Galilee is opposed to Judaea, Judaea breaks down into a tripartite division: Jericho, Jerusalem and Arimathea; Jerusalem is divided between Jerusalem proper and its environs. In the mythological schema these are then further identified with a fundamental opposition between order and chaos, so that now, paradoxically, Galilee stands for order and Jerusalem for chaos, just as the Temple represents chaos and Golgotha a strange, new order.

In so far as the logical hierarchy is meant to represent Mark's linguistic usage, it is unduly schematic; it imposes a binary logic on his use of terms which is bound to suppress the considerable diversity of associations which such geopolitical terms may have in a rich narrative work such as Mark's. Matters are in a sense made worse when the 'real' or latent meaning of Mark's use of these terms is again reduced to a mediation of one fundamental set of oppositions. In what follows, I shall consider recent treatments of Galilee and Judaea, and then in the rest of the chapter attempt to show how Mark is engaged in a complex dialectic with differing views of sacred space which reflect the two dominant ideologies with which he is in dialogue.

## Galilee and Jerusalem in Mark

Scholars since E. Lohmeyer[20] and R. H. Lightfoot have argued that there is a deliberate polarisation of Galilee and Jerusalem in the Gospel, and that it is Mark's creation, as he has drawn together and shaped his traditional material. For Lightfoot, 'Galilee is the sphere of revelation, Jerusalem the scene only of rejection.'[21] This contrast also plays a significant part for Malbon in her tracing out of the logical hierarchy of Mark's geopolitical terms. The contrast between Jewish homelands and

[20] Lohmeyer, 1936.
[21] Lightfoot, 1938, 124. Lohmeyer and Lightfoot have been followed broadly by Marxsen, 1969; Kelber, 1974, 65; Myers, 1988, 432.

foreign lands, which expresses a fundamental opposition between familiar and strange, is replaced by the contrast between Galilee and Judaea, where, unexpectedly (at least for those who have conventional expectations) Galilee, not Judaea, represents the familiar.[22] Indeed this challenging of expectations is underlined by Mark's Gospel which in 1:5 betrays 'an awareness of the positive view of Jerusalem that is challenged and denied in the remainder of the text'.[23] In the opening treatment of the pair of terms Malbon remains content to portray them as sharply contrasted by Mark in terms of familiar and strange. Further consideration of the narrative, however, shows that the familiar home is also a place of difficulty and failure.[24]

Not all scholars, however, agree in seeing the two terms as expressing a central theological point for the Evangelist. Davies questions whether the Evangelist did more than preserve the geographical references which were in the tradition.[25] Galilee is used initially to identify Jesus; while there is a broad geographical division between Galilee (1:13 – 10:52) and Jerusalem (11–16) in the earlier part of the Gospel, Jesus is also found outside Galilee. Crucially, as Davies argues against Lightfoot, Galilee is not portrayed as *terra Christiana*, for he meets there with opposition and outright rejection in his own πατρίς.[26] This, following Jesus' rejection by his family in 3:21, 31–35, shows 'how increasingly his own had rejected Jesus'.[27]

If Davies questions the importance to Mark of the distinction between Galilee and Jerusalem, Freyne resolutely upholds it, but seeks to understand it in terms of its literary associations within the Gospel narrative.[28]

---

[22] 'But the Gospel of Mark challenges such expectations, presenting Judaea not only as a strange place but as a threatening one, and characterizing Galilee not only as the familiar home from which Jesus and the disciples have come but as the final home to which they will return.' Malbon, 1986, 45, referring to Lightfoot, 1938, 124–5 with approval.

[23] Malbon, 1986, 45.

[24] Malbon, 1986, 167, citing Davies, 241.

[25] Davies, 1994, 221–2; see his development of this point, 239–40, where he concludes: 'It seems that, although the necessity that Jesus should go to Jerusalem is strongly implied in Mark, Galilee, as such, can hardly have interested him.' Davies is here echoing the views of K. L. Schmidt, 1919, who argued that the topographical details of the Synoptic Gospels derived in large part from the framework of the oral narrative units and that their largely unedited conjunction by Mark led to much inconsistency and contradiction.

[26] Davies, 1994, 241.

[27] Davies, 1994, 238.

[28] He distances himself, however, from Malbon's structuralist reading, preferring, as he puts it, a reading more in terms of the surface structure of the text than with the deep structures. He agrees with her, however, in wanting to focus less on the extra-textual referents; Freyne, 1988, 34.

His reading characterises Galilee, contrasted with Jerusalem, in terms of a number of further oppositions. (i) Galilee is the place where Jesus is accepted: Jerusalem the principal source of opposition to Jesus. It is the 'scribes from Jerusalem' who accuse him of being in league with Beelzebul (3:22) and join with the Pharisees in the attack on him for allowing his disciples to eat with unwashed hands (7:1–2). The scribes along with the chief priests and the elders in Jerusalem, are his principal opponents in Jerusalem. (ii) Galilee is a place of open boundaries and free movement; Jerusalem is rule-bound and even Jesus' teaching is restricted here to the Temple. Jesus in Galilee is not restricted to any one place;[29] he crosses over into Gentile territory on a number of occasions.[30] (iii) Galilee is 'the place of disclosure and manifestation', while 'Jerusalem is the theatre where the paradox of the Kingdom reaches its climax'.[31] (iv) Galilee is the place where a new understanding of the kingdom, a 'new teaching with authority' (Mark 1:27) is revealed and propagated; Jerusalem is the centre of the old, rule-bound cult which will be replaced with a Temple 'not built with hands',[32] a new mode of existence, characterised by 'radical detachment from family and possessions, similar to that of the main character'.[33]

Freyne's treatment shows precisely the advantages of divesting the straitjacket of a binary, structuralist treatment of such terms: the range of associations set up by the narrative is much richer. On the other hand, one still has to question whether the new pairs of opposition that Freyne identifies apply to Galilee as contrasted to Jerusalem.

(i) If Galilee is in many ways the place which receives Jesus enthusiastically, there is also opposition. The Pharisees oppose him and scheme with the Herodians how they can destroy him (Mark 3:6), challenge him over the washing of hands (7:1–13) and seek a sign from him, which elicits Jesus' warning against the leaven of the Pharisees and of Herod (8:15). As we have seen, in Mark 6:4 Jesus speaks of the refusal of his country (πατρίς), kinsfolk (συγγενεῖς) and house (οἰκία) to honour him (a scene that in some ways echoes 3:31–35). He also meets with a similar mixture of opposition and enthusiastic reception in 5:1–20, when he crosses to the Decapolis. It is true that further opposition

---

[29] Freyne, 1988, 61–2.
[30] Freyne, 1988, 55–6.
[31] Freyne, 1988, 52.
[32] Freyne, 1988, 60.
[33] Freyne, 1988, 64.

comes from Jerusalem, from the scribes, the chief priests and elders. While it is certainly not impossible to see them as the major figures of opposition, we should not overlook the fact that it is the Pharisees and the Herodians who first seek to destroy him.[34] Thus, while it may be argued that the opposition in Jerusalem is implacable and finally destructive, it can hardly be seen as different in kind from that in Galilee. It merely brings to a head opposition that has been there – and virulent – in Galilee since the start of Jesus' ministry. (ii) If the scribes from Jerusalem and the Jerusalem cult represent a rule-bound form of Judaism, then so too do the Pharisees in Galilee. Jesus does not travel equally throughout Galilee: he avoids the main centres of power and keeps to the villages and small towns.[35] Openness to people who are beyond the boundaries of Jewish territory is paralleled in the Marcan Jesus' openness to those who are perceived as deviant within Galilee, 'the tax-collectors and sinners'. (iii) Galilee is by no means only the place of disclosure and manifestation; it also the place of concealment and secrecy (4:11–12). (iv) Galilee is indeed the place where a new teaching with authority is given, but so too is Jerusalem, which is also the place where the veil of the Temple is torn, the centurion makes his testimony, and the women are struck with fear and trembling at the message of the resurrection.

What Freyne's treatment of Galilee then shows is that the important themes of rejection/acceptance, openness/closedness, disclosure/concealment, new/old apply unevenly to the pair of terms Galilee/Jerusalem. Galilee is certainly not simply replacing Jerusalem and its Temple as the place of revelation and fulfilment. What then is happening? Was Davies right to suggest that attachment to the Land is being replaced by attachment to the person of Jesus?[36] Is Malbon right to suggest that it is not so much that Galilee is being replaced by Judaea (though she suggests that as well) as that stasis, a notion of space as

---

[34] So Freyne, 1985, 58, n. 34, citing Cook, 1978, 78.

[35] Freyne, 1988, who somewhat idealises Galilee as the place of openness to the Gentiles, as a rural, boundary-free community, speaks of Galilee as having an 'essentially rural character, consisting of villages rather than cities for the most part' (54). This, as his subsequent work makes very clear, significantly undervalues the importance of the main cities which controlled the surrounding areas politically and commercially; see Freyne, 1995. He rightly contrasts Jesus' 'itinerant ministry of healing and teaching . . . detached from any central holy place' in Galilee with his Temple-based activity in Jerusalem. See, too, Malina and Rohrbaugh, 1992, 214–15.

[36] 'In sum, for the holiness of place, Christianity has fundamentally, though not consistently, substituted the holiness of the Person: it has Christified holy space.' Davies, 1994, 368.

bounded, sacred as opposed to profane space, is being replaced by one of purposeful movement? that it is the notion of the way which carries the final integration?

The story is somewhat more complex. Galilee is indeed replacing Jerusalem; but it is a Galilee which itself is transformed, allegorised. In the allegorisation notions of sacred space are being changed. The cosmology and ethos which emerges is one which casts aside attachments to the Land and to family and possessions and which replaces them with an ideal of the itinerant, preaching and exorcising life of the disciple in imitation of Jesus (Mark 6). In this the notion of the way of the Lord, with which the Gospel opens, plays a key role. It, too, is significantly reformulated. Elements from the tradition: maps and fragments of maps, fragments of narratives of exile and return and their associated world-views are being taken and reshaped.[37] We can only tentatively attempt to trace out how this is happening.

### Contrasting representations of sacred space contemporary to Mark

Let me then spell out how I see Mark's representation of sacred space in the Gospel. As suggested in chapter 2, Jewish views of the world in the first century were by no means uniform. In particular there were sharply opposed views about the nature of evil, its origin and its resolution in

---

[37] C. Lévi-Strauss, in *La Pensée Sauvage,* speaks of primitive thought as concrete thought in which given images and ideas are taken and recombined in a process of *bricolage.* In New Testament studies organic images have been preferred, under the influence of the History of Religions School. Religious ideas are to be explained 'out of' earlier religious ideas: clear connections are to be sought, where antecedent beliefs are related causally to later belief systems. One need not subscribe fully to the almost atomistic account that Lévi-Strauss gives of the process whereby traditional elements are recombined to form new myths and rituals in primal thought. We may allow that in religious cultures with a developed literature and with various élite groups responsible for the preservation of the tradition, there was indeed a great deal more continuity and coherence in the development of religious beliefs and narratives than such a model might suggest. However, Lévi-Strauss' metaphor should encourage us to abandon the strait-jacket of the History of Religions School's insistence on causal modes of explanation and to look for the surprising and the arbitrary elements in the development of religious traditions. There are admittedly some delicate issues here. The History of Religions School attempted to offer an account of religious development which opposed supernaturalist accounts of the origins of Christianity with thorough-going historical ones (see Pfleiderer, 1907, 1–16, for a passionate rejection of such ecclesiastical modes of thought and an equally passionate expression of belief in the 'gesetzmäßigen Ordnung der Welt, die alle menschliche Erfahrung von jeher bedingte'!). In looking for the arbitrary and unexpected in the development of religious cultures, we should be careful not to allow supernaturalist accounts in by the back door.

the divine plan. On one, cosmic dualist, view, evil could be seen as having its source in the disobedience of heavenly, angelic spirits who had infected the world with their rebellion and who would ultimately be destroyed in a cosmic battle in which the forces of God would prevail. In the meantime God had already acted to bind some of the worst spirits, and had chosen a select few to inherit the earth at the end. Such views are to be found in particularly well-defined form in the Book of the Watchers, *1 Enoch* 1–36. On another, forensic, view, evil was the result of men's and women's disobedience, archetypally in Adam, and for this the remedy was the law which had been given through Moses for Israel's instruction and (at least on some views) for the enlightenment of the Gentiles. The final eradication of evil in the world would come at the last judgement, when the righteous would be rewarded and the wicked would perish. Such views can be found in *4 Ezra* and *2 Baruch*.

Moreover, it is possible to discern the influence of such opposed cosmologies on the construction of space in the Jewish literature of the period. Thus *1 Enoch* sees the world as demon-infested, waiting for the time when the Lord will descend on Sinai from heaven to bring judgement and to establish the tree of life in Zion. The sacred sites have significance in his schema only in terms of their roles in the final, cosmic drama. By contrast, Isaiah, and those who drew on the Deutero-Isaianic texts foretelling the return from exile as a model for their own aspirations at the turn of the era, looked to the narratives of Israel's deliverance in the past for grounds for hope in present adversity. God had punished Israel with exile for its disobedience in former times, but so too he had shown mercy and by his guidance and leading had restored them to the Land which he had promised to them in his covenant, if they were faithful to him. Here the notion of the Land is of central importance: it is the goal of their journeyings, of the wanderings in the desert, of the return from exile. It is the place, above all, where on Zion they enjoy the presence of the Lord who preserves them. God's dealings with Israel in the past, his bringing them out of Egypt, his promise of and bringing them into the Land, his dwelling with them in Zion – all these past glories will be repeated in the restoration for which Isaiah and those who drew inspiration from Isaiah longed.

These two very broad and contrasted conceptions of reality with their related notions of sacred space, I suggest, underlie Mark's Gospel. In his views of space, Mark reflects these different notions and is also engaged in a dialectical process of reconciling these oppositions or differences. We shall see that dualistic views of the world, which are linked to beliefs about Satanic dominance, are in a measure overcome and subsumed into views which have their origin in Isaiah's notion of the way of the Lord.

How then does Mark interact with the these two rather different views of sacred space, with their different mappings of localities and their different treatment of the sites of past history? It is possible to reconstruct two different narratives which run through the Gospel and which reflect these two broadly distinguishable notions of sacred space. Neither story represents all that is said in the Gospel. The second in the end, I judge, assumes dominance.

## The influence of cosmic dualism on Mark

The first story portrays Jesus as engaged in spiritual warfare with Satan. Jesus' baptism leads to his recognition as God's Son whose way John has come to prepare. This way immediately leads him, in the Spirit, into the wilderness, where he is tempted by Satan. It is a place of wild beasts, uncivilised and destructive, and it is the place of spiritual conflict between Satan on the one hand and Jesus and the angels on the other hand. It is not, however, clear whether or not Satan is defeated.[38] It is a trial of strength to prepare Jesus for the conflict which is to come: Satan's forces are at work in the world polluting it and corrupting it, holding men and women in bondage. It is characteristic for Mark that demons are referred to as πνευμάτα ἀκαθάρτα, that they are seen as polluting forces in the world (cf. *1 Enoch*). The phrase is relatively rare in the Bible. Apart from Zechariah 13:2, it only occurs twice in Matthew, eleven times in Mark and eight times in Luke/Acts. Significantly, it also occurs in Revelation 16:13; 18:2. As the Revelation texts suggest, unclean

---

[38] Some commentators, e.g. Gnilka 1, 57–8, Allison, 1999, 196–7, see here a scene of eschatological reversal of Adam's loss of Paradise. There is certainly good evidence for a widespread view that Adam 'lived in peace with the angels (Gen 2:18–20; *Jub* 3:1–3, 28; *LAE* 8:1–3; 37:1–3; *Apoc Mos* 15:3; 16:2; 24:4; 29:14, 16; *2 Enoch* 58:2–6), was guarded by and/or honoured by angels (*LAE* 13:3 – 15:3; 21:1–3; 22:1–2; 33:1–3; *Apoc Mos* 29:1–6, 14; *Apoc Sed* 5:2) . . . fed by them (ARN A 1) or ate the food of angels (*LAE* 4:2)'. Best, 1990, 7–19, who believes on the basis of 3:19b–35 that Mark did regard Satan as having been defeated, still thinks that the details of the brief and cryptic account in Mark 1:12–13 do not 'reveal any overwhelmingly convincing theme'. The role of the angels in ministering to Jesus may be in protecting him from the wild animals who are associated with the devil in *T Naph* 8:4, where the angels will support the children. So, too, Hooker, 51.

spirits are associated with violent destructive spiritual powers, dragons and wild beasts, who prey upon human beings until such time as they are themselves destroyed. Their power has the effect not only of maiming, and robbing people of the power of speech and hearing, but of rendering them wholly incapable of any sort of existence in human society, forcing their victims to live in the place of the dead (Mark 5:3).[39] They are alien forces which invade and disrupt human society both in and outside the Land. As such they are like the invading Roman forces which hold the Land in their sway, as is indicated by the demon's name in 5:9. They are to be cast out (ἐκβάλλειν) into the forces of chaos and pollution (as the story of the Gadarene swine dramatically illustrates), just as, interestingly, Jesus was cast out by the Spirit to meet Satan in the desert. The disciples in chapter 6 are commissioned to continue Jesus' onslaught on the unclean spirits. The summary account of Jesus' healings (but no exorcisms) in 6:53–56 paints a picture of a world – in actual fact a region of Galilee around Gennesareth – where the malign and polluting forces of destruction have been vanquished. Galilee represents in some sense a world purged of evil and suffering. It is to this Galilee that Jesus tells his followers he will go before them.

What is missing in this schema is any definite location for the last battle. In Mark 13 wars and battles are predicted. The world will be in turmoil while the gospel is being preached to all nations. The battlefield is the whole world, but it will come to a head when the 'abomination of desolation' is seen standing where it should not. Then those in Judaea should flee to the hills and all should prepare for the end. Jerusalem and the Temple will be destroyed (13:2) and this will usher in a period of tribulation (13:19), so intense that it has to be shortened 'for the sake of the elect' (13:20). False messiahs (the antichrist?) will appear. Then the final stage is presented in thoroughly cosmic terms: the heavens are in turmoil, the 'powers in the heavens will be shaken'.[40] This world will be consumed and the elect will be

---

[39] Cf. here again F. Watson's study of the Gadarene demoniac, in Watson 1995, 248–55.

[40] Commentators, almost without exception, take this phrase to refer to heavenly bodies, equating it with the falling of the stars. *1 Enoch* 86:1–6; 90:20–27 refers to fallen angels who are judged and condemned. Angels are frequently referred to as stars (e.g. Judg 5:20; Job 38:7; Dan 8:10; *LAB* 32:15; *Jos As* 14; Philo, *de Plant* 12; *de Gig* 8). Thus, there may well be here an indirect reference to 'war in heaven' and the overthrow of disobedient angelic spirits.

gathered in 'from the four winds' by angels sent out by the Son of Man (13:27).[41] Then the elect will enjoy the company of the Son of Man, as again *1 Enoch* 62:13–14 describes: 'The righteous and elect ones shall be saved on that day, from thenceforth they shall never see the faces of the sinners and the oppressors. The Lord of the Spirits will abide over them; they shall eat and rest and rise with that Son of Man forever.'[42]

Mark 13 displays a clear tendency to move away from direct and explicit reference to specific locations and to prefer a setting which is unspecified and cosmic.[43] While it is true that the destruction of Jerusalem is referred to (at least for those with sufficient understanding, 13:14), it is no longer the place of final judgement. The final acts are clearly separated from the destruction of Jerusalem by the tribulation, the appearance of the anti-christs and the shaking of the heavens. The motif of the gathering in of the elect clearly echoes Jewish hopes of the gathering in of the dispersed peoples (Deut 30:4; Isa 60:4), but here there is no specifically Jewish reference: it is the elect of the Son of Man, those who have heard the preaching of the gospel and endured to the end (Mark 13:10–13) who will be saved.

It is not clear whether this implies that the world as it now is will be swept away and that the elect will be transported to another world. Jesus' prophecy of the destruction of the holy city seems to indicate that hopes for the restoration of Zion have been abandoned. On the other hand the, admittedly false, accusations against him assert that he foretold the replacement of the old Temple with a Temple not made with hands. Is this the dwelling of Exodus 15:17, the Temple prepared in heaven, ready to descend on Jerusalem in the last days? Or does it refer to a heavenly temple not of this world at all? Were Mark's hopes entirely other worldly? Or does Mark allegorise the notion of the Temple, as in John, taking it to refer to the presence of God among those who are 'with Jesus'? The Gospel ends with the injunction to the disciples to

---

[41] The passage is full of allusions to apocalyptic writings, notably Daniel and *1 Enoch*. The coming of the Son of Man clearly echoes Dan 7:13, but the motif of 'seeing the Son of Man' is perhaps better elucidated against the background of *1 Enoch* 62:3, 10, where the kings and powerful rulers' seeing the Son of Man is linked with their shame and covering with darkness, so Gnilka; 1979, 201. On the other hand, Dan 7 is combined in Rev 1:7 with Zech 12:10 with its characteristic reference to those who 'pierced him' seeing him. The absence of the piercing motif in Mark 13 makes an allusion to Zech 12:10 less likely there.

[42] So Gnilka, 1979, 202.

[43] Cf. Davies, 1994, 370.

follow Jesus to Galilee. Is this to witness the coming of the Son of Man in glory? Is it symbolic of the world to come? Is it the launch-pad for their preaching the Gospel to all nations?

None of these questions is easily answered. Certainly it is doubtful whether Mark envisages a renewed Temple.[44] Why would he command his disciples to go to Galilee, if the culmination of the way was to be in the restoration of the Temple on Mount Zion? Mark's depiction of Jesus as the cornerstone of the new building is much more easily read as a reference to Jesus' relation to his followers, which would be consistent with his characterisation of those who do the will of God as his brothers and sisters (3:31–35). All this seems to point to a final time of fulfilment after the destruction of the powers of evil, when the true followers of Jesus will be gathered into his presence. Is it any different with Mark's dialogue with the Isaianic tradition of eschatology?

## Mark and the way of the Lord

Mark's opening citation of 'Isaiah the prophet' establishes from the outset a dialogue with the Isaianic notion of the way of the Lord, which leads from the desert to Zion. The Gospel starts in the wilderness with John and culminates in Jerusalem with the death of Jesus on the cross. But the way that is taken from the wilderness to Jerusalem is anything but straight, and the story does not end there. John, who appears in the wilderness, is the messenger sent before Jesus to prepare his way. Jesus, after his baptism and divine recognition, and his temptation by Satan, comes from the wilderness into Galilee proclaiming the coming of the kingdom, teaching, preaching and healing, and calling people to repent and believe in the gospel, the good news of divine deliverance and restoration (Isa 40). He calls disciples; people flock to him; but he also encounters opposition, both locally and from those who come down from Jerusalem. While his ministry is centred on Galilee, it is by no means restricted to it, and Jesus frequently enters Gentile territory, of which his various crossings of the Lake are symbolic. On his journey

---

[44] Watts, 1997, 349, concludes his discussion of Mark's parable of the Vineyard: 'And predicated on Jesus, the true son and heir, a new leadership, and presumably a new Temple to which all nations will come, will emerge to take the place of the old.' But he offers no support for this view, unless it be that some restoration of the Temple is envisaged in Isaiah. However, the question which has to be asked is how far Mark has subverted the Isaianic notion of the Way of the Lord and developed very different understandings of the final fulfilment of God's purposes.

into the district of Tyre and Sidon, he encounters the Syro-Phoenician woman, who by the subtlety of her 'word' persuades him to extend his ministry of exorcism to her daughter (7:24–30). From Galilee Jesus moves up to Jerusalem, where he preaches and teaches in the Temple and on the Mount of Olives, and encounters growing opposition which leads to his death in the place of the skull. Here Temple and Golgotha are contrasted: the revelation of Jesus' 'glory' on the cross which evokes the centurion's confession is contrasted with the tearing of the Temple veil. The divine *Shekhina* departs from the Temple and is strangely present in the crucified figure on the cross.[45] But Jesus' way and the way of his disciples does not end here. As he has foretold, he goes before them to Galilee, and the women at the tomb are told to convey that command to his disciples. The ending points forward to Galilee, where the story started.

How does all this fit in with and modify the Isaianic view of the way of the Lord? '[I]n Mark the Deutero-Isaian picture of the Lord's triumphal way has suffered a strange reversal from its intersection with the theology of the cross'.[46] Such is Joel Marcus' thesis in his treatment

[45] The rending of the veil in 15:38 raises a number of problems for exegetes. Does it refer to the curtain that separated the sanctuary from the forecourt or the curtain immediately before the inner sanctum? καταπέτασμα and its cognate is used for both (Exod 26:33, 37 LXX; Josephus, *Ant* 8:72). In favour of the former is its visibility as a sign; in favour of the latter, its greater theological significance (though this is surely only a matter of degree?). Commentators divide over whether this is a sign of the destruction of the Temple which Jesus prophesied and about which he has been mocked; or whether it signifies the end of the cult. The two are by no means unconnected. It seems clear that it points to the coming destruction of the Temple, but that it also indicates that, with the death of the Son of Man, God has already abandoned his Temple. This for two reasons. The verse forms an inclusio with the baptism narrative. Just as Jesus' ministry starts with the rending of the heavens (σχίζω, Mark 1:10) and the descent of the Spirit upon Jesus, so here with the rending of the Temple veil God's *Shekhina* leaves the Temple and his presence with Jesus is recognised by the Gentile centurion. Watts, 1997, 310, n. 85, revealingly declares that he will not be examining the significance of the Temple veil being torn, since it does not 'immediately involve allusions to Isaiah'. *Tg Isa* 5:5 does, however, have 'I will take up my *Shekina* from them, and they will be for plundering; I will break down the place of their sanctuaries, and they will be for trampling'. The implication of the centurion's confession is clear: in the preaching of the gospel of the cross to the nations, the presence of God will be revealed.

[46] Marcus, 1992, 35. Marcus' view is that it is probable that Isaiah 40, with its emphasis on the retreat into the wilderness before the triumphal advance on Jerusalem, played an 'important role in the events leading up to and including the Jewish Revolt against the Romans in A.D. 66–74, which form the background for Mark's Gospel' (22). Certainly Josephus' accounts of various prophetic figures who led their followers into the desert, expecting some kind of dramatic liberation reminiscent of the great events of Israel's

of Mark's 'Gospel according to Isaiah'. If in Deutero-Isaiah the theme of the festal ascent to Jerusalem has 'been fused with that of the holy war of conquest', in the wake of which the people will return to Zion, then in Mark these themes have been radically reworked. For Jesus is going up to Jerusalem[47]

> not in order to triumph over his enemies in a conventional way but in order to be killed by them. Nothing could be more antithetical to conventional notions of victory than Jesus' long prophecy of his own betrayal, condemnation, mockery, physical abuse and execution (10:33–34). Yet, it must be forcefully added, this prophecy is not a *denial* of the Deutero-Isaian hope for a holy war victory: it is rather, a radical, cross-centred *adaptation* of it. For those with eyes to see (see 4:9, 23), the fearful trek of the befuddled, bedraggled little band of disciples is the return of Israel to Zion, and Jesus' suffering and death there *are* the prophesied apocalyptic victory of the divine warrior. The same spirit that will later shape the Marcan passion narrative infuses Mark 8:22–10:52, a unitary redefinition of apocalyptic eschatology that paradoxically hears in Jesus' cry of dereliction the triumph song of Yahweh's return to Zion, that paradoxically sees in his anguished, solitary death the long-awaited advent of the kingdom of God.[48]

This statement sets out with all desirable clarity the claim that Mark offers a highly creative reading of Isaiah.[49] Whereas Isaiah's vision is

---

history, provides evidence for the way that the Exodus-typology shaped Jewish expectations in the first century CE. And this in turn would certainly have influenced the way people read Isa 40 and other similar passages. Whether this quite adds up to the claim that '*both the passage and* the theme' (my italics) were influential in the revolt is another question. Mark's use of the passage represents an original use of a passage which was drawn on by many groups, but the diversity of usage of the passage even in Qumran (cf. 1QS 8:13f.; 9:19–21, which encourages the community to study of the law and separation from the rest of the people, with the martial passage to which Marcus refers, 1QM 1:2–3), suggests that the passage lent itself to varied readings. The Servant Songs would at the very least have given some internal support to Mark's more irenic reading of the Isaiah passage. See the discussion in Braun, 1966b, 17.

[47] ἀναβαίνειν is a technical term for the festal ascent to Zion, see J. Schneider, 'βαίνω, κτλ.' *TDNT* 1964, 1:519; cited Marcus, 1992, 36, n. 86.

[48] Marcus, 1992, 36.

[49] It seems to me that the great weakness of Watts' in many ways learned and informative book, *Isaiah's New Exodus and Mark*, is that it rarely contemplates the possibility that Mark may have significantly reworked the Isaianic motifs which he takes up. He specifically restricts himself to a discussion of themes and motifs which directly correspond to elements in the Isaian schema which he constructs and that involve allusions to Isaiah and Malachi, but this means effectively that he will discuss only those passages which confirm his view that there is a pattern of restoration/salvation based on Isaiah and Malachi that underlies and gives unity to Mark's narrative.

based on the notion of a holy war, in which God will vanquish and destroy his enemies, the central figure of Mark's passion narrative himself dies. His suffering and death *are* the victory of the divine warrior. His people are not the rejoicing returnees from exile, but the 'bedraggled band of disciples' who desert him and flee. True, it is possible to raise questions about the sense in which the resurrection (of which there is, in any case, only an indirect account in the Second Gospel) represents the final triumph over death; it may be possible (I think it is) to argue that the kinds of reworking of the motif of the holy war that we find here are foreshadowed in the servant chapters of Deutero-Isaiah,[50] but there can surely be no denying that there is here a major dissonance between the notion of a triumphal way leading to the enthronement of Jahweh, the restoration of the Land and the Temple and the return of the exiles, and Mark's story of a Messianic figure going up to Jerusalem to meet his death on a Roman cross.

There are, moreover, other points of dissonance not so strongly stressed by Marcus.[51] The festal procession to Jerusalem ends not with the enthronement of the king in the Temple, nor indeed with any kind of celebration in the Temple, but with Jesus enacting and prophesying its destruction (13:2) and with the veil of the Temple torn as Jesus dies. In Isaiah the way of the Lord is a Holy Way over which 'the unclean shall not pass', on which no ravenous beast shall come up (Isa 35:8–9), and which will lead the ransomed of the Lord back to Zion with singing (Isa 35:10); in Mark Jesus' way leads him immediately into the company of wild beasts (1:13);[52] he is confronted by a man with an unclean spirit (1:21–28), by a leper (1:40–45), and this sets the pattern for his

---

[50] There is a significant history of contemporary readings of Isaiah, which is documented by Snodgrass, 1980, and Schwartz, 1987 (not seen). Mark, that is to say, will have come to Isaiah aware and shaped by its significance for his contemporaries.

[51] Though see now Marcus, 2000, 481.

[52] Commentators differ whether the wild beasts are to be seen as part of Jesus' confrontation with the powers of darkness and destruction (Best, 1990, 8, referring back to Lohmeyer and citing Ps 22:13–22; 91:13; Isa 13:21–22, and comparing Ezek 34:5, 8, 25 and Is 34:14 in its Hebrew and Greek forms where Hebrew צִיִּים, 'wild beasts' is rendered by δαιμόνια in the LXX), or already as an anticipation of the new age (so, Gnilka, 1978, 57–8, citing Isa 11:6–8; 65:25; *sBar* 73:6). There is however nothing in the text to suggest that the beasts were in any way friendly and Best is probably right to stress that for Mark's readers wild beasts, either in the wild or in the circus, would be seen as dangerous and destructive, and to point out that they are contrasted with the angels who minister to Jesus. Surprisingly, none of the commentators refers to Isa 35:9, in many ways the most closely associated because of its link with the motif of the way.

encounters throughout his ministry.[53] He himself declares the distinction between clean and unclean to be purely a matter of the heart (7:14–23), and his own journey to Jerusalem finds its end in the place of a skull, of death and impurity. While it is true that his entry into Jerusalem is accompanied by crowds who celebrate him in song, these are only in a very paradoxical way the ransomed or the redeemed. They will shortly turn against him and go up (ἀναβὰς, 15:8) to Pilate to ask him to release Barabbas and to crucify Jesus. Thus it is not only, as Marcus suggests, notions of power and triumph which are being reworked but a range of ideas associated with purity and the Temple. In this there is a radical reformulation of notions of sacred time and place, coupled with a redefinition of who God's appointed, elect are. The *Shekhina* leaves the Temple in Jerusalem (cf. Ezek 11) and this action will be subsequently reflected in the presence in the Temple of the 'abomination of desolation' (Mark 13:14). 'Holiness', purity of heart, is to be found now in those who take up their cross and follow Jesus, enduring to the end in the way which he teaches them (esp. 8:31 – 10:45).

There are other important differences. Galilee plays little or no part in the Isaianic schema, where the triumphal procession leads straight out of the desert to Jerusalem.[54] In Mark, not only is there a long interlude before Jesus moves with his disciples to Jerusalem: there is also the strong motif of return to Galilee (14:28; 16:7). While it is true that Jesus teaches in Jerusalem, the main scene of his teaching is Galilee, and it is here that he reveals the mystery of the kingdom to his disciples. If it is true, as suggested above, that in the Isaianic, forensic, view sin and evil are overcome by the Lord's teaching and leading, then in Mark this is something realised principally through Jesus' teaching of his disciples which occurs in significant measure in Galilee. Significant teaching, not least about Jesus' death and the consequent views of suffering and power, also occurs 'on the way'; and final understanding for the disciples will only dawn when they have completed the journey to the cross and followed him back to Galilee.

---

[53] It is striking that in a number of these encounters the initiative is taken by the unclean person, who approaches Jesus, ἔρχεται πρὸς αὐτὸν (Mark 1:40), as is most clearly expressed in the story of the woman with a haemorrhage who touches him (5:24–34).

[54] With, of course, the notable exception of the Isa 9, 'Galilee of the nations', which Matthew has in his fulfilment citations, 4:15.

What is happening here? Is it any more than that Mark is having to accommodate the known traditions about Jesus' ministry in Galilee into the Isaianic schema? Certainly, as suggested above, Mark is not simply setting up Galilee in opposition to Jerusalem. There are both continuities and discontinuities. On the other hand it is evident that Jerusalem no longer has the central place which it occupied in the Isaianic scheme. Not only is its main institution, the Temple, clearly replaced (the rending of the veil of the Temple): but Galilee is confirmed as the future place of encounter with the risen Lord. Even so, Galilee does not simply replace Jerusalem as the goal of the way. From Galilee the disciples will be sent out to preach the gospel to all nations.

Underlying both Isaiah and the Markan story is a salvation historical view which sees God as enabling his people to overcome sin by teaching and leading them. In Isaiah, God leads his people by punishing them for their disobedience, by exiling them to Babylon, and then subsequently restoring to them their land and sanctuary, leading them in a triumphant campaign back from the wilderness. For Isaiah, the Land provides the currency for God's dealings with his people. In Mark the good news of the way of the Lord is addressed, not to exiles in Babylon, but to those who are weighed down by disease, possessed by demons, who are 'defiled' by 'evil thoughts, fornication, theft, murder, adultery, coveting, wickedness . . .' (Mark 7:21–22).[55] The way of the Lord leads from John's call to repentance in the wilderness to Jesus' prophetic, healing, exorcising ministry, to his journey with his disciples to Jerusalem and then back to Galilee. The currency of God's dealings with people in this story is their being with Jesus. It is to this that the disciples are called (3:14); it is this of which they are deprived through his death by virtue of their falling away (14:27) and to which they will be restored in Galilee and at the appearing of the Son of

---

[55] It is true that this list bears some resemblance to the sins of which Israel and her leaders are accused in Isaiah, but it does not carry strong literary allusions to Isaiah (Matthew has amended it to bring it closer to the text of the Decalogue). Its more obvious similarities are with the lists of vices that we find in Rom 1:29–31; Gal 5:19–21; Eph 4:31; 5:3–5; Col 3:5–8, etc. (see *ADB* 6, 858–9 for lit.) Nor are there any *direct* references in the context either to idolatry or indeed to the kinds of social oppression and exploitation of which Isaiah accuses Israel, and which is linked there with this kind of behaviour. Watts sees the Isaian polemic against idolatry as an important key to Mark, use of the way of the Lord motif, but interestingly he does not discuss this passage. He also gives no weight at all to the prophetic critique of social injustice in Isaiah, which also finds little echo in Mark. But then Mark is not addressed to the wealthy and powerful.

Man.[56] Such 'being with Jesus' is not tied to any particular place, though it is quite specifically localised in the story. It is certainly not restricted to the Land, even though Jesus in his encounter with the Syro-Phoenician woman first protests that his ministry is to be restricted to the children of the household (of Israel). It is a ministry, which even in Jesus' life-time flows backwards and forwards across the boundaries of the Land, and which, after his resurrection, propels the disciples out to the ends of the earth.

## The interrelationship of the two representations of sacred space in Mark

What is happening to the construction of sacred space in Mark's engagement with the Isaianic tradition? And how does it interact with his reworking of the ideology of cosmic dualism? In the first place, Mark is allegorising space.[57] Terms like Galilee and 'the way' are not to be understood as limited to particular places invested with a numinous, sacred quality and contrasted with others which are profane. Rather, they stand for a particular kind of religious experience, which is mediated through Jesus and which can be repeated either inside or outside the Land, in so far as men and women are brought into contact with him. In Mark this is expressed through the invitation to Jesus' disciples to follow him to Galilee. This is clearly not intended as a command to set up a cultic centre in Galilee, as the further implied injunction to preach the gospel to all nations makes clear. To follow Jesus to Galilee is to 'see him', like the Gentile centurion to recognise in him the Son of God, to be led and taught by him (to be instructed in the mystery of the kingdom of God) through the preaching of the gospel and to share in his ministry of teaching, preaching, exorcising and healing. Such 'following' can, in virtue of the resurrection, occur anywhere, and in this sense Galilee is a cipher for this kind of experience. On the other hand, the narrative of Jesus' ministry in Galilee remains a narrative of particular concrete events. What the disciples, and by extension Mark's

---

[56] Jesus cites Zech 13:7: 'I will strike the shepherd, and the sheep will be scattered' and promises that he will, like a shepherd, go before them to Galilee after he has been raised.

[57] One of the most interesting indications of this is the rejection of Jesus by his πατρίς, his relations and his house (Mark 6:1–6). It is not that this means that Galilee cannot be seen as the place of salvation *at all* – 'Not for Matthew nor for Mark was Galilee *terra Christiana*' (W. D. Davies, 1994, 241). Rather it is that Jesus' ministry in Galilee and his dealings with the disciples and the crowds, the sick and the possessed, symbolise the kind of life to which Mark's readers are called. They are not called to go to Jesus' literal πατρίς, but to enter into the new world which he has inaugurated by his ministry.

readers, are called to is just as much a particular experience of the numinous, of the divine, as was the encounter between Jesus of Nazareth and his disciples in the towns and villages of the Galilee prior to his crucifixion.

I take this to be fundamentally in agreement with Malbon's thesis that Mark is substituting for the opposition between random movement (chaos) and stasis (order) the notion of purposive movement as the mediation between the two which is expressed in the notion of the way. '*Hodos*', she writes, 'is more action than a place.'[58] I prefer to say that Mark abandons one of the schemata which express the opposition between order and chaos, namely, that of sacred and profane, which locates God's presence in particular cultic sites, and chooses instead to see the presence of God as disembedded, not limited but irrupting wherever the Gospel is preached and heard.

What this means is that the notions of sacred and profane, which are closely tied to the Isaianic idea of the way of the Lord (the sacred way on which the unclean will not be allowed to tread, the restoration of the Temple as the sacral centre of the Land), are being discarded and replaced with a sense of the irruption of the presence of God 'wherever the gospel is preached in the whole world' (Mark 14:9). This is made explicit in Mark 7 where the notion of external polluting forces is discarded, at least as far as foods are concerned, and implicitly in Jesus' many boundary crossings which demonstrate his indifference to such distinctions of sacred space (the episode with the Syro-Phoenician woman indicates the 'overcoming' of Jesus' inhibitions in this respect). The abandonment of the distinction between sacred and profane as marked out by cultic sites and boundaries is finally dramatised in the narrative of the Passion, where Jesus is crucified, degraded and destroyed in the place of the skull, over against the Temple, at the same time as the protective veil of the Temple is torn, the cultic boundaries removed.

How does this relate to the Markan dialogue with cosmic dualism? One could simply say that what Mark takes up from (*aufheben* in its positive sense) this dialogue is the sense that the battle between the divine presence/will and the forces of darkness knows no boundaries, no clearly defined battlefronts. Just as the encounter between Jesus and 'unclean spirits' may occur inside and outside Galilee, so too the battle for the hearts and minds of men and women may occur anywhere

---

[58]  Malbon, 1986, 164–6.

where the gospel is preached: what is required is that they should have ears to hear. What he sets aside (*aufheben* in its negative sense) is the notion that the source of evil in the world lies in dark angelic powers which subvert the world though the agency of unclean spirits. There is no convincing evidence that this view is sustained *throughout* the Markan narrative, however much it may feature in the earlier chapters.[59] Rather the Isaianic/forensic belief that the source of evil lies in the human heart and can be overcome only through the divine leading and teaching on the one hand and human obedience on the other, is taken up and negates the dualistic view.

That is to say, the particularism of the Isaianic way of the Lord, which is so closely linked to its vision of the restored Temple as the locus of the glory of the Lord, is being overcome by a dialectical process of mediation arising out of the dialogue with *cosmological* dualism; equally the *dualism* of Mark's dialogue partner is being overcome by the influence of the Isaianic vision of human nature and the human heart, in such a way that the battle against evil is now seen essentially as a battle for the human will. This is not a simple substitution of universalism for particularism. Isaiah's way of the Lord has its own form of universalism in its vision of the Gentiles' attraction to the glory of the Temple; Mark's notion of 'following Jesus on the way' is also quite specifically tied to the preaching of the gospel of Jesus Christ, Son of God. His followers, in so far as they do the will of God, are *his* brothers and sisters, not simply children of God: and in any case it is God's will *as interpreted by* Jesus that they must obey.

Thus the new sense of identity which we discussed above is closely tied to this new sense of sacred space. Jesus' disciples are Galileans, literally, as in the case of Peter at his denial of Christ, but metaphorically in so far as the risen Jesus goes before them to Galilee. As the cultic barriers around the Temple and the Land come down, so too the close attachment of Jesus' followers to the Land and its descendants is loosed, and their attachment to him gains prominence. It is no longer physical descent and local attachment which defines a person, but his attachment to the one who comes on the way of the Lord and who leads and teaches them. In this way, those who obey become metaphorically the family of Jesus, the family of God.

---

[59] See the discussion below, chapter 5, 149–52, of Robinson, 1957, Garrett, 1998 and Best, 1990.

# 5

# Conflicting world-views in Mark's Christology

## Introduction

Let me sketch out the central thesis of the two previous chapters concerning Mark. The Gospel of Mark does not present a single ethos, or indeed a single unified view of reality:[1] it can be read in different ways, as a narrative of conversion and radical transformation, or as a narrative of commissioning and restoration; as the story of the purging of the world from pollution by unclean spirits, or as the story of the parodic, strange restoration of Israel's glory and the coming of its light to the Gentiles. Behind these two different, if interwoven, stories, or at least broadly corresponding to them, are two different accounts of the nature of evil and its overcoming, two fundamentally opposed mythologies, neither of which can, on its own, give an adequate account of the human predicament, can make sense of the experience of loss of national sovereignty, of exposure to disease, destitution, pillage and exile which is Israel's (and indeed pretty much everyone else's) in the ancient world. One account suggests that the root of such evils lies in some form of angelic invasion and pollution of the world; the other prefers a primal myth of human disobedience. One sees the resolution of the problem of evil as lying in the divine overthrow and destruction of the dark powers; the other as lying in the moral reformation of men and women (more specifically of Israel) and their final judgement by God. In both cases the world will be finally freed from evil and suffering and the righteous will praise God. The role of Israel may be differently conceived: the central image may be that of the return of the Jews from exile and the flocking of the nations to observe the glory of Zion. Or it

---

[1]  See particularly the work of Räisänen, 1990, and Anderson and Moore, 1992, who have both stressed, against an uncritical narrative reading of Mark, that there is no seamless, coherent story-world, that the narrative is full of seams and gaps and contains *theologoumena* which fit together only loosely.

may be of a cosmic change: the shaking of the foundations of earth and heaven, the establishment of a new heaven and a new earth, where the central sites of God's holiness and glory, Zion, Sinai and Eden, are restored to their primal glory.

It seems clear that the Gospel of Mark is indebted to both these narrative mythologies, as indeed is much of the other Jewish literature of the time. In what sense does the Gospel mediate between them? We have seen, as we have treated different themes and motifs in the Gospel, certain kinds of mediation, of weaving together of the different strands. The disciples are portrayed as disciples of Jesus, commissioned to preach and exorcise like him. They have a particular role in the restoration of Israel: to call to repentance, to preach the good news of God's coming rule and of the 'way of the Lord'. But their exercise of this commission is deeply flawed: they fail to understand, to confess, to watch with him. They desert and flee and deny and betray. The parallels with Elisha's commissioning diminish the more the story progresses. We are shown the depths of human depravity, though interestingly we are not (ctr. Luke 22:3) told that such behaviour is demonic. Obedience is problematised: the demands placed on the disciples break them. They cannot withstand the weight of the cross. They are shining examples of those who do *not* 'endure to the end' (Mark 13:13). On the other hand, Jesus' preaching of the good news is also portrayed as releasing the possessed from their demons, as giving sight to the blind, as extending an open invitation to the outcast and sinners. The models of the human predicament here are multiple: possession, blindness, social exclusion, total breakdown of social communication and control in the case of the Gaderene demoniac. What emerges from this is in no sense a coherent account of human willing and moral failure: it is more that we are bombarded with a set of images which together stress the need for radical change, conversion, restitution, liberation from bondage and restoration to wholeness. What this also does is to give a radically new sense of group identity. Standard markers: kinship, circumcision, physical descent and food-laws are either discarded, absent or metaphoricised. The group is identified as the family of those who do the will of God. Israel is rejected to be replaced by the new building of those who follow Christ, the cornerstone (12:10). The 'elect' are redefined as those who hear the good news and endure to the end.

The interaction, perhaps better, interanimation, of the two myths, is subtle and more than a little elusive. The picture which emerges is lacking in definition, as if two images were superimposed. The forensic view of evil, reflected in the view of discipleship as commissioning, is stretched and subverted by a darker view of human nature as radically corrupt; stretched, but not ultimately broken. The disciples' failings are not, in the end, as in Qumran and Luke (though ctr. Mark 4:15), attributed to evil spirits' leading them astray. But nor is the cosmic dualist view denied. Nothing is done to allegorise the accounts of Jesus' exorcisms or to deny the power of the demons to possess and subject human beings to their will. But these narratives are set in a wider context, alongside accounts of sickness, social exclusion, blindness, moral breakdown and failure, in such a way that they do begin to take on a symbolic significance within the Gospel as a whole, particularly as the narrative focuses more and more on the drama of the Passion, on Jesus' struggle to obey his Father's will, and on the disciples' failure to follow him. Within this context, even though all talk of Satan, demons and unclean spirits ceases after 9:38, the earlier accounts of exorcisms remain as a metaphor for the depth of human perversity which unfolds in the final chapters.

Similarly the world's map is redrawn. The boundaries of Gentile territory and the Land, of Galilee and Jerusalem, are in the first instance clearly marked, but then, variously, subverted. Galilee is given precedence over Jerusalem (whatever qualifications of that statement one might want to make); then boundaries between the Land and Gentile territory are blurred, crossed and re-crossed and their significance famously challenged by the Syro-Phoenician woman. Finally, they are allegorised: 'the Galilee' becomes the place where the disciples will meet Jesus, as it is the place purged of all disease (6:53–56). And as we have seen there are yet other ways in which this sacred geography is undermined. The triumphal 'way of the Lord', along which the exiles will return to Zion, has become a 'circuitous' procession of 'bedraggled pilgrims' to Golgotha. The Temple veil is torn and the divine presence departs at the same time as the Gentile centurion recognises in the face of the dead Jesus the 'son of God'. Jesus, before his death, announces that he will become the cornerstone of a new building and foretells the desecration and destruction of the Temple; Jesus' followers, the new house of God, will be scattered and preach the good news in all the world. Finally, the Son of Man will appear and will send out angels to gather in his elect, those who have accepted the gospel, from the four winds. Thus, a narrative cast in clearly Jewish terms and images is reworked to embrace the church's mission and this in turn opens up a different cosmic dimension of history, where the key to salvation is faithful response to the disciples' preaching.

Here, perhaps more clearly than in Mark's treatment of the discipleship theme, it is the restorationist myth of the return to Zion along the way of the Lord which dominates Mark's narrative. And this is a myth which draws strongly on the notion that Israel's suffering and exile is a divine punishment for its disobedience or, put more positively, that Israel's bitter history is part of God's leading of Israel which will ultimately culminate in the return of the Lord's glory to Israel and in the Gentiles' acknowledgement of that glory. But, as we have seen, this mythological narrative is parodied and subverted. There is a sharp clash here between the restorationist and revolutionist myths with which Mark is engaging. If this whole age lies under the sway of Satan and his forces, then the old distinctions between Jew and Gentile, the Land and the surrounding territories pale into insignificance. The fight against Satanic forces must be pursued where it may: in Tyre and Sidon, or indeed in all the world (13:10). Even if this battle is ultimately a battle for the wills and hearts of men and women (albeit wills and hearts which are deeply corrupted) rather than against spiritual powers, nevertheless it is still a battle which is global, not limited to Israel. The divine presence is encountered wherever the gospel is preached, wherever Jesus' disciples speak in the Spirit. The ultimate victory, however, is not achieved through the overthrow of Satan, but through the hearing of the word of God. It is this which identifies people as the elect of the Son of Man.

## Opposing views of evil in Mark: recent scholarly debate

This view, that Mark is in dialogue with essentially opposed myths about the origins of evil, is not a common one. As we have seen, Martin de Boer[2] has argued in an article that such a dialogue is a feature of Jewish apocalyptic texts of the period and has attempted there to show the relevance of such a view for an understanding of Paul. But that hardly provides a warrant for making similar claims about Mark. I take a good deal of encouragement, however, from the observation that scholarly treatments of Mark over the last forty years have divided radically over the account that they give of Mark's understanding of evil.

---

[2] de Boer, 1989.

The two main positions are well illustrated by the views of J. M. Robinson and E. Best.[3] Robinson argued vigorously that Mark's Gospel was to be read in terms of a conflict between Jesus and Satan and his forces. The Temptation set the tone for the rest of the Gospel, and the conflict between the two opposing forces was continued in the exorcisms with their accounts of the violent struggle between Jesus and the demons, in the conflict stories which were formally most similar to the exorcisms, in the disciples' objection to the Passion,[4] and in the Passion narrative itself, where the disciples fall prey to Satanic temptation and so become Satan's instruments.[5] Even in the subsequent life of the Christian community the conflict continues. The parable of the sower gives an account of the 'understanding' which is proper to Christian faith. It distinguishes between two types of hearing: 'hearing but not under-standing' and true 'hearing (4:3, 9, 23, 24; cf. 7:14). [P]rogress from the first to the second level is blocked by the cosmic enemy of Christ, Satan (v. 15)'.[6]

---

[3] Robinson, 1957, and Best, 1965, 2nd edn with extended preface 1990.

[4] Robinson, 1957, 45, where he attributes Peter's objections to Jesus' prediction of his Passion to the disciples as a whole. A fuller and more nuanced argument is now advanced by Garrett, 1998, 76–82. Garrett compares Jesus' rebuke to Peter with Job's rebuke to his wife in *T. Job* 25:9 – 26:6. But there Satan is depicted as literally standing behind Job's wife, Sitidos: 'Do you not see the devil standing behind you?', whereas in Mark it is Peter who is referred to metaphorically as Satan and who is accused of 'thinking the things of *men* as opposed to those of *God*.' Garrett acknowledges this, 'Peter's perspective on Jesus' impending passion is *strictly a human one*' (my italics), but, goes on to assert, nevertheless, that 'Peter unwittingly serves as Satan's tool to lead Jesus' astray' (79). But while this may be *de facto* true, it does not give an adequate account of the way the agency is conceived by Mark. It is Peter's all too human way of thinking which is the problem here, not Satan's 'first prevent[ing] Peter from seeing the light of the gospel of the glory of the suffering Christ' (79).

[5] The question of Jesus' temptations has been recently examined in more detail by Susan Garrett, 1998, who gives a carefully differentiated account of the development of the figure of Satan and his relation to God, and to the wider theme of the testing of the righteous (19–49). She recognises that there are two rather different strands, one drawn from Near Eastern 'combat myths' and one with roots in the story of Job, where Satan acts more as an agent of God, though one who in the course of the tradition becomes more independent. It is the conjunction of these two traditions which can 'clarify tensions or paradoxes in the New Testament's several references to Satan' (49). This is helpful.

[6] Robinson, 1957, 77. This view is followed by Marcus, 1984, 566: 'Satan is explicitly an actor in leading human beings astray (4:15); implicitly, tribulation, persecution, and the "cares of the age" (4:17, 19) are his agents.' Where is the evidence for this? Marcus believes that, just as in Qumran the angel of darkness is appointed by God, not only to rule over the sons of darkness but also to lead astray the sons of light, so too in Mark it is God who 'unleash[es] the forces of darkness to blind human beings so that they oppose the kingdom which he is bringing in about Jesus Christ' (567). But the notion of divine

This view was comprehensively challenged by Ernest Best, who argued that the outcome of the Temptation in Mark 1:12–13 was not given until 3:27, and that this provides the key to the understanding of the role of Satan in the rest of the Gospel. According to 3:27, Satan is bound, that is to say, is 'render[ed] powerless. Satan bound is not a Satan who can still carry on his activities, tempting and deceiving man within limits, but Satan out of the way'.[7] Thus the subsequent course of the narrative depicts Jesus plundering Satan's possessions as he exorcises demons. Nowhere are demonic forces held to be responsible for moral evil. 'In Mark the evil in men whereby they are led to oppose Jesus is consistently led back to the evil intent of their own hearts: it is from within man that evil comes and goes out from him both to render himself unclean and to injure others. The fact that man's spiritual blindness (iv:10–12) is traced to God shows how far Mark is removed from a Satanic explanation of evil – and from our ideas.'[8]

Best seeks further support for his views by arguing that such a view of temptation to moral evil is part of 'the dominant trend of Old Testament thinking which saw evil as originating within man himself'.[9] This view is to be found in the intertestamental literature, and even though Best acknowledges that spiritual powers have a greater role in apocalyptic literature, he still concludes that the authors do not abandon the dominant trend, which is firmly anchored in *1 Baruch*, Tobit, 1 Esdras, Sirach, Wisdom, 1 and 2 Maccabees.[10]

---

hardening (4:11–12; 8:17–18) does not entail the agency of demonic forces. It can be argued, appealing to 4:15, that the connection is made in ch. 4. But there is a further problem here, for there are other internal inconsistencies in ch. 4. The disciples are said to have been given the mystery of the kingdom, but immediately Jesus complains about their lack of understanding of it (v. 13). The idea of demonic agency is quite absent, however, in ch. 8. Moreover, even in ch. 4, Satan's activity is limited to one class of people who fail to respond adequately to the word.

[7] Best, 1990, 12.

[8] Best, 1990, 37. But, as *Jubilees* 15 and 1QS 3–4 show, it was quite possible for human wickedness to be ascribed to the agency of spirits leading people astray and also ultimately ascribed to God. Best and Robinson both rightly see that there are different views of evil to be found in contemporary literature, but fail to recognise that they can be, and indeed most often are, combined in the same work. It is the failure to recognise this conjunction of views in Mark which leads to such widely divergent accounts of the Gospel.

[9] Best, 1990, 53.

[10] See the discussion, in chapter 2 above, of de Boer's different tracks of apocalyptic eschatology, and, more recently, Garrett, 1998, 19–49.

At one point, however, Best does acknowledge that there is a crack in the picture. How is it that in 4:15 Satan continues to plague the Christians, if he is already bound? Maybe, with other apocalyptic writings, Mark thought that Satan was bound only for a period and then let loose again to attack the Christian community. But Best also acknowledges that Mark may be 'inconsistent at this point'.[11] The problem moreover is not solved by Robinson's account, for he claims that the force of evil is 'conclusively broken' in the resurrection.[12] Indeed the problem 'arises in every writing which speaks both of a conclusive victory over Satan and also sees man as still under assault by evil spiritual forces'.[13] Best comments revealingly: 'The apparent inconsistency that we have found in Mark[14] would thus seem to be written into the texture of the whole New Testament, but to pursue this problem further would take us beyond our present purpose.'[15] True, if the present purpose was to find a unitary reading of Mark. But if the purpose is to understand how Mark formulates his view of the world and the 'long lasting moods' which his Gospel will encourage in his readers, this *aporia*, which equally affects two such opposed readings as those of Best and Robinson, might have proved particularly revealing of the peculiar way in which not only Mark but a whole set of writers in a particular first-century religious tradition thought about the persistence of evil in the world. For does not the fact that two such careful readers of texts can come up with such opposed readings of Mark already suggest that there is something odd here? The very existence of ideas and beliefs which are held to be important and central by the one is denied by the other, and vice versa; and now it is admitted that at one point of no small importance relating precisely to this division of opinion, neither view can achieve self-consistency. Is it not a powerful indication that Best and Robinson share an assumption which needs to be examined, namely, that the religious world-views of the time were, by and large, unitary and self-consistent? Would it not be better to admit that both interpreters have identified important aspects of the sharply contrasting mythologies with

[11] Best, 1990, 184.
[12] Robinson, 1957, 53.
[13] Best, 1990, 186, citing 1 Cor 5:5; 2 Cor 2:11; Gal 4:9; 2 Thess 2:3–10; Eph 6:10ff.; 1 Pet 5:8f.; 1 John 4:3; 5:19; Rev 12:12, as texts where the evil powers still operate, and Rom 8:38f.; Col 2:15; Eph 1:20ff.; 1 Pet 3:22; John 12:31f.; 16:11, 33; 1 John 3:8, as texts where the powers are regarded as already vanquished.
[14] Alluding to his discussion of Mark 12:36, see Best, 1990, 87–8.
[15] Best, 1990, 186.

which Mark is working and to give attention to the way in which he attempts to bring them together?

I suggest that similar changes and modulations to those which occur in the myths that underly Mark's treatment of the themes of discipleship and kinship and of sacred space, are also to be found in his treatment of the central character of his narrative: Jesus.

## Contrasting presentations of Jesus in Mark

Let me start by first sketching out the different strands in the narrative as they affect Jesus. The opening section of Mark's Gospel, as we have seen, shows certain indubitable signs of cosmological eschatology. The introduction of Satan with the Temptation narrative, and the subsequent accounts of exorcisms are clear signs that at least for part of Mark's tradition Satan was active in the world, locked in conflict with the forces of goodness, able to hold men and women in bondage and to disrupt normal modes of communication and sociability.[16] On the other hand, Jesus' proclamation of the Gospel and the fulfilment of the ages is couched in the form of a direct appeal to men and women to 'repent and believe in the Gospel'.[17] What is required is a redirection of their wills, an opening of their hearts to the new reality of God's transforming and renewing rule, and this is coupled with a call to some at least to engage themselves directly in the mission of Jesus.

Thus from the start the two elements of cosmological and forensic eschatology are interlinked. This continues in the stories of the exorcisms on the one hand and the stories of Jesus' appeal to sinners to accept his invitation and to receive the divine forgiveness on the other hand. Similar tensions are to be found in chapter 3. The parable of the kingdom

---

[16] See Watson, 1994, 247–55, for a sensitive exegesis of the Gerasene demoniac narrative, which, however, deliberately underplays the cosmological mythology for which I am arguing here.

[17] Mark 1:15. Marshall, 1989, has rightly stressed the programmatic nature of this statement. Even if he is wrong to give it *prominence* over the cosmological elements in the Gospel, there is no disputing its importance in the work. Any interpretation which fails to do justice to this element *as well*, becomes one-sided. Robinson, 1957, 77, recognises the prominence of the motif, but fails to see any tension between this and the emphasis which he wishes to place on motifs of deliverance from demonic powers. Thus he acknowledges that the deeper level of hearing which is required by the parable of the sower, is concerned with repentance and forgiveness (4:12, cf. 1:4, 15; 6:12). He concludes: 'Thus the struggle for "understanding" is the inner aspect of the eschatological struggle between Satan and God constituting the history of Jesus.' This leaves unresolved how inner and outer aspects of this struggle are related.

divided in 3.23–26 turns on a *reductio ad absurdum* of the charge that Jesus casts out devils in the name of Beelzebul.[18] *If* that were so, goes the argument, then obviously Satan's house would be divided and would be in a state of collapse. But that is evidently not the case, so the argument runs, therefore the charge against Jesus is patently absurd. The whole argument, that is to say, turns on the view which is common to both sides of the dispute, that Satan's power is still strong. But the immediately following parable of the strong man bound seems to run clean contrary to this: Jesus' exorcisms would not be possible, if Satan had not already been overcome. This for many commentators, including, as we have seen, E. Best, is the decisive point. This signals the end of Satan's power; the exorcisms are no more than 'mopping up operations'; the real battle is now for men's and women's hearts and minds, as is made clear by the narratives of Jesus' struggle with the disciples. But, as we have seen,[19] the interpretation of the parable of the sower raises real difficulties for this view.[20]

Once again, the parable of the sower and its interpretation has clearly identifiable apocalyptic traits; but the question is, what kind of apocalyptic? In particular, it bears interesting resemblance to the parable in *4 Ezra* 4:26–32. In *4 Ezra* we have allegorical discourse rather than a parable followed by allegorical interpretation. The imagery of sowing and reaping the fruits of the sowing is central, but developed differently to Mark: there are two sorts of sowing, the evil seed and the good, and two fields, one of which can come into being only when the other has vanished. The image of the sowing of evil into the first field is interpreted in terms of the sowing of evil into the heart of Adam, a theme richly developed subsequently in the notion of the evil יצר. Only when the old Adam has been replaced by the new, so the

---

[18] The conflicting nature of the arguments in the two parabolic sayings, contained in Jesus' reply to the charge of casting out devils in the name of Beelzebul, is lucidly analysed by Marcus, 1999.

[19] Above, n. 3.

[20] It is always possible to respond that there are greater difficulties with alternative views, viz. those of James Robinson; but this is to assume that there ought to be one dominant mode of discourse within the Gospel, which is precisely the view that I am opposing. It is also possible to respond that there are certain inconsistencies in Mark that are simply the result of his having retained elements in the tradition which are opposed to his main drift. This is indeed something that one has to reckon with: what I am trying to show is that there are at least two main strains of thought with which Mark is in dialogue (regardless of his debt to the tradition), and which form too significant a part of his realm of discourse to be regarded as purely accidental accretions.

implication goes, will the good seed be sown into the heart of the new Man. And then what goodness that will bring: 'Reckon this up: if one grain of evil seed has produced so great a crop of godlessness, when heads of grain without number are sown, how great a threshing floor they will fill!' (*4 Ezra* 4:31–32). The resemblances with Mark's parable of the sower and its interpretation are obvious enough; but so are the differences. In *4 Ezra* the two fields succeed each other, have respectively good and bad seeds sown in them and represent then the old and the new Adam, the turning of the ages. Mark distinguishes different types of soil which coexist, which have the same good seed sown in them and which represent different types of response to the same kind of good seed. Whether men and women bear fruit depends on their response to the word, which however is conditioned (determined?) not just by their own inner worth or character, but by factors which bear in on them: Satan, fear of persecution, the attraction of wealth, and other desires.

All of this occurs, moreover, in the context of Jesus' declaration to the disciples that they have received the mystery of the kingdom of God, whereas to those outside, everything has been given in parables to blind them, a saying whose predestinarian ring is unmistakable. What then does all this tell us about the nature of good and evil and about the triumph of the one over the other? In the first place, the time-frame of the two parables is different.[21] In *4 Ezra* the age of the old Adam must pass away before the age of the new can come into being. In Mark, the new age comes with the sowing of the seed by the sower, but it falls on both good and bad soil: the old age is still active, as is evidenced by the failure of the seed to bring forth good fruit. Whereas in *4 Ezra* evil deeds are the result of the sowing of evil seed, in Mark evil results from the failure of soil to provide adequate conditions for growth. This is open to two different interpretations. On the one hand, interpreters like Marcus stress the sense in which the different responses are conditioned: only the good ground can bring forth fruit plentifully; either you are good ground or you are

---

[21] As has been pointed out by Joel Marcus, 1986; see esp. 49–50. But is he right to suppose that the different fields in *4 Ezra* are distinguished as good and evil? Clearly those in whom the good seed has been sown are godly (4:29) and those in whom the evil seed has been sown are godless, but does that imply that they could be distinguished as good and evil *before* the sowing? That would seem to suggest that the first Adam was created evil, which would make *4 Ezra* even more eccentric than is usually suggested.

not.[22] Similarly, the 'poor' soils stand for various forms of subjection under which those who hear the word, but fail to respond stand. Either they are directly constrained by Satan or by his agents, persecution, the cares of the world, or love of wealth.[23] But this at odds with Mark 4:10–12, where it is the parables which are the means whereby God hardens people's response to his revelation.[24]

On the other hand, this is not the only way to read the parable. We can understand the mystery of the kingdom which is given to be the mystery of the coming of the Lord on his way to restore the fortunes of his people, as in Isaiah 40. Those who respond freely and fully to this message will be the ones who bear good fruit, who become faithful servants of the new kingdom; those who allow themselves to be distracted by the difficulties of the way will 'fall by the wayside'. This corresponds to the threefold injunction to hear, at Mark 4:3, 9, 23. It does justice to some elements in the parable, as it chimes in well with the exhortatory tone of much of the rest of the Gospel; it stumbles, at least as a wholly satisfactory reading of the interpretation, on the reference in 4:15 to Satan 'taking away the word' from them. This is not the language of response, but of demonic agency. Again one is led to conclude that there are conflicting voices in the text, which are reflected by different recent scholarly interpretations.

Jesus' actions throughout the first section of the Gospel can be seen again from different perspectives. On the one hand, he is the strong man who, as Robinson argued, binds Satan and launches a sustained assault on his demons. On the other hand, he is the one who announces the good news of the Gospel, who goes along the way of the Lord to bring restoration to Zion. He commissions disciples, teaches the people and leads them to Jerusalem, where however as we have seen, the final drama subverts the Isaianic notion of the coming of the glory of the Lord to Zion.

---

[22] 'Only the one who, in terms of the parable of the sower, is good soil will be addressable, will be able to hear; only the one to whom God has given ears can hear.' Marcus, 1984, 562.

[23] See Marcus, 1984, 556–67.

[24] This is Best's argument against Robinson; see n. 5 above. There is, however, no difficulty in understanding how these two views can be made compatible with each other. If, as in 1QS 3–4, it is God who appoints Satan to afflict and lead astray certain people, then their 'hardening', though effected by demonic spirits, is still ultimately the work of God.

Strongly apocalyptic elements may equally be found in the Markan apocalypse in chapter 13. This presents a catalogue of 'signs' of the end: wars, divisions, persecutions, leading up to the abomination of desolation and culminating in the coming of the Son of Man to gather in the elect 'from the four winds, from the ends of the earth to the ends of heaven' (13:27). But even though there is no doubting the apocalyptic character of the passage, nor indeed the strongly predestinarian nature of some of the language, there are also elements here which do not fit simply into a cosmological dualist framework. In the first place, there are omissions. We hear about angels in heaven and about the Son of Man sending out his angels, but we do not hear of war between the angels, nor indeed of Satan and his forces at all. Again, though this is a passage which contains strongly deterministic language, it also contains a great deal of moral exhortation, principally to be on one's guard. Those who are chosen are to remain steadfast, to be sure that they are not in any way misled by false prophets and messiahs, and above all to watch.

One can draw out from all this two rather different stories which are interwoven in Mark's Gospel. In the first story, which is developed in dialogue with the Isaianic tradition of restorationist eschatology, Jesus comes to follow the way of the Lord, announcing the good news of the fulfilment of the ages, and the coming of the kingdom. He calls people to repent of their past sins and to believe the good news that God is now sending his messenger to proclaim the restoration of his people, an end to their time of trial and punishment. He calls disciples who are to be with him, to receive his teaching about the kingdom of God, and to proclaim it to all peoples. He demonstrates the power of God's forgiveness in his healings and in his invitation to sinners and outcasts to join him. His message is directed to all, to follow him, to take up their cross, to lose their lives in order to save them. Those who follow will enter the new world of the Messiah Son of God, will be renewed in faith and obedience, will think the things of God, and will save their souls. These are the ones whom the Son of Man will uphold when finally he comes to judge the world. Here are all the elements of a restorationist eschatology which sees the root of human suffering as lying in human sin and the divine punishment which it incurs, and which looks to the restorative action of God which will renew his people and bring blessing to the nations, in so far as they respond to his message of salvation. It too looks to a final judgement when all will receive their due reward.

The second story strikes a darker note. Jesus comes into a world which is ruled over by Satan; he confronts him at his Temptation, and engages in conflict with Satan's demons in his exorcisms. He calls whom he will out of the darkness and blindness of this world and initiates them into the secret mysteries of God's dealings with the world. They are the ones who have been chosen to participate in the new world, which will come into being when God's kingdom is finally established and the Son of Man comes to gather in his elect. All the others are 'outside' and are blinded by Jesus' teaching in parables. This blinding occurs through the agency of Satan, who either directly or through the intermediaries of persecutions and temptations of various sorts stifles the word when people hear it. The disciples, too, are led astray by Satan and misunderstand the meaning of Jesus' miracles because their hearts are hardened; they deny and betray him. Nevertheless, they will endure to the end and, with the significant exception of Judas, will be saved.

Again we have all the elements of a cosmological, revolutionist eschatology: the roots of sin lie in the demonic invasion of the world and the possession of men and women. Jesus comes to destroy Satan and to rescue whom he will from his grasp. He gathers around him a community of the elect who will be the heirs to the new world at the end of time; meanwhile, in the overlapping of the ages (which is Mark's special modulation of eschatology), they are to undergo suffering and persecution.

So much for the very broad outlines of Mark's narrative, themes, which of course are interwoven into a single narrative line in Mark. How do they spring into relief when they are developed more fully in relation to Mark's understanding of who Jesus is and what he did? Here for sake of convenience, we shall need to consider first the terminology which Mark deploys to refer to Jesus; and then, second, to look at the way in which the understanding of Jesus' power is developed in Mark's narrative.

## Mark's titles for Jesus

Mark has woven titles for Jesus into his narrative: Son of God, Son of Man, Son of David, Messiah, which serve the dual function of locating Jesus within a certain cultural form of discourse relating to the understanding of Jewish history and the nature of God's dealings with his people *and* of providing an opportunity for Mark to manipulate that understanding. Key among these titles are those which introduce the Gospel: Christ and Son of God, to which must also be added the title Son of Man, which at significant points qualifies those notions.[25]

While the topic of Messianic beliefs at the time of the writing of the Gospels is a complex and contested one, it is generally recognised that there was considerable fluidity in the notion at that time.[26] Of particular interest is the suggestion, most recently by L. H. Schiffman, drawing on the work of G. Scholem, that there were two poles of Jewish Messianism, one 'restorative', the other 'utopian'.[27] The restorative strand hopes for the reform of the present age by the re-establishment of the Davidic kingdom; the utopian looks for a more decisive, divine intervention which will do away with the present age and usher in a new one. He concludes a survey of the Qumran literature: '[t]hose texts which espouse the Davidic Messiah tend toward the restorative. They therefore emphasise much more the prophecies of peace and prosperity, and do not expect the cataclysmic destruction of all evil. The more catastrophic, utopian, or even apocalyptic tendencies usually do not envisage a Davidic Messiah'.[28]

---

[25] Most notably at 8:31 – 9:1, after Peter's confession at Caesarea Philippi, and at 14:62, at the trial before the high priest. In view of the significant debates about the meaning of this term in contemporary Aramaic, we should be cautious of treating it in the same way as Mark's other titles. It is unlikely that he was keying into – and modifying – conventional senses of the term, as he was with his other titles. On the other hand, we should also be cautious about distinguishing too sharply the ways in which Mark deploys the phrases 'Son of Man', Christ, Son of God, Son of David, etc. It is true that Son of Man is used exclusively by Jesus and that it never appears as a predicate like 'You are the Son of Man', so Juel, 1994, 94; but this does not mean that it plays no role in defining who Jesus is. Its role in 8:31 – 9:1 is precisely to qualify and correct Peter's understanding of Jesus' Messiahship. Kingsbury, 1983, 166–73, referring to Uspensky, 1973, ch. 2, helpfully makes the point that the title 'constitutes the "phraseological point of view" of Jesus', but still wishes to limit its use and function in the Gospel. It is a public title which does not 'infringe upon the motif of the secret of Jesus' identity' (171). It merely is used by Jesus to assert his authority over the Jews and to tell his disciples of the fate which he will suffer at the hands of the world. But how can one go on to say that 'it does not inform the reader of "who Jesus is"' (174), when at two important points in the narrative it clearly qualifies the title 'Christ', telling Peter that he is not the *kind* of Christ that he imagines, but one who will suffer, and telling the high priest that he is the Messiah who will come to judge him? Its obvious connections with Dan 7 add further content to the title.

[26] See Marcus, 1989, 134, n. 35, with particular reference to M. de Jonge, 1966, 147.

[27] Schiffman, 1992, 128, referring to Scholem, 1971, and Talmon, 1987.

[28] Schiffman, 1992, 129.

Schiffman provides further evidence of different tendencies within expectations in the Judaism of the first century CE. For our purposes, it is important to see in what way such tendencies are reflected in Mark's Gospel. Here a related proposal by Joel Marcus is of particular assistance.[29] Marcus proposes that we should distinguish between two contemporary senses of Messiah: the Messiah-Son-of-God and the Messiah-Son-of-David. In both these expressions the appositional phrase which qualifies the noun Messiah is used in a restrictive sense (not any Messiah, but this kind of Messiah). Thus when the High Priest asks: 'Are you the Messiah-Son-of-God?' he is asking Jesus what kind of a Messiah he is. Is he the Davidic Messiah or is he something greater? Jesus' reply does indeed suggest 'that "Son of God" (14:61) is understood in terms of participation in God's cosmic lordship (14:62; cf. Ps 110:1) . . . The Markan Jesus implies in 14:62 that he will sit at God's right hand and that he will come with the clouds of heaven . . . An approach to equality with God, then, is suggested'.[30] Such a question, together with Jesus' affirmative answer, would make sense of the consequent charge of blasphemy, which otherwise would be very strange. People may have accused Bar Kochba, when he claimed to be the messiah, of folly but not of blasphemy.

Marcus' proposal allows an interesting reading of the important christological passage in 12:35–37. Here Jesus questions the scribes' understanding of Messiahship, viz. as Messiah-Son-of-David.[31] The problem is that this Messiah's task is to re-establish the Davidic empire and '[s]uch a hope is not big enough to encompass the one who, according to Psalm 110:1, is to be at God's right hand, as he displays his might by an apocalyptic destruction of evil cosmic powers'.[32] This provides us with a further example of the way in which restorationist

---

[29] Marcus, 1989.

[30] Marcus, 1989, 139.

[31] As Marcus points out, the form of Jesus' follow-up question: πόθεν αὐτοῦ ἐστιν υἱός ('how of him is he son?') is odd and puts the emphasis on the αὐτοῦ: How is he then *his* (i.e. David's) son? Juel, 1994, 98, sees this not as a questioning of the scribes' understanding of Messiahship but as the raising by Jesus of a potential contradiction within Scripture in a form of enquiry 'familiar from rabbinic tradition'. He cites Loevestam, 1972, in support. This requires him to read Jesus' opening question as 'a shorthand substitution for the actual citation of passages such as 2 Sam 7:12–14 or Ps 89:3–4'. It is unlikely that this exchange should in context (12:38–40! and the preceding *Streitgespräche*) be read as a piece of disinterested scholarly debate with the scribes.

[32] Marcus, 1989, 137.

eschatology is de-particularised by cosmic dualist notions, even at the same time as these dualist notions are themselves being reshaped. For, as we have already observed, in Mark 13, when the final parousia of the Son of Man is described, there is at best an oblique reference to a cosmic battle and the destruction of apocalyptic powers.

Marcus' views are not representative of the majority of Markan scholars. Both Kingsbury and Juel[33] take Son of God in Mark as a messianic, royal title, identifying Jesus as the Son of David. Support for this can be found importantly in the baptism narrative where Jesus is proclaimed Son by the voice from heaven in language taken from Psalm 2, where God calls the anointed king 'my son'. Again, in the Passion narrative there is much play on the notion of kingship, in Pilate's interrogation of Jesus, in the soldiers' mocking and in the titulus on the cross. They also point out that the title 'Son of David' is used by blind Bartimaeus and by the crowds that welcome Jesus to Jerusalem. It is not difficult to see why such commentators find it difficult to imagine that 'Son of God' has a meaning distinct from 'Son of David'. Not only are the kingship associations well dispersed through the Gospel, there is an ironic treatment of the kingship notion both in the baptism and in the Passion narrative which would be lost if the royal associations of Jesus' Messiahship were unrecognised.[34] At his baptism, Jesus, who has been proclaimed as the stronger one by the Baptist, appears not as a mighty warrior, but among those who have come to repent and receive forgiveness for their sins. The king, saluted by the crowds on his entry to Jerusalem, is mocked by the soldiers and the passers-by, the chief priests and the Pharisees.

Again, there is a dilemma here. To deny that the royal associations of the Messianic title are present is to miss the irony of the narrative. On the other hand, Mark 12:35–37 poses serious problems for this view.[35] So, too, does the centurion's climactic confession of Jesus as Son of God, which can hardly be understood as a recognition of a Jewish Messiah. On the other hand, while Marcus' identification of the Son of God title as a cosmic, rather than a national title seems to me essentially right, even the Son of God title is being subverted. Jesus is not going to

---

[33] Kingsbury, 1983, 47–155; Juel, 1994, 91–105.

[34] So Juel, 1994, 97–102.

[35] As do other points: Bartimaeus refers to Jesus as Son of David when blind; the crowds who welcome Jesus, who salute the one who brings 'the kingdom of our father David' (11:10) subsequently desert him and call for his crucifixion.

engage in heavenly warfare. Moreover, it should not be taken to have totally displaced the Son of David title. Jesus' question 'how is he his son?' does not strictly imply a negative answer: 'he is *not* David's son because he is God's Son', but something more qualified, as Marcus allows: 'Jesus is not *just* the Son of David because he is the Son of God.'[36]

What is at stake here is not only a debate about the nature of the changes which are required or expected in Israel's fortunes, restoration or revolution/utopia; it is also a debate about the nature of the power which will bring about such change. Nor is it a debate conducted only in terms of two contrasted titles: Son of David and Son of God. Importantly, Mark brings into play the somewhat mysterious Son of Man title, which is the title by which Jesus qualifies others' ascriptions of Messiahship to him (8:38; 14:62), but which also runs through the narrative. If Jesus in 12:35–37 is sharply critical of the 'restorative' Messianic title, Son of David, he qualifies the High Priest's question: 'Are you the Christ the Son of the Blessed?' with a clear allusion to the Danielic Son of Man, 14:62. In this way, he gives the authoritative exposition of the 'secret' which has now been officially released to the High Priest: 'I am, and you will see the Son of Man seated on the right hand of power and coming with the clouds of heaven', citing Daniel 7:13. This is significant in two ways. On the one hand, it anchors the title 'Messiah Son of God' back into an eschatological tradition which looks forward to a dramatic reversal of Israel's fortunes, namely, that of Daniel's visions which culminate in the vindication of the Son of Man, identified as the saints of the Most High. On the other hand, it anchors the opening of the secret back into the narrative of the Gospel, where the expression Son of Man has been linked to crucial aspects of Jesus' ministry: his authority to forgive sins (2:10), his lordship over the Sabbath (2:28), the necessity of his suffering and his resurrection (8:31; 9:31; 10:33–34), and his giving of his life as a ransom (10:45). Thus, the use of the title qualifies the rejection of the restorative Messianism in 12:35–37 in the direction of a more apocalyptic hope, which is nevertheless concerned with the restoration of Israel, with the vindication of the saints of the most high, however that is to be understood. At the same time it brings the Gospel narrative fully into play, with its internal references to Jesus' ministry and death as that which defines who he is,

---

[36] Marcus, 1989, 137; my italics.

what the meaning of these titles is when predicated of Jesus. The conventional senses of these terms, that is to say, in so far as they were fixed, are to be understood, and if necessary modified, in the light of that predication. Mark's Christology, like Matthew's, is to be seen as above all narrative-Christology.[37] The nature of the power and authority which is traditionally ascribed to the Christ, and the manner of his victory over the forces which beset his people, are to be seen anew in the light of the story of the life, death and resurrection of Jesus of Nazareth. And that story in Mark is a two-stranded narrative, developed in dialogue with two competing traditions of Jewish eschatology.

*Jesus and power*

The question of power is central both to the restorationist and the revolutionist eschatologies. Both are concerned with the question of the overcoming of Israel's misfortunes, its release from subjection to alien forces, whether by the re-establishment of the Davidic kingdom or by the overthrow of cosmic powers. A glance at the terminology in Mark's Gospel indicates that both these notions of power are in play; further examination of the narrative context of such use will show the extent to which both ideas of power are being reworked.

Mark uses three key terms for power: ἰσχύς, ἰσχυρός, ἰσχύω; ἐξουσία, ἔξεστι; δύναμις, δύναμαι, δυνατόν.[38] The notion of the stronger one (ἰσχυρότερος, 1:7) is introduced early into the Gospel in John's proclamation with its direct citation of Isaiah's Way of the Lord; but the same term occurs in the Beelzebul controversy, in which Jesus is one who binds the strong man (ἰσχυρός, 3:27), where clearly the perspective is more cosmic, reaching beyond a vision of the restoration of national sovereignty.[39] But the verb ἰσχύω may also refer to human capability or incapacity: to subdue the demoniac (5:4), to cast out a spirit (9:18), to watch with Jesus (14:37). People should love God with all their strength (ἰσχύς, 12:30, 33). Jesus, by implication,

---

[37] Cf. here U. Luz's illuminating essay on Matthew's narrative Christology, 'Eine thetische Skizze der matthäischen Christologie', 1991 and Davies and Allison, 1997, 718–21.

[38] ἰσχύς (12:30, 33), ἰσχυρός (1:7; 3:27), ἰσχύω (2:17; 5:4; 9:18; 14:37), ἐξουσία (1:22, 27; 2:10; 3:15; 6:7; 11:28, 29, 33), ἔξεστι (2:24, 26; 3:4; 6:18; 10:2; 12:14); δύναμις (5:30; 6:2, 5; 6:14; 9:1; 9:39; 12:24; 13:25, 26; 14:62), δύναμαι (cf. esp. 1:40, 45; 2:7; 3:23, 24, 26, 27; 7:15, 18; 9:22, 23, 29; 10:26; 10:38, 39; 14:7), δυνατόν (9:23; 10:27; 13:22; 14:35, 36; 15:31).

[39] Cf. PGM 5, 147; 13, 203 for possible uses of ἰσχυρός as a term for Satan; BAG *s.v.*

comes not to help those who are capable (οἱ ἰσχύοντες 2:17) but those who are not, the sinners.

In a similar way, the term ἐξουσία, authority, power, freedom, denotes both Jesus' power over spirits and his authority and freedom in matters of the Law and of God's will (1:22, 27). Jesus has (divine) authority to forgive sins; he also confers on the Twelve the power to exorcise (3:15; 6:7). The key question put to him by the ruling authorities is precisely about his authority to 'do these things' (11:28). It is, as the subsequent parable of the Wicked Vineyarders makes clear, a question about his right to claim that he acts as an agent of God, and about the Jewish authorities' failure to recognise him as such. This is the culmination of questions about Jesus' authority over the Sabbath (2:24; 3:4) and the Pharisees' and the Herodians' testing him on questions about divorce and census money (10:2; 12:14).

Finally, words of the δυν- root are encountered both in contexts which discuss Jesus' engagement with the powers of darkness, notably in the Beelzebul controversy (3:23–27), and in contexts which discuss Jesus' offer of forgiveness (2:7). Herod believes, along with others, that Jesus is John the Baptist, raised from the dead, and that 'is why these powers are at work in him' (6:14). God is the one for whom all things are possible (10:27; 14:36); but so, too, they are to those who believe (9:23). Yet Jesus' power is limited in Nazareth (6:5) and mocked as he hangs on the cross (15:31).

If the language of power is thus woven into the fabric of the Gospel, what is it that Mark has to say about it? We have already seen how Mark transforms the notion of the Way of the Lord from that of a triumphal procession culminating in the return of the glory of the Lord to Zion to the somewhat pathetic story of Jesus and his 'band of bedraggled pilgrims' making their way to Jerusalem, where he meets his death and the veil of the Temple is torn. And we have just noticed the way in which the Passion narrative plays with the notion of kingship, contrasting Jesus' powerlessness and suffering with the title which Pilate gives him and which is echoed in the use of the title Son of David. Such 'sacred parody' must have its roots in a deeply traumatic experience: it is hardly possible to subvert central images of one's tradition without a powerful cause.[40] The taunting of Jesus on the cross may give some

---

[40] See the discussion of Roskies, 1984, in chapter 3 above, pp. 104–9.

pointer to this trauma. '"He saved others; he cannot save himself. Let the Christ, the King of Israel, come down now from the cross, that we may see and believe." Those who were crucified with him also reviled him' (15:31–32). Such taunts will have resonated powerfully with those Christian Jews who fell into Roman hands during the Jewish War, or indeed with those who had witnessed the appalling horrors which Nero inflicted on the Christians in Rome. In what sense could their Son of God stand between them and the powers of this world, who could inflict terrible suffering on them with apparent impunity? What kind of answer does Mark give to such searching questions?

Not, certainly, that God and his Son Jesus are powerless. The miracle stories of the first chapters, the accounts of exorcisms, the parable of the binding of the strong man, all make the claim for Jesus that he is the one who has power to defeat all disease, who can withstand and conquer the worst that the devil can do, and who can overcome the powers of nature. He can indeed provide all that his followers might ask of him. Why then does he not do so?

The answer must lie in the other strand of the narrative which is closely associated (though not exclusively so) with the Son of Man title. Jesus is the one who is baptised with sinners, who has authority to forgive, who calls sinners and eats with them, who must suffer and die, who gives his life a ransom, who acts in accord with the will of God to whom 'all things are possible'. He comes not to destroy sinners, but to call them into the kingdom of God. He calls people to repent, to hear, to think the things of God, not of men. In short, his fundamental struggle is for the human will and heart, and this cannot be won by the exercise of coercive force. On the contrary, it requires that he himself bear the brunt of the use of such force as he is 'delivered into the hands of men' (9:31) who will seize him (κρατέω: 14:44, 46, 49). It is his bearing of this onslaught by 'men' that brings the narrative to the point where the Roman centurion who has executed him makes his confession: 'Truly this man was the Son of God' (15:39). And all this is necessary (δεῖ: 8:31; cf. 9:11; 13:7, 10, 14), if he is to be raised and vindicated and to come, 'seated at the right hand of Power, with the clouds of heaven' (14:62; Dan 7:13).

That is to say, a very different understanding of power is being proposed which entails the vulnerability of those who would exercise it. It is the kind of power which is necessary to overcome the most intractable of the forces which is opposed to the will of God: human perversity, the radical evil of the human heart. That this is the main goal of Jesus' 'coming' is stated programmatically in 2:17: 'I came not to call the righteous but sinners', where the 'righteous' are equated with those who can (οἱ ἰσχύοντες), and the sinners are, by implication, those who cannot do the will of God. Again 'doing the will of God' (3:35) is what characterises those who are his true family, those who have in the full sense, heard his call and responded to it. Jesus' task is to overcome the opposition to God's will in the human heart: to bring people to repentance (1:15) and it is this task which ultimately outstrips all others, all other understandings of his mission, whether it be to bind the strong man, or to overcome the forces of disease and nature and for this a peculiar kind of power is required.

Notions of power in chapters 6–8

The theme is more fully developed in chapters 6–8, where, on the one hand, the narrative of Jesus' mighty works reaches its climax in his stilling of the storm and the feedings of the multitudes, and, on the other hand, Mark introduces, retrospectively, the narrative of John the Baptist's death, and, prospectively, the first prophecy of Jesus' death, with its rejection by Peter. The significance of this passage is brought out partly by Jesus' warning to the disciples to beware of the leaven of the Pharisees and of Herod,[41] partly by the reproof of the disciples for their lack of understanding and hardness of heart (8:17f.; cf. 4:11–13).

The warning against the leaven of the Pharisees and Herod must be read in the context of the Gospel. Clearly the Pharisees and the Herodians are portrayed as failing to understand who Jesus is, plotting to kill him (3:6), and attempting to lure him into difficulty over politically sensitive questions (12:13). But the immediate context of the saying adds further detail to this portrayal. Specifically the reference is to Herod, who is so impressed with reports of Jesus' miracles that he believes him to be John the Baptist raised from the dead (6:16). Mark however does not develop this theme but rather focuses attention on the narrative of John's death.[42] Here again Herod shows signs of

---

[41] Other authorities, p[45], W Δ Θ f[1] f[13], read Herodians (τῶν Ἡρῳδιανῶν), but this is probably a scribal assimilation to 3:6 and 12:13, where the coupling does occur, so Gnilka, 1978, 311, n. 9; Hooker, 194; Lührmann, 138.

[42] Cf. Matthew who portrays his father, Herod the king, as responsible for massacring the children in his attempt to kill the infant Jesus (Matt 2:1–18, suggesting that Antipas is a chip off the old block?) and Luke (23:6–12) who has Pilate send Jesus to Herod Antipas,

recognising John's authority, protecting him, recognising his righteousness and holiness, and hearing him with perplexity and gladness.
But in the end, he is overcome by his weakness for Herodias' daughter
and his fear of loss of honour in front of his guests. Herod becomes
the unwilling instrument of Herodias' desire to kill John.[43] Mark's
remarkable vignette portrays a man's inability to stand up to the
murderous desires of his entourage and to resist the social pressures
which are on him, even against his better, if somewhat confused,
judgement.

The reference to the Pharisees is less easy to construe. Clearly they
are portrayed as those who plot to kill Jesus. In chapter 7 they are the
subject of a fierce attack by Jesus on their hypocrisy in the interpretation
of the Law and their emphasis on laws of purity. Subsequently, they ask
Jesus for a sign, 'to test him' (8:11), and are refused.

It is important not to overinterpret the text at this point. It is clear
from Matthew and Luke's redaction of the phrase that they feel the
need to clarify something that is less than clear. Luke relates it directly
to the charge of hypocrisy, and adds a saying about the revealing of
that which is hidden (12:2–3).[44] It is the Pharisees' hypocrisy, their
secret thoughts and their inner darkness, where there should be
light, which is the butt of Jesus' attack. Matthew pairs the Pharisees
with the Sadducees, attacks them as an 'evil and adulterous generation' for demanding a sign and identifies the leaven as their teaching.
Mark's linking of the Pharisees with the Herodians (cf. 3:6; 12:13)
underscores their murderous intentions towards Jesus. The main force
of his attack is against the Pharisees' teaching on purity, where he accuses
them of 'leaving the commandment of God and holding fast the
tradition of men'. This corresponds closely to Jesus' charge against Peter,
that he 'thinks the things of men and not of God' (8:33), which earns
him the soubriquet, Satan. Here is the fundamental source of evil,

---

who mocks Jesus and sends him back to Pilate without condemning him (23:15,
suggesting that Antipas is part puzzled and intrigued by Jesus, part contemptuous of
him, cf. 3:18–20; 9:7–9?).

[43] It is important to notice that both Matthew and Luke omit this characterisation of
Herod. Luke omits the section (Mark 6:19–29) altogether. Matthew abbreviates, omitting
the motif of Herod's respect for John and suggesting instead that it was fear of the
people which held him back from executing John (14:5).

[44] Luke 12:1, referring back to Jesus' attacks on the Pharisees, 11:37–52; cf. the preceding
pericope, 11:33–36.

the corruption of the heart and mind which comes from its false orientation.[45] Those like Peter who reject the necessity of losing one's life, will indeed lose it. Setting one's mind on human things brings death; being willing to lose it, setting one's mind on the things of God,[46] brings life.[47]

The concentration on the orientation of the mind/heart recalls Mark's commentary on Jesus' sayings about purity which are given to the people after his encounter with the Pharisees in chapter 7: 'What comes out of a man is what defiles a man. For from within, out of the heart of man, come evil thoughts, fornication, theft, murder, adultery, coveting, wickedness, deceit, licentiousness, envy, slander, pride, foolishness. All these evil things come from within, and they defile a man' (7:20–23).

But there is another strand: lack of understanding of Jesus' miracles can lead precisely to such a false orientation. The Pharisees fail to understand the meaning of Jesus' miracles and seek a sign; so too the disciples fail to understand the meaning of Jesus' feeding miracles and are warned that they too are falling into the same danger.[48] What links the two pericopes, 8:11–12, and 8:13–21, is the inability on the part of

---

[45] The disjunction between φρονεῖν τὰ τοῦ θεοῦ and φρονεῖν τὰ τῶν ἀνθρώπων, 'setting one's heart on the things of God/men', recalls a number of similar disjunctions in Paul: most notably in Rom 8:5–7, where Paul contrasts setting the mind on things of the flesh and on the things of the Spirit; and in Col 3:2, where the contrast is between setting one's mind on things above and things that are on earth. The radical nature of the disjunction is clearly brought out by Paul's discussion of the consequences of the two different mind-sets in Rom 8:6–8: the mind that is set on the flesh is hostile to God (ἔχθρα εἰς θεόν); it does not submit to God's law, nor can it (οὐδὲ γὰρ δύναται: Rom 8:7).

[46] Cf. Phil 2:5: 'Have this mind among yourselves, which you have in Christ Jesus (τοῦτο φρονεῖτε ἐν ὑμῖν ὃ καὶ ἐν Χριστῷ Ἰησοῦ), and 2:6–8, the account of his self-emptying and obedience to death.

[47] Cf. Rom 8:6, where the contrast is between death and life and peace.

[48] Two main lines of interpretation are possible: either the Pharisees reveal their obduracy by asking for a sign when Jesus has already just performed exactly what they were asking for; or, in asking for a 'sign from heaven', they are asking for a special sign akin to the raining down of the manna in the wilderness, or some meterological sign (see Gnilka, 1978, 306–8, for details) by which he would prove his Messiahship. The problem with the latter view is (1) that in John 6 the feeding is compared to the manna in the wilderness; (2) that the motif of testing picks up the traditions of Israel's rebellion in the wilderness, see esp. Ps 95:10, where Israel's sin lies 'in doubting the Lord, in spite of the signs which he had performed', Hooker, 192, which makes the fault of the Pharisees their 'inability to see the power of God at work in Jesus' (Hooker, 193). On the other hand, John 6 posits only an analogy with the raining down of manna, in the course of a midrashic interpretation of the feeding narrative; the motif of testing also picks up Mark 1:13, Satan's testing in the wilderness, which at least Matthew and Luke understand as tempting

both the Pharisees and the disciples to understand the power which is at work in Jesus' miracles, though the nature of the misunderstanding is different. The Pharisees fail to recognise in Jesus' miracles evidence of the power of God; they ask for yet more dramatic divine demonstration of power, to legitimate Jesus' Messianic claims, not understanding what the true nature of his Messiahship, and therefore of divine power, is. If they understood that, then they would see his works of power (δυνάμεις), as indeed signs of his Messianic power, the nature of which will be more fully revealed in the remainder of the narrative. The disciples, similarly, fail to understand its nature and are upbraided for their hardness of heart. The passage is cryptic, both in its use of metaphor and in the form of the exchange between Jesus and the disciples. Jesus quizzes them and then leaves them to draw their conclusions. But while commentators may agree that the disciples have failed to understand the meaning of the feeding miracle, there is little agreement about the implications of Jesus' questions.[49]

---

Jesus to give demonstrations of divine power. It, therefore, seems better to read the Pharisees' demand as one for a legitimising sign of Jesus' authority through a mighty divine wonder, which is at the same time intended to expose him as a false Messiah.

[49] Quesnell, 1969, has argued for a thoroughly symbolic interpretation of Mark. The thoroughness with which he has attempted to carry this through has not encouraged others to follow, but there is certainly a case for a broadly symbolic interpretation for this pericope, which must be considered a largely Markan composition, combining, as it does, references to his two accounts of the feedings. The opening contains a minor contradiction: they had forgotten to bring any bread, though they had one loaf. This fact then leads Jesus to make a punning reference to the Pharisees and their demand for a sign, followed by a series of questions which are supposed to remove the disciples' misunderstanding, but which leave the reader mystified. Here Jesus truly speaks in riddles (cf. Mk 4:11–12, where παραβολή = riddles) which are, however, meant to be understood. A symbolic, eucharistic interpretation seems to offer a reading which is consistent with, and indeed illuminative of, the later sections of the Gospel. This is rejected by Hooker, 196, on the grounds that 'this theme is hardly prominent in Mark'. Gnilka also rejects a eucharistic reading, but allows a symbolic reading of the loaf which the disciples have brought with them: it refers to Jesus with whom is the 'Fülle des Heils', 1978, 312. Others, like Taylor, 1966, have argued that the references to the numbers of baskets left over and the different words used for baskets (6:43; 8:8) suggest that Mark is wanting to point to the Gentile mission – a point which is also made in the reference to the crumbs eaten by the dogs in the story of the Syro-Phoenician woman (7:28). Hooker (196) wants to see Jesus' quizzing of the disciples as a reminder 'of the magnitude of the miracles'. But that would suggest that Jesus shares the Pharisaic view of miracles: that they are demonstrations of impressive power. In what follows I want to suggest that a eucharistic interpretation does greater justice to Mark's treatment of the notion of power.

The riddle-like character of this particular narrative demands, I suggest, a symbolic interpretation. Already Jesus' punning reference to the leaven of the Pharisees alerts us to the allusive nature of the discourse. In referring back to the feeding miracles, Jesus stresses the breaking of bread, a feature of the feeding narratives along with taking and blessing, which carries clear eucharistic overtones.[50] The reference to the different numbers of baskets taken up does indeed remind the disciples of the extraordinary multiplication of the loaves. But Mark's point here cannot be to stress the magnitude of the miracle, as if to say that the Pharisees would accept it as a sign from heaven if only they thought about it. For that is precisely what Jesus refuses to give. It therefore seems appropriate to look for a eucharistic sense: in the breaking and multiplication of the loaves is symbolised the fruitfulness of the divine self-giving. Jesus' death, 'his blood poured out for many' (14:24), is the source of life and blessing for many.

## Jesus' victory

The peculiar character of such self-giving love is that the more it gives, the stronger and more fruitful it becomes. It is this kind of power which lies at the heart of Jesus' purpose. The miracles, then, are in a strange sense 'signs' of Jesus' Messiahship. They point beyond the sheer demonstration of the ability to overcome disease, unclean spirits and the powers of nature to a vulnerable kind of power which can overcome even the corruption of the human heart.[51]

How this victory is won is at best hinted at in the narrative of the Gospel. Jesus' vulnerability, however, is clearly illustrated. He lays himself open, by his invitation to tax-collectors and sinners to betrayal and abandonment.[52] The Pharisees' protest expresses the entirely prudent view that it is wise to set boundaries between oneself and those who are untrustworthy. The purity laws which they advocate are designed to provide just such a protective boundary for the community. The consequences of Jesus' imprudence are brought out dramatically in the narrative of Judas' betrayal of Jesus and indeed of Peter's denial. Those

---

[50] As is indeed acknowledged by Hooker, 167.

[51] Thus I agree fully with Robbins, 1976, 28, who writes: 'Evidently for Mk leaven signifies power which inflicts death upon others but refuses to internalize the meaning of suffering and death.'

[52] Cf. Mark 2:17, where καλέω should be taken in the sense of invite, and not, as in the Lukan version, in the sense of moral/religious exhortation to repentance. So, too, Hooker, 97.

closest to him are those who allow the forces of darkness to seize him and destroy him.

This is delicately brought out in the treatment of Judas in the narrative of the Last Supper. The narrative is prefaced in Mark 14 by three scenes: the plotting of the chief priests and scribes to kill Jesus, the anointing at Bethany, and Judas' agreement with the chief priests to betray Jesus. The first of these refers back indirectly to the plotting of the Pharisees and Herodians to kill Jesus (3:6). The second, with its story of the breaking of the alabaster box and the pouring out of the ointment on Jesus' head, provides a powerful metaphor of Jesus' own love which will illuminate the proclamation of the gospel in the whole world. His is a death which is costly both in the sense that it is of inestimable value for those who will receive the gospel, and that it is profoundly costly to Jesus himself. In this sense the pouring out of the ointment is an anointing of his body for its burial.

Then, in the short following scene, Judas' plan to betray him is recorded. Here, and in the immediately following account of Jesus' passover meal with his disciples, Mark's use of adjectival phrases to describe Jesus' betrayer serves to underline his intimacy with Jesus. Judas is introduced as ὁ εἷς τῶν δώδεκα,[53] stressing his membership of the group whom Jesus has called 'to be with him' (3:14). A similar adjectival phrase with the article, ὁ ἐσθίων μετ' ἐμοῦ[54] is used in Jesus' first words at the meal, where he announces that 'one of you will betray me' (14:18); and these two phrases are combined in 14:20, when Jesus answers the disciples' anxious questions: 'It is one of the twelve, one who is dipping bread into the [one] dish with me.' The forces of evil, that is to say, gain their bridgehead in Jesus' kingdom precisely through the work of one of those who has taken up and misused Jesus' offer of fellowship. And, as a final irony, Judas betrays Jesus with a kiss, whereupon the forces of darkness lay hands on him and seize him, take him into their power (καὶ ἐκράτησαν αὐτόν, 14:46).

The subsequent narrative of the trials and crucifixion of Jesus presents the drama as a conflict between two parties wielding very different kinds of power: those who seize, scourge, mock, humiliate and kill

[53] 14:10; literally: 'the one of the twelve', where the article makes the designation almost into a title.

[54] Alluding to Ps 41:9, which again emphasises the sense of intimacy: 'Even my bosom friend in whom I trusted, who ate of my bread, has lifted his heel against me.' Mark's phrase ironically recalls Jesus' call of the disciples in 3:14: ἵνα ὦσιν μετ' αὐτοῦ.

Jesus; and the one who is powerless in their hands, who is passive, silent except for his reply to the High Priest and his brief reply to Pilate. Yet, at the end, it is Jesus who is recognised as the Son of God, the representative of divine power, by the centurion, the instrument of Roman military might. The nature of this victory is not explained: the centurion simply bears witness to it.

What we are given is insight into the internal struggle that lies behind Jesus' victory. This is portrayed principally as a struggle to accept the Father's will. Just as the crucial decision for Peter and the disciples is whether they are willing to lose their lives in order to find life, so too for Jesus the key question is whether he will drink the cup which the Father offers him. Indeed, this parallelism between Jesus' and the disciples' willingness to accept God's will is brought out again in the Gethsemane narrative by the contrast between the sleeping disciples and Jesus' prayer.[55] They are tempted, just as Jesus was tempted at the beginning of the Gospel, but they are overcome by the 'flesh' (14:38). The will of God which Jesus' brothers, sisters and mother must do (3:35) is now revealed in all its terribleness.

But perhaps it is not quite correct to say that the nature of Jesus' victory is not explained. There are hints. On two occasions Jesus speaks about the cup that he must drink (10:38; 14:36). The idea of the cup which God mixes for the people or for individuals is a powerful Hebrew image for the fate which God prepares for them, whether for good (Ps 23:5; 116:13) or ill (Ps 11:6). In the latter sense it is found in Isaiah 51:17 (the cup of his wrath) and in Jeremiah 25:15 (the cup filled with the wine of anger). The literal sense of the 'cup of wrath' is of a cup of wine administered as a means of humiliation (cf. Hab 2:15: making one's neighbours drunk to 'gaze on their shame'; cf. Gen 9:20–22). The victim becomes drunk, loses self-control ('the bowl of staggering', Isa 51:17; 'a cup of reeling', Zech 12:2), behaves shamefully, exposing him/herself (Lam 4:21; Ezek 23:31–34). The shame is the greater in that the instrument of humiliation is itself a symbol of intimacy and fellowship (cf. the ewe lamb which drinks from her owner's cup, 2 Sam 12:3).

Thus the cup is a rich symbol for the humiliation which Jesus must undergo, if he accepts his Father's will. It speaks of the misuse of intimacy, which will be brought out again in the characterisation of his betrayer;

---

[55] The point is well argued by Kelber, 1976, 47–50.

it speaks of the suffering and humiliation which Jesus will undergo: being mocked and stripped and exposed (15:24) on the cross. Does it also indicate that Jesus' death is a punishment for sin which he bears for many (10:45)?

Two things tell against giving prominence to this element, which is undoubtedly present in the Hebrew notion of drinking the cup which God gives. The first is that the Greek λύτρον (10:45) means 'ransom' in the sense of redeeming a slave and is often linked with God's bringing Israel out of Egypt.[56] The emphasis is on the redemptive liberating effect of Jesus' suffering, not on his bearing of a punishment for sin. The second is that in the ensuing narrative of Jesus' arrest and crucifixion the agents of Jesus' humiliation and death are the chief priests and their associates on the one hand and the Romans on the other hand, not God. True, God is characterised as delivering Jesus up into their hands, but they are the ones who seize him and bind him and lead him away to his ordeal. God's delivering him over into their hands is not part of a legal process whereby Jesus undergoes judgement. Rather, Jesus' acceptance of the Father's insistence that he remains true to the purpose for which he has 'come' (2:17; 10:45) initiates the final confrontation between the kind of power which he represents and that which is represented by those ranged against him. His death is the consequence of that decision as indeed was already announced in 3:6. In it the kind of power and authority which he stands for is finally and fully embodied in a human life lived to the end.

## Mark's ending

This is not quite the end of the story. The final scene at the empty tomb confronts the women with the young man who gives them a message for 'his disciples and Peter' (16:7). The message is a message of reconciliation and promise to those, foremost among them Peter, who have denied and deserted him. It is a renewal of the invitation to sinners with which his public activity began (2:17). Despite all that he has suffered at the hands of his people, Jesus remains true to his calling. The women who are the recipients of this message from (beyond) the grave are terror-struck, flee from the tomb and 'say nothing to anyone'.

[56] It is often argued that Isa 53:10–12 LXX forms the background of Mark 10:45, and this is probably right, though others have suggested that Isa 43 should also be taken into account; Hooker, 249, citing Grimm, 1976. However, the Septuagint text does not deploy the notion of sin-offering, as the Hebrew text with אשם does.

This is certainly a profoundly unusual and surprising ending to a book. The language of the last verse with its employment of the terms ἔκστασις, τρόμος and φόβος (in its verbal form) may provide at least a clue to its understanding. There are a number of possible echoes in the Septuagint, though they are no more and no less than that. τρόμος occurs significantly in the LXX text of Exodus 15:15–16 where in the hymn of praise after the crossing of the Red Sea, terror and dread (φόβος καὶ τρόμος, 15:16) fall on the peoples of the Land as the Israelites are invited (παρεκάλεσας) to God's 'holy abode' (15:13) and make their way to the 'ready (ἕτοιμος) dwelling which thou, Lord, didst make, the sanctuary, Lord, which thy hands made ready.'[57] This fear of the godless in Zion is reflected in Isaiah 33:14 and 63:19–64:1,[58] a passage which is echoed in Mark's account of Jesus' baptism.[59] In its context in Isaiah it refers to God's descent from the heavens to 'make thy name known to thy adversaries, and that the nations might tremble at thy presence!'

Similar uses can be found quite widely of the expression ἔκστασις κύριου referring to the fear of the nations at the power of the Lord.[60] Alongside this, the noun on its own is used of the trances which fell on Adam at the creation of Eve and on Abraham before receiving the prophecy of Israel's oppression in Egypt and subsequent release.[61] Both τρόμος and ἔκστασις are combined on occasion with φόβος.

It is clearly important not to press the significance of these possible echoes too far. The senses which come closest to actual scriptural citations in Mark are those connected with the Isaianic Way of the Lord (with its strong correlate in the Exod 15 hymn). Here the emphasis is firmly on the awe which God's redemption of his people inspires in the nations. In this light, the women's fear is like the fear of those who look on as God redeems his people. But, as with many echoes, the fit is not very precise. Strictly speaking, the redeemed would have to be Jesus, who is

[57] 15:17, see Horbury, 1996, 210, and the discussion above in chapter 2, 32–3.
[58] ἐὰν ἀνοίξῃς τὸν οὐρανόν, τρόμος λήμψεται ἀπὸ σοῦ ὄρη, καὶ τακήσονται, ὡς κηρὸς ἀπὸ πυρὸς τήκεται.
[59] Though, as Marcus, 1992, 49–50, has argued, Mark is closer to the Masoretic text at this point. Marcus does believe, however, that Mark also draws on the LXX text (63:14) in his reference to the Spirit at the baptism.
[60] 1 Sam 1:15; 2 Chron 14:13; 15:5; 17:10; 20:29; Zech 14:13.
[61] Gen 2:21; 15:12; cf. 27:33 of the ἔκστασιν μεγάλην σφόδρα which came over Isaac when he learnt of Jacob's deception (discerning the strange hand of God in the action?).

rescued from death. Yet Jesus is himself the redeemer, the λύτρον ἀντὶ πολλῶν; the text is also about the redemption of the disciples and Peter, who have denied him, and indeed contains an implicit word of hope for the women. The new redemptive power is revealed in the invitation to follow him to the Galilee, the offer of renewed discipleship and association. God has worked his redeeming act, not just on Jesus, but on his faltering brothers and sisters, who are invited to start all over again. So too, whether Mark intended it or not, we can just catch a faint echo of the visions of Adam and Abraham. The ἔκστασις which falls on the women hints at the motifs of creation and promise which are associated with the forefathers. Here, as the women flee in awe at the redemptive power of God, is also, *sub contrario*, the moment of revelation, the giving of the mystery of the new creative power of God which will restore his glory and inaugurate a new world, a new family of those who do the will of God.

## Conclusion

It is not easy to give a coherent account of Mark's story, nor indeed to give an account of the way in which Mark sought to communicate his new vision of the world and of human destiny and identity through his narration of the life and death of Jesus. In one sense what he has done is to draw on themes and motifs from his contemporary culture: themes of renewal and restoration, of the age-old conflict between good and evil and its final resolution; and to draw on them in constructing the enormously powerful central symbol of the crucified Christ, a figure of power characterised most succinctly as one 'who should suffer many things and be despised' (9:12, lit. treated as nothing: ἐξουδενηθῇ).[62] It is this shamed figure of no value or honour who is the instrument of God's restoration of his people.[63] Yet, while the story undoubtedly reaches

---

[62] This verb, found only here in the New Testament (though its cognate form ἐξουθενέω is more common), occurs quite frequently in the LXX, notably in Ps 22:6, 24 (LXX 21:7, 25) and also in 1 Sam 8:7, where the people are said to reject God from being king over them, 1 Chron 15:29, where Michal despises David for dancing before the ark, and 2 Chron 36:15–16: 'The LORD, the God of their fathers, sent persistently to them by his messengers, because he had compassion on his people and on his dwelling place; but they kept mocking the messengers of God, despising his words, and scoffing at his prophets, till the wrath of the LORD rose against his people, till there was no remedy.'

[63] Jesus' dishonouring occurs most obviously in his mocking and in his shameful death, which is inflicted on him by his human enemies; but in the motif of the cup which Jesus has to drink at the Father's behest, Mark suggests that this shame is willed on

its climax in the drama of the crucifixion, the disciples' betrayal, denial and flight, Jesus' struggle in the Garden, his rejection by his people, his abandonment and shame on the cross, the 'distant strains of triumph' of the centurion's confession and the message of the young man at the tomb, many strands lead to that final narrative achievement and serve to give it its ironic and parodic force.

For Jesus is presented in the earlier part of the Gospel in terms of many of the key themes of Jewish apocalyptic eschatology: the hope for a restoration of the Temple, for the triumphal return of the exiles and the dispersed people of Israel, for a Messiah to establish once again the kingdom of David and restore Israel's former glory; even more radical hopes, for the expunging of Satan and his cohorts from the world, for divine intervention and subjection of all the forces of darkness to the Messiah-Son-of-God, for a new heaven and a new earth. And in the earlier chapters he appears to fulfil such expectations richly. He does battle in the desert with the devil; exorcises the unclean spirits; he teaches with authority and, like David, arrogates to himself and his companions a certain freedom over against the Law (2:23–28). He is recognised by the suffering people as Son of David. His power over disease and the threatening forces of nature is apparently unlimited. He gathers together a group of followers to lead them to Jerusalem along the 'way of the Lord', which John has announced. He proclaims God's forgiveness to those afflicted with disease and even extends an open invitation to sinners.

Yet already such preaching provokes deep opposition. His consorting with social outcasts and his freedom in matters of the Law strike a warning note among the leaders of the people, who do not recognise his miracles as authenticating signs. But this is as nothing to the subversion of these themes which occurs in the later part of the narrative. Here the hopes for the return of the people and the restoration of Zion are parodied in the narrative of Jesus' progress to Jerusalem and his rejection and crucifixion. The parable of the wicked vineyarders marks the rejection of God's son by the leaders of Israel and points to the creation of a new community of those who follow Jesus; Jesus' death outside the city and the rending of the veil of the Temple signals the

---

him by the Father and willingly accepted by the Son. This is the way that the Son of Man has to go; this is the means by which the Lord will bring victory and redemption to his people.

end of hopes for the restoration of Mount Zion. Only the centurion's confession and the message at the empty tomb tentatively suggest how such hopes may be reborn and reshaped.

Lévi-Strauss, in a telling analogy, has suggested that the pre-scientific thought of the peoples he studied was a form of *bricolage*.[64] In France a *bricoleur* is someone who, unlike the trained tradesman who accepts only work for which he is properly equipped and trained, will undertake a variety of jobs working with whatever materials are to hand. Materials which may previously have served some quite different purpose will be pressed into service for the job in hand. The same object, say a cube of oak, 'could be a wedge to make up for the inadequate length of a plank of pine or it could be a pedestal – which would allow the grain and polish of the old wood to show to advantage'.[65] The analogy serves to bring out the difference between the *esprit de système*, epitomised in the work of philosophers like Spinoza who seek to give an intellectually consistent account of reality with concepts forged specially for that purpose, and the work of mythical narrators like Mark who work within a fairly tightly constrained tradition from which they must select the themes and motifs, with possibly quite sharply opposed senses, out of which to construct their symbolic worlds. It is perfectly possible to dismantle any given piece of *bricolage* and to attempt to identify the original

---

[64] 1972, 16–33, esp. 19: 'The elements which the "bricoleur" collects and uses are "preconstrained" like the constitutive units of myth, the possible combinations of which are restricted by the fact that they are drawn from the language where they already possess a sense which sets a limit on their freedom of manoeuvre. And the decision as to what to put in each place also depends on the possibility of putting a different element there instead, so that each choice which is made will involve a complete reorganisation of the structure, which will never be the same as one vaguely imagined nor as some other which might have been preferred to it.'

[65] Lévi-Strauss, 1972, 18–19. Best makes a similar point when he describes Mark's compositional technique as the making of a collage, 1985, 128, or even, 1983, 121–2, as a 'composer who brings together folk-songs or sea-shanties to make a new unity. Just as each of the original tunes is clearly recognisable, but each has been subtly changed to accommodate it to what precedes and follows, so Mark created a new and exciting whole out of the material available to him in the tradition. He has conserved material, but it would be wrong to say that this was what he primarily set out to do. He has used the tradition, but used it creatively'. The question which all these analogies raise is how different are the senses and functions of the original constituent parts both among themselves and to the purpose to which they are being put. The sea-shanties analogy suggests a rather more harmonious relationship than what I think is the case with Mark, where he seems to combine elements which express fundamentally opposed views of the world. That of the *bricolage*, or indeed the *collage*, perhaps helps to bring this out more clearly.

function of the constituent parts; but the new assemblage has its own unity which both respects the quality of the components and their potential to fulfil a new role, and also freely co-opts them into some quite different purpose.

So too with Mark. He embarks upon a task of great novelty: the narrative of the life and death of Jesus, the Messiah. Whatever models he may have had for the task, they were at best approximate to his particular needs.[66] Contemporary 'Lives' would have provided some parallels; Jewish narrative would have suggested certain narrative styles and techniques; much of his art may have come from folk traditions of storytelling. But where did he get his material from, the pieces of used timber, the nails, the fittings for his 'door-frame'? On the one hand, it appears, he had access to a rich collection of stories, circulating in the early Christian communities about Jesus' life and death, material which included both straight narrative and also discourse, controversy stories, sayings of Jesus, parables, and so on. But he could also draw on a wider tradition of scriptural motifs and ideas, of contemporary expectations and beliefs about the Messiah, about the resolution of Israel's problems and indeed of the world's predicament. As we have seen, in part at least, he was able to fit these together in ways which were innovative, ironic, even subversive. Incorporating motifs like the 'way of the Lord' into the narrative of a religious leader who was executed by a combination of the religious leaders of his people and the foreign occupying forces, significantly changes their sense, and with that the hopes and the expectations that were originally associated with them.

There is another, reciprocal, point. Incorporating the narrative material about Jesus into a set of mythical elements which include motifs and ideas expressing contemporary eschatological expectations and beliefs sheds light on the meaning of the narrative material too. Our view of the central drama with its crucified figure is forever shaped by the powerful expectations of those times, expectations which, as we have seen, may vary widely both as to the account which they offer of the human predicament and of the manner in which it is to be resolved. Here another aspect Lévi-Strauss' use of the analogy of the *bricoleur* may be useful. Lévi-Strauss uses it to bring out the sharp difference between the pre-modern ways of thinking and the *esprit de système* of modernity. Unlike the systematician, who wants to think things through

---

[66] See my introduction to Schmidt, 2001.

to first principles, and so to give a coherent and self-consistent account of things which is firmly grounded in some overall world-view, the 'primitive thinker' simply takes traditional motifs, however contradictory they may be, and forges out of them a view of the world which, while it can be analysed into contradictory parts,[67] nevertheless provides an acceptable unity out of which communities could live and construct their own worlds.

Lévi-Strauss, for the most part at least, is working with communities much less touched by the *esprit de système* than were the communities of the Mediterranean at the turn of the era. We have only to look to Philo for an example of someone who with great rigour attempts, at least, to bring everything back to the first principles of his Platonic world-view, which itself lacks nothing in rigour and self-consistency. By contrast, the Evangelists, not just Mark but Matthew too, clearly saw nothing odd in drawing on ideas that formed parts of quite sharply opposed world-views. This is not to say that they do not attempt to resolve those tensions, to give weight to one view or the other. Mark's focus is, I believe with Best, ultimately on the struggle for the human will as the crucial site of renewal and restoration. Nevertheless, as commentators as perceptive as Robinson, Marcus and Garrett have been at pains to point out, the alternative view that the ultimate source of evil lies outside of human control, that human beings are subject to dark powers which they themselves are powerless to control, is never far away.

Arguing in this way is not to say that this is a particular characteristic of Mark, or indeed of the Gospels or even of early Christianity. On the contrary, this is a widespread characteristic of the ancient texts which lie behind the emerging earliest forms of Christianity. Later Christianity would be greatly influenced by Philo and neo-Platonism and itself embrace the *esprit de système*. The continuing lack of communication between biblical scholars and systematic theologians is part of a general failure to understand the nature of such earlier modes of thinking, of the ways in which mythological narratives mediate between opposing world-views. It is not enough to say that the ancients do not seem to be aware of the differences, that they move quite freely between one kind of eschatology and another, or between eschatology and ethics. We

---

[67] The Beelzebul controversy, analysed above, pp. 162–3, gives a wonderfully clear example of this.

need rather to try to understand the rules of the very different game to that of the systematician that they were playing. Analysing the constituent parts of the *bricolage* is one step towards that; attempting to understand their interplay and weighting, the other.

# 6

# Church of disciples

## Introduction

When we turn to Matthew, the change of mood and context is unmistakable. Questions of the well-being and the maintenance of his community flood in; questions of self-definition are framed as questions about the identity of his – existing – community over against the Jews with 'their' synagogues and scribes. We enter the world of a small community engaged in a visceral struggle for its survival (there is blood in these pages and blood will flow from them down the centuries), yet also still very much in process of forging its own cultural codes.

Clearly we are entering the second generation of Christianity. Matthew, as he writes, already has Mark's Gospel before him and he uses it with great respect, sometimes following the line of the narrative with minor editorial changes; sometimes picking up phrases and sentences and weaving them into his own substantially new narrative; sometimes leaving the Markan narrative on one side for long stretches and then returning to the point where he had left it. Mark's Gospel is a given for Matthew. This is not to say that he cannot use and mould it to his own literary and theological purposes, but it is nevertheless part of his literary and theological tradition, which forms him and with which he interacts.

Mark is, however, not the only part of his tradition. Like Mark, Matthew owes an enormous debt to the Hebrew Scriptures (however they may have been mediated to him textually); unlike Mark, he is also indebted to a Christian tradition, Q, which preserved and meditated on dominical sayings and on which he drew freely for his own major literary creations, his discourses.

We sense too a change of atmosphere in the community. If Mark's community was living under threat of persecution and/or extermination in a fierce war, Matthew's community is fighting at a different level. What is at stake is its own standing within the tradition of the Bible. It is in direct competition for a place within that tradition with the forms of Judaism which are emerging after the destruction of the Temple through the developments in Jamnia and elsewhere. Mark's community was torn between seeing itself as a community totally distinct from the rest of humanity and seeing itself as fulfilling the promises of God to Israel in the Scriptures. Are they a people who have been snatched out of darkness and constituted anew as the family of God, or are they the chosen agents of God as he brings his purposes for his people, and through them for all people, to fulfilment?

For Matthew, there are similar tensions, but they are expressed somewhat differently. On the one hand, he wants to emphasise the roots of the Christian *ecclesia* in the Jewish tradition. He stresses Jesus' descent, as the Son of David, from Abraham; he links Jesus' story with that of Moses; he insists that Jesus fulfils the Law, both in his actions and in his teaching. The church is, above all, the company of the followers of Jesus. On the other hand, he wishes to emphasise his community's distinctiveness over against the Jewish community. Not only does he refer to 'their' synagogues (4:23; 9:35; 10:17; 12:9; 13:54; 23:34) and scribes (7:29); he insists that the disciples' righteousness must exceed that of the scribes and Pharisees; he emphasises the sense in which Jesus' teaching transcends that of the tradition (5:21–48); and finally his Jesus declares that the Kingdom of God will be taken away from the Jewish leaders and given to another people (21:43). On the one hand, that is to say, he appears to want to root the Christian community as deeply and firmly as possible in the tradition of Abraham and the Jewish people; on the other hand, he makes a sharp division between the church and the synagogue, such that it is difficult to see how the rift could be healed.

There is a similar set of tensions in the way Matthew portrays the relationship of the Christian community with the world around it. It might seem, on the one hand, as if the church was called out of the world to be entirely separate from it. The disciples, who are the model for all future believers,[1] are called to leave their fathers, and to follow Jesus without further ado. The abruptness of the break is underscored in 8:21–22 when the would-be disciple is not allowed even to go back and bury his father. In the discipleship discourse in chapter 10, Jesus

---

[1] Ctr. Strecker, 1971, 191–8, who argues that Matthew 'historicises' Mark's Gospel, and this is borne out in his treatment of the disciples, who are identified with the twelve. As Luz, 1971, has argued, Matthew is not interested in the notion of eye-witnesses as guarantors of the tradition; moreover, the fact that there is no account of the creation of

again insists that his followers subordinate all ties of blood to their loyalty to him (10:34–37). Like Mark, Matthew emphasises that Jesus' true family consists of those who do the will of 'his heavenly father' (12:50) He even seems to suggest that they are to discard any notion of human fatherhood (23:9). (This is in marked contrast with the emphasis that Matthew elsewhere puts on Jesus' own genealogy and with his wish to stress the continuities between Christian teaching and the Law and the prophets.) On the other hand, while such emphasis on the break with family and kinship ties might seem to indicate that Matthew is moving in the direction of a very sectarian form of religious community, where only those who fulfil the strict requirements of the community can 'enter the kingdom of heaven', there are other strands within the narrative which point in contrary directions. The call to discipleship is addressed to all. Jesus' teaching on the Mount is given to the disciples *and the crowds* (5:1; see 7:28). The disciples are sent out to make disciples of all nations. The elements of secrecy, of exclusivity, and of predestination, which in Mark seemed to encourage a sectarian outlook, have receded into the background. Our task now is to see how these various elements in Matthew's Gospel combine to give a sense of Christian identity, like but unlike that of Mark. What kind of community would such texts have encouraged? In what sense can it still be described as sectarian? What were its relations to Judaism?

## Matthew's redaction of received traditions about discipleship

Mark's community, we have been arguing, was one torn between a strong sense of its distinctiveness – over against the whole of the rest of creation, which lay under the sway of Satan and his angels – and a sense of its special role within God's purposes for his world, as the true family of the Messiah Jesus, as those who were to continue his task of proclaiming the gospel of the fulfilment of the ages. This tension was expressed in the different ways in which discipleship was

---

the Twelve shows how little Matthew thinks 'historically' (Luz, 1989, 175). Furthermore, Matthew's use of μαθητεύω (13:52; 27:57; 28:19) is a clear indication of his wish to include his readers in his story by allowing them to identify with the disciples. This is obviously also in tension with the emphasis that Matthew elsewhere places on genealogy and physical descent. The point is that for Matthew the disciples have an exemplary function for all believers, and this is reinforced by the pericope about the true family of God. In this respect Matthew's universalism transcends not just the boundaries of Judaism but all ethnic divisions.

presented, partly as a conversion from darkness to light, partly as a commissioning to a specific task within the purposes of God. How much of this is reflected in Matthew's handling of his tradition, which includes, not just Mark, but also Q with its mission charge (Luke 10:1–16), and its instruction to the disciples (12:39–46, 57–59; 13:28–35)?

In the first place, Matthew has dismantled Mark's central section on discipleship, 8:22 – 10:52, which is framed by the two narratives of the healing of the blind men, this despite the fact that he is actually following Mark quite closely at this point. He has omitted the healing of the blind man of Bethsaida[2] and created his own discourse in chapter 18,[3] and inserted the beginning of a major new section of the Gospel at 19:1, as Jesus moves from Galilee to Judaea. Thus, Mark's section on discipleship with its strong images of giving sight to the blind and its sub-themes of the disciples' stumbling growth in understanding, is reshaped into two sections, the first of which has its climax in Peter's confession of Jesus and his renaming and investing with the power of the keys (followed by Jesus' foretelling his sufferings and the transfiguration); the second of which is a community discourse, attending to central matters of discipline and relations within the church.[4] As a

---

[2] As he has the healing of the deaf and dumb man, Mark 7:31–37. However he has compensated for the loss of the blind man of Bethsaida by doubling the number of blind men healed near Jericho (20:29–34//Mark 10:46–52, the healing of Bartimaeus) and has included a further double healing (9:27–31) in his two chapters on Jesus as the Messiah of deed, chapters 8–9. Matthew thus abandons Mark's metaphoric use of the stories to make a statement about the nature of discipleship and instead takes them as stories which illustrate Jesus' compassion and miracle-working power (though certainly 9:29 makes a point about the blind men's faith). This is not unlike the way that the story of the healing of the centurion's servant (Matt 8:5–10//Luke 7:1–10) has been reworked in the similar story of the healing of the official's son (John 4:46–54). In both cases the emphasis on faith/discipleship has been subordinated to the focus on Jesus' miracle-working powers which are heightened, in Matthew by doubling (quadrupling, if one takes both stories as versions of Bartimaeus' healing) the number healed, in John by setting the healing at a distance.

[3] One of the five major blocks of discourse which Matthew clearly signals, both with its opening with the formal approach of the disciples to Jesus (for a fuller discussion, see Davies and Allison, 1, 410–11, and Keegan, 1982) and by the characteristic closure: 'when Jesus had finished these sayings . . .' (7:28; 11:1; 13:53; 19:1; 26:1).

[4] I offer no opinion as to the place of these chapters within the Gospel as a whole. Where Matthew follows Mark as closely as he does here, it is difficult to discern a clear overall pattern: the discourse in chapter 18 is, however, clearly set off from the rest, as is the move from Galilee to Judaea. Luz may be right to suggest that Peter's confession and the promises to him mark the end of a section which sees the transition from Israel to the

result, Mark's section which portrays discipleship principally as a transition from darkness to light, is now presented as a call to membership in a community of faith, schooled in Jesus' teaching, founded on Peter's confession, with its own group norms and discipline.

Further shifts in emphasis can be seen by considering the way that Matthew handles the Markan narrative of the call of the disciples, 4:18–22//Mark 1:16–20. There are few changes of substance in the narrative itself; for the most part Matthew simply tidies up and makes the two stories more closely equivalent. But what he then does is to link the call narrative almost directly into the Sermon on the Mount.[5] After the briefest summary account of Jesus' teaching, preaching and healing activity, and of the crowds which he attracts, the disciples are told in no uncertain terms what their calling is and how it is to be exercised. Their righteousness is to exceed that of the scribes and the Pharisees.

It is interesting to consider in more detail how Matthew is treating the call narrative of 4:18–22. Like Mark's narrative, it bears close resemblance to the story of Elisha's call and highlights the brothers' leaving their nets and their boats and their father (in the second section). It focuses attention on the authority of Jesus' call, to which the brothers respond with immediate and unquestioning obedience. In this respect, there is a contrast with the Elisha story, where Elisha asks permission to take his leave of his parents before killing his oxen and joining the prophet.[6] There is a further contrast with the Elisha story: whereas Jesus makes his call of the disciples without any prompting, Elisha's choice as Elijah's successor is made by God and communicated first to Elijah.

This close linking of the disciples' calling with Jesus' authority is further underscored by the summary which immediately follows. The

---

congregation (Luz, 1990, 381, n. 2). Davies and Allison, 1988, 71–2, think that the transition comes from chapter 14 onwards, with the emergence of the Peter and the feeding narratives which prefigure the Eucharist.

[5] Matthew follows Mark to 1:20, omits 1:21–38, (though he subsequently, at 8:14–17, gives his own version of the healing of Peter's mother-in-law and the summary of 1:32–34), adapts the summary in 1:39 and, then after the whole of the Sermon on the Mount, returns to Mark 1:40. Thus the full three chapters of the Sermon are effectively an insertion in between Mark 1:39 and 40 and function as a commentary on the disciples' call, though Matthew, by linking the Sermon to the crowds, also makes it clear that Jesus' teaching is not for the disciples only, but for all who will hear.

[6] There is ambiguity in the MT as to whether he actually does go back; the LXX and Josephus, *Ant* 8:354, make it clear that he was allowed to take leave of his parents.

disciples are drawn into the teaching, preaching and healing ministry of Jesus, which meets with extraordinary success.[7] Great crowds flock to follow him. We are, that is to say, given a dramatic picture of the kind of life to which they are called as followers of Jesus. They are to be linked with Jesus' work as teacher, preacher and healer; they are to become part of a great band of followers of Jesus.[8]

This twofold aspect of their calling – their linking with Jesus and their becoming part of a band of followers – is again underlined in the opening two verses of the Sermon itself, where Jesus in view of the crowds goes up on to the Mountain and his disciples come to him. It is indeed not clear from these opening verses whether Jesus' teaching is given solely to the disciples (at this stage presumably only the four who have just been called) or to the crowds as well. However, 7:28–29 makes it abundantly clear that he was teaching both the crowds and the disciples.

What is now striking is the way that the whole Gospel becomes a commentary on discipleship. This is achieved by the simple device of tying the Sermon on the Mount into the call-narrative as its commentary and also of tying the subsequent discourses in the Gospel to the Sermon on the Mount, in such a way that the Sermon is itself only the beginning of what Jesus has to say about discipleship.[9] In this way, Matthew can emphasise different aspects of discipleship at different points of the Gospel. The prominent motif in the call-narrative of the breaking of family ties will be developed in the discipleship discourse of chapter 10 (and also in 8:21–22 and 23:9; cf. 12:46–50; 13:53–58); but what is offered by way of introduction in the Beatitudes is at once a characterisation of discipleship and an indication of its goals.

It is clearly not possible in a monograph such as this to treat all aspect of Matthew's presentation of Jesus' teaching. For our purposes let us focus our questions on the topics which relate directly to discipleship. Specifically, I shall look at the understanding of discipleship which emerges from the Beatitudes and at the notion of righteousness which runs through the Sermon on the Mount.

---

[7] At least among the Jewish population of the region: in 4:24–25 Matthew omits Idumaea and the regions around Tyre and Sidon from Mark's account in 3:7–8. He does retain the Decapolis, perhaps because it had a substantial Jewish population; see Luz ad loc.

[8] To this point they are referred to only as those who follow Jesus, which is the same phrase which is used for the crowds. Only at the opening of the Sermon on the Mount will they be called 'disciples'.

[9] See n. 3 above.

## Discipleship and the Beatitudes

Let us consider first a number of questions relating to the Beatitudes.

1. What is the 'logic' of the Beatitudes? Are they declarative statements which set forward certain modes of behaviour which will be rewarded? Are they, that is to say, entrance requirements for the kingdom? Or do they announce God's favour and blessing on certain classes of people, distinguished not by their moral performance but by the fate that has befallen them: the poor, the hungry, those who weep?

2. When will the rewards, the blessings, be apportioned? Will they be apportioned in this life? Or at some future point – the final judgement, the turning of the ages?

3. To whom will the promised benefits be given? To those who measure up to certain standards? To those who fall into certain categories by virtue of circumstance and misfortune?

4. Are the recipients individuals or members of a group? What relation do they bear to the people of Israel to whom God's promises have been made? Are they to be given to certain individuals in virtue of their membership of a given group, the *ecclesia*? Or is the conferring of these blessings and benefits a necessary condition of membership of the preferred group?

One of the factors which complicates discussion of the Beatitudes is their tradition history. We know them in two forms: the Lucan and the Matthaean. Luke has four Beatitudes and four woes, all in the second person. Matthew has eight Beatitudes, which are composed in two sets of four, in the third person, and a ninth in the second. He has no woes. But how did Matthew's nine develop out of an originally shorter (?) collection which we must presume to lie behind Luke?

Luz[10] gives one carefully argued account of the tradition history which I shall take as a basis for this discussion, though disagreeing with it at one important point. The first three Beatitudes in the Q form (Luke 6:20b, 21) go back to Jesus.[11] To these was added a fourth, Matt 5:11//Luke 6:22, which has the effect of directing the promises to the Christian congregation. Between this first Q version and the present version in Matthew, there has been a further expansion by the addition of vv. 5 and 7–9. Here Luz thinks that the first four have been remodelled

---

[10] Luz, 1989, 200–2.
[11] Allison, 1997, chapter 3 argues for an original four.

in the oral tradition to give a set of four π-Beatitudes and that there has been a complex interaction between oral and written traditions, such that the pre-Matthaean form of the first four Beatitudes has influenced the Lukan woes. This stage of the development has also been influenced by the Psalms and Isaiah 61:1–3. How far has Matthew contributed to the process of development? Luz thinks that only the addition of τὴν δικαιοσύνην in v. 6, the whole of v. 10 and βασιλεία τῶν οὐρανῶν can be ascribed to Matthew with certainty. He acknowledges that the strong influence of the language of the Old Testament on the formulation of the additional Beatitudes could be an indication of Matthaean redaction, but firmly asserts that the reformulation of the second Beatitude in the light of Isaiah 61:2 has to be pre-Matthaean.[12]

It is doubtful whether one can be so categorical about the pre-Matthaean origin of the present form of 5:4, but on any view it is likely that Matthew was both sensitive and sympathetic to the dialogue with Isaiah 61, and this may give us important clues as to where Matthew stands in relation to the rather complicated earlier tradition. This in turn may help us to answer the questions posed above.

1. What is the logic of the Beatitudes? Beatitudes occur in Jewish literature principally within the Wisdom tradition, where they typically contain fairly detailed descriptions of the behaviour of the one to be

---

[12] Luz is here engaged in debate with R. Guelich, with whom he mostly agrees that there has been an enlargement of the Q source before Matthew's redaction, comprising vv. 5, 7–9. However, he disagrees with Guelich on the point at which the influence of Isa 61:1–3 bears on the development of the Beatitudes. Guelich believes that this is Matthew's work alone. Luz argues that at least 5:4 in its present form is pre-Matthaean. His reasons for this are (apart from the fact that the change from κλαίω to πενθέω gives a π-series, which would fit well within an oral development) that to suggest that it was Matthew who had made the change would lead to an immensely complicated account of Matthew's relationship to Luke's woes. For, on this view, Luke's woes would have pre-dated Matthew's 5:4. Then Matthew would have taken elements from two of Luke's woes: παρακαλέω, Luke 6.24b, πενθέω, Luke 6:25d and combined them, under the influence of Isa 61:2, This is Schürmann's view, which Luz rejects, as presumably being too complicated. It is almost impossible to disentangle the various lines of influence here: what is clear is that Isa 61:1–3 and quite possibly the whole of the chapter, had a quite widespread influence on the development of this tradition (and, indeed, on other traditions too, see 11QMelchizedek 2), such that we may have to assume that it made itself felt *at different stages of the development*. Even if Matt 5:4 is a pre-Matthaean development under the influence of Isa 61:1–3, this would not in any way mean that Matthew, therefore, had no interest in Isa 61. His own additions of δικαιοσύνη, which occurs in Isa 61:3, 8, 11 LXX, offer prima facie evidence of his engagement with this chapter of Isaiah. For further discussion of this point, see Guelich, 1976, 427–31; Davies and Allison, 1988, 436–9.

blessed. As such they specify ethical modes of behaviour which will bring their own particular reward. Such descriptions, coupled with promises of reward, function effectively as exhortations to such conduct. Sayings like these are predicated on the basis of a belief in the direct connection between deeds and their consequences.[13] Where this breaks down, that is to say, where the righteous are no longer rewarded in this life for their righteous conduct, there emerges a different form of beatitude, one where the apodosis is formulated in the future and relates to the coming of a new age.[14] It is to this latter form that Luke's Beatitudes, and, one may conjecture, Jesus' before them, most closely conform. Quite specifically they promise salvation, release, reversal of their conditions to those who are poor and oppressed. The question which then arises is, how far do the Matthaean Beatitudes conform to this pattern; how far have they become ethicised, that is to say forced back into a pattern closer to that of the Wisdom tradition?

The answer to this question must not be overhasty. There is clear evidence that the descriptions of those to be blessed have developed in the direction of the Wisdom tradition, that is to say, in the direction of a description of ethical characteristics, attitudes and behaviour. The poor are now the 'poor in spirit'; those who hunger are now 'those who hunger and thirst after righteousness'. The Beatitudes which have been added refer specifically to ethical-religious behaviour and attitudes, the meek, the merciful, the pure in heart, the peace-makers. Whatever the meaning of the final form of the Matthaean Beatitudes, it is beyond doubt that there has been a shift in self-understanding within the Christian community which has preserved them, from that of a group of the oppressed and marginalised to one which sees itself as committed to the upholding of certain ethical ideals/norms. There has been a certain kind of interiorisation of the understanding of Christian identity. They are the poor in spirit, the pure in heart. A particular kind of experience marks them out. On the other hand, there is still clear evidence that the eschatological framework of the early Lucan form of the Beatitudes has been preserved. The apodosis is in the future in all but the first and the last two Beatitudes; even there, there is a clearly future dimension to the present declaration.

[13] Ps 1:1–3; 2:12; 32:1–2, etc.
[14] *1 Enoch* 58:2; 99:10; Wis 3:13–14.

Thus there is no clear answer that can be given here along purely form-critical grounds. The Matthaean Beatitudes conform to neither type. They certainly describe ethical characteristics and, if one looks forward to the introduction proper, vv. 17–20, one might say that in this respect they prepare the way for the declaration in v. 20 that 'unless your righteousness exceeds that of the scribes and Pharisees, you will never enter the kingdom of heaven'. On this view, they might well be seen as entrance requirements for the kingdom. On the other hand, the future element is clearly retained and resonates with the future references in the introduction, especially at v. 18, and with the strong emphasis on future judgement throughout the Gospel, culminating in the last discourse, which Matthew has carefully developed in chapters 24–25.

What can we say? There is certainly a shift, from an understanding of the community of the blessed as the poor and the outcast, to one where the community are those who are called to follow Jesus along the 'way of righteousness'; but, as 21:32 suggests, these two positions are not by any means incompatible. Formal considerations alone will not resolve the issue: we need to look at the nature of the goals which are set by the community. We need both to look at Matthew's use of the term δικαιοσύνη, which is one of the few assured marks of his redactional work on the Beatitudes, and to consider whether the addressees of the Beatitudes are a collective or individuals.

## δικαιοσύνη in Matthew

Matthew uses the term δικαιοσύνη seven times, all of them redactional. There are three main options for interpreting the term: 1. as human behaviour; 2. as the gift or power of God; 3. combining both senses, as God's covenantal order which is both a gift and a task.[15]

---

[15] So Luz, 1, 210. Przybylski, 1980, 96, has four: the gift of God; the eschatological vindication of the elect; 'the fulfilment by men of God's will *and* the fulfilment by God of His own purposes of grace and mercy' (Manson, 1949, 48); the right conduct which God requires. Here the eschatological vindication of the elect looks like a sub-set of Manson's more general classification, which broadly corresponds to Luz's second category. It is presumably understood that the elect when vindicated will do the will of God. At issue here is the question whether the righteousness for which Matthew's blessed long is both that which God through his Son is bringing in, namely, an age where his will will indeed be done and therefore also the due performance by the blessed of God's will.

Luz, unhesitatingly, opts for the first of these senses.[16] The term *can* be understood in this way on all occasions; it must be so understood on a number: 3:15; 5:10, 20; 6:1. Let us consider these cases where the majority of scholars opt for an 'ethical' interpretation, that is to say, for a sense according to which δικαιοσύνη refers to a human action.

In 3:15, Jesus says to John that it is fitting for them to fulfil all righteousness: πληρῶσαι πᾶσαν δικαιοσύνην. Clearly this expression embraces the baptism which Jesus is about to undergo and in this respect equally clearly refers to a human action. This action is not however, as Luz clearly acknowledges, prescribed in the Law, nor is it easy to see how it might come under the higher righteousness of 5:20. It is action which is part of the process whereby the kingdom of heaven is to be inaugurated, which is part of John's task in preparing the way of the Lord (3:3), and which will lead to Jesus' acknowledgement as God's Son and his proclamation of the kingdom. It is something which might well be embraced by the expression in 5:17 that Jesus has come to πληρῶσαι[17] τὸν νόμον ἢ τοὺς προφήτας. The phrase πᾶσαν δικαιοσύνην, that is to say, does indeed refer to the 'totality of God's will', as Luz affirms: but this cannot be equated with πάντα ὅσα ἐνετειλάμην ὑμῖν (28:20), as *Jesus*' baptism is clearly something that cannot be repeated: it is a necessary condition of the fulfilment of God's purposes, not an example of kingdom conduct.[18]

---

[16] In this respect, he agrees with Strecker, 1971, 153–8, who equally sees righteousness in Matthew not as a gift from God but as the action of the believers which is in accordance with his will (in this sense it is God's righteousness: 6:33, his righteousness).

[17] πληρόω occurs sixteen times in Matthew of which all but three are related to the fulfilment of prophecy. It specifies, that is to say, actions which accord with God's purposes as foretold by the prophets. Such actions may or may not be in accord with the law. Mostly they are not specifically related to commandments in the law; some quite clearly relate to events which are against the law (2:18, referring to the grief of the mothers of the slaughtered infants). Thus with Meier, 1976, 76–80, it seems right to see here an underlying salvation historical sense. It is action, good or evil, which is part of the process where God will establish his rule over the world. In 3:15, while it is not action strictly in accordance with the law, it is action in accordance with God's wider purposes in establishing his rule. Thus it is missing the larger point simply to insist that because John and Jesus are acting in accordance with Scripture, their actions are to be understood as righteous in terms of 'moral effort or obedience to God's will' (Davies and Allison, 1988, 327). This is true, but their significance is greater than that; they are actions which form part of God's restoration of his rule over his world.

[18] In this respect, I cannot agree with Luz, 1989, 154f., and nn. 32, 37, in his acceptance of earlier and more recent interpretations which see Jesus' coming to John to be baptised as exemplary of humility. Jesus' dialogue with John reveals his authority rather than his humility. More interesting are those interpretations in the Fathers which link Jesus'

The second occurrence of δικαιοσύνη which is said clearly to refer to a human action is in 5:10, 'Blessed are those who are persecuted for righteousness' sake'. This again is indeed undoubtedly so: Christians were doubtless persecuted for their actions. But the phrase ἕνεκεν δικαιοσύνης is interestingly reminiscent of 10:18, ἕνεκεν ἐμοῦ, so that it is perhaps worth considering a somewhat broader sense. Christians are persecuted because of the way of life which they represent and embody. (This would come closer to the sense in 1 Peter 4:16, where ὡς Χριστιανός presumably refers to their identification as members of the group.) That is to say, that δικαιοσύνη, in so far as it refers to actions which are typical of followers of Jesus, is used metonymically for the way of life which they live out, for the corporate existence of the members of the church.

Again, 5:20 clearly refers to human actions, specifically to the actions of Jesus' followers as contrasted with those of the scribes and Pharisees. In context it comes after discussion of the neglect of specific commandments (ἐντολαί). The assertion that their 'righteousness' must exceed that of the scribes and Pharisees, thus seems easily to suggest that Jesus' followers must perform more works of the law than they do.[19]

Even if this is right, the term δικαιοσύνη still refers to their behaviour as a whole and not to the individual acts of which it is comprised. It clearly refers to the behaviour of particular individuals: the phrase 'enter the kingdom of heaven' is uniformly applied to discrete individuals. Nevertheless, the phrase 'your righteousness' as addressed to the disciples still refers to the behaviour appropriate to members of the group, even if in each case such behaviour is constituted by the actions of individuals. Such behaviour is evidence of the dawning reality of God's rule.

Undoubtedly 6:1 seems to refer to specific acts of religious observance which are enjoined under the law or under the teaching of Jesus. The

---

fulfilment of δικαιοσύνη with the Old Testament law and see in this a soteriological-historical motif: Theodore of Heraclea: fr 21 = Reuss 63: Jesus, who is perfect according to the Law attains through his baptism by John to τὸ τοῦ νόμου τέλος. But even here the close identification with the Old Testament law is problematical.

[19] Luz 1989, 240 suggests that πλεῖον indicates a quantitative sense; doing more works of the law than the Gentiles and Pharisees is a condition of entry into the kingdom: 'Πλεῖον legt eine quantitative Deutung nahe: Wenn eure Gerechtigkeit nicht in meßbar höherem Maß reichlicher vorhanden ist als die der Schriftgelehrten und Pharisäer, werdet ihr nicht ins Himmelreich kommen', and goes on to speak of a 'quantitatives Mehr an Toraerfüllung'.

question is whether this sense is to be taken as paradigmatic for all others; or whether such usage is not rather compatible with the broader senses suggested above.

This now brings us to consider those occurrences which less obviously refer to human actions. By common agreement 5:6 is Matthew's modification of the Q Beatitude, 'Blessed are you hungry'. Does the phrase 'hungering and thirsting after righteousness' mean 'striving to perform righteous deeds', or does it mean something like 'longing for the divinely willed new order'? Even allowing that the phrase in Greek can bear either meaning, the apodosis: 'for they will be filled', certainly fits less well with the former sense. Being filled suggests the satisfying of a need and a longing, rather than the achievement of a goal. Clearly, in the light of our discussion so far, if this sense is not to be wholly discontinuous with the other occurrences, it will need to map on to them, but this is not a serious difficulty. For the order for which people long is one where indeed all will perform the righteous will of God, and it is this which makes the metonymic use of righteousness appropriate for the new world-order. And there are other reasons for suggesting such a meaning here. R. Guelich has argued that Matthew is here in dialogue with Isaiah 61.[20] There is widespread agreement among scholars that Isaiah 61:1–3 has been used to shape the first three Beatitudes; Guelich's attractive suggestion is that Matthew's introduction of δικαιοσύνη in 5:6 and 10 is also influenced by Isaiah 61 and that he has given it special emphasis by creating two sets of four Beatitudes, each of which ends with a Beatitude which focuses on 'righteousness'.

This proposal concerns more than the sources of Matthew's usage: it is a substantive proposal about the meaning of Matthew's editorial additions. Specifically, Guelich wanted to challenge those 'who would see primarily an ethical thrust in Matthew's use of δικαιοσύνη'.[21] What precisely is the issue here? Guelich sets out two competing views: on the one hand, there are those who see 'righteousness' in Matthew as 'refer[ring] to conduct in keeping with the will of God set forth in the law as "correctly" interpreted and "fulfilled" by Jesus'. On the other hand, there are those who stress the 'eschatological "gift" character of the Matthaean usage'. What Guelich clearly wants to avoid is the view

[20] Guelich, 1976, 427–31.
[21] Guelich, 1976, 428. At this point Guelich had in mind particularly Bornkamm, 1963, 24–32; Strecker, 70/71, 270–2; 1966, 153–8.

that what Matthew is offering is simply a new set of ethical standards compliance with which is *required* of all those who would enter the kingdom; on the other hand, he also wants to avoid *attributing* to Matthew the view that 'righteousness' is simply *attributed* to the disciples as a gift: it is quite clear to him that Matthew's Jesus demands good works of his followers.

His solution is to identify what is distinctive in Matthew's teaching about righteousness, as contrasted with contemporary Jewish teaching. On the one hand, there is in Matthew's ethical teaching (5:21–48), in his account of the relationship with God (6:1–18), and in his emphasis on persecution (5:10), all of which constitute 'righteousness' for him, something very different from contemporary Judaism with its focus on the Law. On the other hand, the eschatological character of Matthew's presentation of Jesus' teaching means that '"[r]ighteousness" for Matthew involved conduct and relationships nothing short of that characteristic of the promised age of salvation, the presence of the Kingdom. . . . With the dawn of the age of salvation a new relationship with God began for those whose lives were touched by Jesus' person and ministry. . . . One's new relationship with God and the resultant conduct towards God (Matt 6:1–18) and others (5:21–48) was the product of, not the entrance requirements for, the Kingdom'.[22]

Thus there is both a passive and an active aspect of 'righteousness' in Matthew. The passive character is brought out by the redactional addition of δικαιοσύνη in 5:6. The verse describes those who are

> in desperate straits, painful need (πεινάω intensified by διψάω), waiting before God that his will might be done in their lives. This need is not met by the individual himself through a resolute determination to carry out the will of God in one's own strength,[23] a concept completely foreign to the imagery of the Beatitudes as a whole. Rather the promise 'for they shall be satisfied,' implies that God, who comforts the mourning, will satiate their earnest desires by accepting them into a new relationship with himself and enabling them in keeping with the presence of the age of salvation, to accomplish that for which they long, i.e. the will of God. Is not this the 'righteousness' with which God 'covers' one (Isa 61:10) and which he causes to 'spring forth before the nations' (61:11)? Such ones are the 'oaks of righteousness, the planting of the Lord' (61:3).[24]

[22]  Guelich, 1976, 429.
[23]  Guelich cites Strecker, 70/71, 265, 'das angestrengte Sich–Bemühen um die Verwirklichung der Gerechtigkeit . . .'
[24]  Guelich, 1976, 430.

It is hard to avoid altogether the impression that Reformation debates about grace and works are being played out here, with Isaiah's help being enlisted to undergird Matthew's doctrine of grace: viz. that it is by virtue of the '"eschatological gift" of the new relationship between God and the individual' that 'ethical conduct' towards God is made possible. Guelich is precisely right to stress the sense in which 'righteousness' is a gift, that with which those who hunger and thirst after it are *filled*;[25] it is right, too, to emphasise the sense in which God is active in Isaiah 61, causing 'righteousness' to spring up, clothing people with it, planting 'oaks of righteousness'. Such usage is simply too close to the texts with which Matthew 5:1–12 is in dialogue to be ignored. It is hard to believe that Matthew's meaning could be restricted purely to human action. But in what sense does God cause 'righteousness to spring up'? And in what sense is the action of God an action towards individuals? Maybe Isaiah can shed light on Matthew's usage, which we are in danger of confusing, if we see it too much through Reformation spectacles.

We need to consider Isaiah in its final form and to abandon, for the purposes of assessing its influence on Matthew, notions of different sources. That is to say, we need to read Isaiah 61 with the prophecies and woes against Israel in mind from the earlier chapters. Israel's fate of exile and captivity has come upon it because of disobedience. God has punished his people because they have abandoned his ways and brought injustice and oppression into his vineyard. He has given them over to the nations to discipline and punish them, in the hope that he will then be able to raise up a root which will again bear fruit and which will live righteously in accordance with God's will. The prophecy in Isaiah 61 announces the restoration of Israel, the return from exile and captivity and the successful conclusion of God's long and fierce disciplining of his people. Now they will rebuild their cities, and enjoy peace and prosperity, and justice will rule in the land. Those who now inhabit Zion will be called 'oaks of righteousness, the planting of the

---

[25] It is revealing that Luz does not discuss the apodosis of 5:6, in his long comment on δικαιοσύνη in that verse. Even more revealing is Davies and Allison's comment, 1985, 453: The saints' reward might be the vision of God or the eschatological banquet 'or – most probably – a world in which righteousness dwells (cf. Isa 32:1, 16–17; *1 Enoch* 58:4; *T Levi* 13:5; 2 Pet 3:13)'. But this would be to give a very different sense to δικαιοσύνη from that of moral effort. God's gift of δικαιοσύνη here is the gift of a world where his rule runs and his will is obeyed.

Lord': they will act righteously because the Lord has disciplined them and led their feet back into the ways they should go (Isa 57:18; cf. 42:16; 48:17).

This is to say that the righteousness of which Isaiah 61 speaks is indeed based on a relationship between Yahweh and his people (not simply 'individuals'), but that it is the outcome of a long and often painful relationship. Yahweh teaches and leads his people, through the long history of his dealings with them, through the revelation of his law, through the words of his prophets. All this is leading to the point where Yahweh will redeem them and reward them with freedom and prosperity, where the people will finally bear fruits of righteousness. Isaiah can speak of this in terms of an 'everlasting covenant with you' (Isa 55:3), a 'covenant of peace' which 'shall not be removed' (54:10). He opens up a vision of a new Jerusalem whose foundations are on sapphires, and whose children will all be taught of God (למודי יהוה, disciples of God (54:13)).

It is not difficult to see how this bears on the senses of righteousness in Matthew 5. Those who hunger and thirst (cf. Isa 55:1) after righteousness are those who long for the time when Yahweh will restore his people and produce in them the fruits of righteousness: these longings will be filled; the long struggle for obedience and the long history of God's teaching of them will reach its conclusion. Yahweh will teach them his righteousness; righteousness (Matt 5:20–48) and praise (6:1–18) will spring up among them. Similarly, those who are persecuted because they now walk in the way of righteousness will be blessed and enter the kingdom of heaven.

'Righteousness', that is to say, does not refer exclusively either to (unaided) human action, or to a pure gift of God: it is something that springs from the relationship between Yahweh and his people, from his leading (Ps 5:8; 25:9; 27:11; 139:24; Isa 42:16; 48:17; 57:18) and teaching (Ps 27:11; Isa 54:13–14) them and their following him. It is the poor in spirit and the humble and meek who will allow themselves to be led in the ways of the Lord and will therefore inherit the earth (Ps 37:11). As such it requires a fundamental reorientation on the part of those who go along the 'way of righteousness'. But equally it is Yahweh who leads, who through his messenger prepares the way for them (Matt 3:3) and leads those along it who trust in him (21:32). Nor is it something that will only come into being in the final age: it is a way already entered upon and traversed in part; the attainment of its final goal, full realisation, is still awaited (for once the phrase 'now and not yet' has some tangible meaning).

Let us return to our original questions about the nature of the Beatitudes and their relation to the more formal instruction of Matt 5:21–48. The Beatitudes are neither entrance requirements for the kingdom, nor are they simply promises of eschatological blessing. In so far as they are descriptive (and it is undeniable that formally they have in the course of transmission grown closer to the Wisdom Beatitudes than the apocalyptic ones), they describe those characteristics which will enable the disciple not only to enter upon (7:13–14), but which are also required if he is to be led along, the way of righteousness. Nevertheless, despite the greater emphasis in the Beatitudes on description of the moral characteristics of the disciple, the Beatitudes are not to be seen principally as paraenetic, as exhortations to virtue. They are first and foremost invitations to pilgrimage, to travel along the way, to enter into training for the kingdom (μαθητεύεσθαι τῇ βασιλείᾳ, 13:52). On the other hand, such an invitation *is* also an offer of the blessings which await the disciple at the end of the way, just as it is an offer of *training*, which is spelled out in much greater detail in the remainder of the chapter. The Beatitudes are an extension and clarification of the invitation which is made to the disciples at their call in 4:18–22; they are addressed beyond them to *all* who would follow Jesus and enter through the narrow gate on to the way of righteousness.

## Forensic and cosmic dualist perspective in Matthew's understanding of δικαιοσύνη

The centrality which Matthew accords to this understanding of righteousness, with its roots in the hopes for restoration of the people of Israel in Isaiah, places Matthew's Gospel firmly in the tradition of forensic, restorationist eschatology. When the people repent, God will restore them to Zion and they will be free to follow his Law; the nations will see the glory of Zion and will flock to worship God. The emphasis lies clearly on repentance and the freedom of the people to obey or disobey. The role of the prophet/teacher is to encourage and exhort and to warn. This function is more than adequately fulfilled in the Gospel, not least in the five main discourses, which as we have noted are linked formally through their introductions and conclusions. Each contains strong exhortation and equally strong reminders of the consequences of moral choice and action. The Sermon on the Mount concludes with a section on the two ways (two gates: 7:13–14; wise and the foolish man: 7:24–27). The discipleship discourse has references to Jesus' acknowledging or denying those who acknowledge or deny him (10:32–33), to losing and finding one's life (10:39), and to future rewards (10:40–42). The parable discourse concludes with the parable of the dragnet with its interpretation in terms of the casting of the wicked into the furnace of fire (13:47–50). The parable of the unjust steward (18:23–35), which concludes the community discourse, repeats the theme of punishment. The eschatological discourse (chapters 24–25) concludes the whole series with a large-scale allegorical portrayal of final judgement.

Matthew's message is painfully clear: the righteous will be rewarded and the wicked dreadfully punished. Therefore, the duty of Christians is to make disciples and teach all that Jesus has commanded. Therefore, their righteousness is to exceed that of the scribes and the Pharisees.

This powerful discourse of moral exhortation and punishment is qualified, however, in important respects by Matthew's handling of the Q-material on discipleship in chapter 8. Here, in the section which he devotes to Jesus' mighty deeds, he includes material which powerfully emphasises the cost of discipleship (8:19–22//Luke 9:57–60): the homelessness and lack of shelter; the break with family ties. Matthew has again incorporated this Q-material into a Markan pericope, that of the stilling of the storm. Thus 8:18 adapts Mark 4:35 and 8:23 takes up the pericope at Mark 4:36.[26] He emphasises the connection by his introduction to the story of the stilling of the storm, where Jesus precedes the disciples into the boat and they follow him (Matt 8:23). The section opens with Jesus' command to go to the other side of the lake.[27] The challenge is to those who would follow him to brave the dangers and lack of security which the life of discipleship entails. This is brought out in Jesus' reply to his two questioners, where the break with family ties is powerfully asserted. It is brought out symbolically in the subsequent narrative, where the powers of the storm represent the demonic powers which threaten the church and which Jesus

[26]  The classic discussion of this pericope is Bornkamm, 1963a. See too Held, 1963, 202.

[27]  It is not clear whether this command is given to the crowd around him or to the disciples. Barton, 1994, 192 argues for the former, largely because of the prominence which the crowd has had in the preceding pages. Yet the fact that there is only one boat in which to travel suggests that it is directed to his disciples, and this is reflected in the description of the questioners in 8:18–22, if not only 'disciple' but 'scribe' is to be taken as a designation of Jesus' followers.

subdues.[28] The narrative, that is to say, dramatically depicts the forces which will assail those who follow Jesus, just as it indicates that only faith in Jesus' power to overcome them will suffice. What is required here is more than moral exertion: it is entrusting oneself to the Lordship of Jesus who 'subdues the demonic powers and brings the βασιλεία of God'.[29] The disciples of Jesus are not only embarked on a programme of training; they are literally followers of Jesus on his itinerant ministry of healing and exorcism, in his struggle against the dark powers. In this sense those who answer his command to follow him are sharply divided from those who do not. The story becomes an image for the church,[30] as later commentators saw.

This is reflected in a further passage in which the dominant discourse of moral exhortation and punishment and reward falters: in the parable of the wheat and the tares (13:24–30), with its interpretation (13:36–43). For here the world is divided into two, those who are sons of the evil one and those who are sons of the kingdom. The wicked are 'sown' by the devil and as such are sharply distinguished from those sown by the Son of Man. There is a shift here from the interpretation of the parable of the sower. There the seed is the word sown into the heart of the hearer, which seed is then snatched away by the evil one.[31] In the interpretation of the parable of the tares, there are two kinds of seeds which are sharply distinguished: one is destined for destruction, the other to 'shine' in the kingdom of the Father. Seeds of the one sort are sown by Satan and are said to be his sons; those of the other are sown by the Son of Man and are sons of the kingdom. The dualistic, deterministic element here is particularly strong.[32] Such images may be

---

[28] As is underlined by the use of ἐπιτιμάω for the 'rebuking' of the storm (8:26; cf. 17:18; Mark 1:25; 9:25; Luke 4:35; 9:42). Similarly, Matthew has edited Mark's account to bring out the contrast between the σεισμὸς μέγας and the γαλήνη μεγάλη. As Bornkamm, 1963a, 56, points out, the use of σεισμός to refer to the sea is unusual: it is, however, common in references to apocalyptic horrors (Mark 13:8; Matt 24:7; 27:54: 28:2; Rev 6:12; 8:5; 11:13, 19; 16:18).

[29] Bornkamm, 1963a, 57.

[30] 'Matthew is not only a hander-on of the narrative, but also its oldest exegete, and in fact the first to interpret the journey of the disciples with Jesus in the storm and the stilling of the storm with reference to discipleship, and that means with reference to the little ship of the Church'; Bornkamm, 1963a, 55; see references in note 1.

[31] Though even here there are ambiguities as the interpretation shifts to an understanding of the different categories of hearer as different seeds.

[32] As is clearly recognised by Sim, 1996, 79: 'According to this scenario, there is no middle ground in the cosmic conflict between Jesus and Satan and their respective human supporters; one is either a son of the kingdom or a son of the evil one and

199

CONFLICTING MYTHOLOGIES

used in a variety of ways; the interpretation here gives them a clear determinist sense.[33]

The images of the storm-tossed '*navis ecclesiae*' and the wheat surrounded on all sides by weeds, the sons of the evil one, present a picture of the church as beset by powers of evil and destruction. This is again underlined in the commission of Peter in 16:18, with its promise that the 'gates of hell will not prevail against it [sc. the rock of the church]'. The apocalyptic battle between the powers of death and destruction and the powers of heaven will have its assured out-come and good will triumph over evil.[34] Those within the church who endure to the end (10:22; 24:13) will be preserved. Cosmic dualist mythology is certainly present in Matthew's Gospel, but the church, though surrounded by the dark powers is itself a haven from

---

there is no third category.' What is suprising about Sim's thesis is that he takes this kind of apocalyptic eschatology as determinative of Matthew's stance, rather than seeing it as a striking exception to the largely forensic pattern of thought which we find elsewhere in the Gospel. Cf. Beare, 1981, 312, who raises the question whether Matthew has 'borrowed some alien myth without realising its implications'; quoted Sim, 1996, 86.

[33] A further example is provided by the strange passage 12:33–35. Most commentators, e.g. Hill, 218, Luz, 1990, 252, 268, take the phrase, ποιήσατε τὸ δένδρον καλὸν to mean 'suppose the tree is good' (taking ποιεῖν as 'to put the case, to assume that . . .' Liddell and Scott, A VI), giving a sense broadly: 'if you think it is a good tree, you will expect to get good fruit from it'. This would make sense in the context. The Pharisees cannot pretend to speak good. They are evil by nature (through and through?) and therefore can speak only evil. Davies and Allison, 1991, 349, prefer to take it as 'make the tree good and its fruit (will be) good', but do not explain the sense of the metaphor. If Luz and others are right, then the sense in 12:33 is not as strongly dualistic as with the interpretation of the figure of the wheat and the tares in 13:36–43. Such figures of speech can be used in a variety of ways. Luz cites Sir 27:6: 'The fruit discloses the cultivation of a tree; so the expression of a thought discloses the cultivation of a person's mind'; cf. too *T Naph* 2:6 'as is his heart, so is his speech'.

[34] The interpretation of Matt 16:18 is much disputed, as is well documented by the standard commentaries; see e.g. Luz, 1990, 463–4. The major difficulty for an apocalyptic interpretation. (cf. e.g. Marcus, 1988) is that the expression, 'the *gates* of Hades', is not used of the powers which control the gates, only of the area which surround them. However, a metonymic use seems entirely appropriate in the context here, where κατισχύω is most naturally translated as 'prevail against'. As Davies and Allison, 1991, 633, point out, κατισχύω + gen. in LXX is always active. They conclude: 'One should probably think of the end-time scenario, when the powers of the underworld will be unleashed from below, from the abyss, and rage against the saints (cf. *1 Enoch* 56:8; Rev 6:8; 11:7; 17:8). The promise is that even the full fury of the underworld's demonic forces will not overcome the church' (noting that in *T Reub* 4:11 κατισχύω is used of Belial, and in Acts 19:16 of evil spirits).

200

them.[35] Those within the church are to bend their wills to obeying their Lord's commandments, lest they fall.

What sorts of moods and attitudes might such a narrative have inspired, as compared with those which we suggested from Mark? How might Matthew's re-presentation of the story have changed such attitudes and senses of self? Again, we can only approach such questions with great tentativeness. Mark's Gospel is, as it were, suspended between two moods, one which sees Christian existence as lightness after the dark, sight after blindness, albeit a sight only gradually and partially gained; and another which sees it as a particular calling within God's purposes of restoration and renewal of his people, even if the identity of his people has also been subject to radical change.

Some things seem reasonably clear. Matthew has largely abandoned Mark's images of light and darkness, blindness and sight, and instead has stressed the call of the disciples into a teaching and healing community, where it is ultimately the teaching ministry which is of greatest importance. For on the reception, understanding and doing of Jesus' teaching depends one's eternal fate. The disciples as the recipients of Jesus' teaching are to pass it on to the new disciples. The church is the community of those who, if they remain faithful, will be preserved from all the attacks of the evil one.

This imposes immense responsibilities on the community of Jesus' followers. The fate of the nations is in their hands. So, too, is their own fate. If they fail to keep Jesus' commandments, then they know what end awaits them. Moreover, there is the disturbing thought that they might not actually be sons of the kingdom at all: perhaps they are really sons of the evil one. Such doctrines can engender the kind of uneasiness which makes people strive all the more to convince themselves that they are not irretrievably lost. They can also, in other less tender souls, engender a deep sense of confidence and of superiority over all those outside their group. The stark dualism of the wheat and the tares encourages a frame of mind which makes a clear distinction between the group and the world. The field is the world, which properly belongs to them and is the legitimate sphere of their missionary activity; all who do not hear and receive their teaching reveal themselves as sons of

---

[35] Though Matt 7:21–23 states that even within the haven of the church there are those who work ἀνομία. Practically speaking, a community with a need for internal self-discipline could operate with a purely dualist understanding of the division between the church and the world only with the greatest difficulty.

the evil one, as weeds, ultimately to be rooted out. For Matthew's small, beleaguered community such views will presumably have acted more as an eschatological assurance of ultimate vindication than as a stimulus to communal violence against those outside their community.

It is likely, too, that the marked tension in Matthew between strong ethical injunction and emphasis on moral decision-making on the one hand, and the attribution of sin and evil to Satan on the other hand will have led to a high level of moral endeavour and vigilance.[36]

## Matthew's sectarianism

What then of the sectarian nature of the Matthaean community? It is widely agreed that Matthew is a sectarian document, but among those who argue for such a view there is strong disagreement about the precise nature of that sectarianism. There is a general agreement that the community for and to which Matthew writes is a sect in the sense that 'a sect is not only a minority, and not only characterised by opposition to norms accepted by the parent-body, but also claims in a more or less exclusive way to be what the parent-body claims to be'.[37] There is considerably less agreement on the question whether Matthew's divisions with its parent-body have gone so far that it has already parted company with it.

### Recent debates: J. Andrew Overman

A brief review of scholarly debate on this topic may help to introduce a discussion in which I shall attempt to trace the lines of development from Mark to Matthew. J. Andrew Overman initiated recent discussion of Matthew's sectarianism by arguing that Matthew's community, as represented by his Gospel, fitted in well to the pattern of Jewish sectarianism which existed between 165 BCE and 100 CE. The fierce polemic against the Jewish leadership in the Gospel was to be taken not as evidence of the split which had occurred between Matthew's

---

[36] In his excellent survey of recent Matthaean scholarship, Sim, 1996, 2–14, argues that scholars have until recently largely overlooked the dualist and determinist aspects of Matthew's work in favour of a more ethical and paraenetic treatment of it. For scholars like Bornkamm, 1963, Matthew's apocalyptic eschatology is mainly designed to give moral encouragement to the church.

[37] Blenkinsopp, 1981, 1, quoted in Overman, 1990, 8, Stanton, 1992, 90, Sim, 1998, 110.

community and formative Judaism, the emerging Judaism of the post-70 period, but rather of the inner-Jewish polemic. The terms in which it was cast were typical of the 'language of sectarianism', which 'conveys the deep social divisions which seem to have characterised this period'. Terms like 'lawless', 'righteous' occur frequently in apocalyptic literature: *1 Enoch*, *2 Baruch*, *4 Ezra*, as well as the *Psalms of Solomon*, show how widespread was this sectarian usage.[38] Similarly, Matthew's concern for the correct interpretation of the Law is a mark of the sectarian struggle for legitimacy, to show that his community is 'truly the elect, in contrast to the group with which they contend'.[39] It will be evident even from this brief account that it is no easy task to make such judgements secure. The terms 'lawless' and 'righteous' may feature in writings which Overman identifies as sectarian, but they also occur frequently in the literature of mainstream Judaism, in the Book of Wisdom and in the Maccabean literature. It may indeed be that the term 'lawless' comes into currency in relation to the kinds of Jewish reform which emerged in the second century and were opposed by the Maccabean party and that the term was then taken up in other forms of inner Jewish debate. But it is certainly clear that its use alone is in no sense a guarantee of the sectarian status of the user.

In general, Overman's treatment is so broad that it does not do much more than make some interesting suggestions about ways of reading Matthew. He argues that sectarianism was widespread in Judaism throughout the period 165 BCE to 100 CE, but does not consider whether such communities underwent change over the time.[40] Perhaps the greatest difficulty with Overman's treatment is his unwillingness to spell out exactly who it was that Matthew saw his community as being marginal to. We are told that for '*2 Baruch*, *4 Ezra*, or the Gospel of Matthew, these leaders [to whom the writers were opposed] could have been people allied with and sympathetic to the Romans or simply the local leaders and elders in a particular setting or community who had gained power following the destruction of the Temple. In the view of these sectarian communities, these leaders had betrayed the people,

---

[38] Overman, 1990, 16–19. There is a potential problem for Overman here: the more widespread this kind of language, the less likely that it is the language of a minority opposed to the parent body.

[39] Overman, 1990, 24.

[40] Though there is some acknowledgement that the Pharisees may have changed status in this regard.

had turned from God, and had brought upon Israel the hardship the people were now experiencing'.[41] Elsewhere we are told that the religio-political powers to which the sectarians were opposed 'could have been the priests in the temple in Jerusalem or the local *boulē*, or authorities who exercised power because they enjoyed the favour of a ruler or Roman client'.[42] The difficulty here is that this account does not consider clearly enough the implications for Jewish sectarianism of the destruction of the Temple. Once the Temple was destroyed, the whole question of legitimate leadership within the Jewish community became contentious. The priests were cut off from the source of their authority in the cult, and other groups were vying for authority. All were now marginal to the dominant authority, the Romans, an authority which, however, was variously exercised. In this situation it is understandable that there would be a power struggle within the Jewish community. But in what sense would that struggle be sectarian? Once the traditional leaders of the people were disenfranchised, there was in a sense no centre in respect of which groups were marginal. The struggle was for control of a community where there was no established leadership. In such a situation warring parties are likely to exclude each other, as the *Birkath Ha-Minim*, whatever its date, makes clear. The fierce and painful polemic of Matthew 23, and the curse which Matthew puts in the mouth of 'all the people' in 27:25, may be evidence that Matthew feels he has lost the battle for the centre and has broken with the Jewish community altogether (as is the case with John), just as much as it may be for Matthew's continuing struggle for power within the Jewish community.[43]

At the same time, all these different Jewish groups would have all been sharply marginalised with respect to the dominant religio-political power of the Romans and their clients and allies. In Antioch, according to Malalas,[44] the Cherubim were set up on a city gate to humiliate the Jewish community;[45] coinage circulated throughout the Empire portraying *Iudaea capta*. This was not a wholly novel situation. Jews had only rarely been in control of their own affairs in their own land. The Isaianic hopes associated with the return of the exiles along the

---

[41] Overman, 1990, 19–20.

[42] Overman, 1990, 15–16.

[43] This need not imply that any one group yet controlled the centre; only that Matthew believed, for whatever reason, that his community was no longer in a position to influence or control the Jewish community.

[44] 260:21 – 261:14.

[45] See the discussion in Barclay, 1996, 257–8.

way of the Lord were for a restoration of national sovereignty and for the acknowledgement of Israel by all the nations (Isa 60). In this respect the various Jewish groups were not simply battling for leadership positions, but were actively seeking to promote their own visions of the restoration of Israel's independence and its acknowledgement by the nations. It is then not difficult to see how a form of inner-Jewish sectarianism, where the main focus of attention had been on control of the Jewish community, could change to being one where the focus shifted to establishing alternative forms of power to those of the dominant Roman power. This is not to suggest that Matthew was sectarian in the sense that his community sought to take over the leadership of the local Roman cults. Rather, it sought an alternative religious legitimacy: Jesus was to be recognised as the true 'Son of God', as opposed to the emperor, a point underlined by the centurion's acclamation of Jesus at his death.[46] Such notions may well underlie Mark's emphasis on the Son of God title at critical moments of his Gospel. Matthew does not have Mark's opening reference to the Son of God, though he does have the story of the Virgin Birth and follows Mark in his references to the Son of God at the baptism and trans-figuration. Moreover, not only does the centurion acknowledge Jesus as Son of God at the crucifixion; Matthew has the other soldiers with him join in this Roman homage to Jesus (27:54: cf. Mk 15:39).

## Matthew as a deviant sect: Anthony J. Saldarini

The topic of Matthew's sectarianism has been further developed by Saldarini and Sim.[47] Saldarini brings a wider range of social scientific theories to bear on his subject and paints a picture of Matthew's group as a deviant sect within Judaism. It is a community with a strong sense of group cohesion, emphasised in the use of kinship language to describe its members.[48] 'At the core of Matthew's identity is the relationship of Jesus to God as Son and the analogous relationship of his disciples to

---

[46] Cf. Hengel 1976, 95–114, on the Zealots' opposition to the imperial claims to divinity, which he believes is implied in Judas the Galilean's claim that 'God alone is king'.

[47] Saldarini, 1994; Sim, 1998.

[48] Saldarini, 1994, 90–4; 'Membership in the Matthaean group, with its attendant faith in God, acceptance of Jesus' teaching, and obedience to God's will, is understood as a familial relationship with God. However, though Matthew emphasizes that Jesus is the Son of God, he does not call disciples "sons of God," even though God is their Father' (94).

God as sons and servants. These intensive fictive kinship bonds are proper to the household'.[49] Saldarini emphasises the features of the group's organisation which indicate its coherence as a group: it recruits members, develops a coherent world-view, attacks competing social institutions and groups, and develops its own communal procedures, status rankings and community goals.[50] Such patterns of behaviour, he argues, are characteristic of groups that are classified as deviant by other, mainstream groups within their society. But though the evidence Saldarini marshalls demonstrates the group's cohesiveness, it is not, on its own, evidence for the fact that Matthew's group was still within Judaism. The fact that there is evidence of conflict with the Jewish leaders and the development of cohesive forms of group organisation and formation can be seen just as easily as consistent with the behaviour of a group which had parted company with its parent body and which was marginal not only to its former parent body but also to the dominant political force in its world, Rome.

Saldarini sets some store by the fact that Matthew's community was still recruiting from among the Jews: 'the latter half of Matthew 10, contains an extended exhortation to persevere in a Jewish mission'.[51] This is true, but the beginning and the end of the discourse states clearly that this exhortation is delivered specifically to the Twelve. Moreover, Jesus sets a time limit on the enterprise: 'you will not have gone through all the towns of Israel, before the Son of man comes' (10:23).[52] Do these two points suggest that the mission to Israel was strictly limited to the sending out of the Twelve? The matter is far from clear, though this fact is not sufficiently acknowledged either by Sim or Saldarini, both of whom want to argue for the continuation of the Jewish mission till the time of the composition of the Gospel. On the one hand, Jesus' discourse is addressed only to the Twelve disciples and, in this respect, is clearly distinguished from the other discourses. On

---

[49] Saldarini, 1994, 99; though as Saldarini notices (see previous note) Matthew does not expressly speak of the disciples as 'sons of God'; they are Jesus' brothers and sisters, 12:50.

[50] Saldarini, 1994, 112.

[51] Saldarini, 1994, 107.

[52] There is a question here about the translation of τελέσητε τὰς πόλεις. Allison, 1991, 191, considers taking it in relation (i) to preaching: accomplishing the task or finishing preaching in all the cities of Israel; (ii) to flight: you will not have finished going through all the cities. He believes either is possible, given the links with Israel and preaching in Matt 10:5–6 and the immediate reference to flight in v. 23. BAGD opts for 'finish (going through) the cities', linking τελέω directly with τὰς πόλεις. This seems right.

the other hand, it is equally clear that much of the material in the chapter has a wider reference than just to the Twelve. The last verses of the chapter are quite general in their application (v. 39!). Furthermore, the reference to the coming of the Son of Man may seem to indicate clearly that the 'Jewish mission must continue until the parousia'[53] but this has to be set alongside the fact that the coming of the Son of Man is expected very soon, *before* the disciples have got round all the cities, and that it is this which is the source of comfort. There are, that is to say, features which suggest a restrictive application of this exhortation to the Twelve for a limited period; there are other features which suggest that the implications of this charge extend beyond the Twelve and are intended to be of lasting importance.

It is difficult to see how to draw a coherent picture from this puzzling state of affairs.[54] Matthew clearly addresses the charge to go to preach to Israel to the Twelve, but then extends the charge to include experiences which must have been common to many of Matthew's own community. The expectation of a rapid end to this mission is expressed in terms which, if taken at face value, would suggest that the Son of Man had already come, which is contrary to the prophecy in 24:29–31. Perhaps the only solution is, as Luz suggests,[55] in seeing the mission charge in 28:18–20 as a correction of both the restriction of the church's mission to the Jews and of the prophecy in 10:23. If this is right, then, while there is indeed evidence here for recruitment on the part of the community from other Jews at some point, this stage seems to have been superseded. What Saldarini broadly establishes is that it is likely that the Matthaean community was at one stage a deviant group within Judaism; but it is also likely, given the shifts and ambiguities in the text, that the focus has now changed. The experience of expulsion from the synagogue has led the community to see itself as those whose primary

---

[53] Sim, 1998, 158.

[54] Davies and Allison, 1991, 189–90, list possible solutions to the dilemma, preferring the view that the coming of the Son of Man refers to the parousia, and rescuing the verse from the realm of false prophecy (at least during Matthew's life-time) by suggesting that the mission was not in fact accomplished – the disciples' return from the mission is not recorded. This is a possible but not very persuasive view.

[55] Of all commentators, Luz, 1990, 117, is most aware of this dilemma, to which he suggests only a tentative solution: 'Wahrscheinlicher ist mir, daß für ihn nicht nur 10,5f, sondern auch 10,23 durch den Missionsbefehl korrigiert waren.' He argues that 10:5–6 and 10:23 are corrected by the mission charge in 28:18–20 but concedes that whereas there is a reference in 28:18–20 to 10:5–6, there is no such reference to 10:23.

task is to go to the Gentiles. This is not to say that they have thereby abandoned any claim to Jewishness; at the very least as brothers and sisters of Jesus, they are intimately tied to the Son of David and of Abraham. But their identity is established now, not by circumcision as a mark of their participation in the Abrahamic covenant, but by baptism and receiving the teaching of Jesus (28:18–20). We shall return to these issues shortly, when we discuss Matthew's treatment of ethnicity.

The debate here is both intriguing (and could be pursued much further) and also a little frustrating. On the one hand there can be no doubting Matthew's Jewishness, his concern for the Law, and his rich use of material from the Old Testament. If the question at issue is whether Matthew abandons, regards as 'superseded', his Jewish faith, there is little to argue about. The genealogical credentials of his Jewish Messiah are firmly established from the beginning. His Messiah comes to fulfil the Law and the prophets, not to abolish them. The record of fierce debates with the Jewish leadership shows how important to him were matters of the interpretation of the Law. None of this can be seriously doubted. Moreover, if we consider the manner in which Matthew has reworked Mark's Gospel, we can see how he has incorporated into it blocks of material which leave beyond any doubt his belief that Jesus was a teacher of the Law (5–7), who came with a mission to Israel (10), who inculcated into his followers the importance of obedience to the Law in the light of the coming judgement (13) and who, for all his polemics against the Pharisees, still enjoined his followers to obey their rulings, if not to follow their ways (23:2–3), even though these rulings are heavy and Jesus himself comes to offer an easier and lighter load (23:4; cf. 11:30). But, just as in our discussion of 10:23, we saw how difficult it was to weigh this against the final mission charge in 28:18–20, so too here. How does Jesus' injunction to his disciples to do *all* that the scribes and Pharisees tell them relate to the command in 28:20 that the – now eleven – disciples teach their disciples to observe 'all that I have commanded you'. Doubtless at one level, it can be seen as complementary or additional to Jesus' commands. Jesus' scribe trained for the kingdom (13:52) does indeed bring out of his treasure what is old and new, but equally the old and the new are to be kept separate (9:16–17). How in practice was this to be achieved? Did Matthew envisage one set of rules for circumcised Jews and another for un-circumcised converts. Was he giving his community freedom to choose which regulations to apply in different situations? Or was he insisting on full observance of old and new? The existence of these texts, whose precise practical application is lost to us, at least indicates the tension which Matthew's community felt between the old and the new.

The important thing is not whether Matthew regards the Law as superseded, but, in the first place, to determine how Matthew is presenting central Jewish symbols like the Law, the return from exile, the descent from Abraham. One can certainly subsequently ask how far Matthew's community remains within Judaism, but this is foremost a historical question, not only about Matthew's community's perception of its faithfulness to the tradition, but also about other Jews' views of Matthew's reworking of the inherited symbols.

## Kinship language in Matthew

Where I fully agree with Saldarini is in his assessment of the importance of the family image in Matthew's construction of his community's identity. As we have seen earlier, Philo can entertain notions of fictive kinship and speak of all human beings as 'judged worthy of kinship with Him [sc. God] because he shared the gift of reason', in principle at least.[56] In practice, they fall far short, and it is only in exceptional men like the Patriarchs that such true virtues are embodied. Thus such universal kinship with God is in fact only rarely lived out and kinship with those who are descendants of Abraham and Moses and who embody their virtue in special laws (even though such laws are only copies or images of the archetypes which are the lives of good and blameless men recorded in Scripture)[57] is of the greatest importance. How do such parallels illuminate the central role which Matthew gives to notions of fictive kinship?

For Matthew the central mark of the members of his community, which makes them brothers and sisters of Jesus, who therefore share kinship with each other, is 'doing the will of my Father in heaven' (12:50). This, as we have said, is taken directly from Mark, and assigned a central position in Matthew's Gospel, just before the parabolic discourse on judgement in chapter 13. There are however subtle shifts from Mark's treatment. Mark in his account of discipleship underlines the sense in which those who come to be disciples of Jesus move from darkness to light: Matthew's account underlines more strongly the sense in which

---

[56] *De Abr* 41.
[57] *De Abr* 3–5; see discussion, pp. 44–91 above.

the disciples are called to be instructed by Jesus whose teaching is the fulfilment of the Law. Whereas Mark's account is closer to Philo's depiction of the proselyte to Judaism, who abandons the illusions of his former worship of the gods and comes into the 'best of commonwealths',[58] Matthew's account of discipleship stresses the sense in which the disciples enter under instruction. Nevertheless, repentance is an essential part of the acceptance of Jesus' message: both John and Jesus have the same openings to their preaching: repent and believe the Gospel. There is still, that is to say, a clear sense in which those who become brothers and sisters of Jesus by doing God's will leave their former ways behind them and become members of a new (fictive) family centred on Jesus. Moreover this sense of breaking old ties is underlined in the saying about leaving the dead to bury the dead in Matthew 8:22. The sharpest sense of separation from all other groups comes however in chapter 13 itself, when the sons of the kingdom are distinguished from all others, who are categorised as sons of the evil one (13:38), something which is also found in Qumran sectarianism (1QS 3–4). Thus there is a clearly discernible sense in which Matthew is re-Judaising Mark, and at the same time stressing the deep divisions between himself and those Jews who do not belong to his community. None of this breaks the bounds of what one can discern elsewhere in Jewish groups of the time.

What is new in Matthew's account of fictive kinship, however, is the defining role which is given to Jesus. This is expressed partly in the emphasis which is placed on the disciples' relationship to him rather than to God. Though God is spoken of as their father, they are not spoken of as sons of God but as Jesus' brothers and sisters. And while there is nothing in itself unusual in followers of a Jewish teacher being identified by this link, as witness the followers of Hillel and Shammai, in the case of Jesus more is at stake, as we shall see more fully in chapter 8. If the scribes and Pharisees sit on Moses' seat, and derive their authority from him, Jesus has all authority conferred on him and sits at the right hand of the Father. This relationship to Jesus as the authoritative teacher and judge gives the disciples an entirely different authority in matters of the Law to that to which the Pharisees can lay claim. The latter are at best interpreters of the Law once given to Moses; Jesus is the one to whom all authority has been given to teach the will

---

[58] *De Virt* 175.

of God and to judge men and women accordingly. In his teaching he is free to interpret God's will, to develop and expand what has been previously given ('of old') to Moses. The Law is not being set aside as obsolete or outmoded; rather a greater authority to interpret (not the Law but) God's will is here. He is the one greater than the Temple, the Lord of the Sabbath. This is not supersessionism in the sense that the Law is discarded. But it is a form of reworking of the tradition after the destruction of the Temple which radically undermines any attempt to rebuild the community around the authority of those skilled in the traditions of interpretation of the Mosaic law. In this sense a break is inevitable with those who were laying the foundations of rabbinic Judaism.

## Matthew's modification of Mark's sectarianism

This may now allow us to take up our earlier characterisation of Mark's community as a sect and to see in what sense Matthew has modified Mark's sectarianism. Again, we shall follow Wilson's suggested characteristics of a sect. We have already seen how Matthew modifies Mark's strong emphasis on the *exclusiveness* of the group by softening Mark's use of the metaphors of blindness and sight to characterise the transition to discipleship. Matthew does indeed refer to the Pharisees as 'blind guides' (15:14; 23:16, 24), but that, as Saldarini and Overman rightly emphasise, is directed against a specific group within Judaism and not against Jews as a whole. Similarly, Matthew makes little use of Mark's motif of the Messianic secret. On the other hand, he does take over Mark's account of the meaning of Jesus' parables (13:10–3//Mark 4:10–12) and give it programmatic importance in his story.[59] Jesus' parables will fall on deaf ears because Israel does not understand; and this is underlined by the quotation from Isaiah 6:9–10 in 13:14–15. Only those within the community understand the mysteries and will continue to learn from the parables and Jesus' interpretation.

Like Mark, Matthew's Gospel still shows little sign of the development of a *professional* religious group, though we do read of scribes, prophets

---

[59] See Luz, 1990, 311–14, esp. 113, Israel's lack of understanding is a given, not caused by Jesus' parables, which are, rather, Jesus' answer to Israel's failure to understand: 'Deswegen redet er zum Volk in Gleichnissen, weil es sieht und doch nichts sieht. Das Nichtsehen und Nichthören Israels ist für Matthäus eine feststehende Tatsache. Es wird nicht durch Jesus Gleichnesse bewirkt, sondern eher ist Jesu Gleichnisrede "Antwort" auf dieses Nichtverstehen.'

and wise men (10:41; 13:52; 23:34). The Twelve, too, play a specific role: it is to them that the charge to take the mission to Israel is given and then subsequently extended by the risen Jesus to include all nations. Within this group special authority and power is given to Peter.

There is, as in Mark, a strong emphasis on *choice*: disciples are called to follow Jesus and the cost of such a choice is powerfully emphasised by Matthew's inclusion of Q-material in 8:18–22. Matthew does nothing to soften Mark's emphasis on *self-discipline*, adding a variant version of the saying about plucking out one's eye and cutting off one's hand (Mark 9:43–48//Matt 18:8–9) at 5:29–30, possibly taken from Q (but omitted by Luke). Matthew's second version of the saying occurs in the Community discourse in chapter 18, where Matthew outlines the beginnings of communal disciplinary procedures. Finally, the element of *protest* against 'dominant religious groupings' is clearly intensified: not only does Matthew include the long polemical chapter 23, which is directed first and foremost to the scribes and Pharisees, but which widens finally to embrace Jerusalem; he also adds the exchange between Pilate and the crowds in 27:24–25, in which Pilate washes his hands and the crowd call down Jesus' blood on themselves and their children.

There is little in the way of a modification of sectarian patterns of behaviour to be observed in all this. The difference, if anything, seems to lie in the shift in emphasis in the underlying cosmology. Whereas for Mark the emphasis on blindness and the conferring of sight seems to suggest that the world outside the community lies under dark powers, Matthew's emphasis on Jesus' teaching and discipleship as a form of instruction constructs the different worlds in terms of knowledge and ignorance. But even though Jesus teaches the crowds openly, there is still, as Matthew 13 makes clear, a radical (unbridgeable) gap between Matthew's community and the world outside: they cannot hear or understand because their hearts have been hardened. Jesus' teaching in parables only serves to confirm this. The little knowledge that they had will be taken away from them. Perhaps it is the enormity of the thought that God could have blinded his own people and for ever excluded them, that causes Matthew to introduce an alternative account of the rejection of Jesus' teaching in the parable of the wheat and the tares: that those who do not hear are in fact sons of the evil one.

In any case, Matthew draws the lines tightly around his community. If Mark's Jesus, in the story of the strange exorcist, declares that those who are not against them are for them (9:40), Matthew includes the reverse of this saying in Jesus' rejoinder to the Pharisees in the Beelzebul controversy (12:30). The lines between his community and the rest of the world are clearly demarcated: those who do the will of God belong to the family of Jesus, and this will be confirmed at the final judgement (cf. Matt 7:21–23). Matthew's working of his Q-material, with its strong emphasis on judgement, into the body of Mark's Gospel has the effect of reinforcing the forensic strand in his cosmology. With the exception of the mission charge in chapter 10, all the discourses end with warnings of the coming judgement; and this is the theme of the last discourse in chapters 24–25. The emphasis, on the one hand, on doing the will of the Father in heaven, and on the other hand on the authority divinely conferred on Jesus to teach and judge, confirms his faithful followers as the true members of the family of God.

Underlying this is a different kind of response to the world from which they are so sharply divided. As we saw, Mark's Gospel draws deeply on the Isaianic myth of the way of the Lord and the restoration of the Davidic kingdom. This is in Wilson's terms a reformist response: it seeks 'supernaturally given insights about the ways in which social organization should be amended'.[60] But there is a growing realisation through the Gospel that men and women fail to 'think the things of God' and that the human will is in some sense radically corrupt. The Isaianic framework is subverted and the Gospel looks to more radical solutions, the renewal of creation through the overcoming of death in resurrection. The cross is the catalyst for the supernaturally wrought destruction of the natural and social world. In this sense Mark's Gospel is deeply informed by the revolutionist myth of the overthrow of the dark powers, even if it recedes into the background after its initial statement.

Matthew, it would seem, lays far greater stress on the reformist/restorationist myth. Jesus himself is portrayed as the one who comes to give the final authoritative account of the 'supernaturally given insights' which can lead to the restoration of the people of Israel. But as we have seen, this account of Israel's restoration is undercut by Israel's lack of understanding, its refusal to hear. What is required is a change of heart, but the people's hearts are hardened (13:15; 15:8). The Gospel is for the pure in heart (5:8), and requires a deep inner reorientation to counteract the desires of the heart which corrupt and lead people astray (5:28; 15:18–19; 22:37). Jesus' disciples are to learn of him who is

---

[60] Wilson, 1975, 25.

lowly, humble of heart (11:29), and this is expressed in Jesus' forgiveness of sins (9:2–6).[61] In the same way the disciples are also to forgive one another from their heart (18:35). In this sense Matthew's Gospel betrays a strong conversionist character,[62] and the mission to Israel and the hope for its restoration are abandoned and replaced by a universal mission to all nations, in which all are to be made disciples, to learn of Jesus and to be baptised into the new righteousness which he brings.

### Fictive kinship in the Gospel of Matthew: the question of Jewish ethnicity

We have been arguing so far that a social historical reading of Matthew's Gospel strongly suggests that his community was sectarian in nature. The conversionist turn it was already displaying might further suggest that its sense of marginality was not so much to the Jewish community as to the wider world of the Roman principate. Without question it started life as a Jewish group; without question it affirmed its own Jewish roots; but its reworking of central Jewish symbols of law and prophecy, of restoration and return, in the light of the Gospel narrative with its final ascription of all authority to Jesus and 'all that he had commanded', led to the construction of a community ethos and world-view which was incompatible with attempts to base Judaism on the interpretation of the law enshrined in the traditions of the *Hakamim*. It meant furthermore that Jesus' teaching could be used as an authoritative interpretative principle by which to qualify and modify the Law, as the case of divorce and oaths and the omission of any requirement of circumcision for new disciples makes clear.

Much recent discussion of Matthew's Gospel, we have seen, has suggested that Matthew's community was a Christian Jewish community, thinking of itself as Jewish, battling for dominance over the Jewish community as a whole, attacking the leaders of 'formative Judaism', constructing its own particular version of Judaism, shaped by its belief in Jesus as the Messiah. In all this, it was acting as a deviant association

---

[61] Davies and Allison, 1991, 291, write that this is 'yet one more indication that in 11.25–30 Jesus is the functional equivalent of Torah: the Sages learned Torah, the disciples learn Jesus'.

[62] Cf. Wilson, 1975, 22: 'Salvation is seen . . . as available . . . only by a profoundly felt, supernaturally wrought transformation of the self. The objective world will not change but the acquisition of a new subjective orientation to it will itself be salvation.'

within Judaism. Much of this discussion, notably in the work of Saldarini and Sim, is illuminating. The key questions are, on the one hand, when does a deviant association become so isolated that it ceases to see itself as belonging to the wider community from which it diverges? and, on the other hand, what bearing did the radical change in Jewish religious organisation, leadership and institutions, in the wake of the Jewish War and the destruction of Jerusalem, have on the relationship of such Christian bodies to other Jewish groupings?

A further question may help to shed some light on this vexed problem of the relation of Matthew's community to Judaism, namely, that of the significance which Matthew attaches to Jewish ethnicity. Does Matthew still regard his group as having its place within the Jewish *ethnos*? Here I shall be particularly concerned with the arguments of David Sim, who has argued that Matthew's community 'accepted the distinctive Jewish notion of the privileged position of the Jewish nation' and believed 'that only Jews could share in the salvation brought by the Christ'.[63] It would follow, then, that Gentiles would first have to become Jews by being circumcised, and only then could they 'be inducted into Matthew's sectarian Jewish group in the same manner as those who were Jews by birth. Ethnicity was therefore part and parcel of Matthean Christianity and the Gospel which represented it'.[64] This is an interesting, if extreme, position, for two reasons. First, because I think Sim is right to claim that it 'take[s] to the logical conclusion the latest studies on the social setting of the Matthean community which have emphasised its sectarian nature vis-à-vis the remainder of the Jewish world'.[65] It is surely right that, if Matthew saw the members of his community as Christian *Jews*, he would have insisted on maintaining one of the key markers of Jewish identity. One only has to consider a text like *Jub* 15:26, 'Anyone who is born whose own flesh is not circumcised on the eighth day is not from the sons of the covenant which the Lord made for Abraham since he is from the children of destruction', to see how extraordinary it would have been for a Christian Jewish *sect* to have dropped the requirement of circumcision for any but the most unusual and exceptional of cases, if at all. Certainly this does not deal directly with the case of proselytes, but it would be hardly thinkable that, if proselytes were to be made at all, they would not have had to be circumcised. Second, Sim poses the

---

[63] Sim, 1996a, 194.
[64] Sim, 1996a, 195.
[65] Sim, 1996a, 194.

question about Matthew's treatment of ethnicity in his construction of early Christian identity with great clarity.

The subject of ethnicity is itself complex and there is certainly no unanimity among social anthropologists about its nature and maintenance. There are those, like Shils and Geertz, who argue that ethnicity is rooted in common ties of kinship, shared territory and tradition: 'Congruities of blood, speech, custom, are seen to have an ineffable, and at times overpowering coerciveness in and of themselves.'[66] Others, however, have argued that we should be wary of underestimating the extent to which agents within particular ethnic groups can influence their development and growth, as they interact with other groups and cultures. Ethnic boundaries can be maintained, despite considerable changes in culture and the incorporation of outsiders. Ethnic identities, that is to say, can be reworked, 'constructed' through the course of the group's history.[67]

What then of Matthew? More specifically, what were Matthew's intentions in writing his Gospel, in view of the conflicts and controversies within early Christianity about the admission of Gentiles to the community? Where did he stand as between those who insisted that all those who were to be baptised should first (also?) be circumcised and those who saw this as a denial of the gospel? What longer term contribution did his Gospel have to make to these debates?

## Matthew as a Christian Jew: David Sim

Let me start with David Sim's article in *Ethnicity and the Bible.*[68] Sim argues that 'the question of ethnicity was of fundamental importance in all the traditions which comprised first-century Judaism';[69] that it was linked to belief in the Jews' election by God and in the covenant which secured their relationship to him, of which circumcision was a necessary sign; that physical descent was not a necessary condition of membership: Gentile-born males could be admitted, if circumcised. Maybe there was some form of baptism for females.[70] The church was divided over the importance of membership of the Jewish people, that is to say, over the

---

[66] Shils, 1957, quoted in Brett, 1996, 12.
[67] Here the work of Fredrik Barth, 1969, is of the greatest importance. See, for a wider discussion, Hutchinson and Smith, 1996, and Banks, 1996.
[68] Sim, 1996a.
[69] Sim, 1996a, 171.
[70] Sim, 1996a, 171–7.

question whether Christianity (the group of those who accepted Jesus as the Christ) was to remain an ethnic religion, linked to membership of a particular people, with its ties of blood, land and tradition. Those of the circumcision party believed that it should, and that therefore non-Jewish converts should be circumcised as well as baptised. Others, like Paul, believed that abandonment of the pagan cult, baptism and the embracing of the Christian ethos was enough.[71] Matthew, maintains Sim, affirmed the importance of Jewish identity and therefore would have insisted on circumcision for Gentile converts.

His arguments can be briefly summarised: In the first place, Matthew 5:17–19 requires full obedience of Torah. No exceptions are made; in particular there are no distinctions made between the obligations on Jews and Gentiles; only, Matthew's church is to obey the Torah as taught by Jesus, the Messiah.[72] Second, 18:15–17 shows that Matthew still thinks in terms of the old boundaries between Jews and Gentiles: those who are subsequently excluded from the community become as Gentiles. This shows that he regarded as Jews those Gentiles who had been admitted to the church and that they, too, should refrain from contact with Gentiles.[73] Jesus' conduct in the Gospel provides an example of this. In editing Mark 7:1–30, Matthew drops Mark's 'thus he declared all foods clean' and also Mark's subsequent account of Jesus' entering the Syro-Phoenician woman's house. Because this would have implied that he ate with the Gentile householders, Matthew sets the scene outside the house.[74] Further, the fact that in Matthew 28:19 he speaks only of baptising those who are made disciples, and not of their being circumcised, is no counter-argument, for just as at Qumran where initiation rites are discussed, the need would not have been felt to insist on the obvious, namely, circumcision. Circumcision is not an issue between Matthew and Jamnia, the dominant body with which his sectarian community is locked in debate and conflict. Sim also believes it to be unlikely that Matthew's church was itself engaged in Gentile mission (Peter, his key apostle, was charged with the mission to the Jews)[75] and again, therefore, such questions would not have arisen.

---

[71] Sim, 1996a, 177–84.
[72] Sim, 1996a, 186–7.
[73] Sim, 1996a, 190.
[74] Sim, 1996a, 191–2.
[75] Sim, 1998, 196–9.

Let me make some initial response and then broaden the field a little.

The passage 5:17–19 needs of course to be read in the context of the rest of Jesus' teaching, not least the antitheses of the Sermon on the Mount. If Qumran is to be taken as an analogous Jewish sectarian grouping, then it is striking that there is nothing comparable in the community's writings to the contrastive usage of the formula which Matthew uses: 'You have heard that it was said to the men of old, but I say unto you.' If, following Luz, we read this as a divine passive, then there seems to be a clear contrast, not between the teaching of the Pharisees and Jesus, but between what was revealed by God to the 'men of old' and what Jesus has to say.[76] The Messianic teaching of the Law is not simply *opposed* to the law, but is legislation for the new age which the Messiah inaugurates. Here what was previously allowed – divorce on grounds other than of adultery and swearing of oaths in legal proceedings – is disallowed.

It might be argued that allowing divorce on grounds other than adultery was a matter of interpretation of the ruling in Deuteronomy 24:1–4, but the matter is complicated. In the first instance, Deuteronomy 24:1–4 does not regulate the grounds for divorce: it alludes to divorce in the course of a regulation forbidding the remarriage of a divorced woman to her first husband, if she has subsequently remarried and divorced, or been widowed. Thus the first half of the antithesis, 5:31, does not quote Deuteronomy 24:1–4 directly, but gives only a rather loose précis, which may however accurately summarise how the passage was taken in the first century (cf. Mark 10:3–5//Matt 19:7–8). Secondly, the discussion of bills of divorce in the Mishnah, *Gittin*, is almost entirely concerned with the correct procedures for the writing and delivery of such bills. The question of the proper *grounds* for divorce arises only in *Gittin* 10, where it is only the school of Shammai which proposes a limitation on the husband's freedom to divorce his wife. The school of Hillel and R. Akiba both allow a man to

---

[76] Luz, 1989, 249. Luz argues that reading ἐρρέθη as a *passivum divinum* for God's speaking in Scripture is in accord both with rabbinic exegetical terminology (referring to Bacher, 1899: נאמר is the most common for biblical citations) and Matthew's own usage. There is an element of circularity in the latter point as all Matthew's uses come within the antitheses (5:21, 27, 31, 33, 38, 43). Nevertheless, with the exception of 5:43, what is said is to be found in Scripture. Cf. Paul's use in Rom 9:12, 26, and in Gal 3:16 where what is said are the promises to Abraham and his offspring, which again has a clear referent in Scripture.

divorce according to his pleasure or inclination, and it is reasonable to conjecture that this was the majority view, at least among men. In this respect Jesus and the school of Shammai are in agreement in what is clearly both contentious (it is a test question which is put to Jesus to embarrass him, Matt 19:3) and innovative. Against the widespread view, which saw the writing of a bill of divorce as a matter entirely within the discretion of the husband, Shammai and those who followed him, including in this respect Jesus, argued that there should be strict curbs on divorce. Jesus' claim is that Moses' ruling was a means of providing some protection for the women in the face of such 'hardness of heart'. His own ruling is for those whose hearts have been turned and who have thus entered the new realm of the kingdom. Thus Matthew sees this as Messianic legislation for the new age, continuous with, but for his disciples replacing, the old permissions. This clearly informs the sense in which Jesus 'fulfils' the law and the prophets.

Similar points can be made about the section in the antitheses on oaths. Oaths are an important means of regulating civic affairs which are clearly of central importance to Israel, but which Jesus regards as out of place in the new dispensation. This is a radical move which, as the history of its interpretation in the Christian church makes quite clear, could cause deep disturbance in societies where solemn oaths were an important instrument for ensuring that witnesses in formal or informal[77] criminal investigations would tell the truth.[78]

The immediate point of this argument is that Jesus is portrayed by Matthew as fulfilling the law in ways which allow for its modification, to the point of setting aside provisions in the law which are no longer seen as binding in the new dispensation. This would certainly be consistent with the omission of circumcision and the substitution of

---

[77] One need not think only of formal criminal proceedings, though clearly the power of oaths to constrain witnesses to tell the truth, in any society where there is little or no policing and at best rudimentary methods of collecting proof, is extremely important. Informally, too, oaths may be of the greatest significance. In African compounds, if there has been an unexplained theft, members of the household will be asked to swear their innocence on the Bible, oral communication from Dr. Eric Anum.

[78] See e.g. the account of the struggle between the Pennsylvanian Assembly and the British Government over this issue, in Boorstin, 1958, 40–8. The Quakers were allowed to retain the freedom not to swear oaths, but at a considerable political price: they accepted the criminal laws of England with respect to capital punishment, making many more crimes punishable by death.

baptism for Gentiles who would enter the kingdom. Interestingly, at least in the case of divorce, this reflects proposals (albeit controversial ones) which were being advanced by others, the school of Shammai, at this time. In the same way, as the case of King Izates makes clear, there were those who at the time thought that it was possible to forgo the requirement of circumcision for proselytes, even though this was a minority opinion.[79] For Matthew, Jesus' proposals were more radical, in the sense that they were not simply pragmatic concessions but represented legislation for a new age.

The difficulty *on any view* is that Matthew does not discuss circumcision at all. Is this because circumcision would have been regarded as a matter of course? or would the absence of any explicit instruction have been taken as indicating that it was not required? The instruction to the Eleven in 28:18–20, a passage which includes some indication of entrance procedures into the community, refers explicitly to 'teaching them to observe all that I have commanded you'.[80] The most reasonable inference is that it is Jesus' explicitly recorded and transmitted teaching which is normative for the community. On as contentious a matter as circumcision had become in the church after the Pauline mission, the absence of a specific command from Jesus (not least in a context where he does prescribe baptism, which is not in the Mosaic law) would carry the presumption that it was not commanded. How could one possibly persuade a convert that this painful and distressing procedure was required, when he could point to this passage?

An intriguing question is raised by 18:15–17. Does it mean: treat him like *you* treat Gentiles and tax-collectors? or treat him like Jews? The problem is that the use of the phrase to refer to exclusion from the community is very strange (on any view), given the command of Jesus at the end of the Gospel to go and make disciples of all nations.[81] Gentiles are people Jesus usually tells them to go to, not to avoid. Even

---

[79] Josephus, *Ant* 20:38–48.

[80] διδάσκοντες αὐτοὺς τηρεῖν πάντα ὅσα ἐνετειλάμην ὑμῖν. The phrase has a number of significant parallels in the LXX, which are listed by Davies and Allison, 1997, 686: Exod 7:2; Deut 1:3; 6:1; 30:8; Josh 1:7; 22:2; Judg 13:14; Jer 1:7; cf. also *T Job* 4:2; *T Mos* 1:10; *2 Bar* 4:7.

[81] As Davies and Allison point out (1988, 559) such a paradox, concern with Gentile mission and shunning of Gentiles, is not unique to Matthew's Gospel. *The Testaments of the Twelve Patriarchs* both emphasise the salvation of the Gentiles and yet forbid readers to take Gentile wives (*T Levi* 14:6) and to become involved in 'revolting Gentile affairs' (*T Jud* 23:2).

if, as Sim thinks, the Matthaean church was itself not engaged in mission to the Gentiles,[82] it would be odd in the light of 28:19 to use the phrase in a *literal or straightforward sense* to refer to social exclusion. Hence the allusive sense 'like "they" (cf. "their" synagogues) treat Gentiles' is more likely. Former Gentile readers, as well as Jews, would understand what was meant. What of course this text does make abundantly clear is that, however the boundaries of the group were being drawn, whether around a group constituted on the basis of Jewish ethnicity plus acknowledgement of Jesus as Messiah, or of discipleship of Jesus alone, boundaries were indeed being drawn, if reluctantly (cf. 18:22, 'seventy times seven')!

The fact that 1QS does not mention circumcision in its account of initiation into the community seems to provide only a partial parallel to Matthew 28:19. Qumran clearly sees itself as a faithful remnant of the covenant community and its initiation ceremonies as ratifying the election of individual members to the *yaḥad*. The issue of what to do about Gentile 'postulants' and therefore of circumcision hardly arises.[83] In Matthew, it most certainly does: explicitly in Matthew 28:19 and at least indirectly in 21:43, where the kingdom is to be given to a 'nation (*ethnos*)[84] producing the fruits of it'. Yet in neither of these cases does the question of circumcision as an initiation requirement arise.

---

[82] Reading 'all nations' as embracing Jews as well as Gentiles, with the majority of commentators; see Davies and Allison, 1997, 684. But this in turn suggests a certain relativisation of ethnic differences: 'Universal lordship means universal mission ... Inclusion of the Jews harmonises with the universalism of the rest of the passage'.

[83] There is some consideration of it, however, in *Jubilees* 15, a text found in the Qumran library. Here, in the context of a firm declaration that 'anyone who is born whose own flesh is not circumcised on the eighth day is not from the sons of the covenant which the Lord made for Abraham' (15:26), the writer also affirms that the sons of the covenant are not restricted to the direct descendants of Abraham, for 'he sanctified them and gathered them from all the sons of man because (there are) many nations and many people, and they all belong to him' (15:31).

[84] Saldarini, 1994, 59–61, rightly points out that ἔθνος in Greek has a wide range of uses, referring to various kinds of bodies. He objects to its translation here as 'nation' on the grounds that (*a*) the Jewish leaders take it as referring to themselves; (*b*) that the Christian group around Matthew saw themselves as a sub-group and not as a 'nation' in any ethnic sense; (*c*) that the parable in talking about the tenancy being taken away from the tenants is talking about one group being dispossessed in relation to Israel, not to Israel as a whole being dispossessed. Much of this seems to me to be right; I cannot believe that the meaning here is that the church is to be seen as a new ethnic grouping similar to, but wholly distinct from, Israel. But some qualifications do also need to be made. I do not think the self-understanding of the Matthaean community is that of 'a small sub-group' or of a voluntary organisation or small social group. On the contrary, they see themselves

This is particularly revealing in 28:19 where there is reference to rites of entry, namely, baptism. This needs to be read in its wider context in Matthew. This is partly in relation to Jesus' remark to John that his baptism is necessary in order to fulfil all righteousness (3:15). In the light of the discussion above about righteousness, I take it to mean that baptism marks the entry into a new order with its own ethos and group identity. This point is reinforced by John's castigation of the scribes and Pharisees who come to him for baptism, who 'presume to say to themselves "We have Abraham as our father"' (3:9). God, says John, is able to raise up children to Abraham from these stones. What is required in the coming age which will be inaugurated by the coming one, is repentance and baptism in the Holy Spirit. Inscribing the marks of Abrahamic circumcision in the flesh is not important: concern with such questions stands in the way of true repentance and openness to the coming one.[85]

## Ethnicity and kinship

What the discussion so far has done is to show how Sim's points may be met. There are other areas, however, which need to be drawn into the discussion. Though Sim's article is about ethnicity in Matthew, it focuses largely on the question of circumcision of Gentile converts, a matter to which there is not a single direct reference. It does not consider those central elements which by general agreement go to make up ethnicity: 'kinship, shared territory and tradition'. We need now to widen the debate, focusing on questions of kinship and deferring discussion of attachment to the Land to the next chapter. If Matthew were wishing to insist on his own community's inclusion within the Jewish ethnos, he

---

as part of the 'many who will come to sit at table with Abraham, Isaac, and Jacob' (8:11), as those commissioned by the Son of Man, to whom *all* authority has been given, to go and make disciples of all nations (28:19), and this pressing of the metaphor of the vineyard must, sooner or later, lead to its extension. Precisely because of the corporate sense of ἔθνος, one cannot detach the nature of the leadership from the nature of the people they lead. Israel led by the followers of Jesus will be a different kind of grouping from that led by the Jewish leaders opposed to Jesus and Matthew's community.

[85] For most commentators, the question whether Matthew intended it to be understood that all those being baptised would previously have been circumcised scarcely arises. Davies and Allison, 1997, 685, comment: 'Matthew, despite his insistence on upholding the Jewish law, never mentions circumcision. That he expected Jewish Christians to circumcise their male children is plausible; but he evidently did not think such necessary for Gentiles.'

would have been unlikely to play down or ignore elements such as descent from Jewish parentage and ancestors, or indeed attachment to the Land.

We have already seen how central a role the language of fictive kinship plays in Matthew.[86] Much of this is taken from Mark, where it is used to give a sense of belonging and group-definition to the members of a community which clearly sees itself as distinct from the Jewish people, and which sets aside important aspects of the Law (ch. 7). For Mark the disciples are the community of the brothers and sisters of Jesus. Matthew retains this language and intensifies its use. He strengthens the elements in the call narrative which stress the brothers leaving their father.[87] He incorporates the Q-material in 8:18–22 into Mark's story of the stilling of the storm, turning it into an icon of the church; he adds further Q-material (10:34–38) to his Markan material (Matt 10:16–23//Mark 13:9–13) in his depiction of the interfamilial conflicts which await the disciples. Finally, he concludes the section immediately leading into the parables discourse in chapter 13 with the Markan pericope on the family of Jesus. On the other hand, as we have seen, he incorporates into the Markan call narrative the whole of the Sermon on the Mount, making the vital point that those who follow Jesus enter on a path of instruction by the one who fulfils the Law and the prophets.

All this is material which sets aside family ties and introduces notions of a 'family of Jesus'. Matthew also introduces matters of physical ties of kinship. The Gospel starts with a direct reference to Jesus' physical descent from David and Abraham. If Davies and Allison are right that the sense of βίβλος γενέσεως here goes beyond just a reference to the up-coming genealogy, but also embraces the new world which is brought into being by Jesus, then the verse stands for much else that is characteristic of Matthew.[88] On the one hand, right from the beginning, he wants to emphasise Jesus' descent from David and Abraham. Jesus is a Jew by blood, a member of the people. On the other hand, what he brings is a new creation, analogous to, but also transcending ('fulfilling'), what has gone before. The 'fulfilment quotations' make

---

[86] See above, pp. 209–11.

[87] Matthew adds δύο ἀδελφούς twice (4:18, 21; ctr. Mark 1:16, 19), notes that Zebedee their father is in the boat with the two brothers (4:21) and rephrases the last sentence in a way which does nothing to diminish the sense in which discipleship is linked to leaving occupation and family: οἱ δὲ εὐθέως ἀφέντες τὸ πλοῖον καὶ τὸν πατέρα αὐτῶν ἠκολούθησαν αὐτῷ.

[88] Davies and Allison, 1988, 149–54.

the same point, both anchoring the events of Jesus' life in the Jewish Scriptures and at the same time thereby representing those Scriptures as pointing forward to a greater reality (cf. 12:6: 'I tell you, something greater than the temple is here').[89]

But if Matthew wants to emphasise Jesus' Jewishness, other passages undermine the importance of such kinship-ties. We have already mentioned John's remarks to the scribes and Pharisees (Matt 3:9). In 8:10, Jesus commends the centurion's faith and adds: 'Many will come from east and west and sit at table with Abraham, Isaac, and Jacob in the kingdom of heaven, while the sons of the kingdom will be thrown into the outer darkness' (8:11–12). Abraham will welcome un-circumcised Gentiles,[90] while the sons of the kingdom (those physically descended from him) will be thrown out.[91] There is no mention in Matthew of the centurion's love of the Jewish nation (ctr. Luke 7:5); it is solely his faith in Jesus' power to heal which earns him Jesus' commendation. Luz is right to see this as an exemplary story, designed to encourage faith in Gentile readers.[92] Thus Jesus is presented as rooted by virtue of his ancestry in the history of God's dealings with his chosen people; he is also presented as the one who brings a new history which will fulfil the expectations of the prophets and which will embrace all who have faith in him, no matter what their ethnic origin.

This brief survey shows something of the complexity of Matthew's handling of the material he uses which contains references to kinship, literal or fictive. Clearly, commentators like Saldarini can see the sections which emphasise the relationship of the disciples to Jesus as brothers

---

[89] In a similar manner, as Dale Allison, 1993, has shown, Matthew uses the rhetorical device of *synkrisis*, comparing Jesus with Moses to draw out the special and transcendent significance of Jesus. For further discussion, see chapter 8 below.

[90] Davies and Allison, 1991, 26–9, take this to refer to diaspora Jews. Allison, 1997, 176–91, see esp. 190–1, suggests that, while Q probably thought of diaspora Jews, Matthew, in line with Christian usage (John 11:51–52; Jas 1:1; 1 Pet 1:1, 17; 2:11; *5 Ezra* 1:38; Rev 7), was maybe referring to the Church of Jews and Gentiles as the already-being-realised eschatological ingathering of the peoples. This is a highly intriguing possibility which would capture the distinctive mix of continuity and discontinuity with Jewish expectations that is characteristic of Matthew's thought.

[91] Cf. Meeks, 1985, 112, quoted in Saldarini, 1994, 233, who sees 8:11 as a prediction of the rejection of the Jews: 'The implication of this dark saying works its way through the rest of the gospel' to the point where Israel is finally replaced. Saldarini wants to see the pericope as a prophetic warning, designed to 'provoke repentance'. This is all very well, but the verse contains fairly clear allusions to the destruction of Jerusalem which Matthew sees as the fulfilment of the prophetic threat; see again Luz, 1990, 15.

[92] Luz, 1990, 15–17.

and sisters as indicative of the sectarian identity within Judaism of the Matthaean community. However, it seems questionable whether such commentators take seriously enough the passages which explicitly reject the importance of physical kinship-ties. Qumran may provide an instructive parallel. There are important points of similarity between Matthew and Qumran in the tight definition of group boundaries, initiation procedures, polemic against the Temple authorities and the Pharisees, and moral perfectionism. Qumran, like Matthew, also uses the language of fictive kinship to emphasise the distinctiveness of the community over against faithless Israel, and indeed the whole world: 'sons of light/darkness' (1QS 3–4; cf. Matt 13:38: 'sons of the kingdom/ of the evil one'). But whereas Matthew directly attacks notions of physical kinship/descent, Qumran insists on the lineage of the priests in the community as 'sons of Zadok' (1QS 5) and sees the community as a 'faithful remnant' of Israel (CD 1). It retains, that is, the language of kinship and ethnicity, while certainly allegorising it in order to make crucially important distinctions between itself and other Jews. The problem for the Jewish sectarian thesis about Matthew, then, is this: if Matthew's community is a sect struggling for a position within the tradition against the majority who seek to marginalise or exclude it, why would it want to water down or obliterate key factors in the establishment of membership of the group such as kinship? Questions about circumcision of proselytes are, after all, mostly exceptional matters: the key thing is membership of the group by descent and circumcision.[93] If they were all that concerned about circumcision as a sign of the covenant, then surely they would be equally concerned with matters of physical descent, which do of course form a central and interlocking part of the promise to Abraham (Gen 12:2; 15:5; 17:1–14; 22:17–18).

## Conclusion

The picture of Matthew's community which emerges from these discussions is intriguing. Matthew seems on the one hand to be sensitive to many of Mark's concerns. If Mark is developing a community with a strong sense of its own identity over against the wider society in which

---

[93] This would certainly have been true if Matthew's community, as Sim argues, was not engaged in Gentile mission. If they were so engaged, then the whole thesis becomes in any case less plausible.

they live, so is Matthew. And in so doing Matthew will make full use of those elements in Mark's Gospel which stress the group's sense of belonging to a family of God focused on their relationship to Jesus. This will provide a relatively unstructured, intimate group with a sense of strong cohesiveness and no sharp divisions between appointed leaders and the rest of the people. It will be a voluntary group, where members have chosen to adopt this particular pattern of belief and behaviour. It will be a group which will easily tend to divide the world sharply into two: those who are brothers and sisters of Jesus, those who are not; those who are sons of the kingdom, those who are sons of the evil one. The shift from ethnic group definitions with their invocations of (real or supposed) physical descent from common ancestors (sons of Abraham) to allegorised kinship definitions (brothers and sisters of Jesus) *tends* to a more radical division of the world into two. True, Jews can divide the world into Jews and Gentiles; the book of *Jubilees*, in its retelling of Genesis 15 can divide the world into those nations ruled over by spirits who lead them astray and those ruled over by God; but in so doing, it also plays down the importance of physical descent from the ancestors. Qumran, in the section on the Two Spirits, can make similar moves and it too allegorises kinship motifs in referring to its own members. On the other hand, group definitions in terms of descent from common ancestors leave room for alternative kinds of definition of those outside the group, as we have seen in *Jubilees*' use of the Table of Nations to construct a map of the world. The world is divided into the descendents of Shem, Ham and Japheth and territories allotted accordingly. Similarly, distinctions can be made among the descendents of Shem, importantly between the descendents of Isaac and Ishmael. A world of ethnic diversity is created, which allows a place for other groups and nations in sacred history and geography, even if that same history and geography ascribes pride of place to Israel.

What is intriguing about Matthew is the way in which he interweaves these two kinds of group definition. The Matthaean *ecclesia* is the company of the brothers and sisters of Jesus, Messiah, the son of David, son of Abraham. The story which Matthew tells is the new book of Genesis, the story of the new creation which springs out of this new act of God in Jesus. As such, it is continuous with, anchored in the old history, its very fulfilment. But, and this is the crucial difference, it does not allow for alternative group-definitions of a comparable kind, for the new creation has its genesis in Jesus: those who wish to enter into this new world must enter through the narrow gate of his call and teaching. The alternative is the broad gate and the easy way which leads to destruction.

It is then not difficult to see how it was that Matthew could become both the Gospel of the Great Church and of Jewish Christianity. On the one hand, it could be seen as a universal Gospel which would embrace all nations and subordinate their ethnic differences to notions of a universal family of God (albeit with a hierarchical form of love-patriarchy), but which would, at the same time, allow little or no place for other religious groupings. On the other hand, it could become the Gospel of a form of Christian Judaism, which would sever all links both with other forms of Judaism and with the Great Church. They were the only true form of Judaism, and indeed the only true source of righteousness and salvation.

Underlying these two partial, but for all that very powerful, readings of Matthew's Gospel are the two schemata that we have detected. On the one hand, there is the restorationist eschatology which sees the church as the instrument whereby God will restore the former glories of his people, which they lost through their disobedience, but who will be brought back into the ways of righteousness through the instruction which Jesus brings. On the other hand, the cosmic dualist eschatology, which sees the church as the bastion against the forces of darkness, which threaten the world and will finally be destroyed and confined to the places of eternal punishment prepared for them. Closely allied to this is the conversionist view that only those who have undergone a profound change of heart can be members of the new community, the ark of the church which will preserve them from the onslaughts of the evil one.

It is not that the two readings, of Christian Judaism and of the Great Church, simply represent extrapolations of one alone of these two poles of Matthaean cosmology. Rather, they each represent different ways of combining the two. Jewish Christianity, believing itself to be firmly in the succession of the people of Israel, sees itself as perfectly fulfilling the Law and the covenant, and lives in the expectation of the final judgement which will establish God's righteousness over his world. In this sense, it draws freely on the restorationist myth; at the same time, Jewish Christians see themselves as sharply distinguished from all other Jews by virtue of their recognition of Jesus as the Christ, the Petrine faith and confession which is the foundation of their community. This community is distinguished from all other communities as the one which can stand against the powers of darkness.

The Great Church, by contrast, takes up the allegorising strain in Matthew's Gospel, seeing itself as the family of God, which is grounded in its call and instruction by Jesus. Jesus' genealogy and the witness of the Old Testament ensure their place in sacred history, but that history has now moved on: the kingdom has been taken away from the people of Israel and given to a new nation, whose task is to make disciples of all nations, Jews and Gentiles alike. They are heirs of Isaiah's promises of the restoration of Israel's glory and its manifestation to the Gentiles. That manifestation now occurs in the history of Jesus and of his followers' continuation of his teaching mission. The church is the *navis ecclesiae*, the haven for all who seek salvation and liberation from the powers of darkness and who are willing to follow the commandments of the exalted Lord to whom all authority in heaven and earth has been given.

The fact that two such strikingly different readings of Matthew's Gospel were generated in the early centuries of the church is an indication of the oppositions which lie within the Gospel itself. This may in turn help to explain the sharp divisions among present-day commentators over the issue of Matthew's community's relation to formative Judaism. It is a Janus-like book which, more than Mark, looks back to the origins of Jesus' story in the history of Israel and forward to the new creation which he brings, which will embrace the whole world and banish the powers of darkness. The challenge for the contemporary church reader is to hold these two strands, the particularist and the universal together, in ways which allow respect and space for other communities outside the Christian family, while at the same time affirming the universal significance and value of the teaching of Jesus.

# 7

# Matthew and the remaking of sacred space

## Introduction

Matthew's reworking of Mark, we have already begun to see, was in no small way influenced by inner-Jewish debates and conflicts after the destruction of the Temple. Subjugation by Rome inflicted deep wounds. Jews were openly humiliated throughout the Empire, on coins depicting Jewry in chains, and by the public display and profanation of their sacred objects, by the levy of a direct tax to Rome in place of the former Temple tax.[1] Their central institutions were dismantled: physically, Jerusalem, and with it the Temple, was laid low; politically, the ruling élite, the high priestly families, was disempowered and, sooner or later,

---

[1] Thus one central marker of Jewish identity, the Temple tax, was transformed into a powerful reminder of Jewish subjugation, with the added twist that refusal to pay the Roman levy amounted to a denial of one's Jewish identity. The story of the coin in the fish's mouth in 17:24–27 *may* reflect this situation. As it stands, it is explicitly about the tax paid freely (so, rightly, Luz, 1990, 531) to the Temple. It may well be that the story originally comes, as Luz suggests, from a Jewish Christian community before the destruction of the Temple and is critical of the institution of the Temple tax, while upholding the Temple cult (Davies and Allison, 1991, 745). The 'sons of the king' in this reading are then the Israelites who should be free to pay the tax as they wish. It represents a conciliatory attitude towards contemporary Jewish practice; see, too, Bauckham, 1986. The question still remains, why did Matthew include this text, which deals with matters which were no longer relevant after the destruction of the Temple? Luz simply concludes that it was 'out of faithfulness to the tradition' (1990, 536). Another possibility is that Matthew connected it with the paying of the Roman tax into the *fiscus Iudaicus*. If so, what point was he making? If Matthew's community is now thought to have replaced the 'sons of the kingdom', 8:12 (cf. 13:38), what freedom did they have *vis-à-vis* the Roman tax? Would Christians, if circumcised, have been able to escape paying the tax? One can only speculate. It may be that in some centres clear identification with the Christian community would have sufficed to exempt circumcised Jews from paying the tax. Even so, if the notion of the freedom of the 'sons of the king' could be used to justify this act of dissociation, what of the story of the fish's coin? Did it suggest that they should nevertheless show solidarity? Or is this simply a case of selective exegesis: Christians should be free to exercise their right as sons. The story of the fish merely suggests how Jesus solved the practical difficulties which he and his disciples faced.

would be replaced by the rabbinate. Such a devastating series of blows to Jewish pride and self-consciousness would not necessarily have led to the immediate abandonment of all hopes for the restoration and rebuilding of their central institutions and for the recovery of national sovereignty within the Land; two further major uprisings, in the Diaspora and in the Land itself, would follow before such hopes would cease to stir Jews to military action. Yet, while such hopes may have by no means been abandoned in the time at which Matthew was writing, on the practical level, Jews, in order to survive as a community, had to forge new institutions, new patterns of religious life and observance, and to seek new ways of sustaining their sense of identity. They could not carry on as before, because the priesthood had lost its role and the Temple cult was destroyed, and political power over the Land had been denied them; but in forging new institutions and forms of religious observance they had, as far as possible, to maintain a sense of continuity with the past, whether this lay in developing those aspects of Judaism which had not been undermined by the events of the First Jewish Revolt, or in linking new institutions to past history or to promises and hopes, whose realisation would be placed firmly in the hands of God and God alone.

In this respect, there is a major difference between matters relating to ethnicity and those concerning the Land and the Temple. In so far as Jewish identity was linked to physical descent from the Patriarchs and to ties of kinship within Jewish family groupings, it was relatively untouched by recent events.[2] In so far as it was linked to the Land, Jerusalem and the Temple, major change was inevitable. Not that such changes were wholly unprecedented: Jews who had lived in the Diaspora had had of necessity to create a way of life for themselves which for most practical purposes dispensed with the Temple cult and the priesthood. But now such changes were forced on all Jews with a new urgency.

---

[2]  Relatively, because even so the ranking of Jewish families was affected by the priestly families' loss of power and the (more or less) gradual assumption of power by a trained rabbinate whose lines of succession were only partially determined by physical descent. One should probably not underestimate the effects of such changes. Positions of leadership within the Jewish community were now open to all who could acquire the necessary education and learning, whereas previously the highpriesthood had been open only to members of certain families. In this respect Judaism moves closer to existing patterns of access to power in the Graeco-Roman world, where Greek education and learning provides one route which is theoretically open to all.

Matthew went some way to affirming the importance of physical descent, by introducing the genealogy of Jesus at the beginning of his Gospel and by stressing his descent from Abraham and David. Jesus' role as Messiah is, in part at least, authenticated by his descent from the royal house of David. But Matthew restricted the importance of physical ties to Jesus:[3] what was significant for those who wished to be his followers was obedience to the will of God, being trained as disciples to do all that he commanded them. True disciples were those who (as indeed Abraham had done before them) would abandon home and family and follow Jesus into a defenceless existence as his sisters and brothers. In this latter respect, though not in the emphasis on Jesus' Jewish ancestry, Matthew largely follows Mark, though he develops the notion (and most clearly, the content) of Jesus' training the disciples more fully than Mark.

Can something similar be observed in relation to ideas about local attachments to the Land and to the Temple? It is important to recall that for Mark, notions of geography are allegorised. The Galilee which is the scene of Jesus' ministry is a real enough place in the narrative; the Galilee, to which according to the young man at the tomb Jesus has gone ahead, is a cipher for a way of life for those who would follow Jesus. In Isaiah, by contrast, the motif of the way of the Lord is treated typologically: the earlier history of Israel's entry into the land is to be repeated in the return from exile in Babylon to Israel. But in Mark the notion is subverted and loosed from its particular territorial attachments in Isaiah: the Markan way of the Lord culminates not in the triumphal procession of the returnees to Mount Zion, but leads on, from the rejection of the Messiah by the High Priest and his crucifixion opposite the Temple on Golgotha, to his going before the faltering disciples to

---

[3] Even so it is interesting to note that the four women mentioned in the genealogy are Gentiles. While it is hard to know how far to press such details, the prominent position of the genealogy invites the reader to take it seriously. If the Messiah is descended from impeccable Jewish male stock through David to Abraham, he also has plenty of Gentile blood. It is worth while comparing the importance that Josephus attaches to purity of male and female lines, both as a mark of personal distinction (*Vita* 1–6; see esp. his emphasis on his mother and an earlier ancestor, the daughter of the high priest Jonathan), and also as a guarantee of the trustworthiness of the tradition kept by the priests (*c Ap* 1:30–1: 'A member of the priestly order must . . . marry a woman of his own race [ὁμόεθνος], without regard to her wealth or other distinctions; but he must investigate her pedigree, obtaining a genealogy from the archives and producing a number of witnesses'). By contrast, Matthew's flaunting of Jesus' Gentile ancestry is remarkable.

231

'Galilee' whence they will go out to preach the gospel to all nations. The way, for all its mythological overtones in Isaiah, is no longer a specific and finite route from the desert to Zion, but rather a symbol whose precise lineaments are unclear. The coming encounter in Galilee is not related; the nature of the disciples' coming task is at best hinted at in the Little Apocalypse. The Galilee to which the disciples are directed is not just the extension of Isaiah's way by adding another station after Mount Zion. It is an altogether different kind of destination: the opening up of a new way of life to the disciples in which their previous experience in Galilee in Jesus' life-time will be repeated, played out again and again in the very different circumstances of the Gentile mission with which they are charged.

Matthaean redaction of Mark's treatment of the way of the Lord

Is there in Matthew's shaping of sacred space a similar tendency to that which we saw in his treatment of Mark in respect of ethnicity: namely, to earth it more deeply in Jewish history, at the same time as opening it up in a more universal way? Can we even detect a tendency to return to more typological readings of the Isaianic motifs? Prima facie: yes.

## Matthew's fulfilment citations

If in Mark Jesus' circumambulations in and out of Galilee represent anything but straight a way from the desert to Mount Zion, a detour without scriptural precedent (or at least without scriptural argument), Matthew sets about to rectify this, not by straightening the way (he adds a few loops), but by providing scriptural proofs. Wherever his list of Old Testament quotations comes from,[4] scriptural texts certainly serve to present Jesus' whole ministry as the 'fulfilment' of God's purposes. In 2:6 his birth in Bethlehem is related to the prophecy of Micah 5:1.[5] Matthew 2:15 cites Hosea 11:1 and provides a scriptural

---

[4] Cf. the discussion in Luz, 1989, 137–9, Stendahl, 1968, and Davies and Allison, 1997, 573–7.

[5] Though here this is not introduced by Matthew's usual fulfilment formula, but put into the mouth of the scribes in Jerusalem. Luz, 1989, 119–20, argues that this is not primarily to provide 'an OT justification for the historical, biographically locatable beginning of Jesus' life' (Strecker, 1971, 57), but rather, with its double reference to Judah, it makes an anti-Jewish point: they know that he is the expected Messianic shepherd of Israel, but fail to draw the consequences. Luz is right to point out that Matthew's interest here is not primarily historical or biographical (Matthew's portrayal of the alliance between

basis for the flight into Egypt. Matthew 2:18, citing Jeremiah 31:15, supports the story of the massacre of the innocents in Bethlehem. Matthew 2:23, with its mysterious text,[6] is searching hard to find a justification for Jesus' location in Nazareth. Matthew 4:14–16 locates Jesus' ministry in Galilee of the Gentiles. Here Matthew cites Isaiah 8:23 – 9:1, though there is significant compression of the text, such that it is not at all clear which version he is using. The text refers rather loosely to Jesus' move from Nazareth, which is in Zebulon, to Capernaum in Naphtali, and groups these locations together under the heading of Galilee of the Gentiles. The quotation emphasises the prophecy of salvation to those in darkness, and rather indirectly suggests that such salvation is also for the Gentiles. Luz thinks that it is intended to direct the reader's attention to the salvation historical consequences of Jesus' mission, to the coming of salvation to the Gentiles.[7] This, in view of the fact that Jesus' mission in Galilee is restricted to Israel, is persuasive. But again, as Stendahl points out, Matthew's changing the LXX and MT 'walking in darkness' to 'sitting' ($\kappa\alpha\theta\acute{\eta}\mu\epsilon\nu\circ\varsigma$) 'certainly intends to stress again the local, geographical intention of his interpretation'.[8]

These early fulfilment citations all serve, not only to show that Jesus' movements fall within the foretold purposes of God, but to earth them in places which are part of an already established sacred geography. At the same time, as 4:12–17 shows, Matthew's use of the fulfilment citations points beyond the old history and geography to the new world[9]

---

Herod and the Jerusalemites and the scribes is polemical rather that historical). On the other hand, Matthew is concerned to anchor the events of Jesus' life in the history of God's dealings with his people, as Strecker recognises: the saying makes the point that Jesus' mission is directed to the Jewish people. The point is that this anchoring is done geographically: in Bethlehem in the land of Judah is the appointed place for the Messiah's birth.

[6] Does it refer to Judg 13:5, 7; 16:17; or Isa 11:1? or indeed to any particular text at all?

[7] Luz, 1989, 171. Interestingly, Sim does not discuss the wider theological significance of this quotation, only its relevance to the place of composition of the Gospel. Saldarini, 1994, 71, 80, sees it as indicating the inclusion of Jews and Gentile in the promised restoration of Israel; while it 'hints' at the salvation of the Gentiles, 'the primary referents of Isaiah's tribes and nations in Matthew's narrative were Galilean Jews in need of Jesus' teaching and healing'. But this is to underplay the authority which such quotations have in pointing up the significance of the following narrative, which also includes the healing of the centurion's servant and of the Canaanite woman's daughter.

[8] Stendahl, 1968, 105.

[9] Cf. 19:28 for Matthew's sense of the new world which Jesus brings.

which will come into being through the son of David and Abraham. These events have been foreseen and point forward to the Gentile mission when the restrictions ('go rather to the lost sheep of the house of Israel', 10:6) imposed on the Twelve will be lifted and they will be sent to the nations. But it would be a mistake to see here simply a chronological extension of salvation history. The element of comparison and typology is not to be overlooked.[10] Jesus' birth is narrated in such a way as to evoke all kinds of associations with Moses' birth:[11] but he will claim greater authority than that of Moses in the antitheses. Jesus, like Israel, comes out of Egypt to bring salvation to God's people, but this is a new order of salvation which will bring light to all the nations. Matthew, that is to say, is already conscious of the break with Israel's past as well as wanting to insist on the continuity.[12] There is a polemical twist to the quotation from Micah which emphasises that the old Israel has failed to grasp the decisive fact of the coming of the promised Messiah.[13]

Thus Matthew lays the basis for subsequent Christian typological readings of 'Old' Testament history: what has happened/is happening in Christian history is a replaying of sacred history on another level: that of fulfilment. What happens now has been foretold by the prophets and foreshadowed in the great events of the past; but these were all preparatory for the final manifestation of God's saving power which has now occurred with the birth, ministry, death and resurrection of Jesus. In this way the events of Jesus' life take on heightened significance. They are foundational events for the new era of salvation which has dawned with the coming of Immanuel, God with us, to the people of

---

[10] Allison, 1993, esp. 11–23, discusses the use of *sunkrisis* in contemporary (to Matthew) literature and suggests guidelines for its interpretation in ancient texts. See, too, the discussion in Stanton, 1992, 77–84.

[11] This has been argued fully and persuasively by Brown, 1977, 110–19, and Allison, 1993, 140–65; see 140, n. 3 for further bibliographical material.

[12] It is a nice point as to how far σύγκρισις allows for a strong sense of discontinuity as well as continuity. Clearly, if the subject of the discourse is to be praised by comparison with another, it will not do to denigrate the other too far, lest the comparison reflect adversely on the one to be praised. On the other hand, if the 'superiority of the one over the other' (Stanton, 1992, 79) is to be established, differences must be brought out. It is probably right to understand that when Matthew says of Jesus that 'something greater than the Temple is here' (12:6), no anti-Temple polemic is implied (Stanton, 1992, 83); this does not mean, however, that the Temple will continue to have the role and place in God's purposes that it previously had.

[13] A polemic directed not against Israel and its history, but against those who fail to recognise new evidence of God's creative activity.

God. The fulfilment citations underline just this: that the events recounted are the events to which all of sacred history has been moving. Jesus' birth in Bethlehem, his parents' flight with him into Egypt, his childhood in Nazareth, his move to Capernaum at the beginning of his ministry: all this was foretold and has come to pass. But so, too, was his healing (8:17), his preaching and its effects (12:17–21; 13:14–15; 13:35), the triumphal entry (21:4–5), his arrest and passion (26:54), the disciples' flight (26:56) and Judas' betrayal and death (27:9).

In the light of this earthing of his narrative in sacred places attested in Scripture, what of Matthew's overall presentation of the geopolitical and topographical features of the narrative? Does Matthew polarise Galilee and Judaea/Jerusalem, contrasting Jesus' sacred places against the sacred places of Israel? Does Matthew remake sacred space? Does he replace the old sites with new ones? Does he abandon the idea of sacred space and sites altogether? More fundamentally, how does Matthew relate to the dialogue in Mark between dualist and forensic notions of eschatology which shape Mark's understanding of space as they shape every aspect of his work?

Let me recapitulate a little. I argued in chapter 4 that Mark's construction of sacred space was achieved by a reworking of the Isaianic 'way of the Lord' under pressure from more dualistic geographies which saw the whole world as the site of struggle between the forces of light and darkness. The Isaianic view of space was first and foremost conceived in forensic terms. Israel was punished for its obedience by invasion of and exile from the Land and restored to full covenantal relationship with God through the return of the exiles and the rebuilding of the Temple. The drama of God's struggle for the hearts and wills of his people was played out, that is to say, in a world in which pride of place was given to the Land. This view is subverted in the Markan narrative. The way of the Lord culminates not in the restoration of the Temple, but in the crucifixion of the Lord at the place of the skull. The disciples are called to Galilee whence they will go out to preach the gospel to all nations. The medium of God's dealings with men and women is no longer the Land, but 'being with Jesus'. The struggle for the hearts and wills of – all – people occurs wherever the gospel is preached. Just as in the dualist view of the world the boundaries of the Land pale into insignificance, because of the universal presence of evil powers in the world, so here. The struggle, while it is still conceived forensically, ethically, is no longer limited to the people of the Land, but occurs wherever people encounter the will of God. In this way, the geographical details of the Gospel story, though taken from the sacred sites of Israel's history, lose their connection with Israel's hopes for the restoration of Zion and instead become symbolic of the new story of the establishment of God's rule over all human hearts and wills. It is not that Mark elevates Galilee over Jerusalem in order to establish some new *terra christiana*. Rather, both Jerusalem and Galilee are allegorised as the story of the return of the exiles is radically reworked.

Matthew's dialogue with cosmic dualist and forensic nations of sacred space

How does Matthew take up these two geographies which Mark has interwoven in his Gospel? It might appear at first sight that he is interested only in the forensic, Isaianic view; that for him the way of righteousness is connected almost entirely with Jesus' teaching and the disciples' doing the will of God. And it seems beyond dispute that this is a crucial notion for Matthew and that the forensic myth dominates in his presentation of the Gospel material. And yet, before we look at the way in which this has influenced his portrayal of sacred space, we need to consider more carefully how Matthew has interacted with material of a more dualistic character, for surprisingly at certain points Matthew seems to have reinforced this material, too.

In the first place, Matthew has incorporated Q-material into his account of Jesus' Temptation which has significantly increased the role of Satan and which no longer restricts the encounter between Jesus and Satan to the wilderness, as in the Markan account of the Temptation, but extends it to the heart of the Land, as Satan takes Jesus and seats him on the pinnacle of the Temple, and offers him all the kingdoms of the world, which are apparently in his gift. Satan's insidious presence is everywhere; nowhere, not even the holy places, is proof against his corrupting power (4:1–11). Nevertheless, it is Jesus' obedience to the divine will as expressed in the Scriptures (three times 'it is written') that enables him to resist and overcome Satan, even when he, too, cites Scripture. Satan is defeated, *and it is obedience to the Scriptures rather than spiritual warfare which wins the day.* That is to say, it is one man's obedience which defeats the prince of this world, who has power over the nations. This is not a denial of the power of demonic agencies: rather an assertion that the will of the Son of God is able to overcome such power, and so to liberate the wills of men and women to show the same kind of obedience for which they pray (6:9–13) where prayer is also referred to as righteousness (6:1). As in Mark, the site of struggle for the hearts and wills of men and women is universalised under pressure from cosmic dualist mythology, with the interesting difference that now the archetypal conflict, indeed the conflict which will break Satan's rule, is situated at the heart of the 'holy city' (4:5),[14] and that the struggle is one for faithful obedience to the proper interpretation of the Scriptures.

The conflict with demonic forces plays a part again in Jesus' healings and exorcisms, as these are grouped together by Matthew in chapters 8–9. As is often observed, these form a counterpart to Jesus' teaching in chapters 5–7 and present a summary account of his deeds. However, it is far from being a simple collection of miracle stories, giving a sample of his work. It does indeed include a good diversity of types of illness from which people are healed: leprosy, paralysis, fever, haemorrhage, blindness. Jesus also stills the storm, casts out spirits, and raises the ruler's daughter from the dead. Some, but not all, of these illnesses/afflictions are attributed to demonic activity. For the crowds, the healing of the dumb demoniac emphasises the uniqueness of Jesus' exorcistic activity: 'Never was anything like this seen in all Israel'; while the Pharisees confirm the power of his exorcisms by attributing them to the prince of demons (9:33–34). On the other hand, the story of the healing of the paralytic, which Matthew takes over and shortens from Mark (Matt 9:1–8//Mark 2:1–12), emphasises the man's need to be freed from his sins: Jesus offers the man forgiveness and asserts the Son of Man's authority to forgive sins. There seems, that is, to be a clash of interpretations: demonic-dualistic/forensic which is left unresolved. The section runs into the mission discourse which also leaves the matter undecided, commissioning the disciples to go out

---

[14] The phrase 'holy city' occurs widely, not least in Isa (48:2; 52:1), and in the Maccabean literature (1 Macc 2:7; 2 Macc 3:1; 9:14; 15:14; 3 Macc 6:5). It is clearly the focus of the hopes for the restoration of Israel's national fortunes. Its use in Matthew (here and at 27:53) is somewhat puzzling. Here Satan's freedom of access to the heart of the city is paradoxical: it is certainly not a city free of pollution and corruption if Satan can perch himself on the pinnacle of the Temple. Again, in 27:53 the phrase occurs immediately after the tearing of the Temple veil, which indicates the end of the Temple and the departure of the *Shekhina* from it. Davies and Allison, 1997, 635, comment: 'Here the expression is ironic.' The eschatological signs of the shaking of the earth, the splitting of the rocks and the resurrection of the saints (whether before or after Jesus' resurrection) indicate that Jesus' death on Golgotha inaugurates a new world (cf. 19:28). It all starts in the 'holy city' but it inaugurates a world without a Temple, for one greater than the Temple is here (12:6).

with 'authority over unclean spirits, to cast them out, and to heal every disease and every infirmity' (10:1).

Such actions are clearly located in Israel and equally clearly are presented as transcending anything that has previously happened in Israel (9:33). They evoke a divided response: wonder on the part of the crowds and rejection on the part of the Pharisees. They point forward to Jesus' rejection by Israel,[15] but also to the crowd's glorifying him in 15:31.[16] Thus while these are healings which have deep resonances with the Isaianic tradition,[17] they already point beyond Israel, as has been indicated by the earlier healing of the centurion's servant. Here it is the man's faith which has not been seen 'in Israel'. These miracles, that is to say, occur in the Land, but they have meaning for those outside the Land.[18] The Gentile centurion stands for those who will come and celebrate the establishment of the kingdom 'from east and from west', a phrase which would normally refer to the return of the scattered tribes of Israel, but which now is clearly enlarged to include those outside Israel, and which in context may even question whether the sons of Israel will be included at all.[19] By the same token, the discipleship sayings in 8:20–22, which sharply demand the breaking of family ties, focus attention on faith, the unconditional trust in Jesus' helping power,[20] and the willingness to abandon all and follow Jesus unconditionally in a life without home or shelter (8:20).[21] The Son of Man who will judge the whole world sets aside all attachments to home and country, leaves

[15] So Luz, 1990, 63.
[16] Luz, 1990, 440, rightly says that Galilee here is seen, not as 'Galilee of the Gentiles', but as the land in which the Messiah of Israel's activity, which Matthew narrates, takes place for the benefit of his own people. But he does not make the connection with 8:10; 9:33, and so misses some of the tension which runs through Matthew's use of Ἰσραήλ.
[17] As is again brought out at Matt 15:31, with its echoes of Isa 35:5f. and Isa 29:18, 23, see Luz, 1990, 441, n. 15.
[18] Matthew uses Ἰσραήλ both to refer to the people: 10:6; 15:24 (οἶκος Ἰσραήλ), 19:28 (φυλαί); 27:9 (υἱοί) and to the land: 2:20, 21; 10:23. Matt 8:10 must refer to the people; 9:33 could take either sense.
[19] For the association of 'east' and 'west' with Israel, see Gen 28:14; Ps 107:3; Isa 43:5; Zech 8:7; Baruch 4:37; 5:5; but for its association with the nations who surround and threaten Israel and with other powers of destruction, see Josh 11:3; 1 Chron 12:15; Isa 9:12; *4 Ezra* 15:38f.
[20] Luz, 1990, 15.
[21] Strictly speaking the point here is not poverty, but *only* homelessness, *pace* Luz, 1990, 24. Luz rightly brings out the contrast between Jesus' lack of a homeland, 'Heimatlosigkeit', and the role of the Son of Man (here used for the first time) as cosmic judge, 'Weltrichter'.

the land and is driven out of the land of the Gadarenes (8:34). Those who will come from east and west to sit at table with Abraham, Isaac and Jacob will be justified by him; the sons of the kingdom will be cast out (8:11–12).[22] In all this, the particular tension which we noticed earlier in Matthew's handling of questions of kinship and descent again becomes apparent. Jesus and his disciples abandon all local ties and attachments, but the disciples are still promised that they will inherit the kingdom and will participate in the Messianic banquet with the Patriarchs. Nevertheless, it is noteworthy that the promise is formulated in this way, and not as a promise of inheriting the Land.[23]

But if those who inherit the kingdom will not inherit the Land, where will they gather for the Messianic banquet? Does this image at least not require some kind of geographical centre? Certainly 8:11, with its reference to the points of the compass, suggests that the many gather from different directions in one place, and this traditionally would be Jerusalem, Matthew's 'holy city'. But the ironic use of the phrase in 27:53, in a context where the city and its Temple is being split apart under the force of the new world inaugurated by the resurrection,[24] indicates clearly that the 'centre' of the new world inaugurated by Jesus is wherever he is present with the gathered disciples (18:20; cf. 1:23; 28:20).

Thus, there is less a tendency to allegorise the Land, than to regard its boundaries as having been in a sense transcended. The goal of God's actions in Jesus is no longer the restoration of national sovereignty envisaged in Isaiah: it is the bringing of healing to the whole world. Only at one point does Matthew enter the realm of the allegorical. In his weaving together of the section on the cost of discipleship (8:18–22) with the story of the stilling of the storm (8:23–27), he has created an image of the church as assaulted by the powers of darkness, yet under the protection of its Lord who is with them in the boat. The church is the vessel which can provide safe passage and protection for

---

[22] This theme is, of course, already anticipated in John the Baptist's reproach to Pharisees and Sadducees: 'who warned you to flee from the wrath to come . . . God is able from these stones to raise up children for Abraham' (3:7–9).

[23] Could Matt 5:5 μακάριοι οἱ πραεῖς, ὅτι αὐτοὶ κληρονομήσουσιν τὴν γῆν, refer to inheriting the Land? Luz, 1989, 209, has no doubt that the traditional promise of the Land has long since been transposed into a cosmic mode, though not into an other-worldly one: the promise of the earth makes it clear that the kingdom of heaven includes a new this-worldly reality.

[24] See n. 14 above.

those who are exposed to the forces of darkness. It is the company of those who are with Jesus. Here Matthew appears to take up the Markan notion of the disciples' being with Jesus (Mark 3:14, which both he and Luke omit) and develop it in terms of his own Immanuel motif (Matt 1:23). Jesus, the one who has power over the storms (cf. Ps 107:23–32), is indeed 'God with us'. This image of the *navis ecclesiae* suggests a very different understanding of space; God is encountered in the company of those who follow him and put their trust in him, wherever they may be.

## The parable of the wheat and the darnel

This rejection of the importance of local attachments and of the place of the Land in the history of salvation is reflected in a remarkable way in the parable of the wheat and the darnel (13:24–30, 36–43).[25] Here quite clearly the field which belongs to the peasant farmer/householder is the world. The Son of Man, again the cosmic judge, but also the teacher who sows the seed, is linked not to a specific role *vis-à-vis* Israel, but has authority over the whole world. On the other hand, this authority and rule is not unchallenged. The Son of Man's work in his fields produces good results in the form of wheat, the sons of the kingdom; the enemy, the devil, sows darnel, which is identified as the sons of evil/the evil one. Just as the Son of Man has a universal field for his work, so too his adversary has cosmic powers and can challenge him anywhere.

It is interesting to note the role that Matthew's dialogue with cosmic dualism and forensic eschatology plays in this parable and its interpretation. On the one hand, the explanation of evil is entirely dualistic: in so far as an account of the origin of evil is given, it is exclusively in terms of the devil's activity which produces 'sons of evil'. As far as the parable suggests a solution to the problem of evil, it lies neither in teaching and bringing to repentance, nor in some final battle against the powers of evil, but rather in awaiting the final judgement when the wicked will be burnt and the just will shine like the sun in the kingdom

---

[25] In context, the parables in Matt 13 seem to explain Jesus' rejection by the Pharisees in chapter 12, where they plot to kill him and accuse him of being in league with Beelzebul. But it is clear from the end of chapter 12, with its account of Jesus' true brothers and sisters, that this rejection raises questions of continuing relevance for later disciples, with the result that the chapter becomes as much a general statement of the human predicament and its divisions, as it is a particular explanation of the Pharisees' behaviour.

of their Father. It is not difficult to see that there is here a conflation of two broad mythologies. The source of evil in the world is explained in dualist terms; the resolution in forensic ones. What is missing, on the one hand, is any account of the final fate of Satan; on the other hand, any account of the nature of evil which would make a forensic solution appropriate. Strikingly, few commentators draw attention to the role of Satan in the parable and most instead concentrate their attention on the relationship between the church and the world and on the question of inner-church discipline, which is raised in the parable (though not the interpretation) by the dialogue between the householder and his sons over the time to pull up the darnel.

Where does Matthew's emphasis lie?[26] If the parable itself is part of Matthew's own special material, we must look for Matthew's emphasis principally in the interpretation of the parable. This is highly selective, omitting the details of the conversation between the householder and his servants, and offering instead a decoding of the principal terms in the parable (13:37–39), and then a brief account of the harvest in the form of a little apocalypse, whose main emphasis lies on the extirpation of evil (13:40–43). Formally, the dualistic explanation of evil is contained in the glossary of terms, the forensic account of the resolution of the problem in the little apocalypse; the former, as it were sets the cosmological framework, the latter gives the eschatological outcome.

The passage has similarities with 1QS 3–4. In both there is a distinction between two sorts of people: the sons of light and the children of falsehood, the sons of the kingdom and the sons of the evil one; both groups are under the rule or influence of spiritual powers: the prince of light and the angel of darkness, the Son of Man and the devil; both will receive their deserts at the end, at the visitations, when the Son of Man sends out his angels. Both passages occur in texts where there is a strong paraenetic element. There are, on the other hand, differences, some of which may be accounted for simply by the difference in genre. In 1QS, it is God who appoints the two spirits to rule over the two kinds of

---

[26] The parable occurs only in Matthew. Both Matthew and Luke omit Mark's parable of the seed growing secretly (Mark 4:26–29) and it is possible that, as Luz prefers, the parable was formulated by Matthew's congregation as a response to their experience of the continuing presence of evil: 'Sie formuliert die Geschichte Mark 4:26–29 von der Erfahrung her neu, daß das Böse trotz der "Aussaat" des Gottesreichs weiterhin real wirksam ist, und versucht, die "Zwischenzeit mit ihren spezifischen . . . Problemen" vom "Anfang und insbesondere (der) Vollendung der Basieia" her zu verstehen.' Luz, 1990, 323, quoting Dschulnigg, 1988, 496.

people, and equally God who determines the identity of the two kinds; in Matthew, the enemy acts independently of and contrary to the purposes of the Son of Man, whom we assume is alone God's agent. 1QS speaks not only about the spiritual origins of the sons of light and the children of falsehood; it also says that the spirits are appointed to lead the two kinds of people in their ways; Matthew contains only the image of sowing, of origination: the image of two different kinds of seeds and plants is not modified, as is the notion of two kinds of sons with different origins in 1QS, by talk of the spirit of darkness leading astray the sons of light – a rose is a rose is a rose, and the same with wheat – and therefore there is no room within the *framework* of the interpretation of the parable for moral injunction (though as Luz points out this has not stopped later interpreters).[27] On the other hand, in the interpretation itself, clearly the language is predominantly legal and moral. The two groups are now referred to as those who give offence and act against the law, and the righteous. 1QS, similarly, also describes the actions of the two groups in moral and legal terms, though this is still within the overarching description of these groups as 'all those who walk in the ways of the spirit of light/darkness'. There are, that is to say, similar tensions between the two kinds of mythological opposition in Matthew as in 1QS. Within the framework, as opposed to the interpretation proper in Matthew, there is little or no attempt to mediate: just as the two sections are formally distinct, so too the mythology which they each express is radically different.

Is it possible to say whether Matthew expresses an opinion in favour of one of the two opposed mythologies? One might be tempted to decide that the dramatic account of the final judgement must have preference over the more detached glossary of terms. Yet, however much the account of the end of the two groups in Matthew may encourage readers to want to be part of the sons of the kingdom, and indeed to want to bring others to be sons of the kingdom too, the story also reminds them that such a state lies beyond the control of the individual's will, that there are forces at work in the world for good and evil which lie beyond men's

---

[27] Luz, 1990, 347, though interestingly this is often effected by equating the field and the individual: both wheat and darnel are to be found in him, and this is linked to the idea of the freewill: 'If you will, you can change and become wheat!' (Athanasius, *Hom. de semente* 5 = PG 28, 149); but this of course runs counter to the glossary's reading of the field, as well as to the imagery of the two different types of plant: darnel cannot become wheat. See discussion of 12:33 above.

and women's control. This may indeed help to explain the obduracy and malevolence of some; it remains, however, potentially stultifying for individuals in both their moral and their missionary efforts.

What the story and its interpretation, however, do unequivocally achieve, is to universalise the sphere of action of the Son of Man and his agents. The field is the world, and the world is the field of action of the church's mission and of the future judgement of God. The sons of the kingdom are no longer those who belong to Israel geographically and by descent and observance: they are those, anywhere in the world, who are 'sown' by the Son of Man, who follow and obey him wherever he leads. The 'appeal' of cosmic dualism, that is to say, is not only that it offers a way of making sense of the continued existence of opposition to the teaching and commands of the Son of Man (which has been dramatically demonstrated in the previous chapter), but that it also serves to extend the reach of his teaching and commands to the whole world. Christians are not to be surprised, if they experience difficulties and setbacks in their work: Satanic opposition is to be encountered *everywhere*; equally, the work of the Christian mission is to embrace and instruct those who have been sown as 'sons of the kingdom', *wherever* the seed may have fallen, to liberate them from Satan's power, so that they may be among the just when the final harvest comes.

Such language is undoubtedly deterministic and, taken on its own, might well seem to render any kind of missionary activity fruitless. But, as the shift in terminology from 'sons of the kingdom' to 'just', from 'sons of (the) evil (one)' to 'all causes of sin' and all who work lawlessness (ἀνομία) makes clear, the sons of the kingdom still need to do what is right, if they are to 'shine like the sun in the kingdom of their Father'. In this way the metaphor of the seeds and the different plants which they produce, with its clearly deterministic implications, is being replaced by a use of the metaphor which implies both a freely-willed response and a knowledge of what is right.[28]

---

[28]  That this, too, is a matter for further reflection and dialogue within the Gospel is clear from the parable of the sheep and the goats in Jesus' last discourse in Matthew: for there the question: 'Lord when did we see you hungry . . .' (25:44) is asked with equal ignorance by both the just and the unjust. The difference lies not in their knowledge of Jesus' teaching but in their actions: one fed the least of the King's brothers, whilst the others did not. Here the plant metaphor controls the thought: different plants produce different fruits. 'By their fruits you shall know them' (7:16–20). What in the Sermon on the Mount serves as a vivid injunction to put Jesus' teaching into practice, can be read as an

## Jesus and the Canaanite woman

One further text may serve to illustrate how the tradition of Jesus' exorcising serves to break down the boundaries of sacred geography. In 15:21–28 Matthew retells Mark's story of the exorcising of the Syro-Phoenician woman's daughter. To this point in the story, Matthew has emphasised the importance of restricting Jesus' mission to the lost sheep of the house of Israel (10:6). Now, in his reworking of Mark's story of Jesus' withdrawal in the area around Tyre and Sidon and of his encounter with the Syro-Phoenician woman, he is forced to confront the issues of group boundaries more directly. Interestingly Matthew himself underlines the sense in which this story is about precisely the boundaries which protect the Jewish group. The woman's Gentile identity is underlined by using a term rich in associations with Israel's history of the occupation of the Land, a Canaanite; she in turn refers to Jesus as Son of David and Lord. Matthew substantially develops the motif of her rejection, creating a new exchange in which, when Jesus refuses to answer the woman's cry, the disciples appeal to him to send her away, and Jesus, seemingly sharing their sentiment, reaffirms the restricted nature of his mission. In Mark, the woman's appeal is initially turned down on the grounds that the children must *first* be filled. In Matthew, where the woman kneels in front of Jesus and addresses him in the language of the Psalms, the rejection is starker: it is wrong, not καλόν, to give that which is intended for the children to the dogs. There is no suggestion that the dogs might subsequently be fed.

The contrast children/dogs *replaces* the language of clean/unclean of the earlier part of the chapter. Read in this context, it again suggests that the woman is being compared to those who are seen as unclean and outside the group.[29] It is not right to give the children's food to

---

endorsement of the principle that it is people's supernatural origins which determines their behaviour and therefore it is their behaviour which reveals what sort of persons they *really* are. As we saw above, p. 200, n. 33, the language of plants and their fruits has a fairly standard moral sense (Sir 27:6).

[29] Dogs are generally seen as scavengers (Ps 22:16; 59:6, 14), who eat unclean carrion (Exod 22:31), typically in 1 and 2 Kings as those who devour the corpses of the enemy (1 Kings 14:11; 16:4; 21:19, 23, 24; cf. 22:38 where Ahab's chariot is washed after his death and the dogs lick up his blood and the harlots wash themselves in it; 2 Kings 9:10, 36, contrasted with burial; Ps 68:23; Jer 15:3), who inhabit the world outside the gates (Rev 22:15); see Marcus, 2000, 463–4.

those whose proper food is that which is unclean. The woman's reply turns this around. She takes the language of children/dogs to refer to a hierarchical division within the household.[30] That is to say, the dogs are not threatening or out of place; they are part of the group, although of different, lower status. The woman's rejoinder to Jesus is a challenge to him to accept that, within *hierarchies*, there is a common bond as well as differentiation of status: even the dogs get something. Jesus, Son of David, responds to the woman's need[31] and faith is found (as at chapter 8) among the ranks of the heathen (who speak the language of the Psalms). Here salvation-historically profane space has been briefly entered by Jesus, and in this encounter with the woman (which Luz is right to see as more significant than the physical boundary crossing) the revision of social identity which occurs, prepares the way for the subsequent redefinitions of religious boundaries, which must wait till Matthew 28.

This is also a story about an encounter between Jesus and a woman with a daughter who is possessed. However, the theme of demonic possession plays no role in the development of the story (no more than it does in Mark). There is certainly no suggestion that this is more Satan's territory than anywhere else; or that the Caananites are more prone to such possession. The focus is on the woman's need and faith and her fight for her daughter. Her need is universal, and it is Jesus' response to her powerful advocacy of her daughter's plight which leads to the breaking of the traditional boundaries. And this contrasts sharply with the parable of the wheat and the tares, where the ζιζάνια are the sons of the evil one, who are to be left to the end of the age and then destroyed. Here the woman's faith saves her daughter, who is healed/released.

Here, then, it is not so much that the cosmic dualist understanding of space is undermining traditional Jewish notions of the boundaries of the Land. The key to the story is the woman's use of the household imagery. Furthermore, the boundaries of the Land and the related ethnic distinctions are to be overcome/transcended by a new household of

---

[30] See BAG, *s.v.*, and Luz, 1990, 435, n. 59, for classical allusions to household dogs, which were as widespread and popular in the ancient world as at any other time. Cf. his comment: 'In der Antike waren Haushunde in allen Schichten genauso verbreitet und geschätzt wie in irgendeiner anderen Zeit'; 1990, 435.

[31] The text speaks of the power of God's love which bursts the boundaries of Israel, Luz, 1990, 437.

faith, which consists of all those who do the will of Jesus' heavenly Father. Household imagery replaces ethnic/geographic distinctions, an imagery strictly related to Jesus' interpretation of the Law: doing the will of my Father in heaven. Jesus' brothers, sisters and mother now belong to the one who will be given all authority in heaven and earth.

If the dualist mythology, together with the redefinition of the community as the household of faith, serves to universalise the scope and setting of Jesus' and his followers' mission, what of the forensic mythology, which, as we have already suggested for Mark, draws heavily on the language and thought of Isaiah? In the first place, it has to be noticed that Isaiah also has his own universalising traits. If the way of the Lord is one on which the returnees are led in triumph to Mount Zion, it is also one, as Isaiah 60 eloquently portrays, which will lead the Gentiles, willingly or otherwise (60:10–16), to recognise the glory of the Lord and to come and worship – and pay tribute to his glory. It is, nonetheless, a way which leads quite specifically to Mount Zion, and nowhere else, and it is there that the glory of the Lord and his rule will be revealed, that the people will be gathered and the new era of Israel's sovereignty and peace will be inaugurated, bringing blessings on all the nations who willingly recognise God's rule. To what extent is this specific linking of the establishment of the kingdom to a particular territory and a particular city and its sanctuary preserved in Matthew?

## The mountain motif in Matthew

On the negative side, as we have already seen, Matthew does not include the promise of the Land in the Beatitudes or indeed elsewhere: the meek will inherit the earth, not the Land of Israel. Furthermore, there is nothing in Matthew which re-establishes the position of the Temple which Mark's Gospel had thoroughly undermined. Matthew not only keeps Mark's contrast between Jesus' crucifixion on Golgotha and the rending of the Temple veil, together with the reports of Jesus' prophecy of its destruction; he underlines the significance of the rending of the Temple veil by adding to it the earthquake and the opening of the tombs and the appearing of the dead 'after Jesus' resurrection'. In a further intriguing detail, he even suggests that the Temple priests have themselves undermined the very rationale of the Temple cult by 'profaning (βεβηλόω) the Sabbath' (12:5), and that this was in accordance with the Law.

To what extent then does Matthew positively rework the Mount Zion tradition? Not in any very explicit and direct way. On the one hand, he is inevitably brought into relationship with it through his use of Mark, for whom the Isaianic way of the Lord plays a central and formative role. But we have seen that, while Matthew in many ways follows Mark closely and certainly engages with the same kinds of apocalyptic eschatology, he is also quite capable of dismantling Markan interpretative motifs.[32] Certainly, too, mountains play an important part in his editing of the narrative. If for Mark the house is the typical place of instruction and revelation, then in Matthew it is the mountain. The Temptation, the Sermon on the Mount, the Feeding, the Transfiguration, the eschatological discourse on Mount Olivet and the final commissioning are all, wholly or in part, set on mountains. But we should be careful not to push the connection with the Mount Zion traditions too far.[33] Just as the vineyard can stand as a rich symbol for God's dealing and relationship with his people, so too the mountain has strong associations both with the revelation of God's will to his people and with the final restoration of Israel's fortunes. It is reasonable to see the final scene on the mountain as raising general expectations that here the final act in the drama of Israel's and the world's restoration will be played out. But for a closer reading of the

---

[32] Cf. the discussion of the blindness motif in chapter 6 above, pp. 184–5.

[33] According to Donaldson, 1985, the motif of the mountain has a dual role: on the one hand, it serves as a literary motif which draws together certain passages and focuses attention on them; on the other hand, it has a symbolic – theological – content which is related principally to contemporary Mount Zion ideologies. By drawing on contemporary expectations about the eschatological renewal of Israel on Mount Zion, Matthew was able to give a particular content to his narrative. Specifically, he could develop ideas about the Messiah: his obedience, suffering, and vindication; about the gathering of the people of Israel and the Gentiles; and about the nature of salvation history. In the Temptation narrative, Satan offers Jesus the authority which he receives as the Son from the Father after his resurrection and which is declared in Matt 28; in the Sermon on the Mount, Jesus calls to him the disciples and crowds and gives them the instructions which they are to teach to all the nations after his resurrection; the Transfiguration scene is linked christologically, by the theme of the Son's obedient suffering and final vindication, back to the Temptation (obedience) and forward to the Commissioning (vindication); the Feeding is sandwiched between two scenes, which raise the question of the position of the Gentiles which is resolved in Matt 28; Mount Olivet deals with the nature of the church. Matt 28 takes up the motif of the gathering of the dispersion and relates it to the disciples gathered around Jesus. For Donaldson the emphasis is ecclesiological rather than missiological. While there is much to be learnt from Donaldson, it is hard to avoid the conclusion that he presses the connection with Mount Zion too hard. The mountain is a much more polyvalent symbol than Donaldson allows.

passage, we need to play greater attention to its intertextuality, specifically its interaction with Daniel 7 and the commissioning narratives of the Jewish Scriptures.

## The commissioning of the disciples: Matthew 28

The evidence for a close relationship between the two texts Daniel 7:13f. and Matthew 28:16–20 seems overwhelming. Daniel 7:13f. is a text which Matthew has already cited in the trial scene with the high priest; there are strong verbal agreements in this later passage.[34] Thematically the links between Matthew and Daniel 7 are developed quite fully.[35] If this is not sufficient evidence for some measure of intertextuality here, then it is hard to know how these matters should be handled. On the other hand, there are clearly differences in content between the two passages, as commentators have noticed: there is a very different role for the nations, a difference in temporal perspective, and no place for the disciples. But this, *contra* Donaldson, Vögtle[36] and others, seems to be grounds, not for denying the relationship between the two passages, but for suggesting that it is one where Daniel 7:13f. is partially rather than wholly determinative of the meaning of the Matthaean passage. If this makes life more complicated for New Testament exegetes, then this is because linguistic operations are more complicated than this simple view imagines. How does Matthew develop these themes?

Let us start with the references to Daniel. Daniel 7 is in the form of a vision and its interpretation: the vision is of a series of beasts/horns, which inflict destruction on men and women ('flesh') and each other, and are finally overcome by the flames of the Ancient of Days and his judgement, while everlasting dominion is given to the figure like the Son of Man. As with all such vision-interpretations, there is much that is not interpreted. The powerful images of the 'beasts from the sea', who are given human minds so that they have an outward human appearance, are clearly images which have demonic overtones, as is brought out dramatically in the reworking of these images in Revelation 12–13. Nevertheless, in the interpretation the figures of the beasts

---

[34] Dan 7:14 LXX: ἐδόθη αὐτῷ ἐξουσία and πάντα τὰ ἔθνη; the view was first proposed by Michel, 1950–1.

[35] Judgement (19; 25); thrones (in the plural, 19:28); angels/heavenly court (25); coming (10:23; 24:27); the clouds of heaven (24:30; 26:64).

[36] Vögtle, 1964.

are decoded in terms of kingdoms and their rulers; the picture drawn is of a final struggle between the saints of the Most High and the other nations, which has an initial success, followed by a further period of conflict, before the nations are finally judged and submit to the everlasting rule of the one like a son of man.

For our purposes two features are of importance: God is presented as a God of immense power, which exceeds that of all the beasts with their terrifying destructive might. He is also presented as a God of justice and judgement: those who blaspheme against him and destroy his people will be judged and cast into the fire. Thus, the Danielic vision brings together in a powerful and coherent way the two strands of apocalyptic which we have been tracing: the dualistic/demonic and the forensic. The beasts who possess the nations must be destroyed, but their destruction flows from their judgement by God. From there it is only a short step to the point at which the beasts are identified with Satan, who is cast out on to the earth from heaven. Against these forces are ranged the saints of the Most High, those who obey his law and whom he will vindicate – ultimately – by destroying their enemies.

To what extent does Matthew 28:16–20 draw on this complex of ideas? If one compares the echoes in Matthew 28:16–20 with the reworking of Danielic imagery in *4 Ezra* 13 or with Revelation 12–13, it is clear that we have very different uses of this material. *4 Ezra* and Revelation both envisage a final conflict between the forces of evil and those of law and justice, in which the forces massed against the man from the sea (*4 Ezra*) and the Lamb and the saints (Rev 12–13) will be overcome: in *4 Ezra* 13:10 by the stream of fire which comes from the mouth of the man from the sea, in Revelation 12–13 by the blood of the Lamb and the witness of the saints. But as between *4 Ezra* and Revelation, there are important differences too. *4 Ezra* does not develop the imagery of the beasts in Daniel in a dualistic way: the eagle in Ezra's vision (*4 Ezra* 11–12) is explicitly said to represent the fourth beast of Daniel (12:11), but a different interpretation is offered of it. In Daniel it represented the Greek, in *4 Ezra* the Roman empire (*4 Ezra* 12:12–30). This interpretation is based on the identification of the eagle and its wings and of the lion, who is the Messiah who will judge the eagle for his wickedness. The latter was appointed by God, but has failed to act justly.

The use of this imagery in Matthew 28 is far more restrained and Donaldson in this respect is quite right to be cautious about seeing

Daniel 7:13f. as the sole 'source' of the passage.[37] Nevertheless, there can be little doubt that Matthew intends the echo to be understood, as the earlier allusions to Daniel 7:13f. in 24:30 and its citation in 26:64 make clear. In both cases the appearance of the sign of the Son of Man, or of the Son of Man himself, is threatening, as witness the mourning of the tribes of the earth (24:30; cf. Rev 1:7!); the threat however is associated with judgement rather than military conflict, cosmic or earthly. In Matthew 24 the judgement occurs with the gathering of the elect. This is further interpreted by Matthew's parable of the sheep and the goats (25:31–46), which depicts the fate of the nations before the Son of Man when he comes. Those who are judged will be cast into the place of punishment for Satan and his angels. That is to say, already before we read Matthew 28:16–20, the use of the Danielic tradition has been selective: the demonic and conflictual elements have been filtered out of Daniel 7's particularly strong mix of dualist and forensic mythology; the focus of attention has been fixed solely on the final judgement.

In Matthew 28:16–20 the element of judgement is not evidently to the fore. Rather than the nations being judged (as in Matt 25), here the disciples are sent out to make disciples of them (μαθητεύσατε πάντα

---

[37] Donaldson believes that a unitary account of Matthew's redaction can be offered in terms of the Mount Zion motif and its expression in various texts. While there are indeed clear *verbal* parallels between Dan 7:13f. and Matt 28:16–20, the *notion* of the conferring of authority is by no means restricted to Daniel. Ps 2:8: δώσω σοι ἔθνη κληρονομίαν σου, καὶ τὴν κατάσχεσίν σου τὰ πέρατα τῆς γῆς contains 'the essential meaning of' ἐδόθη μοι πᾶσα ἐξουσία and Ps 2:6 refers to the establishment of the king on Mount Zion. In sum, Donaldson thinks that the terms ἐξουσία and ἐδόθη, the reference to the Son, and the mountain background, together point 'to a Zion setting for the enthronement declaration of v. 18b'. Verses 19–20a, with the references to making disciples, baptising, teaching, and to Jesus' commanding, bring the reader to the heart of Matthew's theology. This is not just a mission command. 'In this command to make people disciples who adhere to Jesus' teachings and who are visibly identified with him in baptism, we have the charter of the Church, the constitution of the eschatological people of God' (182). This clearly relates to themes associated with Mount Zion, the return of the peoples and the setting up of the new community in Israel. Is there literary evidence for the link with Zion expectations here? Donaldson finds it in the reference to πάντα τὰ ἔθνη, which while it occurs in Dan 7:14 in the context of their subjugation, also occurs in numerous other passages which link it with 'Zion eschatology'. Notably, Isa 2:2f., 25:6 and 56:7 (183) contain references both to πάντα τὰ ἔθνη and to τὸ ὄρος in passages which also speak of the nations coming to learn the law, Isa 2:3, and of worshipping in the house of prayer, Isa 56:7. The difficulty with all this is that it privileges what are at most rather distant echoes over the quite clear allusions and even citations of Dan 7 in Matthew.

τὰ ἔθνη), baptising them and teaching them to keep all that Jesus has commanded the disciples. The one to whom all authority has been given in heaven and earth appears now, not to call the nations to judgement, but to send his disciples out to offer them the way to life through obedience to his commandments. The motif of the gathering of the elect, which already in Mark had been softened by the interposing of the necessity of the preaching the Gospel 'to all nations' (13:10), is now further qualified by the Matthaean commission to 'make disciples' of all the nations.

But if judgement is not explicitly mentioned, there can be little doubt in the light of Matthew's earlier use of Daniel 7:13f. that it forms the background to the passage. The commissioning of the disciples to baptise and teach all the nations is not, *pace* Donaldson, simply a means to an ecclesiological end, namely, the gathering around Christ of a church of disciples from among the nations, as previously Mount Zion had been the point at which the nations would gather;[38] it now precedes the gathering not just of the elect, but of 'all the nations' (25:32) at the final coming of the Son of Man, and so serves to define the meaning of election which comes into the tradition through Mark 13. If in Mark's apocalypse the notion of election is close to that of predestination, and if in Matthew's parable of the wheat and the weeds this seems to be given an even more dualistic turn of meaning, then here these stark dualisms which allow no room for repentance, conversion and moral instruction are challenged. Judgement is not the moment when it will be revealed who were the sons of the evil one and who were the sons of the kingdom; it is the moment when it will be revealed who has fulfilled the commandments of the one to whom all authority on heaven and earth has been given.

That is to say, here at the climax of his Gospel, Matthew attempts a final resolution of those oppositions which he inherited from Mark and which lie deep in the culture of his time. The world is divided into

---

[38] If further proof of this were needed, then the contrast between this charge and the mission charge in chapter 10 should suffice. There the disciples are told: 'Go not except unto the lost sheep of the house of Israel.' Here they are told to 'go and make disciples of all nations'. In each case they are sent out: what is different is the scope of their mission. Interestingly this contrast brings out another point which I am in danger of labouring: in chapter 10 the disciples are sent out to exorcise, to rescue people from possession by Satan and his demons; in chapter 28 their charge is to baptise and to teach. Baptism for Matthew is baptism of repentance; teaching is instruction and moral injunction. Both are directed to the human will, not against Satanic agencies.

two camps: those who do good and those who do evil. Throughout the Gospel, Matthew wrestles with different accounts of the nature of this distinction. Is it that some are ruled by Satan, others by God or his Messianic king? Is it that God has chosen some for himself and rejected others? Is it that some hear and do the word and others do not? We have suggested that ultimately Matthew abandons demonological explanations, because of his belief that it is through law and instruction that God will shape for himself a new people, while at the same time he cannot escape the strength of such dualist accounts of evil, namely, their drawing attention to the pervasiveness of evil in the world across boundaries of race and nation. Further, for Matthew the notion of election raises sharply and painfully the question of the place of Israel in God's purposes. Matthew has no doubt that God has chosen Israel to be his people, that they are the elect of God. But this is thrown into question by the crowd's rejection of its Messiah (27:25) and of God's rejection of Israel's leaders: the kingdom has been taken away from them and given to a nation producing the fruits of it (21:43). The death of the Son means therefore not simply the end of the identification between Israel and the sons of the kingdom, but rather the recasting of Israel's role in the gathering of the nations, in the process whereby the nations should see the light and 'bring gifts' to Mount Zion (Isa 60:6; cf. Matt 2:11). It is as the disciples gather on the mountain in Galilee at the end of the Gospel, to receive Jesus' commission to go to all nations, that the role of Israel is recast.

Here the links between our passage and other commissioning narratives in the Scriptures and the Moses traditions assume major importance. Here I follow Davies and Allison.[39] There are close verbal links between Matthew 28:16–20 and Old Testament commissioning narratives with links to Moses, as Hubbard has shown.[40] Davies and Allison comment:

> at least four items may be attributed to Matthew's hand: the mountain, the command to go and disciple all nations, the imperative to observe all Jesus has commanded, and the promise of divine presence. We have already observed the significance of the mountain. As for the other three items, each can be

[39] Davies and Allison, 1997, 678–80.

[40] Hubbard, 1974, pointed out that of five such narratives which mention 'all that God has commanded', four contain wording in the LXX similar to that in Matt 28:20, namely, Exod 7:2; Josh 1:7; 1 Chr 22:13; Jer 1:7. Three of these explicitly mention Moses, and Jeremiah is modelled on Moses' call.

related to Deut 31:14–15, 23; and Josh 1:1–9, which are all about God, or God through Moses, commissioning Joshua. Josh 1:2 tells Joshua to 'go' (v. 9) and cross the Jordan. Josh 1:7 enjoins Joshua to 'observe and do as Moses my servant commanded you'. And Josh 1:9 (the pericope's conclusion) promises God's presence: 'for the LORD your God is with you wherever you go' . . .

Matt 28:16–20, like 1 Chr 22:1–16 and Jer 1:1–10, deliberately borrows from traditions about Moses. Readers are to exercise their scripturally informed imaginations and set the end of Jesus beside the end of Moses. Just as Moses, at the close of his life, commissioned Joshua to go into the land peopled by foreign nations and to observe all the commandments in the law, and then further promised his successor God's abiding presence, so similarly Jesus: at the end of his earthly ministry he told his disciples to go into all the world and to teach the observance of the commandments of the new Moses, and then further promised his assisting presence.[41]

This seems illuminating. If Matthew 13 has underlined the cosmic dimensions of Jesus' mission, in respect of the opposition which he encounters and of the divisions between his followers and the world, and the story of the Canaanite woman has undermined the continuing significance of the boundaries around the Land, here the theme of the entry into the Land, Joshua's commissioning to take possession to it, is reworked in such a way as to universalise the New Exodus motif of Isaiah. Just as previously Moses commissioned Joshua to go into the Land and to take possession of it for God's people from the forces hostile to them and to establish God's laws in it, so here Jesus, the new Moses, commissions his disciples to go into all the world, to all nations, to teach his commandments, so that his rule will be acknowledged by all and his kingdom established. The company of the disciples, that is to say, forms the core around which will gather a new people, rooted in the history of Israel, but now embracing Jews and Gentiles. Their territory however is now the world. Their task to teach the commandments of the Son of Man, who will at the end gather all the nations and establish his kingdom with those who have 'observed all that I have commanded you'.

Thus, by the end of the Gospel the question of good and evil has become intimately tied to the reception of the teaching of Jesus, as it is mediated through the teaching of his disciples. This does not mean

---

[41] Davies and Allison, 1990, 679–80.

that forensic accounts of the nature of evil and its overcoming have completely replaced dualistic ones. As chapter 13 shows, the problem is now shifted to questions about the reception of the church's teaching: why do some accept the word and others not? Is it that some hear the church's teaching and others hear false teaching (the parable of the wheat and the darnel)? Is it that Satan suborns some, while others allow themselves to be distracted by their own desires (the parable of the sower)? Matthew's Gospel does not resolve these questions. Dialectical mythology does not give place to (the attempt to write) monological theology in Matthew any more than it does in the New Testament canon with its juxtaposition of four Gospels. Nevertheless, by recasting the ideology of Mount Zion and placing the commission to teach the nations at the culmination of the narrative, Matthew's Gospel has given forensic explanations of evil and its resolution a prominence which will not be easily shaken in the history of Christianity. This is not the same as saying that it has resolved once and for all questions of the nature of evil and its overcoming.

## Conclusion

We must now return to the question of the remaking of sacred space which flows from this reworking of the ideology of Mount Zion. In the simplest terms, Matthew replaces Mount Zion with a mountain in Galilee. He replaces the mission charge to the Twelve in chapter 10, which prohibits them going to the Gentiles or the Samaritans, with the commission to go and make disciples of all nations. If Mark has allegorised space, making 'Galilee' a cipher for the new way of the disciples, how has Matthew used his narrative to redescribe the cosmos?

As we saw earlier, W. D. Davies propounded the thesis that, in the Gospels, theology is de-territorialised and the attachment to Land and Temple replaced by attachment to the person of Jesus.[42] Importantly, this affects the Messianic hopes of the Christian believers: 'life "in Christ", abiding in him, taking the yoke of the kingdom – these signify in the New Testament the fulfilment of the hope for fulness of life in the land that Judaism had cherished'.[43] But while it is 'justifiable to speak of the *realia* of Judaism as being "spiritualized" in the Christian

---

[42] Davies, 1994, esp. 366–76.
[43] Davies, 1994, 374.

dispensation',[44] territory and space are not altogether neglected. History and theology are both responsible for this. There was a need to remember the history of Jesus, the actual places in which he lived. The doctrine of the incarnation 'demanded the recognition that where the Glory had appeared among men all physical forms become suffused with it'.[45] Thus in the New Testament, the Land, Jerusalem and the Temple are transcended; at the same time there is a genuine concern with these realities. 'The New Testament finds holy space wherever Christ is or has been: it personalizes "holy space" in Christ, who as a figure of History, is rooted in the land; he cleansed the Temple and died in Jerusalem, and lends his glory to these and to the places where he was, but, as Living Lord, he is also free to move wherever he wills.'[46]

What exactly is intended by talk of the 'personalisation' of space? It might seem that some doctrine of the interiorisation of Christianity is being put forward, but this is fairly clearly not what Davies intends. A quotation from a letter of Pierre Benoit expresses the matter to Davies' satisfaction: 'le lieu matériel . . . peut être rattaché au cadre religieux du salut comme la coordonnée de l'histoire'.[47] Because of the community of faith's connection with Christ, those places with which he is associated have lasting importance for the community. Whereas Judaism hoped for fulness of life in the Land,[48] Christianity replaces those hopes for the restoration of the Land, the Temple and the gathering of dispersion, which were expressed in the Mount Zion traditions, with hopes for the gathering of the nations around the Messiah Jesus. This is not to be understood in a pietistic, individualistic sense, but rather in a communal one. It is in the gathered church, the new Israel which obeys the commands and teaching of their Lord, that the divine presence and leading is experienced. This means that the community is not tied to any particular space; it also means that those spaces which have played an important part in the community's history do indeed have their own special importance for the 'cadre religieux du salut'.

Much of this seems to be borne out by our discussion of Matthew. It is true that in Matthew Jewish places and sacred sites are

---

[44] Davies, 1994, 366.

[45] Davies, 1994, 366.

[46] Davies, 1994, 367.

[47] Davies, 1994, 367, n. 4: 'material space . . . may be attached to the religious body of salvation like the co-ordinate of history'.

[48] See Davies, 1963, 295–6, for Jamnia's attempts to encourage Jews to remain in the Land.

de-sacralised, in the very real sense that woes are spoken against them. In Matthew 11:20–24 Jesus utters woes against the cities of Galilee where Jesus had performed the majority of his miracles, foretelling their judgement.[49] In 23:37f., at the end of his prophetic discourse against the Pharisees, Jesus pronounces the Temple desolate and forsaken and addresses this to Jerusalem. Moreover, Jesus himself announces that a greater than the Temple is here (12:6) and in the final scene reworks the motif of the entry of the Land in ways which set aside the boundaries of the Land and assert Jesus' claim over the whole world. As a consequence, hopes for the in-gathering of the dispersion on Mount Zion are replaced with the call to make disciples out of all the nations, to draw them into the community of the church in which Jesus is present, in preparation for the final gathering of all the nations when the Son of Man will come to administer judgement and to establish his kingdom by separating the sheep from the goats (25:31–46).

It is right, too, to see in Matthew's Gospel a relocation of the centre of divine power and authority, of 'salvation', from the Temple to the Messiah Jesus. 'All authority has been given to me', and this includes the priestly authority of teaching, as well as the authority to forgive sins and to judge. In this sense, the Temple is superseded by the authority of Jesus; and Jesus as God-with-us is present no longer on the Temple Mount, but 'where two or three are gathered together in my name' (18:20). Nevertheless, the authority which is given to Jesus is not without territorial implications. His – universal – authority is 'over heaven and earth' (28:18). One might perhaps better speak of a de-particularisation or universalisation of the territorial dimensions of Judaism in Christianity, rather than of their personalisation. Jesus now reigns over the whole world: by his authority, his disciples are to go out and to make disciples of all nations; *wherever* they go, he will be with them, as they do battle with the forces hostile to them, of rejection and persecution. At the end he will *come* and all shall see him; Christ will be revealed as judge and cosmocrator.[50] As with Mark, the tendency to

---

[49] Freyne, 69–90, has shown that in Matthew there is no special privileging of Galilee over Jerusalem, as he believes there is in Mark: the whole narrative is too much caught up in the *Auseinandersetzung* with the Jews for one geographical setting to be singled out as particularly responsive to Jesus.

[50] There is a vital distinction to be made here, which will have important implications for discussions of colonialism and the Bible in the last chapter. Davies, 1994, 370, rightly points out that 'the cosmic awareness of primitive Christianity . . . could not but place all Christian speculation on geographical entities that were central to Judaism in a minor

play down the particular divisions of sacred space is linked to the perception that the whole world is under the grip of dark powers and that it is Jesus' and his disciples' mission to overcome them, wherever they may be encountered. But whereas Mark's allegorises Galilee, so that it becomes a cipher for the disciples' field of activity, Matthew works more typologically. As Joshua was commissioned to take possession of the Land with its boundaries, so now the disciples are commissioned to preach the Gospel 'throughout the whole world, as a testimony to all nations; and then the end will come' (24:14; cf. 25:32; 28:19).

Such a typological approach allows Matthew also to do justice to the role which particular geographical sites have played within the divine purposes. The places where Jesus is born and brought up and starts his ministry are all linked to divine prophecy. His life is the culmination of a sacred history which is throughout linked to a particular people, whose story is inseparable from the Land and holy city to which they are led out of slavery, from which they are exiled and to which they long to return. Such restorationist mythology plays a major role in Matthew, as we have seen.

Yet Matthew's Jesus, in announcing that a greater than the Temple is here and declaring that the priests profane the Sabbath, has raised serious questions against the notions of sacred and profane which serve to define sacred space in Judaism. The wandering preacher, whose disciples 'profane' the Sabbath like David and his men, is greater than the Temple. But what is being said here: that his power is greater than that of the Temple because it is not subject to degradation by exposure to the profane? Matthew, unlike Mark, does not interpret Mark 7:15 as a rejection of the food laws and therefore as a categorical rejection of notions of purity. But he does demand a righteousness which is higher than that of the scribes and Pharisees, and that is one which will bring in a new dispensation. The power which Jesus embodies is one which is subject to the ultimate degradation of death and exposure on a cross and which proves stronger than it.

---

key', but such awareness with its 'doctrines of the new creation, the new age, the cosmic Christ, the cosmic Church, and the cosmic salvation through all these' could not but assert the importance of the whole of space and Christianity's claims over it. It is this cosmic dimension which can easily support the development of more aggressive, religiously imperialistic forms of Christianity.

The 'sacred sites' of Christianity are a cross at the place of a skull and a tomb, and yet it is from these that the one rises to whom is given all authority.

Thus, Christianity is linked to sacred sites in a novel way. To say that 'the New Testament . . . personalises "holy space", is at best an analogical statement. The divine power which lies at the centre of the Christian community has its origin in sites which in terms of the Law are impure. The nature of that power is, on the one hand, expressed in its vulnerability, its destruction and lack of divine protection; on the other, by Jesus' resurrection and triumph over the forces of death and destruction. Those who follow Jesus and accept his commission to go and make disciples of the nations do not serve a cult which erects and protects spatial boundaries between its sacred realm and the profane world without, and are not bound to the old regulations which protect the divine from pollution by the profane. They are sent out defenceless on an itinerant ministry, which itself renders the notion of specific cultic sites redundant. And that power, which has its origin in the cross and resurrection, is concretised, is experienced in the worship of the Christian communities for whom Matthew writes.

Is this a sectarian view of sacred space: that the divine power of the cosmocrator is realised, made present in the gathered community? Yes, in the sense that what it implies is that it is the duty of the community to embody that righteousness, that power, in its life and prayer. No, in the sense that such a community should not fence itself off from the world outside, as it were, erecting new 'cultic' boundaries between itself and the 'world'. The power, which it should seek to embody in its own corporate ethos, is one which on the one hand requires a fundamental change of heart on the part of those who enter the community, and on the other hand includes the imperative to *go* and make disciples, not to retreat behind its own doors. And such 'discipling' is above all the bringing of people to recognise the light, the power which is now present among them in the world. It is in this sense, as we have said, a conversionist sect. The world is its mission field.

Again, it should be relatively obvious that Matthew's narrative does not *define* sacred space in a clear-cut way, but rather suggests images and metaphors, which will be taken up by later generations and developed in different ways. The Great Church will use the mission charge in chapter 28 and the image of the harvest fields to develop a view of the world as the sphere of its interaction with 'all the nations'.

Such a mission may be conceived in very different ways. It may be seen as the bringing of divine insight and instruction to all people. As Christianity becomes more powerful, more closely allied to the centres of secular power, so such ideas will become increasingly attractive. It becomes the source of universal divine instruction for all nations. Freed from sectarian constraints, it can become the source of moral and religious authority for civil society. The world is seen as a school, where those who follow Jesus' teaching provide instruction to all who will hear, instruction which will enable them to withstand the final judgement. The boundaries between church and world become more and more blurred and the church is conceived of as a *corpus mixtum*, the company of good and evil, who must exist alongside each other until the end of the ages.

On the other hand, it may see its role in much more oppositional terms. It is in the world to oppose the powers of darkness, to confess that Jesus is the Christ, the Son of the living God (Matt 16:16) and to resist the powers of darkness, until they are finally destroyed at the last judgement. Here the church can be seen as the *navis ecclesiae*, which negotiates the storms of the world, protecting its passengers from the onslaughts of the dark powers. The vision of the world is still one of a world infested by Satanic forces; but the forces of light and life are now established and will not be overcome (16:18). The world is a field in which good and evil exist randomly alongside each other; only at the end will evil be finally rooted out. This is the vision of the North African martyr church, which provoked fierce controversy in the fourth and fifth centuries.[51]

For all the deep differences in the views which we have been sketching in the briefest of ways, they all share one thing: that the church is a universal, catholic church set in the world. Whatever the importance for its history of the links with Israel and the 'holy land', its centres will be in the centres of secular power, in Rome and Constantinople.

By contrast, Jewish Christianity, which saw itself as continuous with Israel, did see the links with Israel and the Land as crucial and read the texts rather differently. Matthew became one of the preferred texts for such groups and was closely related to the *Gospel of the Hebrews*. Nor is

---

[51] The Donatists insisted (with exegetical right on their side) against Augustine that the field is the world and not the church. Such a reading identifies the church as the company of the righteous who will shine like the sun, as opposed to those outside, the sons of the evil one, who are workers of lawlessness (13:41–43); cf. Frend, 1952.

it difficult to see why this should have been. Matthew's underlining of the Isaianic motif of the way of the Lord with the fulfilment quotations, provides one rich vein which could be exploited by such groups, as do the genealogies (though these were not present in all the Gospels which the Fathers attributed to the Jewish Christians).[52] An illuminating insight into the way that Matthew has been received in Jewish Christianity is provided by *5 Ezra*. Here, by contrast to Matthew, where the kingdom is given to an ἔθνος producing fruit, the church is simply identified as the people (except where it is necessary to distinguish it from Israel). 'Israel and the "coming people" are *both* referred to repeatedly as *populus*, and they share the same mother, but Christians are not called a *new* people, as in the *Epistle of Barnabas* 5.7 and in the *Apology of Aristides*, 16.4'.[53] Matthew 21–25, and especially 21:43, are here being taken up and given a particular twist. It is not so much that the kingdom is being taken away from Israel and given to the church, as that the Jewish Christians are now simply identified as the people of God, after the rejection of those who were formerly his people. Similar emphases are to be found in the treatment of sacred geography. As with the former people, the mother of the Jewish Christian church is Jerusalem. The fate of the former people is to be ejected from the Land and scattered among the nations (*5 Ezra* 2:7). The coming people will be given the kingdom of Jerusalem (2:10–32), and finally all those who have fulfilled the law of the Lord will congregate on Mount Zion. Lastly, Ezra is shown a vision of the end, of a 'great multitude on Mount Zion' (*5 Ezra* 2:42) where a tall young man crowns each one who has 'confessed the name of God' and the young man is identified as 'the Son of God, whom they confessed in the world' (2:47). Ezra is then sent to 'tell my people what sort of and how many wonders of the Lord God you have seen' (2:48).

A number of things are remarkable about this text. In the first place, it is written almost entirely in terms of forensic eschatology. Israel is punished for its disobedience; the coming people will fulfil the Law of the Lord. They will receive the rewards for their obedience and faithfulness in confessing the name of God. In this respect, it represents an interesting reworking of the ideology of the way of the Lord. For it

---

[52] Epiphanius, *Heresy* 29.9.4, suggests that the *Gospel of the Ebionites* omitted the 'genealogy from Abraham to Christ'.
[53] Stanton, 1992, 267–8.

is no longer the faithless people who have repented who will return triumphant from exile. Rather, it is a coming people who will be obedient and fulfil the Law as the former people did not. All of this can find strong echoes in Matthew. What is interestingly different from Matthew is the close identification with Jerusalem and Zion. Jerusalem is the mother, the true home of the church. Mount Zion is the place where the faithful will gather at the end and will be sanctified. Ezra's commission is to preach this to the church. Unlike the commissioning on the mountain in Matthew 28, the disciples are not sent out to the nations (it is the former people who will be scattered). Rather they are to live in their home, the Land, and there they are finally to enjoy their rest. In the absence of any dualist elements in the text, there seems to be nothing to disturb the Jewish framework of the text. The key terms are God and his people, the covenant, the Law and the Land.

The reading of this short text demonstrates powerfully how any strictly Jewish reading of the Gospel must force it into a strait-jacket, ignoring those elements which relativise or minimise Jewish motifs of land and descent and which present the struggle against evil as a cosmic struggle against dark powers. It makes it clear how much of a *tour de force* is required to present Matthew's Gospel as affirming Jewish ethnicity, not least as that entails strongly affirming Jewish attachment to the Land. At the same time, the fact that it was Matthew's Gospel which so strongly appealed to the writer of this text, and indeed to Jewish Christians more widely, shows the extent to which Matthew has emphasised elements which Mark had allegorised or ignored. The genealogy, the earthing of Jesus' story in the fulfilment of prophecy, the emphasis on the fulfilling of the law – all these without question lend strong encouragement to such readings.

# 8

# Cosmology and Christology in Matthew

## Introduction

We now need to turn our attention again to the ways in which Matthew has interacted with the different mythologies which, we have been arguing, underly his Markan source and which are indeed widely attested in the Jewish eschatology of his time. What sort of cosmology has Matthew constructed out of the traditional material with which he worked?

One thing which it has been interesting to observe is that Matthew tends to emphasise both the forensic and the cosmic dualist strands of Jewish eschatology. We saw how he develops Mark's discipleship material in forensic terms by inserting the whole of the Sermon on the Mount between Mark's call narrative, Mark 1:16–20, and the next verse of Mark which he cites in order, 1:40. The Sermon on the Mount becomes a commentary on the call to discipleship; the life of the follower of Jesus is conceived of as a training in the special understanding of the Law and God's will that Jesus brings. To become a true follower of Jesus is to become one of his brothers and sisters, to do the will of God (Matt 12:46–50). And this is further underlined by the linking of the Sermon on the Mount with four other blocks of teaching material. Further, Matthew develops the Isaianic way of the Lord motif, with its strong emphasis on Israel's sin and punishment and triumphal return to Mount Zion, notably in the final scene where the disciples are sent out into the whole world to 'disciple', to baptise and to teach all the nations. This emphasis on instruction in the sacred knowledge of God's will which Jesus brings, is underscored by the theme of judgement which runs right through the Gospel, from the section on the Two Ways in the Sermon on the Mount (7:13–27), through the parables in chapter 13, to the final judgement scene in 25:31–46. Thus, the storyline whereby Jesus Christ, Son of David, Son of Abraham, calls disciples, instructs them in the full meaning of the Law and understanding of God's will and commissions them, first to preach to Israel and then to go out and instruct all the nations in his teaching, is brought out very clearly by Matthew's editing of his Markan material and by his overall shaping of his Gospel.

Strikingly however, and this is a point seldom acknowledged by commentators, Matthew *also* pushes his material in the other direction. He uses the Q version of the Temptation narrative, which substantially extends the story and emphasises Satan's rule over all the kingdoms of the world. He sets right at the heart of the Gospel the parable of the wheat and the tares and its interpretation (13:24–30, 36–43), which many take for his own composition, and which divides the world sharply into those who are sons of the kingdom and those who are sons of the evil one. He allegorises the story of the Stilling of the Storm, turning it into an image of the church beset by the powers of darkness, and he weaves motifs associated with a final cosmic battle into the description of the coming of the Son of Man in chapter 24.[1]

Once again, we are confronted on a fairly straightforward surface-reading of Matthew's text with a set of conflicting motifs and storylines. This is further confirmation both of the general thesis that first-century Jewish eschatology was indebted to two very different, indeed conflicting accounts of the nature, origins and ultimate eradication of evil in and from the world; and of the more specific claim that both Mark and Matthew engage with these different accounts, using both to give narrative expression to their view of the nature of Jesus' mission and nature. This is in line, as we saw, with Claude Lévi-Strauss' view of the nature of mythology as attempting to mediate between the deep contradictions in most societies' views of the world and ways of organising their affairs.

A cosmic dualist reading of Matthew's eschatology: David Sim

It is not a view, however, that has much currency among New Testament scholars. I attempted to demonstrate the kinds of *aporiai*, which failure to recognise this kind of oppositionality occasioned, in the study of Mark's Gospel by pointing to the radically different accounts which

---

[1] 24:30 speaks of the σημεῖον of the Son of Man and 24:31 of *his* angels and their trumpet call; see Sim, 1996, 104–8, referring to Isa 18:3; Jer 6:1; 51:27; the tenth benediction of the *Shemoneh Esreh* and the Qumran War Scroll, 1QM 2:15 – 4:17.

scholars like Best on the one hand, and Robinson, Marcus and Garrett on the other hand, offer of Mark's eschatology. Where Matthew is concerned the situation is quite different. With very few exceptions, scholars read Matthew forensically, noting as they go the more dualist elements, and passing on without seriously addressing the challenge which they offer to their chosen paradigm. One of the most notable exceptions to this rule is David Sim, who in his *Apocalyptic Eschatology in the Gospel of Matthew* has argued that the elements of dualism and determinism are dominant in Matthew's treatment of eschatology, and that this is to be explained in terms of the critical situation that Matthew was facing in relation to Judaism, the Gentile world and indeed to other groups within the church.

The major difficulty with Sim's thesis is that, while he is aware that different accounts of the nature of evil and its origins are being offered in various kinds of apocalyptic writing of the turn of the era, he offers no coherent account of how such differing views might be combined. One senses that it is the connections with certain types of social situation that is of primary interest to him and that, while he is very alert to the cosmological beliefs which are expressed in the texts he reviews, he is not greatly concerned with questions of their coherence with one another. This can be illustrated briefly from his treatment of dualism in his section on the 'characteristics of apocalyptic eschatology'.[2] Here he identifies three forms of dualism. There is, first, an historical dualism, whereby two ages are sharply distinguished, the present age and the age to come. Secondly, there is a cosmic dualism which divides the 'cosmos or supernatural realm' into two opposing forces.[3] Thirdly, there is 'human dualism', the division between the righteous and the wicked in the human sphere. Clearly the main problem here from our point of view is the way that the relationship between cosmic dualism and human good and evil-doing is conceived. Is human wrong-doing caused by, or independent of, the actions of cosmic forces of darkness? It is not helpful to use the term 'human dualism', as Sim does, to refer equally to both options. Sim certainly sees quite clearly that there are different views about the relationship between the cosmic forces and human agency expressed in the texts he reviews. In some, the *Testament of Asher*, 1QS 3:13–4:26 and Revelation, 'the dualism on the angelic level and the

[2] Sim, 1996, 35–41.
[3] Sim, 1996, 35.

battle for supremacy it reflects are likewise reflected on the individual human level'.[4] On the other hand, there are other texts which

> say little or nothing at all of the struggle in the angelic orders. While it might be the case that some schemes presume it, it cannot be taken for granted. Yet those texts still accept the basic division of good and evil on the group human level and draw a sharp distinction between those who perform the will of God and those who do not . . . Almost without exception, the documents which emphasise the end of history and the universal judgement take great pains to classify humanity into two diametrically opposed groups. On one side stand the author and his readers, and on the other stand those who are opposed to them. Thus the notion of human dualism is a constant element in apocalyptic eschatology.[5]

But this is to confuse two quite distinct kinds of human dualism. It is one thing to do evil because one freely and knowingly disobeys the will of God, another to do evil because one is ruled over by, is in bondage to evil spirits. It is one thing to choose evil rather than good, another to be 'born of evil'. It is true that in both cases, one can distinguish two different groups of people on the basis of these two opposed definitions of evil in the human sphere; also true that in the apocalyptic writings the author and his readers stand on one side of the divide and their opponents on the other. Either conception of evil will provide, that is to say, powerful ideological weapons against the opponents of a beleaguered group. But that does not make the conceptions themselves identical. The rush to make the social functional point has led Sim to play down the importance of significant theological/cosmological distinctions which will feature in a major way in the subsequent history of reception of these texts.

Once these two different notions are systematically confused, then the way is open to produce a list of characteristics of apocalyptic eschatology which ignores the major differences in conception which are a key feature of this kind of thought. In a similar way, Sim can list together various motifs associated with the turning of the ages, as if they were all equally possible parts of the same schema. But it is important to know whether the notion of some final cosmological battle, when the forces of Satan will be overcome by the heavenly hosts is, or is not, an integral part of a given view of the nature of the overthrow of

---

4  Sim, 1996, 38.
5  Sim, 1996, 40.

evil. And it seems to be clear that it cannot be an *integral* part of a view of the world which attributes evil entirely to human agency. It makes a crucial difference whether men and women have gone astray or have been led astray. If it is the latter, then until such time as the powers that lead them astray are destroyed or bound, there can be no peace, no final overthrow of evil. If the former, then there may be time for people to repent, time for them to hear the proclamation of God's will, and then a time for judgement when those who have failed to respond will be cast out. These are two separate, opposed conceptions; the intriguing thing is that they are frequently to be found in the same writings.

Thus, when Sim comes to consider the evidence of 'apocalyptic eschatology' in Matthew, he similarly lists elements which draw on both opposing cosmologies without any apparent awareness that there are serious conflicts of ideas. What his schema does allow him is readily to identify cosmic dualist elements in the texts.[6] He draws attention to Matthew's use of ὁ πονηρός (5:37; 6:13; 13:19, 38)[7] and argues that Matthew gives the pericope about the return of the unclean spirit (Matt 12:43–45//Luke 11:24–26) a particular twist: when the spirit returns it finds its former home not only swept and in order, but empty. This, argues Sim, gives a warning that the vacuum left by the spirit should have been filled. '[N]eutrality, i.e. emptiness, is not an option in the cosmic conflict: non-alignment with the cause of Jesus means ultimately taking the part of Satan. As with 13:36–43, the dualism of the human world merges completely with the dualism of the supernatural world.'[8]

What is striking, however, is that where Matthew is concerned, Sim wants to take these relatively few explicit references to some form of cosmic dualism to be determinative of the meaning of the rest of the Gospel, specifically of those other passages which divide men and women into two groups, good and evil, righteous and doers of lawlessness, righteous and cursed, wise and foolish, faithful and wise and wicked. This, despite his earlier observation that there are apocalyptic texts where

---

[6] Sim, 1996, 75–87.

[7] Sim, 1996, 77. There are questions here as to whether this should always be taken as a masculine.

[8] Sim, 1996, 80. He notes that commentators like Gnilka, 1988, 649 and Davies and Allison, 1991, 361, n. 113, see Matt 12:43–45 as the only point where such advanced dualism is expressed in Matthew, but comments simply that this overlooks 13:36–43. This still disregards the central point, which is that both these passages appear to conflict very directly with the main drift of Matthew's treatment of good and evil in the rest of the Gospel.

notions of cosmic influence are absent and that in such cases we should certainly not simply assume their presence.[9] The case is certainly different here, in that in Matthew there are clearly identifiable passages which speak of human wrong-doing in cosmic dualist terms. But it is never-theless remarkably bold to go on to claim that all these other references to human wrong and right-doing

> serve to highlight Matthew's dualistic view of the cosmos which he constructed in 13:36–43. The question of morality or ethics is merely one aspect of the conceptual framework in which Matthew's dualistic terminology works. The righteous are good only in so far as they have aligned themselves with Jesus and his forces in the cosmic struggle. On the other hand, the wicked are evil not just because they act immorally, but because their immorality betrays their allegiance to Satan. Matthew's constant use of πονηρός as a descriptive term for the wicked clearly points in this direction.[10]

It is not at all clear what this means. Is Sim claiming that it is Matthew's view that those who do the will of God, but who are not consciously 'aligned with Jesus and his forces in the cosmic struggle', are not good, and will be condemned in the final judgement? That certainly seems to be strikingly at odds with the final judgement scene where those found righteous ask: 'Lord, when did we see thee hungry and feed thee, or thirsty and give thee drink?' (25:37). It is true that here right-doing is identified with ministering to Jesus and his followers: but the implication is that what is righteous about the action is the action of ministering to the hungry and thirsty. Certainly Sim himself at this point, in considering the different accounts of the final judgement that Matthew offers (7:21–23; 19:28), concedes that Matthew was 'by no means a "systematic theologian"' and 'had not himself clearly worked out and assimilated the precise details of the judgement from the disparate traditions at his disposal'.[11] One might, moreover, ask whether the language of alignment and allegiance which Sim uses at this point is not itself unduly ethical. Is the point of cosmic dualism not that it is the evil spirits who lead men and women astray, who are set over them, even from whom they spring, are born? It is the element of dominance and control which is pre-eminent. Sim's account already makes human choice decisive.

---

[9]  Sim, 1996, 40.
[10]  Sim, 1996, 82.
[11]  Sim, 1996, 127.

But, if Sim's characteristically vigorous and frequently perceptive monograph fails to offer an adequate account of the relation of the two types of dualist language in Matthew, what is to be said? The rest of this chapter considers this specifically with reference to Matthew's portrayal of Jesus, something to which Sim here devotes relatively little space. How does Matthew's emphasis on Jesus' teaching role affect his understanding of the role of demonic forces in influencing the actions of men and women? How does his own introduction of cosmic dualistic thought affect his presentation of Jesus as the new Moses, the teacher of Israel, the judge, but also as the opponent of Satan, as the exorcist and the eschatological saviour?

## Matthew's narrative presentation of Jesus: two interlocking stories

Again, it is possible to trace out two rather different lines of narrative which correspond broadly to the two types of contemporary eschatology. In the first, cosmic dualist, story, Jesus the divine figure is born miraculously through the agency of the Holy Spirit, he is baptised, and the Spirit descends and comes upon him and then leads him out to be tested by the devil in the wilderness. The divine saviour figure, God with us, encounters the source of evil and darkness, the ruler of this world, who can offer to him all the kingdoms of the world and their glory. Their conflict is couched largely in scriptural terms but is centred around Satan's attempts to persuade Jesus to use the mighty powers at his disposal to break his fast, to test God to see if he will protect him, to pursue earthly power rather than his divine vocation.[12] Finally, Satan leaves him[13] and the angels minister to him. The conflict is won, for the time being. The nature of the conflict is defined: it is a conflict for Jesus' allegiance. Whom will he worship, obey and follow: God or Satan? And the battleground is specifically linked with the interpretation of Scripture. True hearing of the word of God will lead to doing his will. In this sense the forensic/ethical model is already subverting the dualist story.

Jesus' conflict with Satan continues in the narratives of his mighty works, though it is not greatly stressed. However, Matthew 10:8 explicitly

---

[12] This is preferable to the suggestion that he is being asked to perform some great miracle to demonstrate his Messianic status to the people; so Luz, 1989, 164. There is no mention of the people and no clear evidence for this kind of expectation in relation to the Messiah; see Davies and Allison, 1988, 367.

[13] The present tense may suggest that this is temporary, as is explicitly stated by Luke (ἄχρι καιροῦ); so Hill, 1972, 102.

adds the charge to cast out demons to the mission charge from Q.[14] He greatly abbreviates Mark's account of the Gerasene demoniac (8:28–34//Mark 5:1–20), but retains the basic outline of the narrative. He expands Mark's Beelzebul controversy by adding material from Q (12:25–37//Mark 3:23–30). If Mark's account simply sets the two parables of the kingdom divided and the binding of the strong man alongside each other, Matthew develops the latter parable by adding the saying which explains Jesus' exorcisms, not so much in terms of the binding of the strong man, but by giving an account of the nature of the power by which he is able to overcome the demons: 'If I by the Spirit of God cast out demons, then the kingdom of God has come upon you' (Matt 12:28). The same power, which came upon him in the baptism and led him up into the wilderness to encounter the devil, enables him to cast out the demons and is a mark of the dawning of God's rule over the world. And the dualist element in this understanding, the sharp contrast between the spiritual power of good and evil, is underlined by the Q version of Mark's saying about those who are not against us being for us: 'He who is not with me is against me, and he who does not gather with me scatters' (12:30).

Both these additions to the Markan Beelzebul controversy are consistent with the idea that the struggle between the devil and Jesus, empowered by the Spirit, is a continuing one throughout the Gospel, even if Satan himself may have departed for a while. The battle-fronts are still clearly demarcated. Jesus' exorcisms are not just 'mopping-up operations';[15] they are mighty works of the Spirit working through Jesus, part of the process by which God asserts his rule over a world in the grip of Satanic powers.

Further evidence of Satan's continued activity is provided by references to 'the enemy' (ὁ ἐχθρός) who sows weeds in the farmer's field (13:25, 28, 39) and whose work cannot be uprooted till the final judgement, and by the citation of Psalm 110 in 22:44 (taking this in an eschatological sense). Some of the uses of πονηρός, though by no means all, also point in this direction, most notably 13:19 and 38.[16]

---

[14]  Ctr. Luke 10:9. The point is made by Sim, 1996, 78, though it should be borne in mind that Mark and Luke all include the charge to the disciples in the parallels to Matt 10:1; Mark 6:7; Luke 9:1.

[15]  See Best, 1990, 15.

[16]  Matt 13:19 is unambiguously masculine and makes it more than likely that 13:38 is to be read in the same way. These are the only two occurrences of the singular form which

Despite this, there is no clear depiction of the final victory over Satan. It is true that Jesus declares Peter to be the rock on which the church is founded, against which the gates of Hades will not prevail. There are, too, echoes in chapter 24 of some final battle between the forces of darkness and Jesus and 'his' angels. Sim makes a good case for seeing the reference to Jesus' σημεῖον (his standard, 24:30), the mourning of the tribes of the earth and the σάλπιγξ (trumpet, 24:31) of 'his angels' as all having military overtones. Nevertheless, as he also quite rightly argues, despite the references to the 'eternal fire prepared for the devil and his angels' (25:41), 'Matthew never describes the final conflict between the heavenly saviour figure and his evil opponents. Either his interest in this myth does not extend that far, or it might be the case that he expects an immediate surrender of the armies of the antichrist. . . . Whatever the case might have been, Matthew is more interested in depicting the victory of the Son of Man in terms of the final judgement.'[17] As with Mark, the cosmic dualist story is in the end subordinated to the forensic one, but as with Mark, too, not before it has set up powerful resonances which run throughout the Gospel.

The second, restorationist, story anchors the action firmly in Israel's history by relating Jesus' genealogy, his descent from the forefathers, David and Abraham, and linking the details of his conception, birth, childhood and early ministry to the prophecies of sacred Scripture. It introduces John's proclamation of the way of the Lord with an account of his preaching of repentance in face of the coming kingdom of heaven (Matt 3:3). This is striking, partly because of the way it emphasises repentance as the key preparation for the coming kingdom, partly because Matthew puts the same words into John's mouth as he does into Jesus' (Matt 4:17//Mark 1:15). This emphasis on repentance as the primary 'virtue' is similar to that which we saw in Philo, who identified it as one of the virtues which Abraham archetypally embodied.[18] Matthew's account of John's preaching makes an analogous point when he warns the Pharisees to bear the fruits of repentance and not to rely on their descent from Abraham (3:8–10). Only such repentance will make them receptive to walking along the way of the

---

Luz, 1989, 349 n. 105, allows to be masculine. Others argue also for 6:13, 'deliver us from the evil one', and even for 5:37; Davies and Allison, 1988, 614–15.

[17] Sim, 1996, 104–8, quotation 108.

[18] See above, pp. 44–9, esp. 47.

Lord to which Jesus calls, in the first place, the lost sheep of the house of Israel, and finally, through the agency of his disciples, all the nations.

Matthew significantly modifies the concept of discipleship which he finds in Mark, presenting it as a call, in the first place, to instruction by Jesus, the one who perfectly fulfils the Law and the prophets, and only subsequently as an invitation to go out and preach and teach and, at least where Israel is concerned, to exorcise.[19] Those who follow him along the way are first to be fully instructed in the nature of God's will so that they may truly become members of Jesus' family (12:50).

As the one who instructs, Jesus is presented typologically as the new Moses.[20] Such typological comparison is especially strong in the birth and infancy narratives and in the Sermon on the Mount and generally shapes Matthew 1–7 with the infancy, crossing of the water at baptism, the temptation in the wilderness, and the law-giving on the mountain. Subsequently, there are important further allusions in the saying about the reciprocal knowledge of Father and Son, in the transfiguration, where Moses himself appears, and in the commissioning of Jesus' successors in 28:16–20. This is only one strand in Matthew's presentation of Jesus, but it complements and reinforces the Isaianic way of the Lord. The way on which the disciples are being led runs from the desert to Jerusalem, just as the way of the Israelites led them through the desert to the Land, whence they would travel on to establish the Temple on Zion. As we saw, this movement from the desert to the Temple became greatly schematised in later presentations. In Matthew the way leads on beyond Jerusalem and the cross and resurrection to the mountain from which the disciples are sent out to make disciples of all nations. This is the fulfilment of God's purpose in choosing his people and making his covenant with them. The earlier history is to be recapitulated and transcended as God's rule is finally established over all the world.

The end of this way is, however, no longer Mount Zion. It extends all the way to the final judgement, 'when the Son of Man comes in his glory, and all the angels with him' (25:31). Then he will sit on his throne and all the nations will be gathered before him and he will judge

---

[19] It is important to our argument that the command to exorcise is missing from the mission charge in Matt 28. In this respect it is interesting to compare the longer ending of Mark (16:17) where the disciples are assured that they will 'cast out demons in my name' (16:17).

[20] See Allison, 1993, for a full discussion of Matthew's use of *sunkrisis*.

them. It is an intriguing reworking of the Isaianic theme of the nations flocking to the glory of the Lord on Mount Zion (Isa 60). Here it is the glory of the crucified and resurrected Son of Man to which they come. But before that can occur, the disciples must be sent out to make disciples of all nations and to teach them to do all that Jesus has commanded. The last mountain scene of the Gospel in fact leads on to the judgement scene in chapter 25, which is the true endpoint of the Gospel's trajectory.

## Matthew's use of titles

The attempt to trace two overlapping narratives in Matthew's Gospel helps to show something of the ambiguity of the figure of Jesus he presents. How far can this ambiguity be resolved? Discussions of Matthew's Christology, as indeed of the Christology of other parts of the New Testament, have often focused on the use of titles. This is useful enough, though one needs to be on guard against allowing this kind of discussion to assume too much importance. It is only one element in a complex narrative, and it is probably right to say that in the end it is the narrative, which determines the meaning of the titles, rather that the titles which give meaning to the narrative.[21] Nevertheless, discussion of the titles may help to shed some light on Matthew's dialogue with these two traditions of eschatology.

### Jack D. Kingsbury's treatment of titles in Matthew

Certainly one of the most influential contributions to such discussions has been that of Jack Kingsbury. In *Matthew: Structure, Christology, Kingdom*, Kingsbury argued that 'Son of God' is the 'central christological category of Matthew's Gospel'[22] and that it is in the light of this title that all the others are to be interpreted. 'Son of God' is the one title that is distributed across all the major parts of the Gospel; it is found at the major events of Jesus' baptism (3:17), Temptation (4:3, 6), after the walking on the water (14:33), at Peter's confession at Caesarea Philippi (16:16), at the Transfiguration (17:5), at the Trial (26:63) and Crucifixion (27:40, 54). Kingsbury sees the reference to Immanuel, 'God with us', in 1:23, which is echoed in 18:20 and 28:20,

---

[21] Luz, 1991, 223, 'the Matthaean story of Jesus functions as the predicate and redefines the meaning of the traditional titles'. See too Davies and Allison, 1997, 718–21.
[22] Kingsbury, 1975, 82.

and, he argues, in 14:27, as containing '*in nuce* everything that Matthew otherwise says in 1:1 – 4.16 of Jesus Son of God'.[23] The title is distinguished by being a 'confessional' one (hence its relative scarcity in the long section on Jesus' public ministry, 4:17 – 10:42 – the demon in 8:29 knows who Jesus is, even if he does not confess him); where it is used by non-believers, it is blasphemous. It is revealed to those who make the confession. This distinguishes it from one of the other major titles in the Gospel, Son of Man, which Kingsbury sees as a public title, addressed only to those outside the group of disciples. It does not occur until 8:20, and 'except for the "righteous" in the scene of the Last Judgment, it marks the people in view of whom it is used as being unbelievers or opponents of Jesus'.[24] Its principal interest for Matthew is in its reference to Jesus as the eschatological judge; in this respect it 'coalesces' with the title Son of God.[25]

Later in his *Matthew as Story*, Kingsbury argued the same case on rather different grounds. If in his first book he was working as a redaction critic, looking to see what changes Matthew had made in his sources, attending to patterns of usage and emphasis throughout the book, here he dons the robe of the – ahistorical – literary critic. Historical considerations of setting, sources, mode of composition are laid aside, and we are invited to attend to the composition itself and to the literary conventions by which writers can make themselves heard. Two points are crucial to Kingsbury's argument in this book. First, he now pays greater attention to the placing of the titles within the Gospel itself. Son of God is seen to occur as the culmination of each of the three major sections which Kingsbury has identified: 1:1 – 4:17; 4:18 – 16:20; 16:21 – end. Second, he distinguishes the various 'points of view' which are presented in the Gospel. In simple terms, we need to distinguish between the point of view of the author, of Jesus and of God. It is clear that in the Gospel, Jesus' point of view and that of the author coincide. What is interesting is that these receive ultimate accreditation from the entry of God as 'actor' in the divine voice in 3:17 and 17:5 where God declares Jesus to be his beloved Son. Thus, the ultimately authoritative point of view in the Gospel accredits the title 'Son of God' as the one truly authoritative title in the light of which all others have to be read.

[23] Kingsbury, 1975, 53.
[24] Kingsbury, 1975, 115.
[25] Kingsbury, 1975, 121.

There is a further aspect to this literary approach to the question of Matthew's Christology which concerns his use of the Son of Man title. Kingsbury has argued that it is 'Son of God' as opposed to 'Son of Man' which represents God's point of view in the Gospel, and this is reinforced for him by the fact that in the first section 1:1 – 4:16, which sets out who Jesus is, the title 'Son of Man' does not occur. Furthermore, he argues, its use in Matthew is quite distinct from that of other titles, which are used to say 'who Jesus is', whereas the phrase 'Son of Man' occurs only on Jesus' lips and is never used predicatively (i.e. in the form 'I am the Son of Man'). '"The Son of Man" is not meant to clarify for the reader who Jesus is, but must itself be clarified.'[26]

Rather strangely, Kingsbury finds confirmation of this view in his discussion of the trial scene before the high priest. Jesus' reply to the high priest's demand: 'tell us if you are the Christ, the Son of God' is 'You have said so.' Kingsbury takes this as a straight affirmative and reads Jesus' subsequent remark, 'But I tell you hereafter you will see the Son of Man seated at the right hand of power . . .', as merely a 'tacit reference to himself as "the Son of Man"'.[27] The reason for this is twofold: first, that he rightly observes that the title is nowhere picked up by those to whom it is uttered. In this case the priests in mocking him refer to him as Christ. Secondly, he wants to translate the phrase, not as a special title, carrying certain sense contents, but as a mode of self-reference, 'this man'.

What then is the purpose, according to Kingsbury, of Matthew's use of the phrase? '"The Son of Man" may be defined as the title by means of which Jesus refers to himself "in public" or in view of the "public" (or "world") . . . as "the man", or "the human being" (earthly, suffering, vindicated), and to assert his divine authority in the face of opposition.'[28] By speaking of 'Son of Man' as a public title, Kingsbury means two things: first, that it is principally addressed to the world; secondly, that it can be used openly without any of those who are addressed actually picking it up and using it. How is it to be understood? The key is in the exchange between Jesus and Peter at Caesarea Philippi: Jesus (not Peter, as Kingsbury rather oddly suggests) asks who is the Son of Man and Peter replies, You are the Son of God.

[26] Kingsbury, 1984, 23.
[27] Kingsbury, 1984, 23.
[28] Kingsbury, 1984, 27.

It might seem then that Kingsbury is saying that the term has no content at all. Nevertheless, he does suggest that it is 'associated' with Jesus' assertion of his divine authority and that it is a phrase used specifically in situations of opposition.[29] It signifies the opposition which Jesus encounters as well as pointing to his ultimate vindication, themes which Kingsbury shows, without too much difficulty, run through the Gospel.

Thus Kingsbury's literary critical analysis neatly confirms his earlier findings about Matthew's Christology. While there has been general agreement among scholars that Kingsbury has been right to highlight the importance of Son of God in Matthew's Gospel, there is much less agreement that it should be seen as the central title. One of Kingsbury's most persistent critics, David Hill, has suggested that overvaluing the Son of God title leads to a lack of sensitivity to the many other rich allusions which are to be found in the text. Hill himself has drawn attention to the importance for Matthew of the Servant of Yahweh imagery of Isaiah, which is presented in the long quotation of Isa 42:1–4 in 12:18–21, alluded to by the divine voice in 3:17 and 17:5, and in the citation of Isaiah 53 at 8:17. Hill's point is not that the image of Servant is more important than the title Son of God, but rather that the image gives *content* to the title which otherwise in Kingsbury's treatment seems only to refer to Jesus' authority, whereas the Servant image would associate it with notions of healing and atonement. Hill's own work shows the value of exploring the intertextual relationships between Matthew and the Old Testament. He suggests that the quotation of Isaiah 42 at 12:18–21 is substantially modified by Matthew himself in the light of the divine voice in 3:17, at the same time as the quotation itself shapes chapter 12, emphasising Jesus' empowerment by the Spirit and his humility and his saving concern for 'the weak, the lost and the broken'.[30]

Hill is equally critical of Kingsbury's treatment of Son of Man in Matthew. Of *Matthew: Structure, Christology, Kingship*, Hill says that Kingsbury's treatment of the evidence is 'Procrustean', forcing it to conform to his own preconceived ideas.[31] Why should the scribe in chapter 8 be regarded as in opposition to Jesus? Again, is it credible that 'Matthew can use "Son of Man" at 20:28 only because it is the mother

[29] Kingsbury, 1984, 29.
[30] Hill, 1980, 12.
[31] Hill, 1980, 2.

of James and John (i.e. an unbeliever or opponent?) whose request provokes the utterance?'[32] And he rightly turns to Kingsbury's treatment of the trial before the high priest to ask why there is no discussion there (or anywhere else) of Daniel 7 to which there is clear allusion in Jesus' reply.

Similar criticisms have been made by Dale Allison, who suggests that Kingsbury's concentration on the text alone, irrespective of its roots in and allusions to the Old Testament, denies to him insights which would have enriched his work.[33] Not only are there clear allusions to the Servant of Yahweh from Isaiah, as Hill has pointed out, there is also a strong typological interplay between the notion of Jesus as Son of God and that of Israel as God's Son.[34] It is seen most clearly in the quotation of Hosea 11:1 at 2:15: 'Out of Egypt have I called my son', which in Hosea clearly refers to Israel and in Matthew points to the close parallels between Jesus' story and Israel's. Thus when Jesus is addressed by the divine voice in 3:17 as 'my beloved Son', is he not 'also here identified in some sense with Israel?'[35] Israel's history of exodus, wanderings in the desert and revelation on the mountain is mirrored in Jesus' story in Matthew.

Hill and Allison are surely right to insist that the meaning of terms cannot simply be read off the text without consideration of their associations within a wider body of literature. On any kind of literary view of a text, one needs to pay close attention to the citations and allusions which it contains. But even Kingsbury's handling of the interrelations between the titles on which he so much concentrates is strangely wooden. He observes that in 16:13–20 Jesus' question 'who do men say that the Son of Man is?' is answered by Peter's confession that he is the Christ, the Son of the living God, and concludes that it is the titles contained in Peter's confession which give content to the expression in the question. In a sense this is a fair point. The question asks for further clarification and amplification. If the phrase ὁ υἱὸς τοῦ ἀνθρώπου is taken purely as a self-reference, then it would indeed seem to do no more than ask for such clarification. But while it may be true that in Aramaic this was its main or even sole meaning, there is no evidence to suggest that that is its meaning in Greek. In Greek it is a

---

[32] Hill, 1980, 3.
[33] Allison, 1987.
[34] This has also been argued in Brown, 1977.
[35] Allison, 1987, 76.

strange and puzzling expression with no readily discernible standard or conventional sense. This means that, if it is to be introduced as a meaningful term, its meaning will need to be supplied by its use in a particular community, or in a document or set of documents. In this case there is clearly precedence for its use in Mark and Q, and its further use by Matthew will add definition. What we need is a fuller discussion of the way that Matthew picks up these traditional senses of 'Son of Man' and relates them to other titles and to the narrative in which they are all embedded. A discussion of Matthew 16:13–28 may serve to open up the matter.

## Son of Man, Christ, Son of God: Matthew 16:13–28

In Mark and Q, Son of Man is used predominantly in three ways: in relation to the weakness and unprotectedness of the Son of Man in his earthly existence (Matt 8:20//Luke 9:58); to his coming suffering, death and resurrection (Matt 17:22–23//Mark 9:31); to his authority in matters of the law and forgiveness (Matt 9:6; 12:8//Mark 2:10, 28) and to his future role as judge (Matt 26:64//Mark 14:62). It is also quite clear that in all these traditions the title occurs only on the lips of Jesus.

Matthew then adopts all the ranges of meaning which the title had acquired in the tradition which he inherited. He also uses the title interchangeably with the first person pronoun. What is important now is to see how he combines these traditional features of the title in his own narrative composition. Here the section 16:13–28 is exemplary. By introducing the title at the beginning of the section (16:13, 'who do men say that *the Son of Man is?*' cf. Mark 8:27, 'that I am?'), and again at the conclusion of the section, where he replaces Mark's 'kingdom of God come with power' with 'the Son of Man coming in his kingdom' (Matt 16:28//Mark 9:1), he has created a chiastic structure where a discussion with the disciples about the Son of Man is followed by a discussion between Jesus and Peter, and then, after two brief comments to the disciples, the same elements are repeated in reverse order (A: 16:13–15; B: 16:16–19; A[1]: 17:20, 21; B: 17:22–23; A: 16:24–28).[36]

Thus Peter's confession 'you are the Christ', with its Matthaean addition 'the son of the living God', is embedded in a discussion of the Son of Man's identity which Jesus conducts with his disciples. Peter's

[36] For further discussion, see Luz, 1990, 453.

confession thus becomes both an implicit acknowledgement of Jesus as Son of Man ('*you are* the Christ . . .') as well as an explicit clarification of the Son of Man title: it is in terms of Messiahship and sonship of God that the title is to be understood.

As we have already discussed, there were different strands of Messianism current within Judaism, utopian and restorationist. To what extent does Matthew's addition to his Markan source of 'son of the living God' betray his own views on the subject? Scholarly interpretation differs on the meaning of the phrase 'the living God' in Matthew. Luz[37] locates it in Greek-speaking Judaism and the New Testament, and suggests a missionary context for its use. It is an abbreviated formula for the real God who acts in history as opposed to lifeless, heathen idols.[38] Davies and Allison point also to its usage in the LXX[39] and suggest that its roots are in the Hebrew 'combination of '*ēl* or '*elōhim* with *ḥa(ā)y*'. Rejecting the idea that the primary sense is a contrast with pagan gods who are not alive, they quote John Meier,[40] '"living" is applied to God in the Old Testament and Judaism to stress that God has life in and of himself, and he alone gives it to others'. It is, however, important to be alert to the contrasting senses that are to be found in the later literature, which doubtless have roots in the Hebrew Bible, as Davies and Allison suggest. In *Joseph and Aseneth* 11, Aseneth contrasts her former life when she worshipped 'dead and dumb idols' (v. 8) with what she has now heard of the God of the Hebrews, who 'is a true God, and a living God, and a merciful God' (v. 10). In *T Sol* 1:13; 5:12,[41] the contrast is between the living God and the demons who are anything but dead and dumb: they have power to bring death and to impede the construction of the Temple. Certainly as Davies and Allison suggest, this comes closer to the *immediate* context in Matthew. Jesus' assurance to Peter, that the gates of Hades will not prevail against the church (16:18) is an assertion of the superior strength of the power of the church over the powers of death.[42] For in Jesus, the Son of the living God, the God of life is present. Thus there is a direct line here between contemporary utopian Messianic views and Matthew, which

---

[37] Luz, 1990, 460–1.
[38] Citing 2 Macc 7:33; 15:4; 3 Macc 6:28; Bel Θ 24–25; *Sib Or* 3:760–3; *T Job* 37:2; *T Abr* 17:11 *Jos As* 8:5–6: 11:10; Historicus Callisthenes 44.
[39] Davies and Allison, 2, 620–1, citing 4 Kgdms 19:4, 16; Ps 41:3; Isa 37: 4, 17: Hos 2:1.
[40] 1978, 109.
[41] Cited by Davies and Allison, 1991, 620, n. 60.
[42] So, correctly, the RSV translation.

CONFLICTING MYTHOLOGIES

is probably reflected again in the discussion of the Son of David title in Matt 22:41–44. The Christ, the Son of the living God, has a cosmic function, the subjection of the powers of darkness, which outstrips that of the Messiah Son of David, whose role is to restore the Davidic kingdom.[43] However, within the wider context of the Gospel (28:18–20), it would be wrong to rule out the missionary application of the expression 'living God' altogether.

So far, then, the titles contained in Peter's confession have served to give further definition to the Son of Man title in Jesus' opening question, which is clearly taken to refer to Jesus himself. It is not, however, that the titles, Christ and Son of God, simply supply the content, while Son of Man indicates the reference. Rather the titles interanimate each other: their meaning is to be inferred from their conjunction and development in this narrative. Thus, in the aftermath of Peter's confession, both the prediction of Jesus' coming suffering, now shorn of its Markan reference to the Son of Man (Matt 16:21//Mark 8:31), and the final references to the Son of Man coming in glory to apportion rewards (Matt 16:27–28//Mark 8:38 – 9:1), serve to elucidate further who the Son of Man, the Christ, the son of the living God is. Of particular interest here is Matthew's editing of Mark 8:38 – 9:1. Matthew shortens Mark 8:38 and adds his own comment: 'and then he will repay each one for what he has done'. He further replaces Mark's 'kingdom of God come with power' with 'the Son of Man coming in his kingdom', which points forward to his representation of the Son of Man as king in the judgement-scene in Matthew 25:31. God's kingly rule will finally be established through his Son, when he, the Son of Man, comes in judgement to apportion punishment and rewards.

There is here an implicit dialogue with the traditions of restorationist eschatology represented by the Son of David title with its royal associations. Jesus is revealed as king, but his kingdom will be established only at the parousia, when he comes in judgement. Divine rule, the restoration of law and order in the world, will come not through military engagement with Israel's enemies, nor indeed with the spiritual forces of the evil one, but through the judgement of the wicked and the righteous.

Peter's confession certainly then plays a major role in the development of Matthew's Christology at this point. It authenticates the two titles,

[43] See discussions of this passage in chapter 5 above, pp. 157–62.

280

Christ and Son of God, as divinely revealed (16:17; cf. 11:27) as opposed to the things that 'people say' (16:14) and gives added definition to the title Son of Man with its traditional associations and its further deployment at the end of this section.

In this way 'Son of Man', which introduces the section, becomes a kind of portmanteau title which can assimilate meaning from other titles and also from the narrative of the Gospel itself. He is the Christ, the Son of the living God. But he is also the one who is weak and homeless, who will fall victim to the powers in Jerusalem and be crucified, and whom his followers must follow on the way of the cross, however much this may cut across their ideas of power and salvation. Nevertheless, those who lose their life for his sake will gain it, for he is the one who will come to judge in power and to bring in 'his kingdom'. This final passage in the section reintroduces the Son of Man title and affirms his role as judge over all. The Christ, Son of the living God, is the one who in the words of Psalm 62:11–12, shares in the power of God 'who will repay each one for what he has done'.

The way in which the various titles interanimate each other can be seen again in the trial before the high priest. If Peter's confession that Jesus is the Christ, Son of God, is given in 16:13–28 as an answer to the question of the identity of the Son of Man, here the situation is precisely reversed. Asked whether he is the Christ, the Son of God, Jesus replies with a Son of Man saying, which is taken from Daniel 7:13–14, but also echoes Psalm 110:1. The coming of the Son of Man refers fairly clearly to his coming to earth to judge (not, that is, to his going to the Father to sit at his right hand). It is, on the one hand, a mark of his vindication; on the other hand, the moment of his final triumph over his enemies: the Son of Man will sit in judgement on those who now condemn him.[44]

## Son of David

Thus, in these key passages we have seen a dialogue between three titles, Son of Man, Christ, Son of God. Importantly, the title Son of David was present only by, at best, implication. In Matthew 16, it is not among the opinions listed that people hold – John the Baptist,

[44] Davies and Allison, 1997, 531, argue that it must refer to the parousia since, 'everywhere else in our Gospel the coming of the Son of man refers to the *parousia*; and in 19.28 and 25.31 the sitting on a throne belongs not to the Son of man's present reign but the eschatological future'.

Elijah, Jeremiah, one of the prophets – even though it was suggested by the crowds in 12:23. Luz remarks rather cryptically that this omission is not accidental.[45] In view of the obvious associations between the titles Christ and Son of David, one has to ask to what extent the latter title is intended to be included in Peter's confession, or whether, indeed, it is intended to be excluded by the addition of the phrase 'Son of the living God'.

Two things speak in favour of its intended exclusion: the fact that it has appeared earlier on the lips of the people, whose views are here contrasted with those which are divinely revealed;[46] the fact that the title is later advocated by the Pharisees and subjected to criticism by Jesus (22:41–46). On the other hand, it appears in the opening verse of the Gospel (though Joseph is also referred to as son of David, 1:20), and it is the cry of those who accompany Jesus into Jerusalem (21:9) and is upheld against the criticisms of the high priests and scribes by Jesus, with the – Davidic – words of Psalm 8:2: 'Out of the mouth of babes and sucklings thou hast brought perfect praise' (21:16). This is comparable to the reception of Peter's confession and, like that, alludes back to 11:25–27. These latter points make it clear beyond reasonable doubt that Matthew does not reject the title out of hand. Nevertheless, its absence here, together with its problematisation in 22:41–45, suggests that Jesus transcends the standard meaning of the title: he is indeed the 'Son of David', but in a way that exceeds normal understanding: he is the Son of God, who will be exalted to the right hand of God (Ps 110:1) and who will come to judge the nations and to bring in his kingdom.[47] Its influence on Matthew's presentation of Jesus is indirect. It represents the longings of the people for relief and national restoration. At the same time, the kingdom which Jesus brings both fulfils and transcends such hopes. Matthew, that is to say, roots his understanding of Jesus' identity firmly in Jewish expectations of a Davidic saviour figure, but in the course of the Gospel these expectations are stretched and reworked. Jesus' kingdom will be established not through military conquest, but at his coming on the right hand of power to judge the world.

[45] Luz, 1990, 460.
[46] Cf. 16:23: οὐ φρονεῖς τὰ τοῦ θεοῦ ἀλλὰ τὰ τῶν ἀνθρώπων.
[47] Cf. Hill, 1972, 307: 'the passage is intent on arguing that "Son of David" is not an adequate or complete title for Jesus, since David himself called this son of his "Lord"'.

Again, as with Mark, this raises sharply the question of the under-standing of power which underlies the Gospel. How can it be that the one to whom all authority in heaven and earth is given (28:18), who comes in the glory of his Father with his angels (16:27), and who will raise his standard in the last days (24:30), is the one who will be betrayed/delivered up into the hands of men (17:22; 20:19; 26:2) by one of his own intimates (26:15, 16, 21, 23, 24, 25, 45, 46, 48; 27:3, and indeed whose own followers will be similarly betrayed (10:17, 19, 21; 24:9, 10)?

## *Matthew's narrative Christology: Jesus as vulnerable teacher*

The titles which Matthew uses and the way he weaves them into his narrative can at best give us pointers to his overall meaning. As important is the way he uses narrative, typology, imagery and other terminology to create a texture for his work, which conveys his sense of who Jesus is. We have already referred to his use of Moses-typology to convey something of Jesus' identity, by comparing him favourably with Moses. In similar vein, Jesus is said to be greater than the Temple (12:6), Jonah (12:41) and Solomon (12:42) and, by implication, David (22:41–45). Most evidently the comparison with Moses draws attention to Jesus' teaching, and this is outstandingly the most important aspect of his life as portrayed by Matthew. This is confirmed by the way in which Matthew understands Jesus' authority. Ultimately, the authority given to Jesus entitles him to send out the disciples to instruct all nations in his teaching and commandments (28:18–20). This linkage with his teaching is a characteristic of his authority throughout the Gospel. Thus Matthew omits Mark's opening story of the exorcism of the man with the unclean spirit in the synagogue in Capernaum, where the crowds acclaim the event by referring to a new teaching with authority (Mark 1:27), and transfers Mark's introductory comment (Mark 1:22) about Jesus' teaching with authority and not as the scribes to the end of the Sermon on the Mount (7:29). In this way, he links Jesus' authority specifically with his teaching and detaches it in a measure from his exorcisms and healings, which he nevertheless records fully in chapters 8 and 9. In a similar way, in chapter 21, in the question about Jesus' authority, Matthew explains that the high priests and the elders of the people put the question to him *while he is teaching* (21:23). As a teacher, he can confer his authority on his pupils, as when he gives the Twelve authority to exorcise, to heal and to preach the gospel of the kingdom

(10:1, 7). His authority, however, is not simply a teaching authority. It is forensic: he also has authority to forgive sins (9:6), and this authority is specifically linked to the Son of Man who will ultimately come as judge (13:41–43; 16:27; 25:31–32; 26:64).

What connection does this have with his weakness, his being delivered up into the hands of men (17:22), and indeed with his disciples' similar experience of being handed over to various forms of persecution? The answer must lie in the sense in which Jesus as teacher in Matthew embodies his own teaching in his life, just as his disciples are called to do. Allison has pointed out that a number of the Beatitudes, as well as other aspects of his teaching, find their exemplification in Jesus' life.[48] Jesus is meek (11:29; cf. 5:5);[49] he shows mercy (5:7) to those who cry out for mercy (9:27; 15:22; 17:15; 20:30, 31); he is persecuted and reviled and falsely accused (5:10–11). He keeps the Law (5:20); he does not seek recompense in the face of evil (5:38–42) and does not react when he is slapped on the cheek (26:67). He prays in private (6:5–6; cf. 26:36–46). He renounces mammon (6:24): he has nowhere to lay his head (8:20). Thus Jesus fulfils the Law (5:17), not merely by giving its definitive interpretation, but by embodying that interpretation in his own life.

This is 'his yoke', which he lays on his followers and which he accepts himself. It is the way of the peacemaker (5:9), of the renunciation of violence (5:39), of forgiveness till seventy times seven (18:22). By walking along this way, Jesus realises a new mode of existence which he invites others to follow. Those who follow and do the will of God will form a new family, who will be called into his kingdom, when he finally comes to establish it at the last judgement. But that way, for him and for them, will be the way of the cross. The theological necessity of suffering along the way is brought out by the section 5:38–42.

## Rejection of the *lex talionis*: Jesus as teacher and judge

Jesus contrasts the Old Testament *lex talionis* with the command not to resist evil (the evil one).[50] This is a broad principle, which encompasses

---

[48] This was first drawn to my attention in lectures given in Glasgow in 1996.

[49] Davies and Allison, 1991, 290, see here a further comparison with Moses; cf. Num 12:3; Ecclus 45:4; Philo, *Vit Mos* 2:279; *b Ned* 38a.

[50] The injunction is by no means without parallel. Davies and Allison, 1988, 541, cite Lev 19:18; Deut 32:35; Prov 20:22; 24:29 (Do not say, 'I will do to him as he has done to me; I will pay the man back for what he has done.') Isa 50:6; Lam 3:30;

the following three 'focal instances'[51] about turning the other cheek, about a person taking legal action over clothing, and about being forced to accompany someone on their journey, and runs out into more general injunctions to generosity and sharing one's goods. Davies and Allison suggest that what is enjoined is the refusal to seek restitution or retribution oneself, because God will exact it himself.[52] The difficulty with this interpretation, which clearly chimes in with Matthew's insistence on divine judgement, is that in the 'focal instances', while recourse to violence is ruled out, more is being suggested than simple refraining from seeking restitution. The disciple is being encouraged to think of creative ways in which to respond to situations of violence, injustice and oppression. The one struck is to turn the other cheek, the coat is to be followed by the gift of the cloak, the one mile is to become two. As Luz argues, these examples are hardly intended as practical means of winning over one's adversaries.[53] Rather they are intended to be deliberately provocative,

> a symbolic protest against the inevitable circle of violence. . . . They are the expression of a protest against any and every form of spiral of violence which dehumanises people, and an expression of hope that there can be another form of human behaviour than that which is experienced in everyday life. But that is not all, for they challenge the listener to respond actively. Such action should contain both a measure of protest and an element of provocative contrast against the violence which controls the world. . . . They are, as it were, compressed pictures of a mode of action which has to be discovered and realised in every area of life.[54]

Luz notes that there is no direct reference to the kingdom of God in this passage, but suggests that it explains the particular contrastive character of the passage, which turns normal patterns of behaviour upside

---

1QS10:18–19 ('I will pay to no man the reward of evil; I will pursue him with goodness. For the judgement of the living is with God and it is He who will render to man his reward.')

[51] Tannehill, 1970.

[52] Davies and Allison, 1988, 540, referring to Rom 12:14–21.

[53] Luz, 1989, 294–5.

[54] Luz, 1989, 295. I cannot agree with Davies and Allison, 1988, 542, that this passage is concerned only with person-to-person relations: 'the *lex talionis* is not being wholly rejected – it will be applied by God at the final judgement – but simply branded as inappropriate for personal relations'. They are certainly right to suggest that there are no *easy* inferences to be drawn from this section concerning the proper course of state institutions, but this does not mean that there are none at all to be drawn.

down. Q's framing of this passage (Luke 6:27–28, 35) with the command to love one's enemies, suggests in this context that 'for Jesus the arrival of the kingdom of God is manifested as the boundless love of God for men and women, which in turn makes it possible for men and women to love each other, even their enemies'.[55] He does however detect a certain tendency to 'Christian passivity' in Matthew's summary of the three positive examples in 39b-41 in the negative formula: 'do not resist evil'. Certainly, later church tradition has lost the sense of provocation and contrast which is contained in the following verses.[56]

There is again a delicate balance to be struck here. The element of protest, of reaching out for a new world, which is contained in vv. 39b–42 may indeed be in a measure constrained by the negative formulation of v. 39a, but 39b–42 *and* 43–48 still stand in Matthew as its commentary. Davies and Allison stress the continuity of Jesus' words with the Old Testament *lex talionis*, whose operation is now reserved for the final judgement. The injunction not to resist evil is a temporary injunction to leave vengeance to God. It is limited to the personal, as opposed to the institutional, sphere. Luz sees a more radical, creative ethic in the examples in the passage, while recognising a certain shift of emphasis: less a protest against the powers of this world, coupled with a strong anticipation of a new world with a new ethos, more a distancing of oneself from the operations of the present world.

Luz is right to recognise a certain tension in Matthew between the radical ethic, which Matthew inherits from the Jesus traditions contained in Q, and the Matthaean editing of this material in the Beatitudes and the Sermon on the Mount. There is a certain tendency to inwardness, an element of withdrawal from the world, which may have its roots in Matthew's situation, as his community finds itself more isolated from other Jewish communities. Chapter 18 gives clear expression to Matthew's concern with matters of inner-group discipline and control. But even in his presentation of his source material, which may represent a certain cooling of its creative energy, Matthew still preserves and wrestles with the radical challenge of the Beatitudes and passages like 5:39–42. Davies and Allison rightly emphasise the close connection between the two: 'It may be observed that the spirit or attitude required by 5.39–42 is implicit in the beatitudes. How could the meek, the

---

[55] Luz, 1989, 295.
[56] Luz, 1989, 297.

merciful, the peacemakers, and those who are happy to suffer for the right cause strike back at their opponents?'[57] They are less willing to recognise that there is a clash here between the spirit of the Beatitudes which makes it impossible to strike back and the *lex talionis* whose operation, they believe, is merely restricted to the coming judgement. But in what sense does the Jesus of 11:29, who is meek and lowly in heart, 'reward each according to his work' (16:27)? Is the judgement which Jesus will bring inconsistent with the ethic which he teaches? Surely not.

The problem is thrown up again in chapter 18, where, in the middle of a discussion of community discipline, Peter asks how often he should forgive his brother and is told 'seventy times seven' (18:21–22). This seems to impose impossible burdens on any community,[58] and Matthew provides a commentary on Jesus' saying in the parable of the unforgiving servant (18:23–35). The story itself is simple enough, if wonderfully exaggerated in its detail. It records a servant's enormous debt to his master, which, against all expectations, is forgiven him. When he fails to forgive a fellow-servant, a much smaller debt, his master condemns him to the torturers with the words: 'should not you have had mercy on your fellow-servant as I have had mercy on you?' (18:33). There are clear internal references here: to the need to imitate God's goodness (5:48), to the fifth Beatitude (5:7), to the petition in the Lord's Prayer for forgiveness (6:12). Thus the parable in the first place reinforces Jesus' saying about forgiveness. But the injunction to imitate God also serves to justify the community's practice of excommunication (18:17), for God condemns those who fail to forgive. There is a contradiction here between the implicit injunction to imitate a God who forgives till seventy times seven, and the justification of the Church's practice of excluding people after two attempts at reconciliation on the basis of God's condemnation of those who fail to forgive. This is brought out in the concluding verse where Matthew interprets the parable allegorically: 'So also my heavenly Father will do to every one of you, if you do not forgive your brother from your heart' (18:35). As Luz writes, there is a sense here in which the notion of judgement begins to assume greater importance than the image of God's wholly unexpected and unmerited forgiveness which

---

[57] Davies and Allison, 1988, 541.
[58] See Alan Paton's imaginative account of the difficulties in his short story, 'Sponono', 1961, 99–117.

has dominated the parable: 'The fundamental theological question is whether the judging "father" of Matt 18:35 can still be experienced as the same father who through Christ forgives human guilt out of his infinite love.'[59]

### Jesus' suffering: the relation of Matthew's Christology to contemporary debates about Messianism

In the light of these undeniable theological tensions within Matthew's Gospel, one must return to the question about the necessity of the Son of Man's suffering. Why does the Son of Man have to be delivered up into the hands of men and to suffer and die? Can one say that, for Matthew, it is as Jesus himself gives concrete expression to the spirit of mercy and meekness in his life and death, that that spirit is, as it were, enshrined in the coming judgement, which he will administer when he comes with his angels in the glory of his Father? Jesus not only gives the definitive interpretation of the Law, but, as he fulfils the law in his own life and death, he is given authority to execute judgement; and that judgement has to reflect the spirit of meekness and mercy, of renunciation of violence and refusal to retaliate, of forgiving seventy times seven, which he both preached and lived. It is true that, for Matthew, there is a tendency to see the fulfilment of such conditions as lying in the condemnation of those who have not shown mercy. But the tension between this view of judgement and the injunctions to love one's enemies, as God sends his rain on the just and the unjust, remains and is unresolved.

Similar tensions are to be seen in Matthew's portrayal of the life of the disciples in the church. Certainly, they are to lead the same life of defencelessness, non-retaliation, renunciation of violence and love of enemies as Jesus, and to share the same experience of suffering and persecution as he; it is through their faithfulness that the new family will be born which will instantiate the virtues of the Beatitudes (10; 12:46–50). On the other hand, they are given rules for excluding members from the church and given powers of binding and loosing in earth and heaven, and in this they exercise the authority of the God-with-us, Jesus (18:17–20).

How then does Matthew's picture of Jesus, with all its tensions as the meek and merciful judge, take its place within contemporary

---

[59] Luz, 1997, 76.

debates in Judaism about Messianism? There are certainly echoes of these in the Gospel. Peter's confession raises key questions about the understanding of Jesus' Messiahship. If Matthew adds 'the son of the living God' to Mark's bald statement: 'You are the Christ' (16:16//Mark 8:29), this, and the subsequent discussion, represents a sustained attempt to clarify the understanding of Messiahship. Where does he stand in relation to the different strands of Jewish messianism, restorative and utopian, which we were discussing in relation to Mark?

We have already noticed the somewhat ambiguous role which the title 'Son of David' plays in the Gospel. It is introduced in the first verse. It occurs on the lips of the crowds when they acclaim Jesus (12:23; 21:9); it occurs on the lips of those who seek help from Jesus (9:27; 15:22; 20:30);[60] it is upheld by Jesus when used by children in the Temple (21:16), and it is used by the Pharisees at the end of their attempts to entrap him (22:42). It is not included in Peter's confession. All this, we suggested, argues for a rather nuanced relationship to the title. Matthew certainly wants to earth Jesus in the history of the people of Israel, as his opening genealogy and the fulfilment sayings make clear. On the other hand, there is little in the Gospel to suggest that he harboured hopes for a restoration of the Davidic kingdom in any literal, political sense. Certainly, injunctions to love one's enemies do not fit easily with a military approach to Israel's problems.

There is, however, evidence of an engagement with the 'Son of David' motif in the kingship motif. This is present, from Mark, in the trial, mocking and crucifixion scenes, though Matthew has removed the motif from the scene where Pilate tries to persuade the crowd to ask for Jesus' release, replacing it with the title Christ. Despite this, Matthew's Passion narrative, like Mark's, clearly contrasts Jesus' kingship with worldly forms of royal power. Moreover, Matthew underscores this in his redaction of the entry into Jerusalem, by introducing as a fulfilment saying a mixed quotation from Isa 62:11 and Zech 9:9, which portrays him as a meek king (21:5; cf. 5:5; 11:29).

Most importantly, the notion of kingship is introduced into Matthew's depictions of the final judgement, both in 19:28, where the Son of Man and the Twelve will sit on thrones judging the twelve tribes of Israel, and again in 25:31–46. There is also a further reference in 16:28

[60] Davies and Allison, 1991, 135–6, suggest that there may be a connection between Matthew's portrayal of Jesus the healer as Son of David and the legends, esp. in *T Sol* about Solomon's healing powers.

to the Son of Man coming in his kingdom, which we suggested was also to be taken as referring to judgement. Taking this together with the prominence which Matthew generally gives to the theme of judgement in the Gospel, we can say that Matthew is reworking the Son of David motif, stripping it of its military connotations and of its links with the hopes for a restoration of the Davidic monarchy, and instead tying it into the Matthaean community's hopes for a final vindication at the Last Judgement, when they would sit in judgement over their enemies. It is true that the military associations of the motif show through briefly in 24:30–31, but it is no more than that. Matthew scarcely develops this into the depiction of a final battle between the Son of Man/David and his satanic foes.

What we are observing here is essentially a debate about Jewish expectations and hopes within a strand of tradition which is largely forensic in orientation. Whereas in Mark one can discern a strong dialectic between cosmic dualist modes of thought and forensic ones, here the dominant language is legal/forensic, and the cosmic dualist language, even though Matthew introduces it at points, plays a minor role. In Mark, the Son of David title does not receive the strong underpinning which it has in Matthew. The pericope in Mark 12:35–37 is cast in a much more antagonist mode: 'How can the scribes say that the Christ is the son of David?' The quotation from the Psalm, with its reference to God's subjection of the Messiah's enemies, has resonances with the underlying theme of spiritual warfare which runs through the Gospel. The Son of God title picks up and develops the dialogue with the cosmic dualist strand of mythology.

In Matthew, by contrast, there is much greater emphasis on Jesus' coming to fulfil the Law; the discussion about the nature of Jesus' Messiahship centres on the manner of that fulfilment. Is the Law to be fulfilled by the restoration of the Davidic monarchy, which would insure the observance of the Law as taught and definitively interpreted by Jesus, Son of David? Or will the Law be finally established and fulfilled only when it has been definitively interpreted and proclaimed to all the nations and when the Christ, Son of Man, comes to establish his kingdom, condemning those who have failed to listen and gathering to himself those who have obeyed? The answer to this question is emphatically the latter: the hopes for national restoration are subsumed under wider hopes for a radical transformation of the world as a whole. Something more revolutionary is required than the renewal of the old order at its best, a new schema of things which conserves (*aufhebt*) the best of the old but at the same time transcends it and inaugurates an order which realises hopes springing from the old order itself. That new world (19:28, παλιγγενεσία), the new creation announced in the opening verse of the Gospel, will be inaugurated with the judgement which the Son of Man will bring.

This is not to suggest that cosmic dualism plays no part at all in the development of Matthew's cosmology. It serves primarily, however, to underline the depth of the world's wickedness and so to point to the need for radical solutions. The story of Jesus' Temptation in the wilderness is a story about the ability of Satan to subvert even the means of salvation divinely given in Scripture. At the same time, it illustrates the way in which Satan can operate at the very heart of the Land, in the Temple. The parable of the wheat and the tares portrays the pervasiveness of evil in the world and the impossibility (at least, without doing harm to the sons of the kingdom) of rooting it out in the present dispensation. It also underlines the need for a new beginning: the Son of Man must sow the good seed, which will produce the sons of the kingdom. Only at the judgement, at the time of harvest, can the wicked be removed and the righteous live in peace. The last judgement is the final solution to the ills of the whole world.

## *Relation of Matthew's cosmology to his views of sacred space and ethnicity*

It is worth considering how this account of Matthew's cosmology and Christology relates to our earlier discussions of the Gospel's account of ethnicity, of kinship and sacred space. We saw there how Matthew had re-emphasised traditional Jewish identity markers, descent from the forefathers and attachment to the Land, at the same time as he had also sought to forge an identity for his new community which reached out beyond these markers. The members of the Matthaean community were indeed followers of a leader with an impeccably Jewish line of descent, Jesus Christ, son of David, son of Abraham, but their relationship to him as his brothers and sisters would be defined, not in terms of blood-ties, but in terms of doing the will of God: it was this which would constitute the identity of the sons of the kingdom.

Similarly, while Jesus is indeed the one who comes on the way of the Lord to restore the fortunes of Israel, his way leads to the mountain in chapter 28, whence the Lord of heaven and earth sends out the disciples to make disciples of all nations. Nor does the way stop there; it leads on to the point where he comes again in judgement. Sacred space is no longer defined simply in terms of the Land of Israel, in which the Davidic kingdom is to be reinaugurated and the Temple restored to its former glory, with all the nations flocking to it. The whole world is now a mission field, at any point of which the sons of the kingdom may be encountered side by side with the sons of the evil one. Or it is conceived as a boat at sea, weathering the storms of the forces of evil. The boundaries no longer run along territorial lines: they are defined in terms of conformity to 'all that I have commanded you'. Sacred space is wherever Jesus is present with his followers (Matt 28:20).

Matthew portrays Jesus as the fulfiller of the Law, as the new Moses who fulfils Israel's expectations in ways which both meet and exceed traditional expectations and hopes, as the royal judge who is Son of David, whose kingdom will be established when he comes in glory to judge all the world. It is not difficult to see how this portrait is reflected in and itself mirrors his understanding of ethnicity, of kinship and sacred space. Matthew's claim that Jesus is the one who reveals the true meaning of the Law and who will come again to judge all and to establish his kingdom puts a question mark against all existing social divisions. Only at the last judgement will the true divisions in the world be generally revealed and established. The old lines of descent which defined membership of the covenant community pale into insignificance in comparison with true repentance and the fruits which it bears, which is the only preparation for the coming judgement.[61] And Abrahamic repentance, as indeed Philo saw, was a universal virtue, something that could exist before the Law and which all could realise in their lives, irrespective of their ancestry. What was required was a deep change of heart, a new purity and obedience which would bear fruit in obedience to 'all that I have commanded you', which is the fulfilment of the Law. At the same time, Jesus' emphasis in the Sermon on the Mount on showing mercy, on peacemaking and meekness, underscores elements of the tradition which determine the nature of the coming judgement

[61] May not the exchange between the Pharisees and John the Baptist, 3:7–10, be seen as an indirect answer to the question of circumcision of Gentile converts to the church? It is repentance and the fruits of it which counts. If God can raise up (duly circumcised) children of Abraham from stones, then he can presumably fix anything that is still required for Gentile converts.

(18:35). The Beatitudes are an invitation to all to join Jesus on his way; they also depict the character of those who will be welcomed into his kingdom by the royal judge at his coming. In this sense, again, ethnic boundaries are being relativised: ultimately what counts is not physical descent and membership of a particular group but 'meekness', renunciation of violence and love of enemies.

In a similar way, there is a close correlation between the distancing from the traditions of Jewish restorationist ideology, associated with the son of David motif, and the de-territorialisation of the sense of the sacred that occurs in Matthew. The notion of David as the royal judge is taken up and given cosmic dimensions, as evil is radicalised through the narrative and discursive presentation of the conflict between Jesus and satanic forces. Precisely because evil is portrayed as demonic, as all-pervading, it can no longer be overcome by the re-establishment of the Davidic monarchy, of national sovereignty. Something greater than the Temple, greater than Solomon and Jonah, is needed, the subjection of the evil powers to David's Lord. God through his Son must establish his rule over the whole cosmos, must rid it of the corrupting forces which sow dissension and violence *everywhere*. The power which can resist such forces is now present in the *ekklesia*, where Jesus is with those who confess and acknowledge him.

## Ambiguous character of Matthew's relation to Judaism

This gives Matthew's Judaism the elusive character which it undoubtedly has had for recent interpreters, and which indeed it also had for the early church, where his Gospel found strong resonance both in the Great Church and in Jewish Christianity. On the one hand, he wants to affirm as strongly as he can the rootedness of his story in the history of God's dealings with his people, in the Mosaic law and in the prophetic promises of restoration and fulfilment. Jesus comes from the heart of this people and as the Christ is the object of their deepest expectations. Through him God will be present with his people. Moreover, he is the one who gives and lives out the definitive interpretation of the Law. The judgement that he brings is one based on the Law as he has taught and lived it and as his disciples have passed it on. In all these senses he is fully a Jew and his way is the promised way of the Lord. On the other hand, those who will finally be admitted to his kingdom are no longer defined in ethnic terms. Certainly, Jewish ancestry is no guarantee of inclusion (3:9), but nor are blood-ties the means of defining membership. It is obedience to the will of God. Again, another key constituent of ethnic identity, attachment to the Land, is largely ignored. The mission of the Christ, Son of God, may in the first instance be to the lost sheep of the house of Israel, but at his resurrection he is given all authority in heaven and earth and the mission now extends to all the world. It is Jesus' role as eschatological judge which, in Matthew's scheme of things, de-territorialises him and his followers. He is Lord over heaven and earth. He it is who will send out his angels to root out of his kingdom all who cause offence and all evil doers (13:41). In this sense he can no longer be the Messiah of Israel only, however much his mission is for Israel first; his rule can only be over the whole world.

The most delicate question of all remains, however, how far in all this the inherited understanding of divine power, which lies at the heart of any religious world-view, is being modified. How far does the meta-phoricisation of kinship and the de-territorialisation of sacred space correspond to a shift in understanding of the 'living God'? We have seen how, in Mark notions of vulnerability, and in Matthew notions of meekness and renunciation of violence, are given prominence in the narrative and discourse. Matthew's understanding of divine power is worked out principally in terms of divine justice and its exercise in the giving of the Law and in judgement, as these are linked to the story of the Son of Man. The Son of Man to whom power of judgement is given is the meek and lowly king who himself lives out a life of defencelessness and non-retaliation, is crucified and finally vindicated and invested with all authority at the resurrection. Meekness, mercy and peacemaking, non-retaliation, love of enemies, are the virtues which he teaches and which underly his interpretation of the Law. In no sense is this seen by Matthew as a break with the Law: it is its fulfilment. But it does, nevertheless, raise questions about the exercise of divine power, which in any case is very differently defined in the tradition.

These questions are raised at different points in the narrative in more or less discursive form, in the section on the Son of David (22:41–45) and perhaps most pointedly, in the mocking of Jesus as he hangs on the cross (27:39–44). In the Markan narrative, which Matthew follows here (Mark 15:27–32), the title on which the mocking centres, the King of the Jews, is taken from the titulus on the cross. To this the high priests and scribes add the title, Christ. Matthew twice adds to the jibes thrown at Jesus the title Son of God, omitting the high priests' 'Christ' (27:40, 43). Why can the Son of God who will come seated on the right hand of power (26:64) not come down from the cross? Why will God not save him, if he trusted in God (27:43; cf. Ps 22:8 LXX; Ps 86:2; Jer 39:18)? Just as Satan tests Jesus at the very beginning of his ministry to demonstrate his trust in God's saving power (4:6), so here the high priests and others tempt him to betray his calling as the Son of Man who must suffer, who will not retaliate or answer violence with violence. It is Jesus' last trial, which is followed by darkness for three hours and the final cry of abandonment (27:45–46). It expresses, as Davies and Allison put it, a sense of 'pain in a circumstance in which God has not shown himself to be God'.[62] Jesus, as Son of God, experiences a God who is far removed from the God of salvation of his mockers. God's Son shows his power and obedience to God in bearing the death and shame inflicted on him by his enemies. It is this Son of God, who is recognised by the centurion and by those who were on watch (27:54), who is vindicated and to whom all authority is given (28:18).

Behind these narratives lie (how submerged, it is not easy to say) important contemporary debates about Messiahship. Certainly there seem to be echoes in Matthew. While he upholds the use of the title Son of David, he problematises it and strips it of its territorial and military associations. Jesus' exercise of power, his 'kingship', is over the world, not just over Israel; it is exercised in eschatological judgement, not in ruling over a royal court. Jesus is Son of the living God. He opposes the powers of death and darkness, not in some cosmic battle, but like Job, in the withstanding of temptation, holding fast to the true interpretation of Scripture. He is Spirit-filled and God reveals to him the mystery of his will at the heart of which lie the divine virtues of mercy and meekness. As Son of God who is present with the church, he is the guarantor that the forces of darkness will not overcome it; he does this not by inflicting military defeat on them, but by schooling his followers in the true understanding of the Law and sending them out, defenceless and vulnerable, to teach and make disciples of all nations. He is not a successful national leader, but a crucified Messianic pretender; yet he is the one whom the nations will confess as Son of God and who will judge the whole world.

There is in this kind of comparison with contemporary Jewish views of Messiahship, an all too prevalent danger of engaging in facile contrasts and evaluations. Studies of first-century Judaism, however, make it clear

---

[62] Davies and Allison, 1997, 625.

that there was great diversity of view about how the tradition was to be continued after the fall of Jerusalem and the dramatic change in Jewish religious institutions which it brought about. In struggling for the heart and future of a religious tradition confronted by deep crisis, religious thinkers, leaders and prophets draw on the tradition creatively and selectively. They cannot do otherwise with a tradition as rich and diverse as that of the Hebrew Scriptures. Matthew, moreover, is not writing a treatise about the future of Judaism; he is compiling a Gospel out of existing documents and giving the story which he has inherited his own particular twist. This is his means for leading the tradition in the direction which he advocates. Within these constraints, he produces a Gospel which portrays a figure whose power resides in his faithfulness to the understanding of the Law which has been revealed to him (11:25–27). Such faithfulness leads him to the cross, but also to his vindication and the conferring on him of all authority at his resurrection. It is the particular nature of this authority which represents the distinctive understanding of power in Matthew. It is an authority rooted in his own refusal to retaliate, and yet it is also an authority which by conferring powers of judgement on him entitles him to 'repay everyone for what he has done' (16:27). The *lex talionis*, which he rejects in 5:38, returns as the underlying principle of the judgement which he administers. In the end, Matthew leaves more questions than he answers. He has produced a text which can inspire some of the most radical visions of a new world which would change the very nature of power and its exercise. It can also can be read as the Gospel of an imperial church, preaching an ethic of inwardness and obedience to its subjects who are constantly reminded of the coming day of reckoning; or it can be read as a Gospel of a Jewish Christianity, which sees itself as the people of Israel to whom all will be restored. This strangely elusive character comes from its combination of different elements from the tradition, those which exalt suffering patiently borne and a spirit of meekness, which are evoked powerfully in the quotation from Isa 42:1–4; and others which stress the retributive justice of God. It is these tensions within a largely forensic tradition of eschatology with which Matthew wrestles; his dialogue with cosmic dualism also serves to widen the focus of his Gospel and to relativise the ethnic dimensions of the traditions on which it draws.

## 9

# New worlds and new identities: the Gospels of Mark and Matthew and the beginning of Christianity

### Introduction: traditional and modern senses of identity

The enormous labours which scholars invest in the study of such ancient texts as the Gospels of Mark and Matthew, of which the present bibliography is but the merest scrape of the butter-mountain[1] must surprise the outsider. It occasionally causes concern to those within the discipline, who wonder how long such efforts can be sustained in a world where the communities which have a knowledge of and interest in the Bible are fast diminishing. Who will want to study and buy all these books? Why should modern (post-modern or high-modern) readers occupy themselves with texts which come from a traditional, pre-critical world?

To this it might be answered that there is apparently no diminution in general public interest in the past, and that biblical studies is rapidly re-inventing itself as a branch of classical studies, itself a relative newcomer to emerge out of the old classics departments with their emphasis on philological skills. Within this re-invention of biblical studies, social historical and cultural anthropological studies of the communities to which the texts give us access play a major role. Social scientific studies can show us how these texts once functioned to hold communities together, to allow them to survive and flourish in a variety of cultural, ecological and socio-economic environments. And a study of the history of the reception of the same texts can show the varied ways in which they have continued to generate new communities and to play their role in their persistence.

All this is admittedly a long way from the older style of biblical theology which sought to read these texts in such a way as to hear the word of God speaking through them. Certainly, as we noticed, the beginnings of social historical studies of the New Testament communities were not anti-theological. By showing how the narratives of the Fourth

---

[1]  The phrase is Robert Morgan's, 1988, 117.

Gospel related to the situation of the Evangelist's first readers, Martyn believed he could also discern something of the Evangelist's theological beliefs about the work of the Spirit in relating the community of believers to the Son.[2] But in time social historical studies have become divorced from and indeed often opposed to theological enquiry. They are concerned with a portrayal of the functioning of a community in the past; not with understanding and communicating its theological beliefs to communities of faith in the present.

Thus even where, rather exceptionally as in Sim's monograph which we discussed in chapter 8,[3] theological beliefs form the subject of a major treatment, it is their social function which is the major focus of attention. Sim's account of Matthew's apocalyptic eschatology provides a major clue to the social historical situation of Matthew's community as locked in bitter conflict with other Jewish groups. As such it paves the way for his further study of *The Gospel of Matthew and Christian Judaism*, which is a much more straightforwardly socio-historical study, placing Matthew's community in the developments of first-century Judaism and Christianity.[4]

Such studies have their place within the academic communities of the North (and Australasia). Their history mirrors in certain respects the history of the quest for the historical Jesus. Schweitzer memorably wrote that those who embarked on the Quest set out in the hope of finding the living Jesus behind the later obfuscations of Christian doctrine, but that the more they learnt about the first-century figure, Jesus of Nazareth, the more strange he became to them.[5] In the same way, the more we learn about the communities of the early Christian period and the way they functioned, the more distant these sectarian groupings in the polytheistic world of the first-century Mediterranean come to seem to us. Social-historical study sets a gulf between us and the social worlds of these isolated communities in the world of the Roman Principate, just as it seeks to exclude all theological beliefs and preferences from the process of their historical reconstruction. What is required is historical objectivity.[6] It is true that social scientific study of

---

[2] Martyn, 1979, 129–51.
[3] Sim, 1996.
[4] Sim, 1998.
[5] Schweitzer, 1911, 390–401.
[6] These views were most forcibly expressed by Stendahl, 1984, 11–44, and by Räisänen, 1990a.

the early Christian communities attempts to explain them in terms of certain ideal types of social behaviour. Such explanation may help to draw analogies between them and contemporary religious groupings, and this may equally help to overcome some of the sense of estrangement. On the other hand, it is precisely at this point that social anthropologists warn against pressing the analogies too hard.[7] Most such ideal typologies are drawn from a study of contemporary groups, and their applicability to groups from very different societies two thousand years earlier has to be viewed with caution.

A more strictly social historical approach will underline the major societal and institutional changes that have occurred since the time of the New Testament, and so draw sharper lines between the ways in which social identity was constructed in traditional societies and the ways in which self-identity is treated in high-modern society. Here, as we saw, the work of Anthony Giddens has been influential. For him, there is a radical difference between the ways in which self-identity is regarded as a self-regulating process in contemporary society, where individuals are constantly engaged in the process of constructing and revising their sense of who they are; and the ways in which in traditional society identity is conferred by virtue of birth into a particular position in a particular society at a particular time. Modern or rather high-modern institutions are globalised, disembedded entities, independent largely of local circumstances, and are self-referential, setting their own goals and revising them as they see fit. Similarly, within the high-modern world individuals also feel at liberty to set their own goals and to revise them at will, all the time constructing and reconstructing the narrative of their self-identity. In not dissimilar vein, Charles Taylor has contrasted the modern sense of self with that to be found in traditional, hierarchical societies with their system of *préférences*. It is, he suggests, only with the breakdown of such systems in the eighteenth century that the modern sense of existence (Rousseau) comes into being. More important than who one is, on any social scale or order, is now one's own sense of self.

These are enormously important contributions which should make us much more aware of the great differences between our world and that of the first century. However, there is in the work both of Giddens,

---

[7] Cf. Wilson's warning, 1982, 95–105, about applying sociological models too indiscriminately: 'The type should always turn us back to historical or empirical data so that we can explain those features of a case that contradict our hypothesized common-sense assumptions' (105).

and even of Taylor, a tendency to draw the lines between the modern and the traditional too simplistically. The suggestion that traditional religion simply dictated a fixed mode of existence to people, whereas in modern or high-modern society we have choice and construct our own sense of who we are, needs careful qualification. How on such a model would one explain religious change and development? What account could one give of individual conversions and of change and development in the religious views and practice of individuals? What our studies have shown is that there is a great deal more flexibility in the way that traditions are handled and articulated in the first century than any such simple contrast would suggest. This is as true of Judaism, which is capable of constructing its map of the world in a variety of ways, as it is of the Christianity of the Gospels. It also shows that conversion was something that was a matter of concern to people who were not members of the élite, and that even within the popular literature of the time new world-views were in process of construction.

What this suggests, therefore, is not that we can simply make the Gospels our own, identifying the processes of identity formation in the Gospels with those in high-modern societies: the differences between their situation and ours, between their modes of social organisation and ours, are not to be denied. It shows primarily that the Gospels are part of a living stream of tradition which changes and develops as it makes its way through different periods and different societies. We should not suppose that we can easily identify present communities of Gospel readers (immensely diverse as they are in different continents today) with those of the first century.

But nor should we suppose that they have no connection with us, whether or not we belong to communities for whom the Gospels still have a significant role in determining patterns of behaviour and self-understanding. The first Gospel readers' mode of existence was not simply given, in such a way that they had no part in the shaping of their identity. Processes of identity formation have changed over two thousand years, but they have not changed out of all recognition.

Similarly, the cosmological questions which engaged the minds of popular thinkers and religious authorities like the Evangelists[8] were

---

[8] Whoever asked the Evangelists to *write*? What sort of authority did they enjoy in their communities? The history of the canonisation of the New Testament writings shows how difficult it was for communities in the first centuries of the Common Era to institutionalise writers and writings. Once writings had been accepted as authoritative,

questions which engaged people at all levels in the ancient world and which found many and different responses. Following Lévi-Strauss, I have been suggesting that it is a characteristic of mythological writings like the Gospels (and indeed of much other religious literature contemporary with them) that they attempt to mediate between the contradictions contained in opposed cosmologies. Such mediations can be greatly varied. We have seen this both in relation to Jewish cosmologies and to the different cosmologies to be found in Mark and Matthew. Matthew's reading of Mark continues the debate about the proper way of understanding, in the light of the gospel, the nature of evil and its overcoming. This observation again suggests strongly that the cosmological views of traditional religious communities were a great deal more fluid that is suggested by Giddens and Taylor. It should also be added that the contrasting cosmological views which can be seen to underly the Gospels continue to engross thinkers in the West down to the present.[9]

## Authority and choice in traditional societies

These are very broad claims which cannot be fully substantiated in a final chapter, but let me at least sketch out the way the previous chapters may bear on them. Let me start with the question of the givenness and fixity of the understanding of the self in traditional societies, as articulated by Giddens.

> In pre-modern contexts, tradition has a key role in articulating action and ontological frameworks; tradition offers an organising medium of social life specifically geared to ontological precepts. In the first place, tradition orders time in a manner which restricts the openness of counterfactual futures. People

---

classes of people emerged authorised to interpret them; priests, scribes, bishops and their presbyters and deacons, theological professors in the great medieval universities. But there is never, and in the nature of the case never could have been, a similar institutionalising of the office of sacred writer. Once recognised, they were seen as divinely inspired instruments of the Spirit, the primary agents of a divine revelation which, once canonised, was deemed to be complete and final. Before such recognition was accorded, they could be threatening and troubling figures, to some at least of the Christian communities.

[9] In his *Religion within the Bounds of Reason Alone*, Immanuel Kant asks what light the widespread religious view that the 'whole world lies in the power of the evil one' might throw on his own accounts of human moral failure. This leads to a profound discussion of the problem of radical evil, which continues to engage philosophers today; see Michalson, 1990, and Goodlove, 1997.

in all cultures, including the most resolutely traditional, distinguish future, present and past, and weigh alternative courses of action in terms of likely future considerations. But . . . where traditional modes of practice are dominant, the past inserts a wide band of 'authenticated practice' into the future. Time is not empty, and a consistent 'mode of being' relates future to past. In addition, tradition creates a sense of the firmness of things that typically mixes cognitive and moral elements. The world is as it is because it is as it should be. Of course, in many traditional cultures, and in virtually all rationalised religious systems, explicit ontological conceptions are found – although these may stand in considerable tension with the enactments of traditional practices themselves.[10]

There is much that one can recognise in Giddens' account of traditional society and the manner in which it organises people's ways of acting and understanding their world. He rightly underlines the sense in which social life is organised in terms of certain ontological precepts. Traditionally authorised beliefs about the nature of what there is in the world provide a framework which in turn authorises certain patterns of life and action. Time is not 'empty': there are expectations about the future, just as the past is defined in such a way as to constrain and characterise present action. For Matthew's readers the world was a world which was presently corrupt. Of that there was no doubt, even though the causes of that corruption might be differently defined. But it was also a world where God had acted to remove corruption through a saviour figure who had 'fulfilled the Law' and who would come in judgement to establish God's rule over the world, to separate the righteous from the wicked and so to purify the world. Such a view of the world would undoubtedly significantly constrain action as people weighed 'alternative courses of action in terms of likely future considerations'. At the same time, while one can discern a clear correlation between the cosmological beliefs – beliefs about the way the world is – and patterns of life and action implicit in Matthew's Gospel, there are, as Giddens also notes, considerable tensions between the traditional practices which Matthew advocates and the cosmological beliefs which his Gospel more or less explicitly defines. Foremost among these is the tension between a view of the world that sees evil as the outcome of the intrusion into the world of demonic forces who spawn 'sons of the evil one' and the insistence on obedience to the Law. Those who are controlled by Satan are powerless to do good. Exorcism, not

[10]   Giddens, 1991, 48.

moral instruction, is what is needed. At a more detailed level of practice, there may be strong tensions between some of the traditional requirements of the Law: dietary rules and circumcision and the view that the mission of the church is now to the Gentiles.

All of this fits well enough with Giddens' account of pre-modern societies and illustrates the great gulf which lies between ways of shaping social life in pre-modern societies and the self-reflexive project of the self in the present. At the same time, one needs also to be aware of the elements in pre-modern societies of reflexivity, of reshaping and modifying and questioning the cognitive and moral elements by which 'tradition creates a sense of the firmness of things'. The apocalyptic traditions with which our Evangelists work are directly critical of the way the world is; the world is not as it should be and its present 'works' are all subject to a final divine judgement. There is more fluidity in the creation of that sense of the firmness of things than an unqualified reading of Giddens would suggest. There is also more evidence of individual choice of life patterns and world-view and of the role of individuals in modifying cultural systems than Giddens allows for.

Lest this last reference to individual choice and action be misleading, let me stress that the process of world-building, which we have been attempting to document, was first and foremost a communal one. We have seen how communal traditions collected by Mark and Matthew (his Q material) are taken up by the Evangelists and given narrative form in Gospels. These are works which K. L. Schmidt classified as *Kleinliteratur*,[11] popular works, collecting and preserving communal traditions and designed for public reading in communities whose membership would have numbered few of the élite. They were works which drew on the Hebrew Bible and the Septuagint to tell their narrative and so engaged with the religious traditions of the Jewish people. They were also works which generated a long tradition of communal readings and were embodied in communities of many different kinds.

Within this essentially communal process we have stressed two aspects. The first is the variety of expression which these communal processes allow. The story is told in (admittedly often quite subtle) variant forms, which nevertheless set importantly different accents and emphases. Mark and Matthew emerge as literary craftsmen who know how to shape their narratives, to rework the traditional themes that

[11] Schmidt, 1923.

they take up from Jewish writings in surprising and illuminating ways. The Isaianic notion of the way of the Lord, of the triumphant return of the exiles to Zion, is re-staged in a drama which leads to the crucifixion of the Messiah outside Jerusalem and sends the disciples back to Galilee to resume their discipleship of the risen Lord. Matthew takes the same motif and concludes his Gospel with the final commissioning of the disciples on a mountain, not in Zion but in Galilee, whence the disciples are sent out to teach the whole world, and points beyond this to the final judgement when the Son of Man will return to establish his kingdom. In this sense time – and space – is filled in ways which differ significantly from those of traditional Jewish expectations.

The second aspect to underline is the peculiar role of the Evangelists in shaping their traditional material and presenting it to the Christian communities. Mark's achievement was to have transposed the oral tradition into written, narrative form. As K. L. Schmidt argued, what characterised the Gospels was their closeness to, their transparency to, the early Christian tradition of sayings and narratives about Jesus.[12] Mark took the traditions and created out of them a narrative work which was more a collage, more the work of a *bricoleur*, than a sustained and systematically ordered *Life*. The simple process of juxtaposing traditional units of material inevitably led to inconsistencies and roughnesses in the on-going narrative, as Schmidt vigorously argued; it also created tensions between the different cosmologies which informed the narrative and discourse material, tensions which, we have argued, the Evangelists were capable of exploiting. Certainly, Mark created a form which was quickly imitated by others. Its material could be reordered and added to or abbreviated; the introduction of new material could lead to shifts of emphasis, subtle changes of ethos and cosmology. Within a relatively short space of time, numbers of such Gospels were circulating within the Christian communities of the Mediterranean.[13]

This impressive rush to literacy, which is reflected in Matthew's redaction and expansion of Mark's Gospel within some twenty years, sheds light on the ways in which tradition is being handled in the early Christian period. What kind of authority did Mark's Gospel have for Matthew, if he felt able to write his own Gospel, which retold it with some considerable freedom? The answer is not simple. *Jubilees*, for example, retells the Genesis story and allows itself very considerable

---

[12] Schmidt, 1919.
[13] For a full treatment, see Koester, 1990.

freedom in the retelling, while still obviously following the main lines of the narrative. Matthew, if anything, follows Mark more closely than *Jubilees* does Genesis. Both interweave considerable amounts of additional material as well as redacting their *Vorlagen*. There can be little doubt that Genesis was regarded by the author of the book of *Jubilees* as authoritative Scripture; so did Matthew regard Mark in the same way? This is unlikely, as Matthew's use of 'Scriptures' (21:42; 22:29; 26:54, 56) and 'it is written' (2:5; 4:4, 6, 7; 4:10; 11:10; 21:13; 26:24, 31) refers to the Scriptures of the Hebrew Bible/LXX and not to Mark's Gospel. It is the former texts to which he appeals editorially, and to which Jesus himself appeals in his dealings with the devil, the crowds and his opponents. These Scriptures have the kind of traditional authority which can resolve disputes and give authoritative shape to Matthew's retelling of Mark, and in that sense they must be considered to have had greater authority for Matthew than for Mark. This is not to say that Mark was without authority for him, any less than were the other traditions which he incorporated into his narrative. Matthew clearly treats them with considerable respect and care, preserving the majority of Mark's Gospel and incorporating even quite small snippets of Markan material into his narrative. And we must remember that within a hundred years both Mark and Matthew will be regarded by the church as Scripture.

So how are traditional scriptural authorities being handled here? In strangely unconventional ways, perhaps. Matthew claims for his story the authority of the Jewish community's Scriptures, but then claims for the central figure of his narrative 'all authority in heaven and earth' (28:18). It is in him that the 'Scriptures' are fulfilled. In this way, Matthew's Gospel indirectly claims greater authority for itself than that of the traditional Scriptures, for, unlike those Scriptures, it gives access to the teaching and life of the supremely authoritative Son of Man. And yet it is not alone in giving access to this supreme authority. It is itself derivative from another such Gospel, and will ultimately stand alongside another two in the canonical Scriptures of the church which will base itself on them. The Gospels with their rich borrowings and reworkings together form the scriptural authority for the new church.

Nor are the Gospels in this respect radically different in character from the writings of the Hebrew Bible. There, too, one will find rich borrowings and intertextual echoes, themes taken up and reworked, different versions of the same narrative. The fact is that traditional literary authorities like the Jewish Scriptures and the Gospels betray a considerable freedom in the way they handle the sacred symbols of their community and fashion out of them new worlds and new patterns of living. This is seen in an explosive way in the writing of the Gospels, where in the space of some thirty years no less than four Gospels were circulating among the Christian communities scattered round the Mediterranean. The very form in which they circulated, the codex, encouraged a kind of portability for the new traditions. At the same time, their very mobility meant that they were vulnerable, open to interpretation outside of any established framework, open to reworking and refashioning as other Gospels, suggesting other forms of community and world-view. There is a flexibility and pluriformity about the literature of the Gospels, which is evidence of the extent to which these early communities were active in the process of shaping their new lives and world-views. At the same time, it suggests that those who were caught up in this dynamic religious movement would be transported into other worlds from those which they had formerly inhabited.

Quite clearly there is evidence in this literature not only of communal and individual crafting of the tradition to create subtly variant forms of ethos and world-view, but also of individual changes of allegiance from one form of traditional mode of living to another. Our discussion of Mark showed how he portrayed discipleship as a form of conversion from blindness to sight. To enter the Christian community was to be freed from a world of illusion, of enslavement to forces of darkness, and to enter the light of the gospel of Jesus Christ, Son of God. Yet, alongside this was another model of discipleship, which saw it as a commissioning to follow the Messiah in his work of preaching the gospel and inaugurating the reign of God. Nor is it just a question of two models of discipleship which are juxtaposed. The drama of the narrative shows how the disciples are broken by the demands of loyalty and obedience which are placed upon them. In the portrait of Peter's denial, Mark opens up a new form of sensibility, and, in Auerbach's judgement, inaugurates a new form of social realism.[14] Mark's Gospel provides evidence, not only of individual conversions at a popular level,[15] which are far removed from the mass conversions which scholars like

[14] Auerbach, 1953, 42.
[15] This contrasts with Nock's view that conversion in the ancient world was restricted to an élite form of conversion to philosophy (Nock, 1933). Cf. the discussion and critique of Nock's views in Shumate, 1996.

Macmullen have posited as characteristic of a later stage of the church's development,[16] but also of personal development and crisis within individual histories within the community of faith. It is not straining the point to say that the view of the formation of the self which emerges from a close reading of Mark's Gospel is a dramatic one which requires a complex narrative to encompass it, and which places heavy demands on individual decision and on the willingness to break with traditional roles and patterns of association. The sectarian nature of the communities behind the Gospels, equally, points to the importance of individual choice. Sects were voluntarist groupings

Such processes of identity formation as we may discern in the Gospels are clearly very different from those in which people in high modern society are presently engaged. The first Christians were trying to find their place in newly emergent communities, which were in process of redefining the parameters of their world. They were not, like people today, trying to form their identities in a world which is wholly (largely?) undefined, where the process of constructing a narrative of the self is far less constrained by traditional patterns, expectations, by 'authenticated practice' and accepted 'modes of being'. Time and space for them were by no means empty; but their dimensions were not yet fully or finally defined. The future was marked out by the coming of the Son of Man, but rather different accounts were offered of this coming: he would send out the angels and gather in his elect (Mark 13:26–27); he would come in judgement to establish his kingdom, to gather all the nations and separate the righteous from the wicked (Matt 25:31–46). Similarly, the boundaries of the world were being redrawn: the Galilean ministry was to become the pattern for a mission to preach the gospel to the whole world (Mark 14:9; cf. 13:10); the church's mission was no longer to be restricted to the lost sheep of the house of Israel (Matt 10:6), but was to be extended to all nations (Matt 28:18–20).

The process of identity-formation which we may, albeit somewhat tentatively, posit for those who gave their allegiance to the early Christian communities, is thus quite distinct from that described by Giddens for those in high-modern societies today. In the first place, it was a communal process: new adherents found themselves within a new community of faith, which shared a common confession, even if it was one whose details were still to be worked out. It was not a matter of

---

[16] Macmullen, 1981, 95–6.

individuals constructing a narrative of their own. Secondly, it was one where the adoption of communal beliefs about the nature of time and space played an essential part. However fragmentary or unformed or conflicting these beliefs may have been, they nevertheless gave shape to the emerging identity of those who joined these new communities, as we shall shortly explain more fully. Such identities were not constructed in a cognitive or moral void. Nevertheless, we should not underestimate either the dynamism of this process, or the element of choice. The tradition was pluriform and manifested itself in different transformations. Sectarianism, which entails individuals' choosing to associate with a group marginal to the main stream of society, was common.

## The politics of recognition

Here one needs to enter a caution against an unqualified acceptance of Giddens' account of self-identity. What is illuminating about Giddens' account are the correlations he makes between the 'project of the self' in high-modernity and the reflexivity of institutional processes at a time of increasing globalisation. It is the freedom of transnational institutions to set and constantly revise their own goals, without regard for local conditions and beliefs, that distinguishes them from previous institutions; in the same way, individuals construct and constantly revise their sense of who they are, without regard for traditional beliefs and values. Characteristically, people constructing their own narratives in this way will turn to self-help manuals, which are non-prescriptive, but which offer assistance in the process of the formation of self-identity. This corresponds broadly to the search for a 'sense of existence', and to the notion of 'self-determining freedom' both of which Charles Taylor traces back to Rousseau.[17] Self-determining freedom is the idea 'that I am free when I decide for myself what concerns me, rather than being shaped by external influences . . . Self-determining freedom demands that I break the hold of all . . . external impositions and decide for myself alone'.[18]

---

[17] Taylor, 1991, 27, citing Rousseau: 'Le sentiment de l'existence dépouillé de toute autre affection est par lui-même un sentiment précieux de contentement et de paix qui suffiroit seul pour rendre cette existence chère et douce à qui sauroit écarter de soi toutes les impressions sensuelles et terrestres qui viennent sans cesse nous en distraire et en troubler ici bas la douceur.' Rousseau, 1959, 1047, citation Taylor, 1991, 126, n. 21.

[18] Taylor, 1991, 27.

Similar ideas were articulated by Herder, who asserted that everyone has his or her own 'measure, as it were a manner peculiar to him/her in which his or her sensual feelings harmonise with each other'.[19] To be true to oneself, one needs to listen, not to the voices of society telling one who one is and what one's station is, but to the inner voice which puts one in touch with one's own originality, something that only the individual can articulate. Yet, importantly, for Herder such originality was encountered at two levels, at the level of the individual and at the level of the culture-bearing people. In Herder's case, this was identified with the *Volk*, with its own particular cultural genius.

Taylor's account of the history of the idea of authenticity, of the pursuit of individual and communal self-fulfilment and self-realisation provides an interesting context into which to set the developments which Giddens is attempting to plot. The notions of selfhood and originality which emerge at the time of Rousseau and Herder, are very much concerned with the discovery and development of the individual's own particular self. It is in a sense a given, though it is a given which individuals need to discover and cultivate, something that they can properly do only if they break free from external influences. Giddens' view is somewhat different. The individual is free to set goals and revise them at will. The narrative which individuals construct for themselves may be almost constantly in process of revision. There is no given, other than the individual's ability to work out and modify their own self-identity as they make their way through life.

Neither Giddens nor Taylor is uncritical of these developments. Giddens in his recent Reith Lectures argued that a pure individualism, which simply pursued its own, revisable goals, would lead to a society without overarching values, a society which had nothing to die for. Traditions, which are themselves the product of society's search for common values and regularly invented, preserve group-values and give dignity to the society.[20] Taylor, similarly, argues that the search for self-realisation is not something that can be achieved on one's own. For the

[19] 'Jeder Mensch hat ein eigenes Maass, gleichsam eine eigne Stimmung aller seiner sinnlichen Gefühle zu einander.' Herder, 13:291, quoted in Taylor, 1994, 30, n. 6.

[20] In this sense Giddens in no way disagrees with our view that in traditional societies there is change and innovation. He concludes, 1999, 7: 'All of us need moral commitments that stand above the petty concerns and squabbles of everyday life. We should be prepared to mount an active defence of these values wherever they are poorly developed, or threatened. None of us would have anything to live for, if we didn't have something worth dying for.'

'crucial feature of life is its fundamentally *dialogical* character. We become full human agents, capable of understanding ourselves, and hence of defining our identity, through our acquisition of rich human languages of expression'. Taking 'language' here in its broadest sense to encompass all forms of human expression, Taylor argues that we learn such language only through contact with significant others.[21] It is only as we engage in dialogue with those close to us, who have influence for good or ill within our lives, that we can achieve a sense of our own identity. Without them, we do not have the language in which to do it; without their recognition as we struggle to define ourselves in our relationships and dialogue with them, we cannot fully come to ourselves.

It is this factor of recognition which principally informs Taylor's account of the distinction between traditional and modern forms of identity-formation. Dependence on others for one's sense of identity is not something new. 'The socially derived identity was by its very nature dependent on society. But in the earlier age recognition never arose as a problem. General recognition was built into the socially derived identity by virtue of the very fact that it was based on social categories that everyone took for granted. Yet inwardly derived, personal, original identity doesn't enjoy this recognition *a priori*. It has to win it through exchange, and the attempt can fail. What has come about with the modern age is not the need for recognition but the conditions in which the attempt to be recognised can fail.'[22]

This both qualifies Giddens' view of the self and sets up another distinction between modes of identity formation in ancient and modern societies. Taylor stresses, unlike Giddens, the recognition and dialogue that is for him an essential part of the formation of the self in any society. This is well illustrated for ancient society by the ways in which the Evangelists engage with their communal traditions, as found in Jewish Scripture and in the oral traditions of the earliest Christian communities. They do not construct new senses of social identity for their churches out of nothing. The narratives and discourses, which form the basis of the new worlds, and new identities which they are forging, are written out of a dialogue which operates at many levels. They engage with Jewish hopes and expectations which are expressed in Scripture. Isaiah's motif of the way of the Lord is a

---

[21] Taylor, 1994, 32.
[22] Taylor, 1994, 34–5.

foil to both Mark and Matthew. Contemporary ideas about the Messiah, the son of David and the Son of God are also woven into the narrative and, as with Isaiah's way of the Lord, reworked and modified. They engage with central concepts of the Jewish religion, such as the Law. Matthew's dialogue with his 'significant other', the Jewish community struggling to re-form after 70 CE, centres on this topic and involves his insistence that Jesus and the *ekklesia* 'fulfil' the Law (a recognition almost certainly withheld by the synagogue), and at the same time the claim that Jesus and, by delegation, the church, now have all authority in heaven and earth, something that other Jews would not claim even for Moses, with whom Matthew pointedly compares Jesus.

On the other hand, Taylor, still sharply distinguishes ancient and modern modes of identity formation by contrasting 'socially derived identity' with 'inwardly derived, personal, original identity'. The problem here is that, by his own account, modern forms of identity are themselves, in a measure at least, socially derived. 'The genesis of the human mind is . . . not something each person accomplishes on his or her own, but dialogical . . . We define our identity always in dialogue with, sometimes in struggle against, the things our significant others want to see in us. Even after we outgrow some of these others – our parents, for instance – and they disappear from our lives, the conversation with them continues with us as long as we live.'[23] This is something that could be said about Matthew and his relationship with Judaism, and would provide an interesting perspective from which to view debates about his church's position in relation to the parting of the ways. Matthew certainly learnt his theological language from Judaism; he struggled with the synagogue's refusal to recognise Jesus as the Messiah and his community as faithful exponents and practitioners of the Law. Even after his community had failed in their attempts to persuade the synagogue of the truth of their claims about Jesus, and their ways had parted, Matthew still wrote a Gospel which was dominated by comparisons between Jesus and Moses, by notions of Jesus as the true teacher of the Law, yet which ends by declaring that his authority far outstrips any authority held by anyone within the synagogue or indeed in the whole history of the Jewish nation.

[23] Taylor, 1994, 32–3.

On the other hand, there is clearly a difference between the attempt to construct a world-view for a community which will be determinative of the ethos of its members and the imparting of a language of personal, original identity, which encourages people to be true to themselves and to resist the pressures of society to conform to established patterns of behaviour. Certainly, to encourage people to see themselves as 'brothers and sisters of Jesus', in so far as they conform to particular forms of 'authenticated practice' (Mark 3:35; Matt 12:50), represents a very different view of the importance of conformity to group norms from the kind of ethical stance which demands respect for anyone's chosen or indeed constructed values. Yet Taylor's account of the history of the idea of authenticity makes it clear that such a precept is indeed socially transmitted, and in that sense the identity of those who embrace it and live it out in their lives is also socially derived. And as Taylor himself argues, it is even questionable whether such ethics of authenticity can survive without some transcendental framework to support it, without some sense of belonging to 'a wider whole'.[24]

This is not to argue that the processes of identity formation which we can discern in the Gospels are repeatable today within modern globalised societies. I have been trying to show where the lines of discontinuity and of continuity lie. The world of the first century, with its closely defined communities, but also its great social dynamism and mobility, was more fluid than is sometimes supposed in the sharp contrasts which are drawn between ancient and modern. We have plenty of evidence for the dialogical character of earliest Christianity, however it may have evolved in later forms of orthodoxy. We have evidence for considerable diversity of views within the Gospels.[25] Yet it is emphatically diversity in search of a clearer sense of the wider whole to which the members of the church belong. It is not the attempt to construct a narrative of the self in a void. It is a search which was conducted on a community level, as well as by individuals of remarkable imaginative power and narrative skill. It involved dialogue with different traditions within and outwith the church. It was, above all, one which attempted to redraw the dimensions of its world and to grapple with the underlying questions of the nature of evil and its resolution which troubled its contemporaries.

[24] Taylor, 1991, 91.
[25] Cf. again the judicious assessment of early Christian sectarianism by Markus, 1980, chapter 1 above, n. 7.

## Some conclusions: the worlds of Mark and Matthew

Finally then, let me draw together some of the conclusions of this study to show what sort of worlds these early communities and writers were fashioning.

Much recent study of Mark and Matthew has been directed to an understanding of what has been termed their sectarian nature. In what sense were the communities, with which Mark and Matthew were closely associated, *sects*? This has often been linked to and in a measure confused with the question of the ethnic character of these emergent communities, specifically with the question how far they remained within and continued to see themselves as part of the Jewish community. In what sense were they *Jewish* sects?

### The sectarian nature of Mark's and Matthew's communities

Sects, it is generally agreed, are groups which, *inter alia*, are marginal to the wider society in which they live. This raises difficult questions in relation to the emerging Christian communities, for they were, on the one hand, in process of parting company with the Jewish people; on the other hand, they were a new religious grouping, whether inside or outside Judaism, which would soon be the subject of fierce and barbaric, though sporadic, treatment from the Roman state. They were, that is to say, marginal both to the Jewish communities, of which they for a time formed a part, and also to the Roman principate which would regard them with suspicion for some three centuries. The problem is substantially compounded by the fact that there is no agreement among scholars about the precise location of the communities from which the Evangelists came. Scholars are divided whether we should locate Mark's immediate community in Rome shortly after the Neronic persecutions or in Syria during the Jewish War. The Syrian location in the Jewish War would certainly suggest stronger Jewish ties in the very recent past. On either view their position was fraught with danger, and they were hardly exaggerating when they saw themselves as 'hated by all for my name's sake'.[26] It was in short an extremely liminal community,[27] and as

---

[26] Matt 24:9//Mark 13:13; Matthew intriguingly reads 'hated by all *nations*', echoing the mission charge in Matt 28:19.

[27] Cf. Victor Turner's discussion of liminality in Turner, 1974. Turner has argued that liminal figures, by working with powerful metaphors, bring 'the unknown a little more into the light'. Such metaphors share with symbols 'a certain kind of polarisation of

such was able to reach out and anticipate new worlds in ways that other more established groupings rarely can.

This dual relationship to the Jewish people and to the Roman principate needs to be emphasised, not least in discussions of Matthew's Gospel. Here, in recent discussions, it is more often the tendencies to stabilisation of the community, towards its legitimation over against the mainstream Jewish community, which have earned scholars' attention. But apart from the fact that the Jewish community itself was divided into parties and, especially after the destruction of the Temple, did not have a central core,[28] there is a further question whether a community which was solely or indeed principally intent on consolidation would have been creating such diversity in its own central authoritative texts. There is no need to deny that Matthew was concerned with developing the structures of the Christian church and that his chapter 18 is a kind of 'manual of discipline' for the fledgling community. But this should not blind one to the way that Matthew is also even there deploying metaphors for forgiveness and judgement which carry a subversive charge as well as a stabilising message. There is certainly, as we have said, a change of mood from Mark to Matthew, but still there is a great energy in Matthew, which works away at Mark's central metaphor of the way of the Lord and uses it to develop his own vision of the universal mission of the church.

What is most useful in the application of modern sociological discussions of religious sects to these early Christian communities is to consider the different responses to the world which they give. Mark and Matthew both operate with two broad mythological schemata, the notion of a cosmic conflict between God and Satan and that of the

---

meaning in which the subsidiary subject is really a depth world of prophetic, half-glimpsed images, and the principal subject, the visible fully known (or thought to be fully known) component at the opposite pole to it, acquires new and surprising contours and valences from its dark companion' (51). He believes that such revealing metaphors 'appear in the work of exceptionally liminal thinkers – poets, writers, religious prophets, "the un-acknowledged legislators of mankind" – just before outstanding limina of history, major crises of societal change, since such shamanistic figures are possessed by spirits of change before changes become visible in public arenas' (28).

[28] This is reinforced by recent scholarship, which has been critical of the view that the Academy at Jamnia immediately assumed control over Judaism after the destruction of Jerusalem. The preferred description of Judaism in this period is 'formative Judaism'. But if Judaism was in process of (re-)formation, then there was as yet no clearly defined centre of power in respect of which Matthew's group could be marginal.

'way of the Lord', of the new exodus and restoration of Zion. The first of these advocates a revolutionist response to the world: God must intervene to sweep away the present evil age and the dark powers which control it and replace it with a new world. The second is basically reformist: the world will be set to rights when the people have accepted God's teaching, are forgiven, and follow him along the way, returning to a restored Zion. Both these myths undergo substantial transformations in the Gospels. In the end, both in Mark and in Matthew, it is the reformist myth that gains the upper hand; people must accept Jesus' call and teaching, must learn to do the will of God and to become his brothers and sisters. Only such people will be gathered in and, will be upheld in the judgement, when the Son of Man comes. This is not to say that the revolutionist myth is simply set aside. In the first place, it continues to function as a metaphor for the radical nature of evil. The perversity of the human will, which is exemplified in the moral failure of the disciples, while not directly attributed to the devil and his agents (though cf. Mark 4:15), is not explicable in terms of a simple malfunction of the will. The will breaks under the pressures to which it is subjected. Similarly, discipleship is not conceived simply in terms of instruction and obedience to the commands of the teacher Jesus, though this clearly plays an enormously important part in Matthew. It is also contrasted with the darkness of the existence of those who are not followers of Jesus. They are like blind people in need of healing (Mark 8:22–26; 10:46–52); they are like bad seed sown by the devil (Matt 13:36–43). These images play a powerful role in both Gospels and keep alive a deep sense of the divide between the world of the community and the established world outside it, just as they inculcate a mood of deep moral seriousness and a sense of the need for a radical change of heart (Mark 6:52; 7:6, 21; 8:17; 11:23; 12:30, 33; Matt 5:8, 28; 6:21; 11:29; 12:34; 13:15, 19; 18:35; 22:37). This tendency is pronounced in Matthew, where there is much greater emphasis on the purity and meekness of heart which is required of those who follow Jesus. Mark talks more about the hardness of heart of others. In this sense there are strong tendencies towards a form of conversionism. What perhaps is most instructive about this is the dynamism of the responses to the world, which is found in these early witnesses to the Christian tradition. It is clear, on the one hand, that they are filled with a deep consciousness of the need for the world outside the community to be radically transformed. Equally, on the other hand, this poses deep questions about the proper form of response by members of the community. The story of the disciples, their deep failings and their restoration, their instruction and their misunderstanding, their commissioning and the assurances given to them, their need for moral perfection (Matt 5:48!), becomes a rich vehicle for developing the ethos of the new community. Its restless dynamic will take many forms: introspective, perfectionist, even triumphalist.

## Mark's and Matthew's communities as *Jewish* sects

All this certainly indicates that the communities which read and received these Gospels had a sharp sense of their own distinctiveness over against the world and all other groups. In what sense did they see themselves as *forming* a *Jewish* sect? We have argued that Mark's Gospel betrays a clear sense of distance and separation from the Jewish people. The parable of the Wicked Vineyarders takes the motif of the vineyard and fiercely parodies it. The loving relationship between God and his people is reduced to a contractual one which is discarded and awarded to others. Mark's Jesus sets aside provisions in the Law relating to purity (Mark 7:19). The veil of the Temple is torn and the Shekhina departs, while a Gentile centurion recognises the Son of God in the crucified Jewish Messiah. The idea of the Land, which is central to the covenant relationship between God and Israel and to Isaiah's notion of the way of the Lord, with its themes of exile and return to Zion, is metaphoricised and notions of the restoration of the Davidic kingdom and of the glory of Mount Zion are deeply subverted. In all this it is evident that key components of Jewish ethnic identity, that of the covenant relationship, of the binding force of the Law and of the distinguishing mark of food laws, of the attachment to the Land, are all being set aside. Mark, by contrast, sees the identity of Jesus' followers as being crucially linked to Jesus: they are his brothers and sisters in so far as they do God's will, and this means following him, leaving family and occupation, taking up their cross, losing their life, and returning to Galilee to go out to preach the Gospel in all the world.

What is remarkable in all this is how deeply rooted Mark's Gospel, nevertheless, is in Jewish Scripture and tradition. Much of his language, and the main images and motifs which structure his Gospel, are drawn from them and he shapes the identity of his community in dialogue with them. His saviour is a thoroughly Jewish saviour figure, the Messiah. His Gospel reflects debates about the nature of the

Messiah, whether he is Son of David and or Son of God, but in all this Mark does not stray outside Jewish language and thought. Despite the clear signs of distance between his community and the Jewish people and their traditions, he thinks and writes in thoroughly Jewish terms. As Taylor suggests, senses of identity cannot be developed in isolation; we need to be taught a language and to engage in dialogue with significant others. Mark has clearly been schooled in Jewish ways of thought and expression; he equally clearly has a deep antipathy to certain sections of the Jewish people, as is shown by his portrayal of Jesus' opponents. Yet no matter how much he may have moved on after parting company with the Jewish people, his thought-forms remain indebted to Judaism. At the same time, the communal narrative traditions of the Christian community which he preserves present a new story, giving a new dimension to Jewish hopes and expectations and constituting a new people, a new family of brothers and sisters of Jesus.

If so much is reasonably certain, the question of Matthew's stance *vis-à-vis* Judaism is much more contentious. In the first place, Matthew underscores the Jewish roots of the story of Jesus by prefacing his Gospel with a genealogy reaching back via David to Abraham (albeit one which contains four Gentile women). His story is further presented as the fulfilment of prophecy and Jesus as the one who in his teaching and life fulfils the Law. Jesus is compared, favourably, with Moses and his credentials as Messiah are established. He is Son of David but his Messiahship goes beyond what is implied by this notion and is linked with the Danielic Son of Man: Jesus, Son of God, Son of Man will come in royal power to judge all the nations (25:32). He is the one whose authority transcends all earthly and heavenly authority. Something greater than the Temple and Solomon and Jonah is here (12:6, 41–42).

There can be no denying Matthew's wish to claim the Hebrew Scriptures and tradition for his church. This is not simply a case of someone so deeply embued with Jewish language and thought that he remains indebted even when he has long parted company with his parent body. Matthew is actively disputing the tradition with the synagogue. In one fairly obvious sense, it is right to describe Matthew's Gospel as a work of Christian Judaism, if by that one means an account of Christianity which claims it to be the authentic development of Judaism. The problem comes precisely with the question of ethnicity. Does Matthew still insist that members of the church must be circumcised?

Does he still regard Jewish descent as a major mark of membership of the group? What role does attachment to the Land and the Temple play in his understanding of Christianity?

I have suggested that in each of these key areas which mark out Jewish identity, Matthew gives either very ambiguous or quite negative answers. There is silence over the issue of circumcision (as there is in Mark, though not in Luke, who reports John's and Jesus' circumcision, 1:59; 2:21, or John where Jesus alludes to it as one of 'your' customs, 7:22–23) but a Gentile mission with circumcision *in the church of the eighties* CE is hardly thinkable. The importance of Jewish descent for salvation in face of impending judgement is explicitly down-played (Matt 3:9) and, as in Mark, it is discipleship and doing the will of God which leads to people becoming part of the true family of Jesus. Finally, the Land plays no part in Matthew's scheme of things: the notion of the way of the Lord, which Mark had taken up and subverted, is not restored to something like its Isaianic form, with a literal goal in the restoration of the Temple. The Temple's destruction is prophesied; the veil is torn; the way leads to the mountain in Galilee, whence Jesus sends his disciples out into the whole world, and reaches its goal when Jesus comes seated on his throne in judgement. Jewish ethnicity is no longer a key marker of Matthew's community whatever its Jewishness in other respects.

What then, to tackle the most sensitive of issues, does this have to say about the Jewish people and the 'ethnicity' of the ἐθνός to whom the kingdom has been given (21:43)? Why does Matthew stress the importance of Jewish ethnicity in some respects (Jesus' Jewish descent, his fulfilment of the Law, even the prophecies of the place of his birth and ministry) and yet in other respects play it down, belittling the importance of descent from Abraham (3:9), stressing the new – fictive – kinship relationships to Jesus of those who do the will of God, recasting sacred geography, as he sends his disciples to make disciples of all nations, and promises his presence with them wherever they go? The answer seems to lie in the radicalness of his vision of the nature of evil. Evil is so pervasive in the world that it is not possible to root it out. Only at the final judgement, when the Son of Man who fulfils the Law comes to establish his kingdom, will the world be purged of those who do evil, and a new world be established. What this means is that there can be no assurances that any given people, defined in terms of descent, adherence to ancestral customs and attachment to a particular territory, will be free of such corrupting influence. Even the Jewish nation is subject to corruption in this respect, as the narrative of its leaders' opposition to the Messiah Jesus makes clear and as is bitterly underlined by the Jerusalem crowds when they turn against Jesus and call down his blood upon themselves and their children (27:25). Thus only a very different ἔθνός, composed of 'sons of the kingdom', those who do the will of Jesus' Father in heaven and who are his brothers and sisters, will ultimately enter his kingdom, when he comes in judgement. Thus just as Mark allegorises the motif of Galilee, so Matthew metaphoricises ethnicity. The community of Jesus' disciples, of those who follow him and do all that he commands, is an *ethnos* only in a fictive sense. Above all, it is an *ethnos* which is yet to be fully realised.

But where does that leave the Jewish people? Essentially as the people who gave the world the Law and the Messiah, but who like every other nation prove to be comprised of good and bad alike. It is from the Jewish nation that the Messiah and his first disciples come; it is also from the Jewish nation that come those who oppose Jesus and call for his death. What is, for Matthew, of abiding value in this is the Jewish Law as interpreted by the Jewish Messiah. Kinship and territorial attachments are metaphoricised. It is in this strictly limited sense that Matthew advocates a form of Christian Judaism.

It is important to be as careful as one can about the history here. However much scholars may want to present their work as an objective, distanced study of the topic, it is not possible in a post-holocaust, multicultural setting to approach this particular topic without an awareness of the wider political implications of what one says. Mostly these are left unstated, but there is evidently an entirely proper concern to avoid giving support to some of the terrible uses of the Gospels, not least of Matthew (27:25), in Christian attacks on Jews. It is not clear, however, that this is best served by presenting the Gospel of Matthew as Jewish, in the sense that it makes Jewish ethnicity a necessary condition of membership of the *ekklesia*.[29] I have given my reasons for thinking that this is in any case not right, but it is worth considering what the wider political consequences of such a view might be. In the first place,

---

[29] Not that there is in any way a consensus on this issue. While Sim is emphatic that circumcision would have been regarded as a condition of entry into the Christian Jewish church, Saldarini, 1994, 160, is less confident. Probably some Gentiles in Matthew's group were circumcised and some were not. 'The relationship each had with God in faith through Jesus was the central focus of their commitment.'

it would indicate that one of the canonical Gospels was correctly read by Christian Jews and misread by the Great Church.[30] On this view of Matthew, the church was wrong to see itself as a third race/nation, distinct from Jews and Gentiles. It should have remained within the Jewish people, insisting on circumcision and attachment to the Land and Temple (as James the brother of the Lord continued to worship in the Temple). By setting up a separate nation, claiming that the kingdom had been given to another 'nation', the Great Church implied that the Jewish nation had been dispossessed, judged and cast out. 'Supersessionism' is unmasked as, implicitly, the outlawing of Judaism. This effectively declares the main stream of the church's development from the second and third centuries onward to have been fundamentally misdirected, and leaves the way open for the church to strike out on an entirely new course, which would leave the whole history of anti-Semitism behind. Practically, this is unlikely to prove persuasive to many, but it might at least encourage some to entertain new modes of Christian living and association.

But how might this be done? Sim encourages his readers to 'take seriously his (sc. Matthew's) alternative Christian Jewish version of the gospel',[31] but what this means is less than clear. Would it mean embracing all forms of Jewish legal observance, including male circumcision? Or would it, as Saldarini suggests,[32] be more a matter of 'forc[ing] Christians to confront again and again their Jewish roots', so ruling out Marcionite options? The problem with the first view, apart from the obvious obstacle of male circumcision, is that it would not necessarily make for easy Jewish-Christian relations. For, as Matthew's Gospel well illustrates, relations between Christian Jews and other Jewish groups were far from cordial. Chapter 23 and the curse put into the mouths of the Jerusalem crowds may be explained as typical of the rhetoric of inner-group polemics, but they remain deeply offensive whatever their context, and

[30] This is Sim's view. Speaking of the extensive reinterpretation which the Greek Gospel of Matthew went through at the hands of its new owners, the Gentile Christian churches, he writes, 'Quite contrary to the intentions of the evangelist, the Gospel was now interpreted along Pauline lines and it was used to demonstrate the superiority of (Gentile) Christianity over Judaism.' Some Matthaean Christians, however, remained true to Matthew and developed into the sect of the Nazarenes which continued to read it 'in terms of law-observance and anti-Paulinism' (Sim 1998, 302).

[31] Sim, 1998, 302.

[32] Saldarini, 1994, 205.

make the point that simply emulating the situation of Matthew's community will not serve to right the wrongs of the past.

The problem is that such polemic emerges from the profound sense of pain of the Christian Jewish community at the majority's refusal to give it recognition, specifically to recognise its claims that Jesus was the Messiah, and that as Messiah he had given the definitive interpretation of the Law and would come to judge all the nations. It would mean facing up to the question of blasphemy which Matthew (following Mark) attributes to the high priest (26:65) in response to Jesus' acceptance of the title Son of God and his saying about the Son of Man.

On the other hand, Saldarini's view, that Christians should confront their Jewish roots, is also something that would follow from the kind of presentation which we have offered. Matthew, if he is seen as someone who engages deeply with the Jewish tradition and uses it to give form and expression to the new world and the new sense of identity which he is advocating, is certainly someone who forces Christians to confront their Jewish roots. The same would indeed be true of Mark, even though the break he makes with Judaism appears to be much cleaner. What does it add if Matthew is seen as a Christian Jewish Gospel, in the sense that he sees Jewish ethnicity as an integral part of Christian life?

The key issue here is the relation of the church to Israel. On my view, Matthew sees the church as an eschatological community, which will be fully realised only at the last judgement. Meanwhile, the church is the company of those who follow Jesus and obey all that he has commanded. On Saldarini's view, it is the group that has replaced the Jewish leaders as the leaders of Israel. Whatever the historical rights or wrongs of this claim, it is extremely doubtful whether claiming that a group of followers of Jesus calling themselves the church are the true leaders of Israel, as opposed to the leaders of formative Judaism and their heirs, would bring much relief in Jewish-Christian relations. Whether the church replaces Israel and so declares it to be cut off from God's purposes; or whether it claims to be the true leadership of Israel and so outlaws non-Christian Jewish leaders and all who follow them, is a theologically significant distinction; which of these ways of refusing recognition to Jewish communities would cause greater offence is hard to say.

This is a difficult discussion, not least because the political views of the major discussants are only lightly sketched. At times it is hard to avoid the impression that there is a kind of essentialism at work here.

Sim is keen to restore interpretations of Matthew that do justice to the Evangelist and his intended readers. The suggestion seems to be that we need to recapture, and in a measure recreate, the original and therefore essential meaning of the text, as it was understood by its first readers. This is a very partial view of the text, which in the case of Matthew has a rich pre-history and an equally rich after-life. What I have been trying to show is something of the tensiveness of the text which renders it patient of many different readings, such that it makes little sense to appeal to the original intention of the author. But something of the same is true of the attempts of the early Christian communities to construct new identities for themselves. They are part of a process which is highly dialogical. It is, I have wanted to emphasise, a dialogue with Jewish Scripture and also with the traditions about Jesus. It is, on the one hand, part of a continuing process of trying to mediate between different world-views, a cosmic dualist and a forensic eschatology. On the other hand, it is part of a search for a sense of identity by a people who see themselves as a peculiar people, chosen by God to be his instruments in the world. The tension between ethnic particularity and universality is part of the Jewish tradition, as we saw in our discussions of *Jubilees* and some of the Qumran texts. God disposes over all the world, and his designs for his people are part of his purposes for the world. This is particularly true of the Mount Zion traditions in Isaiah, which speak of the nations flocking to the glory of the Lord on Zion.

The fact then that both Matthew and Mark in their different ways stress the universalising elements in the tradition is not something that automatically means that they part company with Jewish tradition.[33] There is an in-built dilemma: how to reconcile God's will to establish his rule over the whole world and his particular attachment to Israel. These elements are variously emphasised in the two myths which engage Mark and Matthew, that of the cosmic battle between Satan and God and that of the return of the exiles to Zion. The myth of the invasion and corruption of the world by demonic forces, and the final destruction of these powers in a cosmic battle, is certainly one which pays little attention to the details either of Israel's history or its geography, though

---

[33] It is interesting to recall that Daniel Boyarin, 1994, raises similar issues in relation to Paul, whom he presents as a cultural critic of Judaism, a radical Jew. The problem for Paul, he hypothesises (39–40), is how to reconcile a religious tradition which imposes obligations on its members that sharply distinguish them from the rest of the peoples, with a creator God who rules over the whole earth.

as the Qumran texts make clear, at least there is a remnant to whom God has revealed his mysteries and who are to bear witness to his purposes. The myth of the return of the exiles to Zion, on the other hand, is first and foremost a story of the restoration of the people of Israel to their land and monarchy. Nevertheless, it is also a story about the restoration of cosmic order. When the glory of the Lord returns to Zion, then all the nations will flock to Zion and recognise Israel's God and righteousness and praise will be established throughout the world.

What we have suggested is that in both Mark and Matthew it is the Isaianic way of the Lord which dominates the narrative, but that the myth of the cosmic battle works to universalise and to blur the boundaries of the group and the land.[34] Precisely because the myth works as a constant reminder of the universality of the corruption of the human condition, there is a constant pressure to develop the universalising elements in the myth of the return. The way of the Lord does not reach its terminus in the restoration of the glory of the Lord to the Temple and the vision of that glory by the Gentiles. Instead, the Temple veil is torn and the Gentile centurion perceives the glory as he looks at the dead Christ, while the disciples are sent back to Galilee, whence they will continue their itinerant ministry as they preach the Gospel to all nations. In Matthew, for all his re-emphasis of Jewish elements in the narrative, these universalising elements are brought out even more strongly. The faith of the Gentiles is recorded already during Jesus' ministry; from the crucifixion and the centurion's confession, the narrative moves to the mountain in Galilee whence the disciples are sent out into all the world to preach and make disciples of all nations. The final drama will come when the Son of Man comes to judge the world and establish his kingdom and all will appear before him.

It is true that there is a certain sense of completion, of closure, in these narratives. The very fact that one can offer such a summary of Mark and Matthew indicates as much. But such summaries should not be confused with the works themselves, or indeed with the wealth of meaning which will be drawn from them in the course of their reception

[34] See Davies, 1994, 370: 'the cosmic awareness of primitive Christianity . . . could not but place all Christian speculation on geographic entities that were central to Judaism in a minor key. Judaism had this cosmic dimension also. To that extent it, too, depressed the doctrine of Jerusalem and the land. But that dimension is far more immediate and ubiquitous in its intensity in primitive Christianity, and the consequent depression greater.'

both in the Great Church and within Jewish Christianity. It is much more important to see them as part of a dynamic tradition which is constantly engaged in a dialogue with both Jewish Scripture and the ongoing experience of its readers.

This means that we have in fact to be very careful about using the Gospels in too simple a normative sense. They are more a language school, training their readers in a complex mode of expression, which draws on a broad range of prophetic and apocalyptic traditions with deep roots in Jewish Scripture, and trains them, not just by teaching the rules of the language, but by deploying it in the telling and retelling of the narrative of Jesus Christ. It is this language which Christian communities have drawn on down the ages to articulate their own sense of their identity and they have done so in a great diversity of ways, as is richly illustrated by Luz in his commentary. To suppose that there was one normative way, a Christian Jewish way, to read one of these texts is to abstract the text from its literary history.

## Multiculturalism and the Gospels

One last matter must be touched on. The discussion of the relation of Matthew's community to Judaism raises sharply enough questions which have a strong contemporary relevance, questions of ethnicity and multi-culturalism. We saw above how both Mark and Matthew take Jewish traditions which variously contain universalistic and particularising elements and stretch them, emphasising the universal, though also, notably in Matthew's case, not losing sight of the particular, of the importance of tradition, descent, local community, local hopes and aspirations. Jesus in Matthew is rooted in Jewish history and in Jewish prophecy; even the places of his birth and his ministry, it is claimed, are recorded in sacred Scripture as part of God's purposes. His actions recall the great figures of the past, and in so doing repeat and affirm Jewish history. For all that, in Matthew as in Mark it is the universalising elements which get the upper hand. The Jewish nation is no longer, as such, the subject of the Isaianic prophecies. It is Jesus, and with him the band of followers, of those who do the will of God, who are his brothers and sisters. Fictive kinship replaces bonds of flesh and blood. The world is divided into sons of the kingdom and sons of the evil one.

In this there is a clear transcendence of ethnicity, a relativising of particular groupings of family, clan and ethnic group in favour of a universal dualism of good and evil. In the same way, territorial divisions are relativised or allegorised. Galilee is no longer in Mark the piece of Jewish territory in which Jesus of Nazareth conducted his ministry; it is a figure for the whole world which is now the stage on which the disciples will move.

How can such traditions, with all their dynamism, contribute to the contemporary debates on multiculturalism? We need, first, to be fully aware of the dangers of such traditions. At their most aggressive, universal categories of fictive kinship, children of the earth, sons and daughters of God, comrades, render all other forms of classification redundant and effectively colonise all other groupings. There is no space left for those who wish to uphold other forms of classification and to reserve a place on the earth for Jews and Gentiles, for Hausas and Ibos, for Quebeckois and English-speaking Canadians.[35] If, moreover, the world is divided into sons of the kingdom and sons of the evil one, and the sons of the kingdom are defined as those who follow or will follow Jesus, then this reclassifies all those who do not recognise Jesus as the Messiah as sons of the evil one. What might appear to be a liberalising development, transcending 'narrow' ethnic boundaries, may easily turn out to be a culturally imperialistic move.

There are in effect two countervailing tendencies at work here. On the one hand, there is a universalising tendency which seeks a common ground for all, which reacts against those forces in society and culture which separate and divide and which uphold forms of inequality. Such tendencies may be embodied in divisions of race, gender, class, language, and many others. According equal dignity to all is a modern democratic imperative, and notions of universal human rights have their roots in this period. The theological imperative is of a different kind: it derives from a sense of the impartiality of a universal God who is 'no respecter of persons' (Acts 10:34), a belief that all are created equal in the sight of God.

---

[35] This is well illustrated by Taylor, 1994, in relation to the dilemma within liberal philosophies of human rights and the conflict between a politics of equal dignity and one of difference. Is the role of government in a modern democratic society to uphold certain universal rights for all: housing, freedom of religion, universal suffrage . . . under some bill of rights? or is it to recognise the 'unique identity of this individual or group' (37–8), without which recognition such groups may be seriously affected. There is a clear conflict of interest here, as illustrated in the controversy over French-schooling in Quebec. Is it proper to introduce legislation to require that all inhabitants (with the exception of Quebec-born English speakers) should attend French-language schools, in order to preserve the French language and thus the Quebeckois as a group?

The other tendency seeks to accord recognition to minority groups and others who are discriminated against, acknowledging that without such recognition they will be unable to achieve their full development. Recognition by significant others is an essential part of any individual's or group's development and it is part of the state's duty to accord it. There are theological roots for such tendencies, in the special status accorded to particular groups by particular deities, or indeed by a universal God. The Table of Nations in Genesis 10 is an example of such recognition of different nations and peoples by a universal creator God; it is developed in *Jubilees' mappa mundi*, as each nation is given a particular territory. Israel's election as a particular people is an example of theological recognition of a group.

What we have seen in Mark and Matthew is at first sight an underscoring of the universalising tendencies in the theological tradition. All may be deemed brothers and sisters of the universal saviour Jesus, who, though a Jewish Messiah, brings a gospel of God's rule which is to be preached to all nations and which will be established over all. The pressure for this came from a radical view of evil as pervasive throughout the world and as requiring therefore a universal solution. But we should not read either Mark or Matthew in one-dimensional ways. Complex dialogues are being conducted in both Gospels, and one needs to be sensitive to different voices. Just as Matthew emphasises the universal authority which has been accorded to Jesus, who commissions his disciples to go to all nations to proclaim his teaching and demand obedience to it, as once Moses commissioned Joshua to take possession of the land, so he also emphasises Jesus' deep roots within the Jewish people. He affirms central values of the Jewish community, with his strong affirmation of the validity of the Law, and yet he also relativises matters of kinship and territory. Judaism is not outlawed, but it is shown to demonstrate the same moral ambiguity as the world as a whole: it contains both good seed and bad. The same nation from which the Messiah and his, albeit sometimes faltering, disciples come, also contains a leadership which will plot his death and crowds who will both celebrate him and cry out for his crucifixion. *Such groupings are not rejected*; their value is affirmed, but they are also subjected to a deep critique. A solution is sought to the world's ills which will only be resolved at the coming of the Son of Man. A new *ethnos* is announced, subject to the same critique, which will only finally be established at the judgement, when the Son of Man establishes his kingdom and when all who have obeyed his commands will be gathered together. An element of radical provisionality is added, at least for those 'with ears to hear'.

It would be naïve to suppose that these theological debates from the first century could simply be transposed into the twenty-first century and provide answers to the debates which we have briefly noticed. I have been trying to guard against such essentialism in resisting a mono-dimensional reading of Matthew as a Christian Jewish document. Its positive reception by both Jewish Christians and the Great Church demonstrates its deep ambivalence about questions of ethnicity. Contemporary Christians must be free to participate in contemporary debate and to back their instincts in the struggle to balance the need for recognition of minority groups with the need to pursue justice and equality for all. I hope this study may contribute to that necessary freedom by showing how both the universalising and the particularising tendencies are represented in the Gospel tradition and that there is no definitive position. Matthew is as much part of a developing and dynamic process as is Mark. The process does not stop with the writing of the canonical Gospels; rather the Gospels are themselves the initiators of a continuing process of theological dialogue and reflection which will spawn many and varied life-forms over two millennia of Christian history.

What is remarkable about this process is the interanimation of, on the one hand, contrasting modes of group definition, universal and particular, and, on the other, of opposed cosmologies, dualist and forensic. The interanimation is complex, as the richness of its many different social embodiments demonstrates. The polarities between universal and particular, dualist and forensic, make possible a variety of correlations which have inspired very different kinds of communities with intriguing diverse forms of ethos and cosmology.

## Closing remarks

Attempts to show the relevance of social historical studies of the Gospels to contemporary debates are fraught with dangers. It is too easy to fall into the trap of attempting to derive norms and 'authenticated practices' from ancient documents for an age profoundly sceptical of all such practices. While the Gospels we have been examining did indeed seek to establish such practices, it may be that their contribution to contemporary debate will be less in the provision of precise models of behaviour than in the provision of a language with which to engage in contemporary issues of identity formation. While the canon of Scripture has often been understood as a normative canon, generating rules for its community, it has also, and arguably more influentially, functioned as a formative canon, as a rich and diverse body of literature providing the language with which communities could make sense of their experience and shape their corporate and individual identities.[36] It was indeed a constant resource, as each generation sought to adapt to changing circumstance and context.

Moreover, the particular character of the linguistic traditions of the Gospels is well suited to fostering such revision and change in the communities which make them their own. Here, as we have seen, the language of apocalyptic is of central importance. Its insistence on the radical corruption of 'this present age' is a direct challenge to cosmologies which regard the way the world is as essentially in conformity with the divine will. Belief in the corruption of the present world may inspire many different responses; it certainly creates a deep sense of alienation from the existing order and is often allied to an equally profound conviction of the rightness of one's own community. In time, however, such language may be turned against the communities which have made it their own; sectarian communities carry with them the seeds of their own dissolution or fragmentation.

There are however, as we have seen, other sources of diversification contained in the language and imagery of the Gospels. Images of demonic invasion and possession vie with the language of moral exhortation and images of a final assize. The world is divided into the wicked and the righteous, but the linguistic codes which give definition to such distinctions are varied and radically opposed. The Gospels represent different articulations of such conflicting codes; they do not ultimately resolve the oppositions, however much they may seek to mediate between them. It is as if the experience of conflict and disorder and its resolution which they seek to convey cannot itself be encompassed by any single cosmological perspective. The Gospels present us with a series of such attempted mediations, rather than with a final synthesis. They are the source of a rich literary history of reception and initiation, a stimulus to further thought and reflection, rather than definitive statements of the church's beliefs.

[36] See the important discussion in Halberthal, 1997.

# Bibliography

ALEXANDER, P. S., 'Geography and the Bible (Early Jewish)', *ABD*, New York: Doubleday, 1992, 2, 977–88.

——, 'Notes on the *Imago Mundi* in the Book of Jubilees', *JJS* 33 (1982) 197–213.

ALLISON, DALE C., 'The Son of God as Israel: A Note on Matthean Christology', *IBS* 9 (1987) 74–81.

——, *The New Moses: A Matthean Typology*, Minneapolis: Augsburg Fortress Press, 1993.

——, *The Jesus Tradition in Q*, Harrisville: Trinity Press International, 1997.

——, 'Behind the Temptations of Jesus: Q 4:1–13 and Mark 1:12–13', in Bruce D. Chilton and Craig A. Evans, eds, *Authenticating the Activities of Jesus*, Leiden: Brill, 1999, 195–214.

ANDERSON, JANICE C. and MOORE, STEPHEN D., eds, *Mark and Method: New Approaches in Biblical Studies*, Minneapolis: Fortress Press, 1992.

AUERBACH, ERICH, *Mimesis: The Representation of Reality in Western Literature*, Princeton: Princeton University Press, 1953.


BACHER, W., *Die exegetische Terminologie der jüdischen Traditionsliteratur: I, Die bibel-exegetische Terminologie der Tannaiten* (1899), Darmstadt: Wissenschaftliche Buchgesellschaft, 1965; *II, Die bibel-exegetische Terminologie der Amoräer* (1905), Darmstadt: Wissenschaftliche Buchgesellschaft, 1965.

BANKS, MARCUS, *Ethnicity: Anthropological Constructions*, London: Routledge, 1996.

BARCLAY, JOHN M. G., *Obeying the Truth: A Study of Paul's Ethics in Galatians*, SNTW, Edinburgh: T&T Clark, 1988.

——, *Jews in the Mediterranean Diaspora: From Alexandra to Trajan* (323 BCE – 117 CE), Edinburgh: T&T Clark, 1996.

BARTH, FREDERIK, 'Introduction', in Frederik Barth, ed., *Ethnic Groups and Boundaries: The Social Organisation of Cultural Difference*, London: George Allen & Unwin, 1969.

BARTON, STEPHEN C., *Discipleship and Family Ties in Mark and Matthew*, SNTSMS 80, Cambridge: Cambridge University Press, 1994.

BAUCKHAM, RICHARD, 'Jesus and the Wild Animals (Mark 1:13): A Christological Image for an Ecological Age', in Joel Green and Max Turner, eds, *Jesus of Nazareth: Lord and Christ: Essays on the Historical Jesus and New Testament Christology*, Grand Rapids: Eerdmans, 1994, 3–21.

——, 'The Coin in the Fish's Mouth', in David Wenham and Craig Blomberg, eds, *The Miracles of Jesus*, Gospel Perspectives 6, Sheffield: Sheffield Academic Press, 1986, 219–52.

——, ed., *The Gospel for All Christians: Rethinking the Gospel Audiences*, Edinburgh: T&T Clark, 1998.

BEARE, FRANCIS W., *The Gospel According to Matthew: a Commentary*, Oxford: Basil Blackwell, 1981.

BERGER, PETER, *The Sacred Canopy: Elements of a Sociological Theory of Religion*, Garden City, New York: Doubleday, 1969.

BEST, ERNEST, 'Mark's Preservation of the Tradition', in William Telford, ed., *The Interpretation of Mark*, London: SPCK, 1985, 119–33.

——, *Mark: The Gospel as Story*, SNTW, Edinburgh: T&T Clark, 1983.

——, *The Temptation and the Passion: The Markan Soteriology*, SNTSMS 2, Cambridge: Cambridge University Press, 1965, 2nd edn, 1990.

——, 'Mark III.20, 21, 31–35', *NTS* 22 (1975/6) 309–19, in Ernest Best, *Disciples and Discipleship: Studies in the Gospel according to Mark*, Edinburgh: T&T Clark, 1986, 49–63.

——, *Following Jesus: Discipleship in the Gospel of Mark*, JSNTSup 4, Sheffield: JSOT Press, 1981.

BLENKINSOPP, J., 'Interpretation and Sectarian Tendencies: An Aspect of Second Temple History', in E. P. Sanders, ed., *Jewish and Christian Self-Definition*, vol. 2, Philadelphia: Fortress Press, 1981, 1–26.

BOORSTIN, DANIEL J., *The Americans: The Colonial Experience*, New York: Vintage Books, 1958.

BORNKAMM, G., 'End-Expectation and Church in Matthew', in G. Bornkamm, G. Barth, and H. J. Held, eds, *Tradition and Interpretation in Matthew*, London: SCM Press, 1963, 15–51.

BORNKAMM, G., 'The Stilling of the Storm in Matthew', in G. Bornkamm, G. Barth and H. J. Held, eds, *Tradition and Interpretation in Matthew*, London: SCM Press, 1963, 52–7.

BRANDON, S. G. F., *Jesus and the Zealots: A Study of the Political Factors in Primitive Christianity*, Manchester: Manchester University Press, 1967.

BRETT, MARK G., ed., *Ethnicity and the Bible*, Leiden: Brill, 1996.

BROWN, RAYMOND E., *The Birth of the Messiah*, New York: Doubleday, 1977.

BULTMANN, RUDOLF, *The New Testament and Mythology and Other Basic Writings*, London: SCM Press, 1985.

BURRIDGE, KENNELM O. L., *New Heaven, New Earth: A Study of Millenarian Activities*, Oxford: Blackwell, 1969.


COHEN, ATHNOY P., *Self-Consciousness: An Alternative Anthropology of Identity*, London: Routledge, 1994.

COHEN, SHAYE J. D., 'Crossing the Boundary and Becoming a Jew', *HTR* 82:1 (1989) 13–33.

COHN, ROBERT L., *The Shape of Sacred Space*, Chico: Scholars Press, 1981.

COLLINS, JOHN J., *Between Athens and Jerusalem: Jewish Identity in the Hellenistic Diaspora*, New York: Crossroad, 1986.

——, *The Apocalyptic Imagination: an Introduction to Jewish Apocalyptic Literature*, Grand Rapids: Eerdmans, 2nd edn, 1998.

CROSS, FRANK M., *Canaanite Myth and Hebrew Epic: Essays in the History of Religion of Israel*, Cambridge, Mass.: Harvard University Press, 1973.

CROSSAN, J. DOMINIC, 'Mark and the Relatives of Jesus', *NovT* 15 (1973) 81–113.

——, *The Historical Jesus: The Life of a Galilean Peasant*, San Francisco: HarperCollins, 1991.


DAVIES, W. D., *The Setting of the Sermon on the Mount*, Cambridge: Cambridge University Press, 1963.

——, *The Gospel and the Land: Early Christianity and Jewish Territorial Doctrine*, Sheffield: JSOT Press, 1994.

——, *The Territorial Dimension of Judaism: With a Symposium and Further Reflections*, Minneapolis: Fortress Press, 1991.

—— and ALLISON, DALE C., *Matthew*, ICC, Edinburgh: T&T Clark, 3 vols, 1988, 1991, 1997.

331

DE BOER, MARTIN C., 'Paul and Jewish Apocalyptic Eschatology', in Joel Marcus and Marion L. Soards, eds, *Apocalyptic in the New Testament: Essays in Honor of J. Louis Martyn*, JSNTSup 24, Sheffield: JSOT Press, 1989, 169–90.

——, 'Paul and Apocalyptic Eschatology', in John J. Collins, ed., *The Encyclopaedia of Apocalypticism*, vol. 1, *The Origins of Apocalypticism in Judaism and Christianity*, New York: Continuum, 1999, 345–83.

DE JONGE, MARINUS, 'The Use of the Word "Anointed" in the Time of Jesus', *NovT* 8 (1966) 132–48.

DONALDSON, TERENCE L., *Jesus on the Mountain: A Study in Matthaean Theology*, JSNTSup 8, Sheffield: JSOT Press, 1985.

DOUGLAS, MARY, *Purity and Danger: An Analysis of the Concepts of Pollution and Taboo*, London: Routledge & Kegan Paul, 1966.

DSCHULNIGG, P., *Rabbinische Gleichnisse und das Neue Testament: Die Gleichnisse der PesK im Vergleich mit den Gleichnissen Jesu und dem Neuen Testament*, Bern: Peter Lang, 1988.


ELIADE, MIRCEA, *The Sacred and the Profane*, New York: Harcourt Brace, 1959.

ESLER, PHILIP F., 'Mountaineering in Matthew: A Response to K. C. Hanson', *Semeia* 67 (1994) 171–7.


FOHRER, GEORG, *Elia*, AThANT 31, Zurich: Zwingli Verlag, 1957.

FREND, WILLIAM H. C., *The Donatist Church*, Oxford: Clarendon Press, 1953.

FREYNE, SEAN, Galilee, *Jesus and the Gospels: Literary Approaches and Historical Investigations*, Philadelphia: Fortress Press, 1988.


GAGER, JOHN, *Kingdom and Community: The Social World of Early Christianity*, Englewood Cliffs: Prentice Hall, 1975.

GARRETT, SUSAN R., *The Temptations of Jesus in Mark's Gospel*, Grand Rapids, Michigan: Eerdmans, 1998.

GEERTZ, CLIFFORD, 'Religion as a Cultural System', in C. Geertz, *The Interpretation of Cultures*, London: Fontana, 1993, 87–125.

GIDDENS, ANTHONY, *Modernity and Self-identity: Self and Society in the Late Modern Age*, Cambridge: Polity Press, 1991.

——, *Politics, Sociology and Social Theory: Encounters with Classical and Contemporary Social Thought*, Cambridge: Polity Press, 1995.

GIDDENS, ANTHONY, 'Tradition', *The Reith Lectures*, 1999, BBC web site.

GNILKA, JOACHIM, *Das Evangelium nach Markus*, EKKNT II/1–2, Einsiedeln: Benziger, 2 vols, 1978, 1979.

——, *Das Matthäusevangelium*, HTKNT, Freiburg: Herder, 2 vols, 1986, 1988.

GOODLOVE, TERRY F., *Religion, Interpretation and Diversity of Belief: The Framework Model from Kant to Durkheim to Davidson*, Macon, Georgia: Mercer University Press, 1997.

GRIMM, W., *Weil Ich Dich Liebe: Die Verkündigung Jesu und Deutero-Jesaia*, Bern: Peter Lang, 1976.

GUELICH, R., 'The Matthean Beatitudes: "Entrance-Requirements" or Eschatological Blessings?' *JBL* 95/3 (1976) 415–34.

——, 'Anti-Semitism and/or Anti-Judaism in Mark?' in Craig A. Evans and Donald A. Hagner, eds, *Anti-Semitism and Early Christianity: Issues of Polemic and Faith*, Minneapolis: Fortress Press, 1993, 80–101.


HALBERTHAL, MOSHE, *People of the Book: Canon, Meaning, and Authority*, Cambridge, Mass.: Harvard University Press, 1997.

HALL, ROBERT G., 'Circumcision', *ABD*, New York: Doubleday, 1992, 1, 1025–31.

HANSON, K. C., 'Transformed on the Mountain: Ritual Analysis and the Gospel of Matthew', *Semeia* 67 (1994) 147–70.

HENGEL, MARTIN, *Die Zeloten: Untersuchungen zur jüdischen Freiheitsbewegung in der Zeit von Herodes I bis 70 n. Chr.* AGAJU, Leiden: E. J. Brill, 2nd edn, 1976.

——, *Studies in the Gospel of Mark*, London: SCM Press, 1985.

——, *The Charismatic Leader and His Followers*, SNTW, Edinburgh: T&T Clark, 1981.

HERDER, JOHANN G., *Ideen*, in Bernard Suphan, ed., *Herders Sämtliche Werke*, vol. 13, Berlin: Weidmann, 1877–1913.

HILL, DAVID, *The Gospel of Matthew*, NCB, London: Oliphants, 1972.

——, 'Son and Servant: An Essay on Matthean Christology', *JSNT* 6 (1980) 2–16.

HORBURY, W., 'Land, Sanctuary and Worship', in John Barclay and John Sweet, eds, *Early Christian Thought in its Jewish Context*, Cambridge: Cambridge University Press, 1996, 207–24.

HUBBARD, B. J., *The Matthean Redaction of a Primitive Apostolic Commissioning*, SBLDS 19, Missouola: Scholars Press, 1974.

HUTCHINSON, JOHN and SMITH, ANTHONY D., eds, *Ethnicity*, Oxford: Oxford University Press, 1996.

IERSEL, BAS VAN, *Reading Mark*, Edinburgh: T&T Clark, 1989.

ISER, WOLFGANG, *Der Akt des Lesens: Theorie ästhetischer Wirkung*, Munich: W. Fink, 3rd edn, 1990.

JACKSON, R. H. and HENRIE, R., 'Perception of Sacred Space', *Journal of Cultural Geography* 3 (1983) 94–107.

JAUSS, HANS-ROBERT, 'Literaturgeschichte als Provokation der Literaturwissenschaft', in *Literaturgeschichte als Provokation*, Frankfurt: Suhrkamp, 1970, 144–207. English, 'Literary History as a Challenge to Literary Theory', in Ralph Cohen, ed., *New Directions in Literary History*, Baltimore: Johns Hopkins University Press, 1974.

JUEL, DONALD H., *A Master of Surprise: Mark Interpreted*, Minneapolis: Fortress Press, 1994.

KEE, H. C., *Community for a New Age: Studies in Mark's Gospel*, Philadephia: Westminster Press, 1977.

KEEGAN, T. J., 'Introductory Formulae for Matthaean Discourses', *CBQ* 44 (1982) 415–30.

KEEL, OTHMAR and KÜCHLER, MAX, *Orte und Landschaften der Bibel: ein Handbuch und Studienreiseführer zum Heiligen Land*, Zurich: Benziger, vol. 1, 1982.

KELBER, WERNER H., *The Kingdom in Mark: A New Place and a New Time*, Philadelphia: Fortress Press, 1974.

——, 'The Hour of the Son of Man and the Temptation of the Disciples (Mark 14:32–42)', in Werner H. Kelber, ed., *The Passion in Mark: Studies on Mark 14–16*, Philadelphia: Fortress Press, 1976, 41–60.

KINGSBURY, JACK D., *The Christology of Mark's Gospel*, Philadelphia: Fortress Press, 1983.

——, *Matthew: Structure, Christology, Kingdom*, Minneapolis: Fortress Press, 1975.

——, 'The Figure of Jesus in Matthew's Story: A Literary-Critical Probe', *JSNT* 21 (1984) 3–36.

——, 'The Figure of Jesus in Matthew's Story: A Rejoinder to David Hill', *JSNT* 25 (1985) 61–81.

KINGSBURY, JACK D., *Matthew as Story,* Philadelphia: Fortress Press, 2nd rev. edn, 1988.

KOESTER, HELMUT, *Ancient Christian Gospels: Their History and Development,* London: SCM Press, 1990.

LAMPE, GEOFFREY W. H., 'St. Peter's Denial', *BJRL* 55 (1972–3) 346–68.

LEACH, EDMUND, *Lévi-Strauss,* London: Collins, 1970.

LEVENSON, JON D., *Theology of the Program of Restoration in Ezekiel 40–48,* Harvard Semitic Monographs 10, Cambridge, Mass.: Scholars Press, 1976.

——, *Creation and the Persistence of Evil: The Jewish Drama of Divine Omnipotence,* Princeton: Princeton University Press, 1994.

LEVINE, AMY-JILL, *The Social and Ethnic Dimensions of Matthean Salvation History: 'Go nowhere among the Gentiles . . .' (Matt. 10:5b),* Lewiston: Edwin Mellen Press, 1988.

LÉVI-STRAUSS, CLAUDE, 'The Structural Study of Myth', *Journal of American Folklore,* 68 (1955) 428–43.

——, *The Savage Mind (La Pensée Sauvage),* London: Weidenfeld & Nicolson, 1972. [French: 1962].

——, 'The Story of Asdiwal', in *Structural Anthropology 2,* Harmondsworth: Penguin, 1977, 146–97.

LIGHTFOOT, R. H., *Locality and Doctrine in the Gospels,* London: Hodder & Stoughton, 1938.

LOEVESTAM, EVALD, 'Die Davidssohnsfrage', *SEA* 27 (1972) 72–82.

LOHMEYER, ERNST, *Galiläa und Jerusalem,* FRLANT 34, Göttingen: Vandenhoeck & Ruprecht, 1936.

LÜHRMANN, DIETER, *Das Markusevangelium,* HNT 3, Tübingen: J. C. B. Mohr (Paul Siebeck), 1987.

LUZ, ULRICH, 'Die Jünger im Matthäusevangelium', *ZNW* 62 (1971) 141–71.

——, 'Markusforschung in der Sackgasse', *ThLZ* 105 (1980) 641–55.

——, 'Eine thetische Skizze der matthäischen Christologie', in C. Breytenbach and H. Paulsen, eds, *Anfänge der Christologie,* Göttingen: Vandenhoeck & Ruprecht, 1991, 221–35.

——, *Das Evangelium nach Matthäus,* EKKNT I/1–3, Zürich: Benziger Verlag, 3 vols, 1985 (2nd rev. edn, 1989), 1990, 1997.

McKELVEY, R. J., *The New Temple: The Church in the New Testament*, Oxford: Oxford University Press, 1969.

MacMULLEN, RAMSAY, *Paganism in the Roman Empire*, New Haven: Yale University Press, 1981.

MALBON, ELIZABETH STRUTHERS, *Narrative Space and Mythic Meaning in Mark*, San Francisco: Harper & Row, 1986.

——, 'Disciples/Crowds/Whoever: Markan Characters and Readers', *NovT* 28 (1987) 104–30.

MALINA, BRUCE, J. and ROHRBAUGH, RICHARD L., *Social-Science Commentary on the Synoptic Gospels*, Minneapolis: Fortress Press, 1992.

MANSON, THOMAS W., *The Sayings of Jesus*, London: SCM Press, 1949.

MARCUS, JOEL, *The Mystery of the Kingdom of God*, SBLDS 90, Atlanta: Scholars Press, 1986.

——, 'Mark 14:61: "Are You the Messiah-Son-of-God?"' 31, 2 *NovT* (1989) 125–41.

——, 'The Jewish War and the Sitz im Leben of Mark', *JBL* 111 (1992a), 441–62.

——, *The Way of the Lord: Christological Exegesis of the Old Testament in the Gospel of Mark*, Louisville: Westminster/John Knox Press; Edinburgh: T&T Clark (SNTW), 1992b.

——, 'The Intertextual Polemic of the Markan Vineyard Parable', in Graham N. Stanton and Guy G. Stroumsa, eds, *Tolerance and Intolerance in Early Judaism and Christianity*, Cambridge: Cambridge University Press, 1998, 211–27.

——, 'The Beelzebul Controversy and the Eschatologies of Jesus', in Bruce D. Chilton and Craig A. Evans, eds, *Authenticating the Activities of Jesus*, Leiden: Brill, 1999, 247–77.

——, *Mark 1–8: A New Translation with Introduction and Commentary*, AB 27, New York: Doubleday, 2000.

MARKUS, ROBERT A., 'The Problem of Self-Definition: From Sect to Church', in E. P. Sanders, ed., *Jewish and Christian Self-Definition*. vol. 1, *The Shaping of Christianity in the Second and Third Centuries*, London: SCM Press, 1980, 1–15.

MARTYN, J. LOUIS, *History and Theology in the Fourth Gospel*, Nashville: Abingdon, 2nd edn, 1979.

MARXSEN, WILLI, *Der Evangelist Markus: Studien zur Redaktionsgeschichte des Evangeliums*, FRLANT 67, Göttingen: Vandenhoeck & Ruprecht, 1956.

MEAD, GEORGE HERBERT, *Mind, Self and Society*, Chicago: Chicago University Press, 1934.

MEEKS, WAYNE A., 'The Man from Heaven in Johannine Sectarianism', *JBL* 91 (1972) 44–72.

——, 'Breaking Away: Three New Testament Pictures of Christianity's Separation from the Jewish Communities', in Jacob Neusner and Ernest S. Frerichs, eds, *'To See Ourselves as Others See Us': Christians, Jews, 'Others' in Late Antiquity*, Chico: Scholars Press, 1985, 93–115.

——, *The Origins of Christian Morality: The First Two Centuries*, Yale: Yale University Press, 1993.

MEIER, JOHN P., *Law and History in Matthew's Gospel*, Rome: Biblical Institute Press, 1976.

——, *The Vision of Matthew: Christ, Church, and Morality in the First Gospel*, New York: Paulist Press, 1978.

MEYERS, CAROL L. and MEYERS, ERIC M., *Haggai, Zechariah 1–8: A New Translation with Introduction and Commentary*, AB 25B, New York: Doubleday, 1987.

MICHALSON, GORDON E., *Fallen Freedom: Kant on Radical Evil and Moral Regeneration*, Cambridge: Cambridge University Press, 1990.

MICHEL, OTTO, 'Der Abschluß des Matthäusevangeliums', *EvTh* 10 (1950–1), 16–26.

MORGAN, ROBERT, with JOHN BARTON, *Biblical Interpretation*, Oxford: Oxford University Press, 1988.

MYERS, CHED, *Binding the Strong Man: A Political Reading of Mark's Story of Jesus*, New York: Orbis, 1988.

NOCK, ARTHUR D., *Conversion: The Old and New in Religion from Alexander the Great to Augustine of Hippo*, Oxford: Clarendon Press, 1933.

OVERMAN, J. ANDREW, *Matthew's Gospel and Formative Judaism: The Social World of the Matthean Community*, Minneapolis: Fortress Press, 1990.

PATON, ALAN, *Debbie Go Home*, London: Jonathan Cape, 1961.

PFLEIDERER, OTTO, *Die Entstehung des Christentums*, Munich: J. F. Lehmann, 1907.

Przybylski, Benno, *Righteousness in Matthew and His World of Thought*, SNTSMS 41, Cambridge: Cambridge University Press, 1980.

Quesnell, Quentin, *The Mind of Mark: Interpretation and Method through the Exegesis of Mark* 6.52, AnBib 38, Rome: Pontifical Biblical Institute, 1969.

Räisänen, Heikki, *The 'Messianic Secret' in Mark*, SNTW, Edinburgh: T&T Clark, 1990.
——, *Beyond New Testament Theology*, London: SCM Press, 1990a.
Rensberger, David K., *Overcoming the World: Politics and Community in the Gospel of John*, London: SPCK, 1989.
Riches, John K., *Jesus and the Transformation of Judaism*, London: Darton, Longman & Todd, 1980.
——, *A Century of New Testament Study*, Cambridge: Lutterworth, 1993.
——, and Millar, Alan, 'Interpretation: A Theoretical Perspective and Some Applications', in *Numen* 28 (1981) 29–53.
——, and Millar, Alan, 'Conceptual Change in the New Testament', in *Alternative Approaches to New Testament Study*, Anthony E. Harvey, ed., London: SPCK, 1985, 37–60.
Robbins, Vernon K., 'Last Meal: Preparation, Betrayal, and Absence (Mark 14:12–25)', in Werner H. Kelber, ed. *The Passion in Mark: Studies on Mark 14–16*, Philadelphia: Fortress Press, 1976.
Robinson, James M., *The Problem of History in Mark*, SBT 21, London: SCM Press, 1957.
Roskies, David R., *Against the Apocalypse: Responses to Catastrophe in Modern Jewish Culture*, Cambridge, Mass.: Harvard University Press, 1984.
Rousseau, Jean-Jacques, *Les Rêveries du Promeneur Solitaire*, in *Oeuvres Complètes*, vol. 1, Paris: Gallimard, 1959.
Rowland, Christopher, *Radical Christianity*, Cambridge: Polity Press, 1988.

Saldarini, Anthony J., *Matthew's Christian-Jewish Community*, Chicago: University of Chicago Press, 1994.
Schell, Marc, *Children of the Earth: Literature, Politics and Nationhood*, Oxford: Oxford University Press, 1993.
Schiffman, Lawrence H., 'The Concept of the Messiah in Second Temple and Rabbinic Literature', *RevExp* 84 (1987) 235–46.

SCHIFFMAN, LAWRENCE H., 'Messianic Figures and Ideas in the Qumran Scrolls', in James H. Charlesworth, ed. *The Messiah: Developments in Earliest Judaism and Christianity*, Minneapolis: Fortress Press, 1992, 116–29.

SCHMIDT, KARL L., *Der Rahmen der Geschichte Jesus*, Berlin: Töpelmann, 1919.

——, 'Die Stellung der Evangelien in der allgemeinen Literaturgeschichte', in *Eucharisterion: H. Gunkel dargebracht II*, FRLANT, Göttingen: Vandenhoeck & Ruprecht, 1923, 50–134; ET, *The Place of the Gospels in the General History of Literature*, translated by Byron McCane; introduced by John Riches, Columbia S.C.: University of South Carolina Press, 2001.

SCHMITHALS, WALTER, 'Introduction', in Rudolf Bultmann, *The Gospel according to John*, Oxford: Blackwells, 1971, 3–12.

SCHOLEM, GERSHOM, 'Toward an Understanding of the Messianic Idea in Judaism', *The Messianic Idea in Judaism, and Other Essays on Jewish Spirituality*, New York: Schocken Books, 1971.

SCHWARTZ, DANIEL R., 'Temple and Desert: On Religion and State in Second Temple Period Judaea', in *Studies in the Jewish Background of Christianity*, WUNT 60, Tübingen: J. C. B. Mohr (Paul Siebeck) 1992 (Hebrew original 1987).

SCHWEITZER, ALBERT, *The Quest of the Historical Jesus: A Critical Study of its Progress from Reimarus to Wrede*, London: A & C Black, 2nd English edn, 1911.

SHILS, E., 'Primordial, Personal, Sacred and Civil Ties', *British Journal of Sociology* 8 (1957) 130–45.

SHUMATE, NANCY, *Crisis and Conversion in Apuleius' Metamorphoses*, Ann Arbor: University of Michigan Press, 1996.

SIBLEY, DAVID, *Geographies of Exclusion: Society and Difference in the West*, London: Routledge, 1995.

SIM, DAVID, *Apocalyptic Eschatology in the Gospel of Matthew*, SNTSMS 88, Cambridge: Cambridge University Press, 1996.

——, 'Christianity and Ethnicity in the Gospel of Matthew', in Mark G. Brett, ed. *Ethnicity and the Bible*, Biblical Interpretation Series 19, Leiden: Brill, 1996a, 171–95.

——, *The Gospel of Matthew and Christian Judaism: The History and Social Setting of the Matthean Community*, SNTW, Edinburgh: T&T Clark, 1998.

SMITH, JONATHAN Z., *Map is Not Territory: Studies in the History of Religions*, Leiden: Brill, 1978.

——, *To Take Place: Toward Theory in Ritual*, Chicago: University of Chicago Press, 1987.

SNODGRASS, KLINE R., 'Streams of Tradition Emerging from Isaiah 40:1–5 and their Adaptation in the New Testament,' *JSNT* 8 (1980) 24–45.

STANTON, GRAHAM N., *A Gospel for a New People: Studies in Matthew*, Edinburgh: T&T Clark, 1992.

STENDAHL, KRISTER, *The School of Matthew and its Use of the Old Testament*, Philadelphia: Fortress Press, 1968.

——, 'Biblical Theology: A Program', in *Meanings: The Bible as Document and as Guide*, Philadelphia: Fortress Press, 1984, 11–44.

STRECKER, GEORG, *Der Weg der Gerechtigkeit: Untersuchung zur Theologie des Matthäus*, FRLANT 82, Göttingen: Vandenhoeck & Ruprecht, 1962.

——, 'Die Makarismen der Bergpredigt', *NTS* 17 (1970/71) 255–75.

SYME, RONALD, *The Roman Revolution*, Oxford: Oxford University Press, 1960.

TALMON, S., 'Types of Messianic Expectation at the Turn of the Era', *King, Cult, and Calendar in Ancient Israel: Collected Studies*, Jerusalem: Magnes Press, 1987.

TANNEHILL, ROBERT, 'The "Focal Instance" as a Form of New Testament Speech: A Study of Matthew 5:39b–42', *JR* 50 (1970) 372–85.

TAYLOR, CHARLES, *Sources of the Self: The Making of the Modern Identity*, Cambridge: Cambridge University Press, 1989.

——, *The Ethics of Authenticity*, Cambridge, Mass.: Harvard University Press, 1991.

——, 'The Politics of Recognition', in Amy Gutmann, ed., *Multi-Culturalism: Examining the Politics of Recognition*, Princeton: Princeton University Press, 1994, 25–73.

THEISSEN, GERD, *Miracle Stories of the Early Christian Tradition*, SNTW, Edinburgh: T&T Clark, 1983.

——, 'Jesusbewegung als charismatische Wertrevolution', *NTS* 35, 1989, 343–60.

——, *A Theory of Primitive Christian Religion*, London: SCM Press, 1999.

TRACY, DAVID, *Plurality and Ambiguity: Hermeneutics, Religion, Hope*, London: SCM Press, 1988.

TRILLING, WOLFGANG, *Das wahre Israel: Studien zur Theologie des Matthäus-Evangeliums*, SANT 10, Munich: Kösel Verlag, 3rd rev. edn, 1964.

TROCMÉ, E., *The Formation of the Gospel according to Mark*, London: SPCK, 1975.

TUCKETT, CHRISTOPHER, ed., *The Messianic Secret*, Philadelphia: Fortress Press, 1983.

TURNER, VICTOR, *Dramas, Fields, and Metaphors: Symbolic Action in Human Society*, Ithaca, N.Y.: Cornell University Press, 1974.

TYSON, J. B., 'The Blindness of the Disciples in Mark', *JBL* 80 (1961) 261–8.

USPENSKY, BORIS, *A Poetics of Composition*, Berkeley and Los Angeles: University of California Press, 1973.

VÖGTLE, ANTON, 'Das christologische und ekklesiologische Anliegen von Mt 28,18–20', *SE* 2 (1964), 266–94.

WATSON, FRANCIS, *Text, Church and World: Biblical Interpretation in Theological Perspective*, Edinburgh: T&T Clark, 1994.

WATTS, RIKKI E., *Isaiah's New Exodus and Mark*, WUNT 2. Reihe, 88, Tübingen: Mohr Siebeck, 1997.

WILKEN, ROBERT L., *The Land Called Holy: Palestine in Christian History and Thought*, Yale: Yale University Press, 1992.

——, *The Christians as the Romans Saw Them*, New Haven: Yale University Press, 1984.

WILSON, BRYAN, *Magic and the Millennium*, St Albans: Paladin, 1975.

——, *Religion in Sociological Perspective*, Oxford: Oxford University Press, 1982.

# Index of biblical references and ancient sources

# Index of modern authors

Grimm, W. 172 n.56
Guelich, R. 102–4, 107, 108 n.99, 188 n.12, 193 and n.21, 194, 195

Halberthal, M. 328 n.36
Hall, A. G. 49 n.51
Hanson, K. C. 116 n.3
Held, H. J. 198 n.26
Hengel, M. 22 n.4, 86 and nn.43, 46, 104 n.84, 106 n.91, 205 n.46
Henrie, R. 24, 25 n.6
Herder, J. G. 18, 308, 309 n.19
Hill, D. 200 n.33, 269 n.13, 176, 277, 282 n.47
Hooker, M. 70 n.4, 84, 110, 132 n.38, 165 n.41, 167 n.48, 168 n.49, 169 nn.50, 52, 172 n.56
Horbury, W. 32 n.22, 33 n.23, 38 n.31, 173 n.57
Hubbard, B. J. 252 and n.40
Hutchinson, J. 216 n.67

Iersel, B. van 75 n.13

Jackson, R. H. 24, 25 n.6
Jakobsen, R. 122 n.14
Jauss, H.-R. 15
Juel, D. 158 n.25, 159 n.31, 160

Keegan, T. J. 184 n.3
Keel, O. 116 n.2
Kelber, W. H. 75 n.14, 126 n.21, 171 n.55
Kingsbury, J. D. 158 n.25, 160, 273-8
Koester, H. 304 n.13

Leach, E. 54 n.56, 122 n.14
Lévi-Strauss, C. 12 and n.20, 54 and n.56, 74 n.11, 122 and n.14, 123 n.15, 125, 130 and n.37, 176 and nn.64, 65, 177, 178, 301
Lightfoot, R. H. 126 and n.21, 127
Loevestam, E. 159 n.31
Lohmeyer, E. 126 and n.21
Lührmann, D. 165 n.41
Luz, U. 8 and n.12, 162 n.37, 182 n.1, 184 n.4, 186 n.7, 187, 188 and n.12, 190 n.15, 191 and n.18, 192 n.19, 195 n.25, 200 nn.33, 34, 207 n.55, 218 and n.76, 224, 229 n.1, 232 n.5, 233, 236 nn.15, 16, 21, 239 n.23, 241 n.26, 242 and n.27, 245 nn.30, 31, 269 n.12, 271 n.16, 273 n.21, 278 n.36, 279, 282, 285, 286, 288 n.59, 324

Macmullen, R. 307
Malbon, E. S. 73 n.9, 122–6, 127 and nn.22, 28, 129, 142
Malina, B. J. 129 n.35
Manson, T. W. 190 n.15
Marcus, J. xii, xiii, xv, 7 n.7, 22 n.4, 33 n.24, 60 and n.61, 62 n.63, 79 n.26, 82 n.34, 83 nn.35, 36, 90 n.50, 97 n.64, 103–11, 136 and n.46, 138, 149 n.6, 153 n.18, 154 n.21, 155 n.22, 158 n.26, 159 and n.31, 161, 173 n.59, 178, 200 n.34, 244 n.29, 265, 312 n.25
Marshall, C. D. 70 n.3, 73 n.8, 79 n.28, 81 n.31
Martyn, J. L. 5 and nn.3, 4, 83 n.34, 298
Marxsen, W. 126 n.21
Matera, F. J. 70 n.4
Mead, G. H. 100 n.71
Meeks, W. 7, 224 n.91
Meier, J. 191 n.17, 279
Meyers, C. L. 32 n.19, 126 n.21
Meyers, E. 32 n.19
Michalson, G. E. 301 n.9
Michel, O. 248 n.34
Moore, S. D. 74 n.10, 145 n.1
Morgan, R. 297 n.1

Nock, A. D. 306 n.15

Overman, J. A. 7 n.10, 202–5

Paton, A. 287 n.58
Pfleiderer, O. 190 n.15
Przybylski, B. 190 n.15

Quesnell, Q. 168 n.49

Räisänen, H. 71 n.6, 74 n.10, 145 n.1, 298 n.6
Rensberger, D. K. 5 n.3
Riches, J. K. 118 n.6, 125 n.18, 177 n.66
Robbins, V. K. 169 n.51
Robinson, J. M. xii, 143 n.59, 149 and nn.4, 6, 150 n.8, 151, 152 n.17, 153 n.20, 155, 178, 265
Róheim, G. 119
Rohrbaugh, R. L. 129 n.35
Roskies, D. R. 104 n.82, 163 n.40
Rowland, C. 97 n.65

Saldarini, A. J. 7 n.10, 205–9, 221 n.84, 233 n.7, 319 n.29, 320
Sanders, E. P. 89 n.49

# Index of subjects